THE
STRUCTURE AND FORM
OF THE
FRENCH ENLIGHTENMENT

Volume II

The
Structure and Form
of the
French Enlightenment

VOLUME II: *Esprit Révolutionnaire*

Ira O. Wade

PRINCETON, NEW JERSEY
PRINCETON UNIVERSITY PRESS
1977

To *Mabel* . . .

Entre le vide et l'Événement pur,
J'attends l'écho de ma grandeur interne,
Amère, sombre et sonore citerne,
Sonnant dans l'âme un creux toujours futur!

Le Cimetière Marin
Paul Valéry

CONTENTS

CONTENTS

ABBREVIATIONS

The Cabeen Bibliography contains a rather full list of abbreviations generally used. I have adopted the following:

Annales	*Annales, Economies, Sociétés, Civilisations*
Annales JJR	*Annales Jean-Jacques Rousseau*
APSP	*American Philosophical Society, Proceedings*
APSR	*American Political Science Review*
Archiv	Archiv für das Studium der neueren Sprachen und literaturen (Herrig)
ASP	*Annales des sciences politiques*
AUP	*Annales de l'Université de Paris*
B or Best	Theodore Besterman, *Voltaire's Correspondence*, Geneva, 1953–. 108 vols.
BM	British Museum
BN	Bibliothèque Nationale
CAIEF	*Cahiers de l'Association internationale des études françaises*
CDU	Centre de documentation universitaire
DS	*Diderot Studies*
FAR	*Franco-American Review*
FQ	*French Quarterly*
FR	*French Review*
FS	*French Studies*
JHI	*Journal of the History of Ideas*
JMH	*Journal of Modern History*
LC	Library of Congress
MLN	*Modern Language Notes*
MLQ	*Modern Language Quarterly*
MLR	*Modern Language Review*
MP	*Modern Philology*
PMLA	*Publications of the Modern Language Association of America*
PSQ	*Political Science Quarterly*
PUF	Presses universitaires de France
RCC	*Revue des cours et des conférences*
RDP	*Revue du droit public*

RDS	*Revue du dix-huitième Siècle*
Rfr	*Révolution française, revue d'histoire moderne et contemporaine*
RHL	*Revue d'histoire littéraire de la France*
RHM	*Revue d'histoire moderne*
RHRF	*Revue historique de la révolution française*
R. Int. Phil	*Revue internationale de philosophie*
RLC	*Revue de littérature comparée*
RMM	*Revue de métaphysique et de morale*
RR	*Romanic Review*
RSH	*Revue des sciences humaines*
SP	*Studies in Philology*
Symp	Symposium
SVEC	*Studies on Voltaire and the Eighteenth Century*
YR	*Yale Review*
YRS	*Yale Romanic Studies*

PART III
The Building of Organic Unity

FOREWORD

THOSE of us who began our studies around the end of the First World War will recall that in spite of the constant attacks made upon his historical criticism, Taine's method of literary analysis with its emphasis upon the little significant facts leading to the larger generalizations remained the accepted method in academic criticism. We of the profession spoke more quietly of "race," "moment," and "milieu," and especially of "faculté maîtresse"; we used more discreetly such terms as "psychologie littéraire" or "caractérologie," while more imaginative newcomers engaged in "close reading" or "literary analysis." It is well that our studies have been enriched by these more perceptive approaches. However, there comes a time in the work of art, in the biography of an important figure, in the organization of an historical period, when we would like to grasp its total effect, penetrate to that quality which gives it its vital unity, seize it, as Kafka says about life, "like a little ball."

On those occasions, we are apt to revert to our early training, to seek to coordinate the procedures of that training so beautifully exemplified by Lanson and his students with the more esthetic approaches of the "new" criticism and to hope that we may forge some sort of genetic criticism which will solve our problem. We are always slightly apologetic when we suggest this genetic process, though, possibly because it is neither fish nor fowl and therefore doubtfully organic itself and also because of a certain fear that we will be called old-fashioned, if not something more unpleasant. However, I know no other way to see the "whole" work of art, or the "whole" life of an important creator, or the "whole" spirit of a historical period. And I am surely not inclined to reject it because I learned it in the historical criticism of Voltaire and the esthetic criticism of Diderot, which is where Taine found it, I suspect. Perhaps, some of my more prudent friends will suggest that it is better not to undertake these enterprises when we know we are incapable of handling them. However, *Candide*, Voltaire, and the Enlightenment are living realities; there ought to be ways which will permit us to penetrate their inner meaning.

I am going to hazard here a method which is a combination of

Taine's historical criticism continued by the structure-form analysis of the "new" critics, or, if one prefers, the historical criticism of Voltaire modified by the esthetic criticism of Diderot. It begins with the raw product, follows it through the artist as he makes his selection of the material, seizes the "idea," makes his internal model, and begins to structure his work. We try to see both artist and work as the latter develops in the milieu and the tradition. We endeavor to grasp the vitality which the work absorbs from the tradition, from the milieu, from its creator, and we pursue relentlessly that inner vitality as the work of art takes over from the artist and assumes responsibility for its reality as a total effect, an organic entity of permanent value.

If we succeed, which means, I suppose, in the language of our time, that we have penetrated the work's reality with our consciousness, that we have, quite literally, "seized it like a little ball," we are then prepared to pass to the inner reality of the artist, and from there to that of a historical period. For our assumption here is simple: every man is his own artist and makes his life in the same way as he creates a work of art—*his* work of art. Life is organic whether it is seen in art, in an artist, in history, in thought, or in itself. It certainly has to be portrayed as it is.

If that is old-fashioned, my prudent friends will have to make the most of it, until they have developed a better, "more modern" method. They don't seem to have done so up to now. I am quite aware that they are trying, though, and I wish them luck.

Despite the clear risk I run of being misunderstood, I do have a critical doctrine to defend and an earnest desire to defend it. It consists in proving that the task of the critic is the application of an analysis to the point where the critical act has been transformed into a creative act. It is understood in this process that the critic is proceeding exactly as the creative artist does; he is penetrating in an imaginative way the raw material which has been offered to him, his goal being "to possess" that material. Possession in these terms means that the critic has discovered a way to organize it as a coherent, continuous, consistent entity which because of these qualities now has power of asserting its livingness. I am, of course, well aware that all of this is subject to the accusation of being just so much critical jargon and consequently of no great value in explaining phenomena.

I am just as aware that whenever a critic, great or small, enters upon this task in whatever field of human endeavor, whether artistic, historical, autobiographical, political, economic, moral, scientific, or philosophical, his one overpowering desire is to explain, interpret, organize, and present it in such a way that it becomes alive. I realize only too well that this inordinate desire can prove unsuccessful and lay the critic open to the romantic myth of "playing God."

The critic is convinced that if he can succeed, the organized something takes on human value through the sheer capacity to further its own existence. It is in these terms that I speak of its "organic unity," meaning simply that it works as a living unit, and the livingness derives from the organized unity of its parts. It would be wiser perhaps to exclude the term and replace it with the term "total effect," meaning that we human beings are not only involved in living, we have some unquenchable desire to identify ourselves with things which have lived or can live. So far as I know, those things are works of art, important artists, important thinkers, ideas, systems of thought and action (we call them philosophies), and historical periods. It is my contention that any one of these things can be explored and exploited in the same analytic manner and with the same goals always in mind. It is tantamount to saying that the quality which binds them all together is the quality of being human.

All of this which I am trying to make appear easy to comprehend is in reality tremendously complex and I should confess that I have no great hope of ever advancing in more than a very modest way (if at all) the task which I recognize as my job.

I should perhaps add one more word of explanation. This organic unity which we harp upon so continually is not, as I see it, some mystic quality for something which has never existed; it is just the reverse, something which is very much alive. Nor do I wish it to be considered merely a bit of academic jargon, although I must admit to the possibility of its being misunderstood, and consequently thought only academic. It is, indeed, synonymous with the term "total effect" which has been in the service of literary criticism for at least fifty years. Nor do I wish it to be confused with contemporary theories of "structuralism" although it is committed to the notion that an analysis of the structural elements will always bring out the qualities of the form. Those who coined the expression assumed that a literary masterpiece, as well as a historical period, a philosophy, or the intellectual biography of a man of distinction—that is to say, the analysis of any human phenomenon in the areas of art, thought, and life—can best be understood if they are conceived as being composed of coordinated elements and that they can best be judged if those elements are analyzed for the qualities which each displays. The standard of judgment thus becomes the harmonious coordination of all the qualities in all the elements. When this harmony is of a high order, we deem that we are dealing with something which is superior and we express our appreciation of it by suggesting that it is very much alive. We thereby assert its livingness and speak freely of this livingness (erlebnis) as the "inner" reality of the thing we are trying to comprehend. It is true that we, like Voltaire, regard this "inner reality" as being more durable than "outer" reality. We would, like Voltaire, wish to think that it lasts forever, but we don't know what the word forever means. What we do know is that things to which we agree to attribute the quality of "inner" reality are very apt to last longer than we do; we don't know how much longer, of course. What enhances the livingness of the thing is coherence, consistency, and logical continuity; what threatens it is incoherence, inconsistency, and a lack of logical continuity. These latter things we usually call contradictions, and we are only too aware that we ourselves are full of them. When occasions present themselves where these contradictions appear, we assume that it is our job as critics to explain them if we can, or try to eliminate them if we cannot.

ORGANIC UNITY IN VOLTAIRE

Rien n'est plus difficile que de porter un jugement d'ensemble sur Voltaire.—G. Lanson, *Histoire de la littérature française.*

IN THIS essay, I would like to investigate Voltaire's inner reality in these terms in an effort to understand his livingness. I have considered Voltaire's intellectual development elsewhere. Here, I am more anxious to show that, having assembled an immense amount of material, Voltaire was forced to organize it in the terms I have described for any critic or any artist. Having organized it in his way, he then had to integrate it into the organizations of others —Montesquieu, Rousseau, Diderot, the *Encyclopédie*—to create an Enlightenment. In investigating that activity, I feel that I have to ask certain questions continually. What is there in Voltaire's activity which contributes to an understanding of him as an indispensable Enlightenment man? What are the sources of this particular activity and how did they modify Voltaire and Voltaire's time? How does each activity contribute to a better understanding of Voltaire? What difference does that make to us? And I shall have to repeat these questions for Montesquieu, Rousseau, Diderot, and the *Encyclopédie*.

These questions have been asked time and time again by my predecessors. All my academic language can hardly conceal that in many respects I am doing what any positivistic critic of the twentieth century has attempted in his "l'homme et l'œuvre." I have, in fact, in my first attempt at this kind of analysis recognized cheerfully my debt to a number of them (particularly Lanson, Brunetière, Bellessort, Morley, Taine, and Faguet.

Despite indiscriminate pronouncements concerning Voltaire's total worth, there have been only very few who have given more than passing consideration to the problem or the way it was organized. I have tried to gather the opinions of the outstanding critics of Voltaire in an article entitled "Towards a New Voltaire" (American Philosophical Society, Transactions: *The Search for a New Voltaire*, n.s., vol. 48, part 4, 1958, pp. 107 ff.). Even in Voltaire's day, there was a tendency to denigrate his worth, as can be seen in the two remarks of Marivaux: "M. de Voltaire est la perfection des choses communes," and "M. de Voltaire est le premier homme du monde pour dire et penser ce que tout le monde a dit et pensé." Fortunately, all judgments about him have not been so acid, although it must be admitted that he has had his share. Mr. Besterman in the *Travaux sur Voltaire*, (I, 141–143), has quoted Flaubert in an opinion which seems to me better balanced than that of Marivaux: "Je m'étonne que vous n'admiriez pas cette grande palpitation qui a remué le monde. Est-ce qu'on obtient de tels résultats quand on n'est pas sincère? . . . Bref, cet homme-là me semble ardent, acharné, convaincu, superbe. Son "Ecrasons l'infâme" me fait l'effet d'un cri de croisade. Toute son intelligence était une machine de guerre." Flaubert, however, stressed that the key to the understanding of Voltaire can be found in the artistic expression of his personal opinion: "On s'extasie devant la correspondance de Voltaire. Mais il n'a jamais été capable que de cela, le grand homme! C'est-à-dire d'exposer son opinion personnelle; et tout chez lui a été cela." Flaubert acknowledged that Voltaire was "pitoyable" in his theatre and poetry, but he admitted that he had composed a novel "lequel est le résumé de toutes ses œuvres." The best part of that, Flaubert added, are the four pages devoted to the visit which Candide made to Pococuranté's estate, "où Voltaire exprime encore son opinion personnelle sur à peu près tout." Flaubert calls these four pages "merveilles de la prose. Elles étaient la condensation de soixante volumes écrits et d'un demi-siècle d'efforts." Flaubert concludes nonetheless that what was lacking in Voltaire, in spite of his ability to create laughter or weeping, was the art of inducing revery, which incidentally was the grand art of Rousseau, whom Flaubert had just proclaimed that he detested: "Or, j'aime le grand Voltaire autant que je déteste le grand Rousseau."

Since Flaubert's day, there has often been a tendency, in speaking of Voltaire's worth, to place him in the dichotomy of poet or philosopher, artist or thinker. John Morley put it in an epigrammatic way when he wrote in his *Voltaire* (1909) that "Voltaire went to England [1726] a poet, and returned [1729] a philosopher." This bifurcation of Voltaire into poet and philosopher, artist and thinker, has been thought a sort of touchstone whereby he can be grasped as a reality. Morley left no doubt as to his own stand; for him, Voltaire was the representative man of his age: "Yet Voltaire was the very eye of eighteenth-century illumination. It was he who conveyed to his generation in the multitude of forms the consciousness at once of the power and the rights of human intelligence . . ." (p. 5). Thus, Voltaire's tremendous production is indicative of the encyclopedic spirit of curiosity. Morley adds that he was as much the heir of the thought of the past as he was the leader of the thought of his time. He was, Morley added, "a stupendous power, not only because his expression was incomparably lucid, or even because his sight was exquisitely keen and clear, but because he saw many new things, after which the spirits of others were unconsciously groping and for which they were mutely yearning."

Morley's view seems to have been shared in large part by Lanson who wrote in his *Histoire* (p. 771): "aussi est-il le philosophe qui peut-être a le plus fait pour préparer la forme actuelle de la civilisation." Lanson, however, had a greater understanding of Voltaire the literary artist than did Morley in his *Voltaire*. The former presented chapters upon *Le Goût de Voltaire* and *L'Art de Voltaire* along with those upon *Voltaire Historien* and *La Philosophie de Ferney*. It is obvious, in spite of Lanson's effort to put together the poet and the philosopher, that in the opinion of the critic, Voltaire's true worth for the twentieth century lay in his thought, particularly as it was directed to political and social matters. His remark in the *Histoire* (p. 769) seems to give the case away: "Son style n'est nullement artiste. Il voit toutes choses du point de vue de la raison; l'idée du vrai est comme la catégorie de son esprit, hors de laquelle il ne peut rien concevoir." It is true that in his *Art de la prose* and in his later revisions of the *Histoire*, Lanson made some concessions to the literary artistry of Voltaire. In general, though, Lanson lays greatest stress upon what he calls Voltaire's "œuvre de démolition de l'ancien régime" and the "réconstruction de la société moderne." His profound statement that "Voltaire nous a donné notre liberté et a préparé notre justice," though undoubtedly exaggerated, still remains one of the wisest judgments ever made about Voltaire.

On the contrary, Faguet, who in a way represents the university attitude toward Voltaire during the opening decades of the twentieth century, is much more negative and categorical in his judgment. In his *Voltaire* (p. 194) he says: "Voltaire n'a pas été artiste pour une obole." The critic declares, in addition, that "Il n'a ni le détachement du philosophe, ni l'élévation philosophique." He concedes that "il aimait passionnément la littérature," but insists that he does not understand literature. Faguet emphasizes that "il n'a point d'idée à lui, ni de conception artistique personnelle, ni même de tempérament artistique distinct et tranché à exprimer dans ses écrits." He is "un très bon écrivain" and knows that "il écrit bien." But his lack of comprehension stems from the fact that he was no poet: "cette complexion même à être un ouvrier infiniment adroit et prestigieux, qui, sans bien sentir l'art, se donne, et même aux autres, l'illusion qu'il est un artiste."

It can be asserted that these judgments, which are certainly important, make no pretense of being total, although they do tend to be arbitrary. It could be argued, I suppose, that all personal opinions tend to the arbitrary and consequently that literary, philosophical, and historical judgments are always arbitrary, sometimes interesting, but rarely true. There are some, however, who would like to develop a criticism which would not depend to such an extent upon personal opinion and possess more truth and less arbitrariness. Such an attempt in Voltaire's case was made in R. Naves's *Voltaire: L'Homme et l'œuvre* (Paris, 1958), in a section entitled "The Unity of his Thought." Naves notes that there have been those who have insisted that Voltaire constantly contradicted himself. Fréron, for instance, selected Voltaire's quotations out of context and arranged them in contradictory fashion; more serious critics, such as Châteaubriand, insisted that Voltaire eternally upheld the pros and the cons; Nisard often praised him for his thought but attributed to him diabolical intentions; Faguet characterized all his thinking a chaos of clear ideas. Naves finds these procedures unworthy and maintains that only when viewed from an unhistorical point of view can these impressions be justified. When restored to a historical basis, he insists that there is in Voltaire's thought *a psychological unity*: everywhere the same impatient desire to know, curious, hostile to all mystery, desirous of clarity. This attitude is presented as the basis for Voltaire's philosophy, which, Naves feels, always demands freedom of the mind. Naves also detects in Voltaire's thinking *a critical unity* which he defines as a dislike of absolutes, certainties, and all fanatical extremes. He confesses, however, that, despite this inner unity of mind and spirit on Voltaire's part, there is evident an evolution toward a more relaxed, broader taste, and a movement, philosophically, toward determinism. This movement, said Naves, is rather modest in the areas of philosophy and esthetics and is more pronounced in history, where Voltaire confessed that he was himself unaware that his object was the study of civilization. Naves insists that there is a third unity in Voltaire, what he calls *a practical* or *constructive unity* —Voltaire's wisdom. Naves confesses that it is his intention to utilize this concept to combat those like Bernardin de St.-Pierre who maintained that Voltaire was concerned with little else than to destroy, or like Bellessort, who asserted: "He founded nothing." Naves does not look with favor upon these criticisms, not so much because they are totally negative. Though fully as severe, a criticism such as Vinet's should be examined with care, in Naves's opinion, because it is characteristic of so many others. Vinet wrote: "Voltaire does not allow for the noblest elements of human nature, faith, the infinite, Providence; he is acquainted with the lower and middle regions of the soul. He came to know only the social side of man; he does not know what man is, face to face with himself, and all the less face to face with the infinite. He lacked a true sense of moral values; in morality, he has instincts, prejudices, habits, but no principles."

We have collected, it seems to me, a sufficient number of opinions, and varied at that, to warrant the view that ever since Voltaire's day there has been much fluctuation as to what constitutes his reality and that there would be a wide diversity of answers if we inquired as to his worth. What kind of a writer are we dealing with—a literary man, a critic, or a thinker? We could expect very different answers to this question. Some would certainly say a literary man, since Voltaire wrote fifty-four plays, an epic poem, at least two mock epics, twenty-two philosophical tales of varying length, and a large number of formal Horatian poems (satires, épîtres, odes in imitation of Horace), eight or ten poems called "philosophical" poems, an equal number of poems called "contes en vers," and a correspondence of about 20,000 letters. But he also wrote volumes of histories (universal, European, French) and many volumes treating religion, politics, economics, ethics, and natural science. Are we dealing fundamentally with a literary writer, a critic, a philosophical critic, or a thinker? If we insist that he really is a writer, is he predominantly lyric poet, epic poet, dramatist, writer of satiric "contes," novelist, or correspondent? Or is he a critic interested in encouraging others to write good literature or in discussing what constitutes good literature, history, politics, morality, philosophy, natural science? Has this latter preoccupation become so dominant in his mind that he has surrendered art for thought, thought for reform, or reform for revolution? More important than all this, perhaps, has he really abandoned his high regard for letters and his desire to be a great poet in an effort to make a new world? A world which has become a world of thought? Where ideas go running around with all the vitality of human beings? Poet, critic, thinker; thinker, reformer, maker, poet? Is that the way the mind of Voltaire works? Is that his reality, so much so that only by the power of ideas is reality, and poetry, possible? Does the critic of Voltaire have to work the same way in order to understand what Voltaire is doing? Is the critic of Voltaire left, after all his efforts, with a new definition of poet, a different sort of critic, a new kind of philosopher, or with an eighteenth-century enlightened man, an "encyclopedic" man, who is convinced that he is now prepared by enlightenment to remake his world, even if he has to destroy the one in which he is living, which turned out not to be such a bad world after all, even in Voltaire's own enlightened estimate. But, of course, Voltaire, who frequently used the metaphor of reading the ultimate answers in the book of life, seems not to have known any more than we do what these ultimate answers are. Still, he thought that it was his job to keep looking for them—just as we do.

It was Voltaire who almost single-handedly collected and brought into the eighteenth century all the currents of literature and thought from which the Enlightenment sprang. From the classical writers of antiquity, he elected to follow Horace and Virgil, Lucretius and Cicero. In that group, Virgil appeared to him the perfect poet, but Horace appealed to him more, perhaps because of his satires and epistles, his ability to converse with his readers with ease and grace, and his role as the classical literary critic. His first acquaintance with Horace probably came from his Latin teacher, Père Tarteron, who had translated and published the Latin poet into French. Voltaire, however, appreciated more highly the ten-volume translation with commentaries by Dacier. Lucretius appealed to Voltaire because of the *De rerum natura*, which tended particularly toward a kind of Anti-Christian Epicureanism that Voltaire sometimes expressed in his early years, but as far as I can see the influence of Epicurus was a passing one. What attracted Voltaire to Cicero was probably the *De natura deorum*, which was rather widely read and quoted in the clandestine deistic manuscripts of his time. In later years, Cicero loomed large, because of his authority in moral matters.

From the classical writers of the preceding century, he chose Boileau, Racine, and La Fontaine; Boileau because he was the French Horace with his satires and epistles and his role as critic; Racine because he, like Virgil, was the perfect poet; and La Fontaine because of his gracefulness, his charm, his quiet mirth, but, above all, because of his ability to produce "contes en vers." Voltaire admired all three of these poets because of their command over the language. He never failed to stress their ability to say exactly in poetry what each wanted to say. While they were his masters, though, Voltaire undoubtedly felt a greater affinity to the free-thinking Horatian poets, who were abundant in France in the seventeenth century beginning with Théophile de Viau, Des Barreaux, Blot, De Hénault, Mme. des Houlières, Chaulieu, and La Fare. Voltaire knew the works of all; the two whom he particularly cultivated were Chaulieu and La Fare. Voltaire knew them personally at the Temple. Of these two, he imitated especially Chaulieu. Of the Utopian novelists, he knew the works of Rabelais, Cyrano, and Fénelon, and eventually those of Foigny, Vairasse, Tyssot de Patot, La Hontan, and Gilbert. At first only the *Télémaque* appealed to him, probably because of the wide popularity it enjoyed, but in the late 1720s and the 1730s, both Cyrano and Rabelais became more important because of Voltaire's infatuation with Swift. Before the end of the Cirey period, all the Utopian novelists were united with the oriental tales to furnish the background for the *Contes philosophiques*. It was at this time also that Voltaire delved heavily in all the free-thinkers from Montaigne to Bayle: Charron, Naudé, La Mothe le Vayer, and Saint-Evremond. He was particularly attracted at first to Saint-Evremond, but in the 1740s both Montaigne and Bayle commanded his attention.

Voltaire became acquainted with every one of the great European philosophers of the seventeenth century from Bacon to Fontenelle: Hobbes, Descartes, Gassendi, Pascal, Spinoza, Leibniz, Malebranche, Bayle, Newton, and Locke. Those whom he tried to reject were Descartes, Pascal, and Leibniz, without too much success, however. Finally, those whom he treated with the greatest caution were

Malebranche, Bayle, and Spinoza. He became acquainted with these philosophers at various intervals; he had at least a passing acquaintance with Malebranche, Descartes, and Bayle before going to England. Of these three, he showed more interest in Malebranche at that time. While in England, he had a passing acquaintance with Bacon, Newton, and Locke. He worked hard with Descartes, Newton, Locke, and Leibniz from 1734 to 1740. The philosopher whom he regarded with the gravest suspicion was Spinoza, because of his alleged atheism. Curiously, though, the two who seemed to intrigue him most at the end of his life were Leibniz and Spinoza, and the one whom he openly adopted at the end was the one whom he had relied upon at the beginning—Malebranche. I think it is significant that he saw in Malebranche a philosopher-poet. In those preferences and dislikes, Voltaire's opinions appear more or less in accord with the public opinion of his time. The two points of serious deviation were Bacon, whom he regarded as a precursor and whom the *Encyclopédie* adopted as the founder of their epistemology, and Hobbes, whom Voltaire tended to neglect probably because Hobbes, like Spinoza, was regarded as an atheist and because acceptance of Locke precluded too much interest in Hobbes. However, in the *Philosophe ignorant* (1766) and thereafter, Hobbes assumed a greater importance, probably because of Diderot's article in the *Encyclopédie* which Voltaire greatly admired.

The English writers varied greatly in their influence. The two whom he investigated with the greatest care, but with least results, were Shakespeare and Milton; the three who exercized the most influence upon his own work were Dryden, Pope, and Swift. The most influential moralists were Bolingbroke, Mandeville, and Shaftesbury; the English deists whom he studied were Toland, Woolston, Collins, Middleton, Annet, and Tindal. Of the corresponding French deists, he was well acquainted with Meslier, Boulainvilliers, Dumarsais, Fréret, Mirabaud, and Lévesque de Burigny. The two deists whom he used more than the others were Meslier and Woolston. Finally, Voltaire was forced to coordinate all these selections from the past with his interest in contemporaries, particularly Melon, Dutot, the Abbé de Saint-Pierre, Montesquieu, Diderot, the encyclopedists, and Rousseau.

What stands out from this large enumeration of classical French and English writers and thinkers is the tremendous diversity of his interests. In fact, in the past we have tended to stress that they may be arranged in many distinct groups: the classical writers of antiquity, the French classical writers of the preceding century, the Horatian Epicurean free-thinking poets of the previous century, the Utopian novelists of the sixteenth and seventeenth centuries, the free-thinkers from Montaigne to Bayle, all the outstanding philosophers of Western Europe from Bacon to Bayle, the outstanding English writers of the sixteenth and seventeenth centuries, the English moralists at the end of the seventeenth century, the English deists, the corresponding French deists of the first part of the eighteenth century, the political and economic writers, and the French and some English historians of the same period. All told, these diverse interests ranged from poetry, drama, epic poetry, and literary criticism to history, politics, and economics, to the study of civilization, to morality as the science of man, to natural sciences and life sciences, to religion, to that philosophy which consists in trying to see life whole and in attempting to create its possibilities. Such extraordinary diversity certainly leaves us with the feeling that we are dealing with a universal, encyclopedic man. There is no wonder that at the Bibliothèque Nationale he is classed among the "polygraphes"—meaning, I suppose that he is totally unclassifiable. Still, one would like to be able to bring all this together and give it a focus. That undoubtedly is what Voltaire eventually had to do. He himself stated that he organized everything around the concept of "la morale" ("Je ramène tout à la morale"). He insisted that despite the fact that there is a continual difference of opinions and ideas on the principles of things, this "morale" is common to all men of all times and places. It is universal, and it comes from God who has granted it to all through reason. While it would not be impossible, I imagine, to accept Voltaire's own opinion of his unity, it would not be easy to demonstrate how his enormous production fits into the concept of "la morale" or contributes to the formation of a vital morality or a dynamic view of the sciences of man or the expression of a new humanism or even a declaration of "the party of humanity." Some recent historians have tried in the last few decades to do this. I have no objection to assigning to Voltaire a deep interest in the problems of humanity; indeed, all his activity in attempting to bring into existence a better world is very important. There are, however, other important aspects of Voltaire which can be incorporated under this rubric only with difficulty—his art, for instance.

The tremendous breadth and diversity of influences to which Voltaire submitted either expressed or led to a great diversity of interests. In Voltaire's own activity there has been apparent throughout his long life a constant desire to be the leader in many fields. Indeed, we have interpreted this desire for leadership as one of the outstanding reasons for his evident lack of focus. For instance, he wanted to be France's foremost playwright in the Enlightenment, France's superior poet, France's epic poet of all time, France's leading cultural historian, a superior scientist, an outstanding thinker, and so on. The result of this constant diversity of interest and this ambition to become preeminent in all these areas was that, even in his day, there was tendency to regard him as peculiarly shapeless, unorganized, contradictory, and somewhat superficial. But it also left the impression of an extraordinary mobility, which is certainly another of his important characteristics. He constantly moved from one place to another—Paris, London, Cirey, Berlin, Lyons, Lausanne, Geneva, and the German principalities. He also moved from one intellectual pursuit to another—from poetry to history, criticism, natural science, politics, and religion; from one idea to another—freedom, justice, natural law, and deism; from one genre to another—epic, mock epic, drama, "conte philosophique," essay, dialogue, "facétie," history, and correspondence; from one philosophical attitude to another—determinism, Epicureanism, stoicism, optimism, meliorism, pessimism, skepticism, deism, and pantheism. He even skirted a kind of atheism at times, while professing a horror for such a move. Finally, he moved from one theory to another: justice, doctrine of progress, theory of utility, personal interest, theory of attendant circumstances, of the spirit of nations, of public education, of tolerance, liberty, equality, fraternity. All this mobility, both physical and intellectual, contributes to a further impression of scattered diversity, discontinuity, and incoherence.

In order to comprehend this diversity, mobility, and dispersal, we usually adopt some sort of genetic process which consists in dividing his long life into periods. The method was utilized by Desnoiresterres in his massive eight-volume *Voltaire et la société française au dix-*

huitième siècle, and was adopted by Lanson in his short but excellent *Voltaire*. In general, all of us have followed this procedure; specifying the period of Voltaire's youth (1694-1725), the English period (1726-1729), a Cirey period (1733-1749), a Berlin period (1750-1753), a Geneva period (1754-1758), a Ferney period (1759-1777), and finally the return to Paris (1778).

There are certain hazards in this method, to be sure. In the first place, there are some unexplained gaps in this kind of arbitrary periodization, between England and Cirey, for instance, or between Potsdam and Geneva. The last half of the Cirey period (1740-1749) was called by Lanson the most arid part of Voltaire's intellectual career. These gaps have a tendency also to break the continuity, the consistency, or the organic unity of his intellectual career. We are all too ready to assume that when Voltaire moved from one aspect to another, or from one period to another, he abandoned his former interest in favor of a subsequent but different one, and that he thereby broke the continuity of his work. The assumption, however, is not correct in Voltaire's case. He had a way of changing the priority of his material, but rarely did he drop some part of it and replace it by another. As a result, the longer he lived, the more complex his intellectual life became, the more difficulty he experienced in keeping it integrated, and the more difficulty we experience in keeping it unified. Moreover, there occurred in Voltaire's life, as in everybody's, a certain length of time in which a new experience was undergone, followed by a longer time when the new experience was integrated and interpreted to Voltaire's audience. The English period is a good case in point. Voltaire underwent it in two years, more or less, but it took some six years to absorb it and the rest of his life to integrate and interpret it to the French. Finally, in the formal periods as we establish them, there are usually shorter periods of great intensity in which Voltaire condenses an immense amount of intellectual energy. They should be regarded, I suppose, as crisis periods, since they are, indeed, "le moment de la crise." Such a critical time occurred from 1719 to 1723 when Voltaire entered upon his career as poet and when he produced in rapid succession a tragedy (*Œdipe*, 1719), a philosophical Horatian poem (*L'Epître à Uranie*, 1722), and an epic poem (*La Ligue*, 1723). A second of these moments of intensity occurred at the time of the English sojourn; a third came in 1734, when Voltaire retired to Cirey with Mme. du Châtelet and literally reeducated himself in a modern way during the next four years. Berlin offered Voltaire the counterpart of England, but this time, the result was a defeat. It was a critical moment and an exceedingly intense one, but for once Voltaire judged it wrongly out of a wounded vanity. Be that as it may, the next crucial period lasted from 1758 to 1762 (it coincided precisely with the most crucial moment of the Enlightenment). This time Voltaire was prepared, thanks to the defeat at Potsdam. The last of these crucial periods extended from 1768 to 1772 when he was faced with the final organization of Voltaireanism. Each of these short periods of intensity in which Voltaire's involvement is at a climax is preceded and followed by longer stretches when absorption and organization are more important than intensity. The striking thing about this rhythm, however, is the clear way in which the consistent and continuous flow of Voltaire's activity harmonizes both movement and change. It is rather imperative that we grasp this rhythm, otherwise we run the risk of slipping into a tendency of seeing incoherences where there are only perfectly normal growth and change.

There is, however, a final difficulty in rightly interpreting the meaning of Voltaire. This difficulty springs from the clandestinity which is so very typical of all his activity. It is, to be sure, a rich source of his satire and irony, and basic to his wit. But it is not easy to know just how to interpret it. Perhaps the best way of proceeding is to remember that Faguet's statement that Voltaire is a "chaos of clear ideas" derived from a misunderstanding on Faguet's part of the meaning of this clandestinity. It is not enough to regard it as a simple subterfuge to elude the censorship, although doubtless that is the way it got its start. We must recall that it was a stylistic device for bringing together normally incompatible opposites and even contradictory phenomena—illusion and reality, for instance, or the assumption of a mask to conceal a truth or even vice and virtue. It is also a powerful artistic device, so powerful, indeed, that it may delude the creator as well as his audience. Under these circumstances the possibilities of self-delusion are practically infinite; carried too far, they may induce pain and frustration rather than enlightenment and happiness. There are, for example, situations in which Voltaire actually deluded himself, thinking all the time that he was merely fooling his audience. *Candide* is one of them.

Be that as it may, we must now return to Voltaire's determination to be the Poet. Miss Gilman in her *Idea of Poetry in France* (Cambridge, Mass., 1958) has quoted a remark from the Abbé Trublet's *Essay*, "De la Poésie et des poètes": "As reason is perfected," Trublet wrote, "judgment will more and more be preferred to imagination, and, consequently, poets will be less and less appreciated. The first writers, it is said, were poets. I can well believe it; they could hardly be anything else. The last writers will be philosophers." Miss Gilman has utilized Trublet's remark to point up a particular attitude toward the relationship of poetry and philosophy in Voltaire's day. There is certainly implied in the remark that poetry is characteristic of the world's youth, while philosophy is characteristic of its maturity, with the further assumption that philosophy must be richer, more important, and consequently something other than poetry. That could be a prejudice. The curious thing, though, is that Voltaire made very similar remarks in Lacombe's *Poétique de Voltaire*.

Nonetheless, Voltaire's plan for becoming the Poet has all the appearance of being both total and organic. He would essay all kinds of poetry: lyric, dramatic, and epic. He would pick as his masters those who in his opinion were preeminent in antiquity—Horace and Virgil—and those who were superior in France in the glorious century which had just preceded him—Boileau, Racine, and La Fontaine. He would choose as his sponsors the Horatian free-thinking lyric poets of seventeenth-century France. His immediate guide in all this would be the Abbé Dubos, "l'homme de très bon sens" (there's that judgment getting ready to torpedo the "poetic imagination"). The lighter verse of the miscellaneous poems—the epigram, chanson, society verses of a satiric order—was to follow Horace in structural form and the free-thinking poets of the Temple, especially La Fare and Chaulieu. To them should be added the more sublime poetry of Virgil and Racine: the epic and drama should be joined to the épître, the ode, the satire of Boileau, the "Horace français," and the "poésies légères" of La Fontaine along with the Horatian free-thinkers. Finally, the expression was to be patterned upon the art of Virgil, Horace, Racine, and La Fontaine. It was an art which consisted in saying, clearly and precisely, exactly what the poet wanted to depict; in the desire to bring together "pensées vraies" with "expressions justes," not merely "mots justes"; in the conformity of the thought with the style. Appreciation of the art was guaranteed by the taste of the poet and that of his audience. Thus the poet would express himself in all poetic genres, but in a modern, contemporary way. To his ambition to become the poet of his day, Voltaire aspired above all to a preeminence in poetic expression, hence his determination to outdistance Chaulieu and La Fare, Boileau and Horace, Virgil and Racine. He would write the French epic poem, since France had never succeeded in having a modern epic; his drama would naturally have to be superior to all other preceding drama of Racine and Corneille. Since the Greeks had been said to have an interesting drama and some superior playwrights, he began with the greatest of all—Sophocles—and imitated his greatest play—*Œdipus*. It was a rash move, but in popular opinion it succeeded just as the *Ligue* succeeded, chiefly because no one understood Sophocles or Homer or Horace, with the possible exception of M. and Mme. Dacier. If, however, I exaggerate—and a few did— mostly priests, there is no great importance in the fact, because the modernity of Voltaire could not possibly be present in Sophocles and Homer; Voltaire, though, insisted as much on being modern as being poetic.

There were other difficulties in executing this program. There was a distinct feeling on the part of many that poetry had declined, even that it was no longer possible to justify it. Voltaire himself entertained this notion and explained it by insisting that France was resting after the glorious previous age. Under the quarrel of the ancients and the subsequent attack against Homer, it was understood that what had brought about this threatened sterility in poetry was failure to become modern. Since the time was characterized by the gradual disappearance of poetry, it was not long before the suggestion was made that if poetry consisted in "pensées vraies" and "expressions justes," one would do well to suppress the poetic expression and develop the philosophical content. La Motte, with his "Géométrie," actually advised abandoning poetry for prose, maintaining that the restraints of verse handicapped the clarity of expression. He actually began writing prose drama and congratulated Mme. Dacier, a bit ironically, for translating Homer into French prose. Voltaire nonetheless refused the advice and struggled for twenty-five years to be the Poet, with great success in the opinion of his contemporaries, while insisting that the difficulties of verse, which he conceded, added additional beauties to the subject-matter.

There were other impediments, though, which we can only enumerate for the moment. Voltaire may have had a superficial acquaintance with Sophocles and Homer, but he had no understanding whatever of their merit. Having written and performed his *Œdipe* he wrote a critical essay comparing his play with that of Sophocles and with Corneille's imitation of Sophocles, from which he had actually taken his subject-matter. Corneille's play was almost as mediocre as Voltaire's, if one may risk such an inconsequential literary judgment. The latter was sufficiently astute to recognize that, but the real difficulty stemmed from the fact that he had no comprehension of the worth of the Greek play. Furthermore, it is clear that Voltaire's whole concept of the art of drama was built upon a false understanding of the value of technical, literary rules and upon the assumption that the author was master showman and had full control over the actions of the protagonists. He therefore maintained that it was he who ordered them what to say and when to say it, what to do and when to do it. He invented the situation, assigned the theme, organized the emotions, and produced the effects. In some peculiar way, he looked upon the playwright as a sort of a "chef-d'orchestre." That would work in a theatre of marionettes or in any kind of magic lantern performance, both of which Voltaire adored, but it was scarcely the accepted procedure for a classical dramatist.

The English experience of 1726 to 1729 had brought about some modification of Voltaire's plan to become the total poet. We all assume that his intention of going to England consisted in enriching French letters with English letters. At least, we assume that, since he was permitted to spend his exile in England, the natural thing for him to do would be to get acquainted with the English literary production of the time. That may well have been a major preoccupation with him. In general, though, Voltaire does not seem to have enriched his own poetry to any great extent by any penetration of English poetry, despite the fact that his visit was heralded in the journals of the time as that of a famous French poet. There were, however, some notable exceptions—Pope, whose literary production appealed to him immensely, to the point where he thought him the greatest poet in the whole world. Pope had some influence upon Voltaire's shift from light Horatian verse to Horatian philosophical poetry; he at least confirmed the French poet in his desire to make the shift. Voltaire also admired and imitated the Englishman's literary criticism, his "morale," while in the field of philosophy, Voltaire equated him almost with Locke and Newton. Swift with his satire was almost as interesting. Voltaire merged the satiric utopianism of the English novelist with Rabelais, Cyrano, and the utopian French, and eventually created a new form of philosophical *conte*. Shakespeare, whom he tried to use to renew French drama, and Milton, from whom he hoped to extract new styles in epic poetry, both proved disappointing. In the theatre, Dryden alone was useful but only because, like Pope, he had already submitted to the classical doctrine of Boileau. In letters, Pope, Swift, and Dryden, represent the literary impact of England upon the French poet. It would certainly be unwise to be persuaded that the influence of English letters was anything exceptional.

We should not forget at this point, while talking of Voltaire the poet in England, two tendencies which he had shown even before his arrival in London. The first is that Voltaire subscribed fully to Boileau's division of the poetic art into thought and expression. But Voltaire tended to equate the thought with philosophy, the expression with art. Boileau had no intention of drawing such a conclusion. Voltaire was closer to the mark when he said that these classicists could say precisely what they wished to say. Voltaire's conclusion went much farther. It was what inclined him even in his early poetry to pack into his poetry a good deal of free-thinking. Indeed, the *Epître à Uranie*, one of his earliest poems, is as philosophical as any of his later philosophical poems. This fact also brings out a second tendency already evident in Voltaire's poetry. We are likely to get the impression that he came to the decision to be the poet without any hesitation. As a matter of fact, there is some evidence, and Pomeau was among the first to point out its significance, to indicate that Voltaire was in his early days drawn to religion and religious discussion as much as to poetry. The most telling part of this evidence can be deduced from the source of the thought of *L'Epître à Uranie*, which was taken from three combined poems of Chaulieu under the general title of *Trois façons de penser sur la mort* (after the principles of Christianity, of deism, and of Epicureanism). If one stops to reflect upon these three *façons de penser* he will see clearly that Voltaire faced in this one poem problems which involved not only poetry but religion and ethics. In fact, he was preoccupied not only with religious problems but with political and ethical ones as well, particularly in his drama and in his epic.

The consequence of these two tendencies was that Voltaire was not totally unprepared to meet with the strength and diversity of English thought. By reputation, England was the land of thinkers, and Voltaire found that it indeed was. Besides, two of its thinkers, Locke and Newton, had only recently been recommended by Bolingbroke. Voltaire was now busily engaged in making their acquaintance and he had become impressed to the point that he judged each to be the greatest philosopher in the whole world. He was convinced that England was the land of philosophers and that he should acquaint the French with these strange people.

Hence, if his first aim in journeying to England was to familiarize himself with English poetry and poets, a second aim certainly involved getting acquainted with the civilization of England and introducing it to the French. The project naturally necessitated an alteration in his poetic enterprise: all the more since Voltaire held to the formula of "vraies pensées" with "expressions justes," that is of thought and art. He now conceived of the British as more competent in thought, while the French were in his view superior in art. He envisaged, however, that British thought and French art, well integrated, laid the foundation for a very acceptable European civilization. This was the basis for the merging of the two, but he was forced first to study the problem of getting at the inner reality of a foreign civilization.

At first it was a personal problem. Voltaire's experience in England had made him keenly aware that there were some striking differences between life in London and life in Paris. He had some difficulties in assembling these differences, as every traveler does, but fortunately he had Thiériot upon whom he could try them. For the moment, these differences seemed to be mainly idiosyncrasies and contradictions, strange and bizarre. The trial letter which he sketched but which never entered into the *Lettres philosophiques* stressed with some wit these peculiarities. At the same time it is evident that he was busy trying to make some basic generalizations about the English people. "England is a nation of thinkers; the Englishman is public-spirited." It is evident that Voltaire, like all travelers in another country, was prying into the manners and customs of the people in order to understand their reality. But he quickly understood that this manner of proceeding, while interesting and amusing, was not sufficient. Sometime between 1728 and 1733 he devised another way of analyzing the inner reality of a people. What characterized a society, he decided, was its religion; its political and economic organization; its social structure, its philosophical thought; its science, its arts, and its letters; its institutions for advancing art and science; and its treatment of the leaders in these fields, particularly, since he himself was a poet, its poets. These were the subjects treated in the *Lettres philosophiques*. Where Voltaire found this scheme is still not very well known. Some of it undoubtedly came from the travel guides on England—Leti, Guy Miège, and Chamberlayne; some from the more sophisticated travelers—Muralt and Prévost; some from the English writers on this subject—Addison, and the contributors to the periodicals of the time. But I know no place in which Voltaire could have discovered that a civilization consists in the way a society lives its religious category, its political category, its economic category, its social category, its philosophy, science, and art categories, and its institution category. What was even more specific was Voltaire's discovery that the characteristics which a society discloses in one of these categories will likely be the characteristics which it will show in other categories. Hence it is possible to put together the manners and customs, the political and social institutions, and the arts and sciences of a people and define that people's civilization. It is even possible to define this civilization in such a way that it will be understood as desirable by another people and even absorbed by that other people if it so wishes. Finally, it is possible to merge the manners of living of the two different peoples in such a way that the superior qualities of each may be united with those of the other and thereby create an advanced civilization.

All of these considerations led in a perfectly logical way to the concept of a new kind of history. I am not sure we have understood very clearly what this new history is about and what role it played in Voltaire's philosophy and in the development of enlightenment as a whole. We have some fine analyses of Voltaire's histories, one of the best being Professor Brumfitt's *Voltaire Historian* (Oxford, 1958). For the most part, they are concerned with Voltaire and his predecessors in the art of history, with his own views upon the major problems of scientific history, and with his deficiencies looked at from the point of view of twentieth-century historiography. It is not my intention to enter into a discussion of these perfectly legitimate matters. What I want to do here is to stress that the historical problem underlying Voltaire's histories is the extent to which one's thought is what one says, does, and is. Voltaire seems committed to the belief that a society is consequently what it thinks, says, does, and is. Ideas are the source of man's activities. We take all these things for granted these days and do not even accord them any great importance. But we do refer to them, without giving them a thought, as intellectual history. Voltaire, however, came upon the problem in a much more specific way—in the conditions which he had just experienced. His first formal historical work was composed in England—*Histoire de Charles XII*. Voltaire undoubtedly undertook it because he thought it was amusing. He didn't undertake it, however, because he wanted to write a "new" kind of history; it was "romanced" history of the sort produced by writers like Courtilz de Sandras. Even now it makes grand fiction, beautifully related. But Voltaire gave it a "philosophical" focus; it was the history of a king who ruined his country. Voltaire announced his purpose in his prefaces, and he pointed up his seriousness of purpose by constantly contrasting Charles, the king who ruined his country, with Peter, the czar who civilized his, that is, he gave it a civilization. But Voltaire had just come from a country where discussion was relatively widespread as to whether Louis XIV had given France the glory of the superior civilization of Europe or whether he had bankrupted and exhausted it by his incessant wars. We practically always assume that when Voltaire composed his *Siècle de Louis XIV*, he accepted the first view and defended it, but those few who saw the manuscript around 1738 and 1739, when it was considered all but finished and ready for publication, asserted otherwise (both Valdruche and Goujet). The Abbé de Saint-Pierre's *Annales*, which was also finished and ready for the printer around

1739 and was known to Voltaire, affirmed the second point of view. Voltaire's *Siècle*, though presumed ready for publication in 1739, was not published until 1751. We have always thought that he waited to publish it until Berlin because he felt that it would not be tolerated in Paris. It now seems more likely that Voltaire needed much of the time between 1739, when the trial chapters were launched, and 1751 to revise the point of view. At all events, the *Siècle* is not the blueprint for the analysis of a civilization. The blueprint for the "new" kind of history was the *Lettres philosophiques*. It was in that work that Voltaire made his discoveries in the method of analysis, in the study of the seven categories of every civilization, in the search for the manners and customs of the people (their *mœurs*), the penetration of their political and social institutions, and the knowledge of their arts and letters, their science and their history. If the *Lettres philosophiques* was the blueprint, the *Essai sur les mœurs* and *La Philosophie de l'histoire* were its culmination. But much had to be learned before Voltaire arrived at this point. (See the excellent introduction of Professor Pomeau to his edition of the *Essai sur les mœurs*, Paris, 1963, 2 vols.)

The execution of this second project in the *Lettres philosophiques* rendered necessary a third enterprise which consisted in a whole reeducation on the part of Voltaire. At first he saw it as an education in English civilization, and he began to boast to Thiériot of having become a self-made Englishman. Very quickly, though, he understood that this project entailed training in the analysis of all categories of life, but it particularly required skill in the merging of art with thought and poetry with philosophy, what Voltaire constantly referred to as "poétiser et philosopher." It was this reeducation and this merging process which became the basis of his desire to become the encyclopedic man.

In reality, this third enterprise involved not only a tremendous increase in knowledge but also a totally new epistemology and a basic shift from the dominance of formal poetry to that of philosophy. Not only did Voltaire undertake such subjects as biblical criticism, cultural history, politics, economics, "la morale," metaphysics, and physics, he undertook to assemble the history of ideas in these subjects, to organize a whole new way of thinking, and to give to that thought a philosophical orientation. This brought up the adoption of a whole new set of choices: the Epicurean free-thinking poets now yielded to the prose essayists and free-thinkers from Montaigne to Saint-Evremond; a whole long line of philosophers from Bacon to Bayle had to be consulted and, where relevant, to be merged and absorbed. Preferably, the French philosophers were to yield to the English; the scientists were to precede the metaphysicians; and the historians and political thinkers, that is to say, the moralists, were to take precedence over the natural scientists. The two subjects of supreme importance became critical deism and history. The former was to lead to the reform of all previous assumptions, the latter was to devise means to give impetus to the march of the human mind. But Voltaire was unwilling to renounce art for philosophy. While he did deemphasize the formal poetic genres, he gave a high priority to a new kind of philosophical novel. From 1758 to 1762, he completed the process. He had transformed himself from the poet to the encyclopedic man. Everything he touched became philosophical: poetry, drama, "conte," essay, correspondence, science, history. What remained now was to establish some kind of a focus and to find a way to interpret that philosophy into action.

Thus all the currents of seventeenth-century thought and art enter into the eighteenth century through Voltaire; he is the terminus of a long line of Epicurean poets, followers of Horace, Lucretius, utopian novelists, erudite free-thinkers, classic authors, philosophers, political theorists, modern scientists, English and French deists. Voltaire actually unifies all the diversity of classicism. Not only does he close the movements represented by these groups, he seems to dominate each essential eighteenth-century movement of ideas which derives naturally from them: the quarrel of the ancients and moderns; the formation of the doctrine of progress; the quarrel of the Jesuits and the Jansenists; *La Géométrie poétique*; French and English deism; the development of modern science in England, Holland, and France; the development of political ideas from Bodin to Rousseau, of moral ideas from Montaigne to Diderot, of esthetic ideas from Boileau to Diderot. Voltaire does not always carry these movements of ideas to the apex of their development. He never attained the quiet simplicity of Montesquieu's republicanism, nor the profound political thought of Rousseau, nor the magnificent esthetic doctrine of Diderot. But he always seemed to take the initiative in some sort of way in starting these and many other things on their way.

Voltaire's two fundamental enterprises of becoming an encyclopedic man and of preparing himself through the intellectual processes of the encyclopedic man for the making of a new organic way of life required a new epistemology and a new conception of history. The sheer massiveness of the material was staggering and any one item could justify a full life: poet, Newtonian scientist, political and economic thinker, literary critic, historian, critical deist, moralist, encyclopedist. It is clear that Voltaire wished his understanding to embrace all the categories of life, and he wished to integrate coherently and put into action the sum total of this understanding. Because he accepted the responsibility for structuring all these preoccupations into a new conception of life, he literally had to forge a philosophy, a philosophy which was at the same time an art—the art of living. He had to investigate the scope of this philosophy, he had to organize it into a coherent whole, and he was obliged to develop an action in accord with his new vision. But this was not all. He seemed determined to give a new direction to life by changing the general direction of thought, and through this shift in direction, he was determined to change the march of civilization.

The procedure which he employed to achieve this was a merging process. Beginning with the Cirey period, he frequently talked of merging poetry with some other intellectual activity—with science, with history, with "la morale." Over and over he refers to this merging with the expression "poétiser et philosopher." He actually wrote to Cideville and Formont, his two Rouen friends, that he was distributing intervals of his time between poetry and science; then between poetry, science, and history; finally, between poetry, science, history, and morale. The next step was to merge all this into philosophy. In this way, he prepared himself diligently to become a philosopher, a free-thinker, an encyclopedic man, a "philosophe," and, at the same time, to remain a poet. It is obvious that in each case, he thought his preparation qualified him to become a critic of previous philosophers, a historian of ideas, a defender of certain particular ideas, and an initiator of certain thoughts of great importance for the welfare of man.

As a result of the constant merging, he became involved with a difficulty. There can be no doubt that he, like his century, was caught in the "content-form" dilemma. Form, having failed first because of a scarcity of content, failed a second time because of the overpowering massiveness of the new content and also because of the nature of much of the new content. Voltaire was faced, like Montaigne, two centuries before him, with assembling the wisdom of his time. His task, however, was more complicated than Montaigne's. His intellectual baggage no longer comprised one thousand books of the past; it comprised between five and six thousand works from the past and the present. It contained not predominantly humanistic learning, but liberal learning; that is, it was at the same time more broad and more specialized. It was not simply Mediterranean, as Montaigne's had been, it was Nordic as well as Latin. Naturally, Voltaire had difficulties in organizing this disparate material. His Notebooks offer some evidence of the confusion which he experienced. Nonetheless, they display four distinct currents of interest: literature, history, "la morale," and science. They give a picture of a man desperately concerned with incorporating his knowledge into a unity. The problem of organic unity was for him, as for us, almost overwhelming.

We have to take into account that what was happening to him was also happening to his contemporaries, but each naturally had his particular way of responding to the situation. When, following the discussion of geometry with La Motte, the age turned from poetry to prose as the dominant form of expression, Voltaire opposed the move. His English notebooks were cluttered with selections, not from Locke and Newton, but from English verse not always of the best, and they attest to the fact that his dominant interest was still poetry. He returned from England nonetheless prepared to make a compromise. He would continue writing poetry, but he would write prose, too. It was at that moment that drama became prose dialogue, the epic formal history; the épître, the prose epistle. And there was a terrain dealing with moral philosophy which he put indiscriminately into prose (*Traité de métaphysique*) or verse (*Le Mondain, Discours en vers sur l'homme*). It is significant, though, that he published the poetic version, and laid aside the prose.

Then natural science took the place of formal literature in popular favor. Voltaire recorded the trend and his opposition in a letter to Thiériot, but to no avail, since the new intellectual current was strongly oriented toward the science. Voltaire was most distressed by the fact that Newtonianism was ill-suited to formal literary genres. He now decided upon another compromise. He would give part of his time to the arts, part to science, alternating between poetry and science. This did not prevent him from attempting to put Newtonian science into verse (*Epître à Mme. du Châtelet*), but Newtonian science was, he discovered, somewhat unpoetic. Moreover, his turning to history merely complicated his difficulties, and there was also the Biblical criticism, the literary criticism, and letters. He had finally reached the moment when he had no literary genre which could contain all this indiscriminate material.

It was at this point that he invented a kind of philosophical symposium, called a *Conte philosophique*, which, strictly speaking, is a cross between a dialogue (or series of dialogues) and a restricted essay. The new form, original enough, can be broken up into either dialogue or restricted essay, and when so broken up becomes admirably adapted to the varied materials he had to treat. It is protean-like also, since it may be a letter, fiction, narrative, or an actual event; a very abbreviated essay, or a series of essays; a dialogue, that is, a true dialogue between two named characters, or sometimes between two opposing ideas under the symbolic names of characters, or a series of Dialogues (as in *Micromégas* and later *Candide*), or an imperfect dialogue (which is a letter between Voltaire and his correspondent). Its elasticity presents a real advantage—it gave Voltaire limitless possibilities to "stretch a point." It is adjustable to any content or to any amount of content. By separating each little essay, one can clarify each idea in turn; by uniting a handful of little essays, one has a treatise; by uniting a series of treatises, one creates a massive work. Thus Voltaire's whole nonformal production (excluding drama, epic, mock epic, light poetry), including both histories and contes, is an encyclopedic production using encyclopedic techniques. Indeed, in many cases (*Lettres philosophiques, Examen important, Dictionnaire philosophique,* and *Questions sur l'Encyclopédie*) it follows an encyclopedic order. There is really no difference between a personal letter and a letter in the *Lettres philosophiques* (except in the addressee), a letter of the *Lettres philosophiques* and a chapter of the *Traité de métaphysique* (except in arrangement); a chapter of the *Traité de métaphysique* and an article in the *Dictionnaire philosophique* (except the alphabetical order), between an article in the *Dictionnaire* and a chapter in *Candide* (except in the fictional plot); between a chapter in *Candide* and a "facétie" such as *Frère Berthier* (except in completeness); and between a "facétie" and a dialogue such as the *Dîner du Comte de Boulainvilliers* (except that external gestures and fictional plot have been removed). Everywhere the unit is the short, restricted essay which bursts at any moment into monologue or dialogue. To be sure it is exceedingly diversified, marvelously contradictory, very ironical, and delightfully paradoxical. All of these qualities are what we call "witty"; they are techniques to protect or to defend, to attack or to ridicule the ideas; they are devices whereby ideas can be incorporated into life or disengaged from it, persuasions of a master showman who prides himself above all upon his "style," his "class," his "art of persuasion." The whole operation vitalizes ideas, it breathes into them all the dynamic livingness people think they alone possess. The assumption here is that an idea can do anything a person may do and, provided it can make contact with a human mind, can do it better, because having been once brought to life it never dies. It is "l'esprit, l'esprit humain, l'esprit du monde, l'esprit des nations, l'énigme du monde."

Voltaire discovered this technique early (by 1734), although it came from La Mothe le Vayer and all those from Montaigne on who talked about the meaning of *Pensées*. Voltaire, who talked often as his century did of "esprit," was slow in finding a name for it. If we examine the *Œuvres* of 1741, it is evident that the process has begun. In Volume IV of this edition, the *Lettres philosophiques* have become *Mélanges de littérature et de philosophie*. They are now in chapter form and other chapters, not part of the original *Lettres*, have been added (Chapter I: "De la Gloire, ou entretien avec un Chinois"; Chapter II: "Du Suicide, ou de l'homicide de soi-même"). In the 1742 edition of the *Œuvres* (Vol. V), the technique progressed; there he published as little essays items which entered into the *Mélanges* of 1756 as separate articles, and into the *Dictionnaire philosophique* of 1764 in alphabetical order. For instance, "Déisme" in the *Oeuvres* (Volume V, of 1742) became *Théisme* in the *Mélanges* of 1756 and *Théisme* in the *Dictionnaire philosophique* of 1764. The articles "Bulle," "Contradictions," "Fanatisme," "Histoire," "Directeur," have a similar fortune, the only difference being that sometimes the article finds its way not to the *Dictionnaire philosophique*, but to the *Questions sur l'Encyclopédie* which is the nine-volume *Dictionnaire philosophique*. The surprising thing about all this is that Voltaire in 1741 and 1742 was already preparing articles for the *Dictionnaire philosophique* before he had a *Dictionnaire* or even an idea of one, and long before that memorable discussion which is supposed to have taken place at Potsdam in 1752 and is said to have inaugurated the initial impetus for that work.

The technique of reducing ideas to separate articles and arranging them in an encyclopedic order reached its climax in the evolution of the *Dictionnaire philosophique* into the *Questions sur l'Encyclopédie* when, in a period of six or seven years a volume of some 72 articles was expanded into a nine-volume series of some 375 articles. This expansion, however, holds no surprise. In a way these "cahiers" represent a perfectly natural development of the *Notebooks* which dated from the English period to the middle of the century at least and which were composed of "thoughts."

Voltaire continued the publication of these post-1734 articles throughout his life. His collected work (*Œuvres*) after 1741 has sections of volumes, sometimes whole volumes given over to them. The *Mélanges*, and the *Nouveaux mélanges* which grew to nineteen volumes, were made up of them. As a matter of fact, Voltaire came to regard a play or a poem as an article. *Les Scythes* or *Le Triumvirat* would be printed in the *Mélanges*, or the article "Philosophe" would be published in the *Lois de Minos*. Any one of the *Discours en vers sur l'homme* equals a chapter in the *Traité de métaphysique* as we have seen. Only the *pièces de circonstance*, the *Œuvres mêlées*, and the *Henriade* have retained a conventional form; everything else has been cast, for better or for worse, in the philosophical mold.

Voltaire eventually found a name for this short essay, little letter, or dialogue form. He called it his "Petit Chapitre." Mme. Denis wrote to Cramer on 1 March 1755: "De plus, il [Voltaire] fait continuellement de petits chapitres . . ." It was apparently the first reference to them. Voltaire often mentioned them to Cramer thereafter. In a letter to Mme. d'Epinay (1 March 1760), he even suggests that he wrote them on schedule: "Vous sentez bien qu'on fait peu de petits chapitres lorsqu'on a la guerre avec des commis; on ne peut pas chanter quand on vous serre la gorge. Si vous daigniez faire encore un voyage dans ce pays-ci, on vous donnerait un chapitre par se-maine."[1] Voltaire was more explicit still in a letter to Lacombe (1 July 1766), whom he was trying to interest in their publication: "Si en attendant vous êtes toujours dans le dessein d'imprimer les petits chapitres par ordre alphabétique, on vous fera tenir des addi-tions. Vous observerez, s. v. p., qu'il se trouve plusieurs chapitres sur la même matière. Il ne vous sera pas difficile de conformer les titres aux objets qui sont traittés dans chaque chapitre, ou de mettre le tout dans un ordre convenable" (F. fr., 12942, p. 99).

One may ask whether it is very significant that Voltaire is an en-cyclopedist whose complete work is a number of agglomerated encyclopedias, indefinitely renewed, of which the smallest unit is not an "atome," or a "monade," but a "petit chapitre," the subject of which is an idea, or an infinite number of expanding ideas. Such a view at least explains his constant tendency to reduce a formal work to an encyclopedic article: thus *Candide* is an article on "optimisme," *Zadig* is an article upon "providence," *Jeannot et Colin* is an article upon "equality," *Socrate* is an article upon "tolérance," the *"Dis-cours en vers sur l'homme"* is a series of articles upon "happiness." But it also explains the reverse movement. There was a story current in the seventeenth century and early eighteenth century that Des-cartes had once said: "Give me matter and movement and I'll make you a world." Voltaire knew the story and was properly scandalized by it, or at least, pretended to be, since he saw in the remark proof that Descartes was a materialist and an atheist. He needn't have been so picayune, since essentially what he is saying is, "Give me an idea, and I'll make you a 'conte,' or write you an essay, or compose you a 'facétie' which will be a monologue, or a dialogue, a letter, whatever you will. I will add only one substance: human wit. Then with all these ideas and this human wit, I'll remake your world." It was not a small order.

Such was Voltaire's preoccupation with the structure of his work. In general, it can be seen as a wide and varied organization of his world—almost, one could say, a complete liberalization of his art. Moreover, it represented to the fullest the rationalization of reality,

---

[1] For Voltaire, "chanter un petit chapitre" is the same stylistic, poetic order as "chanter un poème sur le bonheur."

or perhaps one had better say the realization of reason. The concept which most often confronts the reader is the sense of limits, and very often he, the reader, is tempted to conclude that all one finds displayed in this structure is negative. It is true that Voltaire conceives of all human phenomena as circumscribed by time and place and by the inevitable limitations of the human. The light which Voltaire ultimately brings to bear upon man and his world is controlled by a hard-headed common sense which we generally misinterpret as the renunciation of optimism or the affirmation of pessimism. As a matter of fact, it is very difficult to make of Voltaire either an habitual optimist or a confirmed pessimist. Skeptic he most assuredly was, possessed of a skepticism which consisted in weighing scrupulously the truth or falsehood of his material. But Voltaire's skepticism was always countered by his childish curiosity. He was always looking for "something," constantly seeking himself in it. It is the combination of these two traits which, working together, have established reasonable limits in a universe which is avowed unreasonably limitless. What holds things in some sort of equilibrium is "esprit critique." One is tempted to liken this critical spirit to Montaigne, but it would be wiser perhaps to see it as an extension of Pierre Bayle's *Dictionnaire historique et critique.* Like Bayle, Voltaire was rational in human history. The best way to get at these two ideas is through the articles "Histoire" and "Esprit" in the *Encyclopédie,* both by Voltaire. They must, however, be approached with the understanding that the world of Voltaire is a world of ideas living in time and space and being organized, disorganized, and reorganized by the human mind. When the process is rightly performed, sparks fly and enlightenment occurs; when something goes amiss, one enters into the dark age. But mainly man lives in a universe of light and shade, of "rapport" and préjugé." Voltaire acknowledges that total enlightenment (what he calls the ultimate principles) is impossible. He harks back to the "que-sçais-je" of Montaigne or better still to the "Docte ignorance" of Nicolas de Cusa. Since he is living in a universe where the sources of ideas are the sensations, one experiences contact with the objects of the external world rather than with a world conditioned or inspired by innate ideas. Hence, the immediacy of the universe is much greater than it had ever been in the past with the consequence that there is a

tendency to treat ideas in the same way a normal literary man formerly treated characters.

All of this, however, does not make it any easier for present-day
critics of the Enlightenment to stress their importance. The usual
way is to analyze them in connection with an author's special interest
(science, history, literature, religion, government, society), or to
merge all these special interests and treat them as an aspect of
philosophy, or to analyze the outstanding ideas in the key works of
the author, or to sum up the ideas which have prevailed throughout
the life of the author, or finally to point out a particular person's
attitude toward a certain number of ideas which have been thought
to have prevailed during his lifetime. The grave difficulty which
vitiates any of these approaches lies in the fact that we are inclined
to believe that we know what important ideas we are seeking before
we begin our search. Voltaire, however, has a tendency to aid his
critic, because he is constantly trying to account to himself how he
views certain ideas. Thus, in 1734, he began a *Traité de métaphysique*
which was destined to give his reply to five essential questions. This
questioning method helps considerably. His tendency to arrange the
ideas in alphabetical order and to define clearly at the beginning of
his article what he understands the idea to be can also be of great
assistance. Finally, both Voltaire's contemporaries and later critics
have often assembled these ideas. When he published, for instance,
his *Dictionnaire philosophique*, there appeared a *Dictionnaire anti-
philosophique*. In 1759, *L'Esprit de Voltaire* appeared. A collection
of Voltaire's ideas since the beginning of his career to *Candide*, it was
republished in 1761 and 1765.

We have already cited the period from 1758 to 1762 as one of the
critical periods in Voltaire's life. Indeed, it is above all, in our opinion, the critical moment of his life. We regard *Candide* as the summary of all of Voltaire's past; it presents a blueprint for works of
the remainder of his life, a blueprint which consists in asserting the
dynamic power of thought and its intimate relationship with action.
Since we have a collection of Voltaire's basic thoughts down to
Candide in the little work entitled *L'Esprit de Voltaire*, we would
now like to compare *L'Esprit de Voltaire* with *Candide* to see how
Candide changed the "esprit" of Voltaire. First we shall endeavor
to review Voltaire's basic works before *Candide* and to give suc-

cinctly the basic intellectual content of each work. Then we shall turn to the attitude of Voltaire toward the ideas seen in the *Esprit de Voltaire*, and from these we shall attempt to discover Voltaire's way of handling ideas after *Candide*.

The basic works before *Candide* are well known: *L'Epître à Uranie, Le Traité de métaphysique, Les Lettres philosophiques, Le Mondain, Les Discours en vers sur l'homme, Les Eléments de la philosophie de Newton, Le Siècle de Louis XIV, Le Poème sur la loi naturelle, Le Poème sur le désastre de Lisbonne*, and *L'Essai sur les mœurs*. In these works we shall endeavor to distinguish between the "idea" (that is to say, the core idea around which all Voltaire's ideas, opinions, and experiences gravitate) and the ideas themselves (the intellectual flashes of insight contributing to or deriving from the "idea").

The central idea of the *Epître à Uranie* is the existence of a God more universal in scope and power than any anthropomorphic, denominational, or private Deity. From this assertion is derived a series of private opinions, both destructive and constructive: the falsity of every organized cult, the superstition of every dogma, the treachery and intolerance of every priesthood, but also the universality of God, the immediacy of the relationship of Creator and created, and the autonomy of moral law.

The *Traité de métaphysique* attempts to answer five basic questions concerning the existence of God, the immortality of the Soul, the origin of thought, the nature of free will and the nature of good and evil. Voltaire's answer to each is a succession of destructive and constructive opinions that pertain not solely to the religious field but also to the metaphysical, moral, and physical fields. He had hardly begun his intellectual career before he became overwhelmed with difficulties that he attempted to minimize by insisting upon a deistic providentialism which, in a way, offers total security. As long as God is in His heaven, Voltaire feels that all is right with the world. He feels so secure, in fact, that he decides that all that man needs to do is to find ways of enjoying himself. The *Lettres philosophiques* has as the central idea the concept that freedom of being is possible in this world, provided one lives in the right place, at the right time, with the right manners, customs, and culture. Ideas proliferate in every direction from this central theme, practically all of them concerned with the principles and practices of civilization. Foremost among them is the notion of man's making his freedom by judicious adjustments in all his categories of living: religious, political, economic, philosophical, and esthetic. But just as important is the thought that by studying man in his various categories, one can understand what his vitality is. Most important is the idea that man can make the "conditions" which guarantee his freedom. The human creature can do little to influence Providence in his favor, but if he assumes that Providence is on his side, or at least neutral, he can do much in shaping his own destiny. Thus happiness is humanly possible. This becomes the central idea of both the *Eléments de la philosophie de Newton* (for physical nature) and the *Essai sur les mœurs* (for moral man).

Once again, we note the instability, incoherence, ambiguity, and contradiction of the opinions derived from these "key" ideas. Indeed, Voltaire would seem to have no ideas, only impressions; no body of thought, only chaotic notions; and he attaches no particular importance to his deficiencies, contradictions, and incoherences. Indeed, he has a deep feeling of security, complete confidence that although everything may be wrong, there is no reason to be concerned. Of course, there are moments when personal experiences shake that confidence, they do not shatter it. Only at the moment of *Candide* did the crushing blow fall, when Voltaire was unprepared for it.

It could be, though, that my opinions have grossly colored Voltaire's. It is for this reason, that we should turn to the *Esprit de Voltaire* where Voltaire has the floor. The list of subjects chosen by the editor from Voltaire's own texts is as follows:

God and Religion

Etre Suprême, Dieux, Théisme, Athéisme, Christianisme, Persécutions, Confession, Pénitence, Enfer, Rome, Pontifes, Politiques, Excommunications, Dispenses Schisme, Eglises Latines et Grecques, Ecclésiastiques, Sorbonne, Sociétés religieuses, Jansénisme, Convulsions, Disputes théologiques, Sectes, Fanatisme, Inquisition, Hérésies, Guerres de religion, Ligue, Massacre de la Saint Barthélemi, Religion mahométane, Païenne, Oracles du paganisme, Prodiges.

Man and morality

L'homme, Nature, Humanité, Vertus, Amitié, Courage, Fermeté, Grandeur d'âme, Héroïsme, Générosité, Modération, Sagesse, Gloire, Liberté, Fidélité, Sincérité, Reconnaissance, Amour de la patrie, Honneur, Amour du travail, Raison, Sagesse, Amour de l'ordre, Usage, des Conseils, Passions, Amour, Le Temple de l'amour, Conscience, Remords, Amour-propre, Vanité, Fatuité, Pédanterie, Envie, Jalousie, Rivalité, Médisance, Discorde, Tracasserie, Ingratitude, Inconstance, Intérêt, Ignorance, Faiblesse, Ambition, Hypocrisie, Crime, Honte, Désespoir, Suicide, Esprit du monde, Conduite, Conversation, Liberté, Gaieté, Jeu, Retraite, La Cour, Le peuple, Naissance, Noblesse, Réputation, la Mode, le Temps, Vérité, Mensonge, Mœurs et usages, Opinions, Préjugés, Femmes, Mariages, Destinée, Biens et maux.

Man and the State

Gouvernement, Monarchie, Rois et sujets, Républiques, Hommes publics, Ministres, Ambassadeurs, Grands hommes, Etats généraux et conciles, Parlement, Commerce, Luxe, Circulation, Loix somptuaires, Finances, Monnoie, Usure, Marques de la pauvreté publique, Etablissements utiles, Ecole militaire, Travaux publics, Justice, Lois, Jurisprudence, Législateurs, Droit public, Loi naturelle, Usages, Loi salique, Fondateurs d'empire, Conquérants, Guerres civiles, Conspirations, Ambition criminelle, Favoris, Tyrans, Despotisme, Nations, Leurs Caractères, Chinois, Américains, Juifs, Russes, Suisses, Anglais, Français.

Man, Science, and Philosophy

Philosophie, Médecine, Inoculation.

Man and Art

Génie, Invention, Génie des nations, Poésie, Spectacles, Tragédies, Comédies, Opéra, Arts, Talents, Artillerie, Mines, Librairie, Imprimerie, Langues, Littérature, Imitation, Traduction, Littératures Etrangères, Anciens et modernes, Progrès et bornes des connaissances humaines, Goût, Littérature, Satire, Critique, Histoire, Académie, Eloquence de la chaire, Oraisons funèbres.

In reading this list, one is impressed by the vast scope of Voltaire's observations, which range from metaphysics to religion, ethics, politics, economics, and esthetics. Conspicuously absent is natural science; conspicuously present is the subject of history and civilization, what Voltaire calls "mœurs et esprit des nations." The list could easily pass for the table of contents of a modest *Distionnaire philosophique*. Taken in bulk, these ideas leave the impression of great confusion, since the author has thoughts on many subjects along with many thoughts on any subject, but they do not hang together too well. Many of them appear to be affirmations, but closer examination shows them to be about equally divided between construction and destruction. What is more disturbing is the circuitous way in which they are presented. To a considerable extent, they represent impressions rather than truths, beliefs rather than knowledge. It would be a difficult task indeed to bring order out of this chaos, and the difficulty increases whenever Voltaire undertakes an opinion of the Catholic cult. In general, he has an optimist's belief in reasonableness, in moderation, in philosophy as he understands it, and he naively defends the goodness of man. He declares him the most perfect and happiest of creatures, a combination of virtues and crimes, of grandeur and baseness, neither great nor small—in short, as he should be. In reality, he regards man as having two natures: one common to all men (human nature) and governed in its actions by a small number of principles (natural laws); and a second one, common only to individuals of a certain group (spirit of a people) and governed in its actions by customs, manners, and precepts— infinite in number and endless in variety—that are peculiar to the group. The human and uniform nature is invariable, and its precepts are few—the Golden Rule, love of God, patriotism: "Adore Dieu, sois juste, et chéris ta patrie." The other nature is modifiable in every respect by education. Virtue and vice are therefore relative to the customs of the group; reform (or even revolution) is merely a change of one's habits, although it may be disagreeable, painful, and even dangerous. Voltaire feels naively that as long as this second nature is controlled by fundamental laws, all is well.

He is not too sure, however, that all is well. Persecutions, intolerance, and superstitions abound, and what we call "the human lot" though it has its pleasant moments, also has its days of pain and misery:

> Notre cœur égaré, sans guide et sans appui,
> Est brûlé de désirs, ou glacé par ennui.

Voltaire counsels brotherly love and stresses humanity, the virtue including all others. His admonitions are abundant: let us live in peace, adore our common Father, help each other to happiness. It is not enough to be just and fair, one must also render service. There would be little inclination today to criticize this attitude adversely, since the doctrine of fraternity which he contributed to the democratic creed has become almost a second nature.

The supreme difficulty lies in the fact that man—Western man at any rate—has built up a code of action which he calls his morality and according to which certain qualities of action are considered virtues. Friendship, courage, firmness, high-spiritedness, generosity, heroism, moderation, wisdom, glory, freedom, fidelity, sincerity, gratitude, patriotism, honor, and industry are all virtues. By contrast, egotism, vanity, pompousness, pedantry, envy, jealousy, discord, minor irritations, ingratitude, inconstancy, personal interest, ignorance, weakness, ambition, and hypocrisy are all vices. However, Voltaire leaves the impression that all these things, whether virtues or vices, are conventional attitudes, not living realities; they are poetic fictions if you will but, in the long run, dead abstractions. It is not surprising that his moral world is full of contradictions and inconsistencies, and he prates about it in well-turned banalities. The truth is, he is as disengaged and as indifferent as the world about him. His picture is of a petty, picayune world, of men who "cabalent": "on joue, on soupe, on médit, on fait de mauvaises chansons, et on s'endort dans la stupidité, pour recommencer le lendemain son cercle de légèreté, et d'indifférence."

Negative banalities, contradictory truths, insignificant platitudes, renunciation of the theological and metaphysical, betrayal of the moral, ineptitude in dealing with the political—such seems to be the quality of Voltaire's thought until 1758. There is a constant effort to channel all these ideas, to give them a certain order, a certain rhythm. They clearly move from the theological to the metaphysical, to the moral, to the social, to the political. They follow a plan; they pass from category to category, but they come to naught. Within the category, they pass constantly from affirmation to denial, or from denial to affirmation. In this respect also the movement is clear, but again it comes to nothing; the eternally contradictory produces a static (and sterile) condition which negates reality.

It is evident that Voltaire had a possible structure for all these indiscriminate ideas, but in 1758 he had no form into which they may be vitally cast. If ideas are a source of power, and power is action, then action is a form of being. This relationship between the "fond" and the "forme" is reasonably clear, but somehow Voltaire seems unable to grasp the relationship. He is too negative, too positive, too categorical, or not categorical enough, too skeptical, too mystical. In other words, it is not easy to mark out Voltaire's intellectual response to the challenge of 1758. The first difficulty stems from our inability (and Voltaire's, too) to see where he is going intellectually between 1719 and 1758. Is he passing from a deep intellectual concern for theology to an ever increasing interest in philosophy? In philosophy, is he shifting from metaphysics to physical science? Or is he shifting from metaphysics to morality, as he said? Is it Leibniz with his principles, or Newton with his physical laws, or Locke with his natural morality who will give Voltaire a foundation for these new ideas? Is it possible to combine these impressions, these beliefs? Is it possible to find a form to contain them, a method for reconciling them? Are there any principles to which we may adhere? Only one, the existence of God, all wise, all good, all powerful. Are there any beliefs to which we may cling? Yes, there is the belief in man's freedom, in his goodness, in his ability to know, not first principles, but within limits; belief in the unity of knowledge; belief that happiness is possible and that knowledge is a way to happiness, that man can be modified in diverse ways and that intelligent modification is desirable; belief, finally, that every man progresses materially, spiritually, and esthetically. Thus, to belief in man's freedom is added belief in his reason, to which is united a belief in the possibility of progress. In short, we can still have confidence in life, if only the principle by which we abide holds firm.

Voltaire clung desperately to this one principle, as Professor Pomeau has shown, but even so his beliefs waver: man has taken a long time, and profited from fortunate circumstances, to rise above his primitive state; occidentals owe everything to time, commerce, and slow industry. The advance of civilization is the progress of the human mind, but this progress leads to no principles of living; we have no real way of knowing: "J'ignore comment je vis, comment je donne la vie, et vous voulez que je sache comment j'ai des idées." Voltaire came close to embracing Bayle's pyrrhonism: "Il faut tout lire avec défiance, l'analyse est la seule manière de raisonner sur les choses . . . Tout ce que nous pouvons faire est de sentir notre impuissance, de reconnaître un Etre tout-puissant, et de nous garder de ces systèmes."

Under the impact of events between 1753 and 1758, doubt entered Voltaire's mind. His sole abiding principle was suddenly put to question. The one guarantee against banalities, contradictions, and absurdities, against his own powerlessness was removed, leaving a world in chaos and Voltaire himself a helpless old man. He went through a rapid succession of startling emotional responses: terror, anger, irreverence, revolt, and, finally, submission. One of the most extraordinary things about *Candide* is that Voltaire's thought, almost explicitly stated, is incorporated in the work. It abounds in platitudes, contradictions, and absurdities; there is a savage destruction of that thought, a grim delight in the holocaust. Voltaire becomes a wicked self-tormentor, and in this full confession of man's defeat, he lays bare with sadistic pleasure his intellectual shame. With fiendish glee he asserts that thought is not power, that ideas lead nowhere, that mind has no control over matter, until he nearly believes it himself. But in the end chaos has been given a form; the irreconcilable has been harmonized; destruction, which was well-nigh complete, has become creation. In the full meaning of art, *Candide* has become the structured reality of *L'Esprit de Voltaire*.

This last statement forms the crux of the matter: what Voltaire was seeking, what we must seek, is the structured reality of his "esprit"—not what he thought but the spirit of what he thought. Here Voltaire adds a remark of great consequence: "Quand on est bien pénétré d'une idée, quand un esprit juste et plein de chaleur possède bien sa pensée, elle sort de son cerveau toute ornée des expressions convenables, comme Minerve sortit toute armée du cerveau de Jupiter" (p. 257). He believes that "on est resserré dans les bornes de son talent," and that the greatest genius is "celui qui ne donne l'exclusion à aucun des Beaux-arts," but adds, "Heureux l'esprit que la philosophie ne peut dessécher et que les charmes des belles-lettres ne peuvent amollir." Here Voltaire made a discovery of great value: thought which is an end in itself is sterile, at best it becomes an abstraction or a commonplace. Neither its quantity nor its weight nor its depth has relevance to the living process. Its sole value is its active ingredient, it is valid only insofar as it produces action. It is thus a release to life, freeing all the possibilities within one; it is the liberating spirit. It transforms the negative into the positive, sterility into creativity, despair into effort. It is, in short, the release of the human spirit. But the human spirit is also the release of thought. Voltaire saw plainly that thought could no more do without wit than wit without thought. It is the combination of the two that leads to action and to active creation.

"Esprit" is then an instrument for uniting thought and penetrating ideas, and it is also a form of expression. It is "une qualité d'âme"; it is not judgment, genius, taste, talent, penetration, expansion, gracefulness, and finesse, "mais il doit tenir de tous ces mérites." Voltaire calls it "raison ingénieuse" and ascribes to it a definite connection with genius. He defines many other relationships of "esprit": "esprit de corps," by way of expressing the customs and manner of speaking in a group; "esprit de parti," to denote what binds a group together; "esprit d'une loi" as a way of distinguishing intention; "esprit d'un ouvrage" as a means of bringing out its character, its aim, what it "says." Finally, it means sometimes "la plus subtile partie de la matière." We are far from the concept of "esprit" as penetration, organization, expression; it has now become for him a resultant, a tendency, and, as we say in English, a spirit, connected with breath, wind, soul. Of still greater moment, it has to do with *ingenium*, wit, witty, in the original sense of "born free" and "sage," because "esprit" in this sense of resultant, or tendency, is the instrument seeking to release the genius of man. At this point Voltaire's thought rejoins Diderot's. "Esprit" has now become an instrument, an energizing force of life. It releases from inner man those things which he is capable of creating, vitalizing, forming. Its ultimate synonyms are "fantôme, imagination, rêverie, sottise, friponnerie." Once more, Voltaire joins Diderot and even Rousseau. We are really not far from the romantic concept of creation: indeed we are surprisingly close to Diderot's and Rousseau's concept of creation as liberation. It is the one universal principle of the Enlightenment, like lying in Kafka. Though a universal principle, it is, of course, the very opposite of Kafka's. It has something to do with truth.

If "esprit" has become in Voltaire's opinion such an effective personal source of creative power, it must manifest itself in some collective way as the "esprit des nations." That Voltaire understood this to be the case can be seen in the fact that what he entitled at first

"Histoire universelle" or "Histoire générale" ultimately was entitled *Essai sur les mœurs et sur l'esprit des nations*. Voltaire conceived by the simple principle of analogy that "esprit," which is in the individual the source of his *moi*, his personality, and consequently his character, and which inevitably leads to his action, power, and creation, becomes collectively the source of the society's *moi*, its personality, its character. Inevitably it leads to action, power, and creation, whether in one person or in a nation. In either case it is the key to human thought, movement, and being. Such a concept can explain what is meant by the remark we have been using so often: what you think is what you say, do, become. Thought produces action, meaning, which in turn leads to set goals and accepted values. Voltaire identified it with history and insisted from the first, that is in the first *Essai* (1745) in the *Mercure de France* where he published the early extracts of the *Universal History*, that it was a new plan for the history of the human mind. The editor added that the work was "une espèce d'histoire universelle," and suggested that it might well be entitled *L'Histoire de l'esprit humain*.

We have noted elsewhere the immense importance which Voltaire assigned to this "new" history, particularly in connection with his newly-contrived concept of civilization which he used both in the analysis of England in the *Lettres philosophiques* and the establishment of a plan for the merging of English and French civilizations combined into a "new" European civilization. We have shown elsewhere that the idea was not unique to Voltaire, but originated with Espiard's two works and could be found in both French and English contemporary historians. We have not forgotten to stress also the importance of Voltaire's article on history in the *Encyclopédie*. What we would like to examine here is the importance of "esprit" in the evolution of history, and the consequent relationship between the evolution of history and the development of manners and customs, between the development of manners and the transformation of society's institutions, between these institutions and the goals of life thought to be desirable. (See the excellent two volumes of Professor Pomeau's edition of the *Essai sur les mœurs*, especially his Introduction and his Appendix, and Voltaire's Introduction and Conclusion: *Résumé de cette histoire*, II 800–812.)

The *Résumé* of the *Essai* (Chapter 197) is instructive in that respect. Voltaire now insists that he has traversed the vast "theatre" (it will be recalled that he thought that history could best be understood by the writer of drama) from Charlemagne to Louis XIV. He now enquires into the utility of this vast panorama. He notes that "on a vu les faits et les mœurs," suggesting that the historian normally moves from the incidents to their effect upon the manners and customs. The true light in which this operation can be analyzed, he urges, is the elimination of fables and myths caused by fanaticism and undue credulity. This verification of facts will disclose at the same time the change in "mœurs" in Europe since the twelfth century. The arts around that time "adoucissent les esprits en les éclairant," but their beneficent effect has been countered by "les plus lâches et les plus absurdes superstitions." Voltaire enumerates the consequent defects: the barbarity of the popes, the bloody wars of religion, the quarrels between the pontiffs and the emperors, and "la fureur dogmatique" ("le sang a coulé dans les campagnes et sur les échafauds, pour des arguments de théologie . . . pendant cinq cents années . . . parce qu'on a toujours négligé la morale pour le dogme). Voltaire concludes that this history is a long enumeration of crimes, follies, and disasters, along with a few virtues and some moments of happiness. One of these moments, he said, was assured by Pope Alexander III.

Voltaire notes that the Western part of Europe has in its "mœurs" and its "génie" a characteristic not present in the nations of Eastern Europe and Asia. In the West, three things contribute to modify "l'esprit des hommes": climate, government, and religion. They are the three things which can explain "l'énigme du monde." The East lacks a body of nobles, such as there is in the West, and the little republics have all been swallowed up by the big empires. Particularly different is the Western way of treating women (it was one of Espiard's important points, too). Voltaire proclaims that in fact "tout diffère entre eux et nous": religion, police, government, "mœurs," nourishment, clothing, manner of writing, of expressing one's self, of thinking. West and East have in common brutality and destruction in war. Nonetheless, he concedes that both East and West have a latent "amour d'ordre qui anime en secret le genre humain." A restriction is everywhere placed upon arbitrary power by law. Manners and customs have become a unifying force, and everywhère religion teaches a common morality to all people. Voltaire adds that when religion and war unite, though, there results "le plus horrible des fléaux." He concludes that throughout the world, religion has been used "pour faire le mal," although it was certainly established "pour porter au bien." He condemns dogmas but praises morality, which inspires to peace.

His final conclusion is that everything which derives from human nature is held in common by all, that everything which depends upon custom is normally different. "L'empire de la coutume est bien plus vaste que celui de la nature; il s'étend sur les mœurs, sur tous les usages." It scatters throughout the universe a constant variety while nature spreads a constant unity. "Ainsi le fond est partout le même, et la culture produit des fruits divers. (This was also Espiard's point.) Moreover, the greatest plague is civil war, but it can often be counter-balanced by human industry. Voltaire adds optimistically that "quand une nation connaît les arts, quand elle n'est point subjuguée et transportée par les étrangers, elle sort aisément de ses ruines, et se rétablit toujours."

The *Essai sur les mœurs et sur l'esprit des nations* is thus a major contribution to the thought of the time; indeed, to the thought of all time. Voltaire, in his correspondence between June 1752 and the end of 1754, makes numerous efforts to explain his purpose in composing the *Essai*. To the *Bibliothèque impartiale* (5 June 1752) he explains that he first formed the plan for the work fifteen years previously (1737). He wanted it to be for his own instruction. This assertion is practically always repeated: to Schœpflin, the professor of history, he stated that the *Essai* is "un compte que je me rends librement à moi-même de mes lectures." He often confesses to an additional purpose which was more professional and less personal: usually an explanation of his manner of treating the subject. To the *Bibliothèque impartiale* he wrote, for instance: "je me proposais de m'instruire des mœurs des hommes," rather than to concern himself with the details of their biography. He explained that he devised a plan which would bring out the "esprit" of a society, century by century. To Schœpflin, after his remark quoted above, he added, by way of further explanation: "Mon principal but avait été de suivre les révolutions de l'esprit humain dans celles des gouvernements." Voltaire wondered how so many wicked men backed by so many evil rulers have been so successful in establishing societies where arts, sciences, and virtues have been cultivated. Finally, an "avertissement" to Lambert's 1754 edition explains: "Son [Voltaire's] but étant moins de faire des narrations que de nous peindre la science du monde telle que la voit l'œil du philosophe."

It is this latter intention which seems to Professor Pomeau to be the most significant. He therefore stresses that Voltaire is inclined to see the past through the eyes of his philosophy. He notes, however, that in writing the history of a civilization, Voltaire was naturally constrained to choose among the scattered monuments. Voltaire, though, in his rebellion against Bossuet's principles of universal history, had given himself a stupendous task of writing the history of humanity. Being overwhelmed by his vast material, he used the concept of the power of the human mind in creating human events and in using changing events to transform man's manners and customs.

Voltaire certainly clung to these relationships, as we have shown above. He had studied with some care the historical method of Bayle, as well as that of Fontenelle and Lenglet-Dufresnoy (see *The Intellectual Development of Voltaire*, "Voltaire and History"; and Brumfitt, *Voltaire Historian*) to whom he now adds Espiard. The result of all this study is that he, like Bayle, attempts to fortify himself against his overwhelming difficulties by using just the proper amount of skepticism. Like Fontenelle, he tries to protect himself against the fables and myths of the past. From these two ancestors, Voltaire learned to separate myth from history and to forge a rather negative interpretation of the whole of Christianity: Creation, the Fall, the Awaiting of the Messiah, Incarnation, Redemption, the Final Judgment. Voltaire rejects this history of the establishment of Christianity. It was the title of one of his unfinished books, in fact. The rejection rendered necessary a replacement in the historical process. What Voltaire had to seek as a consequence of this rejection was the answer to three crucial questions: How can the historian now determine what are the significant events of history, how can he validly present their causes, and, above all, how can he penetrate "l'esprit des hommes"?

This, of course, does not mean that Voltaire cannot be led astray by his own prejudices. But his insistence upon the freedom assured

by a search for truth in history is in itself healthy. "Ceux qui dé-
trompent les hommes sont leur véritables bienfaiteurs," he wrote.
Pomeau remarks here that Voltaire is among the first historians who
was at the same time revolutionary, in the sense that he intends by a
study of historical processes to bring about a "revolution" in the human mind. It could be that Pomeau is correct, but I see things at this
point a little differently. Voltaire does not seem to me to suggest the
possibilities of "revolution" to the human mind. Rather, he seems
to me to have "discovered" that the possibilities of revolution are
always present in the human mind; they evolve whether the historian is revolutionary or not, or even whether there is such a person
as the historian. Voltaire does not appear to have asked himself what
is the responsibility of the historian in encouraging or in modifying
this "revolution."

He does recommend that the historian would be wise to follow
certain procedures which are very specific. (1) Choose only those
events which are clearly of consequence to the "mœurs" and to the
"esprit du temps." (2) Turn the march of history from the events
which are clearly only of concern to the prince to those of interest
to the people. (3) Lay the important emphasis upon "mœurs, gouvernement, usages" or upon the prevailing category of life in a particular century. (4) Study the relationship between "esprit" and
"mœurs." Voltaire, as do Vico, more particularly Espiard, and a raft
of others, sees a correlation between the "esprit" of man and the
"mœurs du temps." Thereupon he presents as fundamental to a
civilization the merging of the collective mind with history. As
Pomeau presents the situation: "l'influence du moral collectif se
trouve conditionnée par les situations historiques." (5) Thus the
Essai sur les mœurs leads naturally to the importance of the "esprit
des nations." Here Voltaire profits immensely from Espiard's *Esprit
des nations.*

Thus Voltaire's "l'énigme du monde" takes on two different
meanings. First of all, it means to deduce from the effects of "mœurs"
and "esprit" the meaning of history. For instance, Voltaire wants to
know what are the forces which move humanity. If one can clearly
distinguish these forces and the way they operate in history, one is
well on his way to a possible interpretation of universal history.
Voltaire refused, as historian, though, to see in this "esprit des

hommes" the working of God in history. The second meaning he gives to this "énigme du monde" means for him that there is something in the Western European mind which makes it very different from the universal mind of man. He attributes as cause of this difference, that peculiar something in the mind of the Western European which has been modified by his "mœurs." As he sees the situation "le mental individuel et collectif" has only a natural interrelationship. It is affected by climate, government, and religion; they are the forces which forever determine the mind of man. By studying their influence, and only in this way, one can arrive at a cogent explanation of "l'énigme du monde," in both senses of the expression. The situation offers the historian opportunity to learn something about the nature of man and also something about the mission of the European. The power controlling man's life has been thereby brought from the Courts of Heaven to man's habitat without diminishing the spirit of man.

One wonders whether we have not finally penetrated to the very core of Voltaire's reality, whether, in fact, it was not this "découverte métaphysique de l'homme" which Voltaire made in his *Essai*. Thanks to this discovery, Voltaire eventually found ways to change the thinking and actions of man as a means of reorienting him in his thinking and consequently in his action. Such an interpretation would go far to explain certain aspects of Voltaire's thought which we have always found unclear, particularly his assertion that he tried to bring everything back to "la morale." The *Essai* would thus become the "key" work in the making of Voltaire's unity.

This remark, tentative though it is, certainly takes us back to our central problem. We must ultimately determine, in our search for Voltaire's unity, in what work or works it can best be found? We have a good deal of difficulty, however, in going about looking for that work or works which will pull all the aspects of Voltaire together, because we are not terribly clear what are the elements which have to be unified. In *The Intellectual Development of Voltaire*, I took the stand that I had the right to select the essential works arbitrarily. I am not inclined any longer to defend that point of view. It now seems more reasonable to find that Voltairean philosophy— what we usually call his Voltaireanism—either in the complete works or in the combination of those works which Voltaire has clearly designated as containing his philosophy. I presume it is reasonable to state that the two dominating elements are poetry and philosophy; that is, if it does not sound too presumptious, creating a new world by the power of thought, but it could be history and natural history, or taste and esthetics, or metaphysics and morality, or even revolution and reform. What have to be harmonized are expression and thought, structure and ideas, which is what poetry has always been expected to do.

In this case, we have to analyze the total massive production of Voltaire to find out what are his important thoughts and to seek the characteristics of his style. This is by no means an impossible task. It is possible to assemble the thoughts at least to the point where they can be classified; there would be religious, metaphysical, political, economic, social, moral, scientific, historical, and esthetic ideas and a whole body of ideas from many of Voltaire's predecessors and contemporaries which are discussed endlessly by Voltaire. For example, as Pomeau has shown, he continuously discussed the ideas basic to the Catholic religion, such as the immortality of the soul, the nature of the soul, the origin of good and evil, and many others. He discussed voluminously the ideas of Descartes, of Newton, of all of the twelve outstanding European philosophers, and the countless number of thinkers and free-thinkers of his time. In fact, Voltaire's discussion of their ideas, particularly in his massive correspondence, is almost unending.

We are certainly not sure that such an enterprise can best be approached by transforming artistic form into living content or, if you will, by harmonizing living expression with dynamic thought or, more simply put, by placing into right perspective the proper balance between art and philosophy. It is certainly true that we have no ready explanation how these things occurred to Voltaire and some of his contemporaries with startling frequency between 1760 and 1789. In fact, these explanations seem overwhelmingly beyond the pale of reality. But they are no more silly than the statement, for instance, that Bacon wanted to make a new England, not a new philosophy. And if a perfectly reasonable Englishman can have such a vision, I suppose it is not imagining too much for some Frenchman to get a vision of a possible new world. As a matter of fact, Voltaire, in talking of Descartes always seemed to revert to the remark that he was, as a philosopher, a kind of poet, a dreamer. He often said the same thing about Malebranche. And to prove his point he finally told the anecdote that the father of modern philosophy was reputed to have once said: "Give me matter and movement and I'll make you a world." At any rate, that was certainly what Cartesianism was about. It could be that Voltaireanism also had some such silly idea.

It might be worth an effort, therefore, to seek that work of Voltaire which best offers the most poetic expression, or that work which consists in the fullest and profoundest body of ideas, or those works which he states were designed to give to himself an account of his beliefs. It could be, of course, that the same work could perform all these tricks. In that case, we could probably suggest *Candide* or perhaps some other philosophical tale or even all of them. I doubt that it would occur to any of us to suggest a play, an epic poem, or even a dialogue or an essay. Someone could have the audacity to suggest Voltaire's *Œuvres complètes—Correspondence, Notebooks,* histories, and all. I doubt, though, that anyone is yet fully equipped to handle that much material. Voltaire himself, who had to do so, is reputed to have expressed some hesitation about going down to posterity encumbered by so much intellectual impediments. Our usual way of handling this difficulty is to either settle for Voltaire the artist or to revert to Voltaire the thinker (or the man of action). A perfectly normal procedure occurs in Mr. Gay's *Party of Humanity* where he uses as the core of Voltaire's thought the *Dictionnaire philosophique* with a page or so (incidentally, very good) on Voltaire's style taken more or less from Auerbach.

Professor Gay insists that Voltaire put into his *Dictionnaire philosophique* practically everything he knew. He concludes that the work actually did contain what Voltaire had learned from 1719 to 1752, when he began to compose the *Dictionnaire* after the momentous gathering at Potsdam in which he brought forward his plan of procedure. This remark, however, is factually inaccurate. We know, for instance, from the Miller papers in Leningrad that certain articles destined to appear in the *Dictionnaire* or one of its subsequent editions (that is, *La Raison par alphabet* or *Questions sur l'Encyclopédie*) appeared already in the early *Œuvres complètes* of 1741 or 1742, and we have a letter of Cramer to Grimm around 1764 to 1768 which states that Voltaire had been working on the *Dictionnaire* for over twenty years. The gathering at Potsdam may have occurred, but it is evident that Voltaire had been writing dictionary articles before he had an official plan for the *Dictionnaire philosophique*. Moreover, Gay is none too explicit (nor is Bengesco, for that matter) about the detail of Voltaire's plan. And he is inadequate about what Voltaire learned between the presentation of his original plan (1752) and the publication of the first edition of the *Dictionnaire philosophique* (1764). It would be interesting to know how Voltaire modified that plan during that twelve-year interval. Still, I think that Gay is essentially correct in believing that Voltaire originally intended and actually planned to present the *Dictionnaire* as a summary of his philosophy, though certainly not in the terms in which Gay understands that event. Voltaire stated that he considered it an account of everything he ought to think about this world and the next. He assured Mme. du Deffand that it was for his own edification, and perhaps after his death for that of all "honnêtes gens." One could be easily justified in examining the work as Voltaire's intellectual last will and testament. But on second thought, Voltaire was such a clandestine writer that some caution is recommended. In this particular case, there are certain difficulties. In the first place, Voltaire had a tendency to frequently explain the reason for the composition of a work as a desire on his part to clarify for himself what he thinks about certain particular problems. It was his way of explaining the composition of the *Traité de métaphysique* back in 1734. Since he made three versions of the *Traité* and never published a one of them, I see nothing else to do than to adopt his explanation. He reverted to the same sort of remark when he was composing the *Universal History*, although, on this occasion, he used Mme. du Châtelet as an additional explanation. The two explanations, however, are not contradictory, they are merely supplementary. After the early editions of the *Dictionnaire philosophique*, Voltaire wrote and published *Le Philosophe ignorant* (1766). This time he again reverted, in an obvious way, to his formula by making the whole work an exposition of his opinions, his doubts, and his questionings. Indeed, one of the editions was entitled *Questions d'un homme qui ne sait rien* (when it was published in the *Mélanges*) and very frequently *Questions* is used to introduce the doubt—in fact, the opening consists in a group of questions. To Mme. du Deffand he wrote, "je me suis mis à rechercher ce qui est." Curiously, the five problems discussed in the *Traité* reoccur as the core of the *Philosophe ignorant.* One could argue, I suspect, that the basic philosophic problems were treated in the *Traité de métaphysique* and thereafter they remained the foundation of his philosophy. I don't think that would do, however, since they would represent only his metaphysical problems as he deduced them from his study of Locke. Moreover, they would not incorporate the role historical criticism played in that philosophy as both Lanson and Pomeau have characterized it. Whether this is correct or not, the existence of two or more ways of bringing together Voltaire's philosophy certainly tends to handicap the possibility of bringing out the unity of that philosophy.

What is more, Gay's own method of solving the problem brings out a further difficulty. In his English translation of the *Dictionary* (see Voltaire, *Dictionnaire Philosophique*, translated, with an Introduction and Glossary by Peter Gay, New York, 1962, 2 vols.) he has added a note (II, 653–656) in which he explains that he has selected as his text the *Raison par alphabet* of 1769 (2 vols.), just as Naves and Benda had done in their French edition of 1935. The *Raison par alphabet* of 1769 is certainly an extension of the *Dictionary* of 1764, since it contains the 73 articles of the first edition, but it contains 45 more articles. One wonders on what grounds the *Raison* can be justified rather than the *Dictionary*. If the answer is that after 1769, the *Dictionary* is to all intents and purposes completed, one wonders how such a statement can be justified, when the 73 articles of the edition of 1764 have become 118 in the *Raison par alphabet,* and 375 in the *Questions sur l'Encyclopédie.* In short, if any group of articles cast in the form of philosophical articles in alphabetical order can qualify no matter whether it is the original *Dictionnaire philosophique* or not, is it to be taken as the organic expression of Voltaire's philosophy and looked at as contributing to the unity of his philosophy? In that case, it seems to me that the *Dictionnaire philosophique* as it appears in the Moland edition of the *Œuvres complètes* would offer the best text since it is a composite of the early *Dictionnaire philosophique,* the *Raison par alphabet,* and the *Questions sur l'Encyclopédie.* Or the *Questions sur l'Encyclopédie,* coming last in the series (1770–1772) and reprinted almost up to the end (1777) could serve as the best text.

Professor Pomeau has added some very serious complications to an already complex problem. He sees the *Dictionnaire philosophique* as a work which took its origin in the misfortunes of the Seven Years' War and the suppression of the *Encyclopédie*. He notes that the "tradition intellectuelle du pays se délabre, supplantée par la philosophie . . ." along with "Révolution dans les idées." Pomeau has noted further that under these unhappy circumstances, Voltaire has transformed the *Dictionnaire* article into a literary genre, situated half-way between the "essay" of Montaigne and the *propos* of Alain. (This, however, had been started as early as 1742, as we have seen above.) And he adds the *Dictionnaire* presents an empirical philosophy. This was the philosophy which Voltaire brought into a more elaborate order and published in 1765 as *La Philosophie de l'histoire*. In this work, Voltaire, says Pomeau, lays aside the importance of the chronological order, just as the *Encyclopédie* did, and undertakes an inquiry into the origins of history and the origins of the human race. It is at this point that Pomeau concludes that Voltaire was among the first historians who was at the same time revolutionary, in the sense that he intended by a study of historical processes to bring about an "evolution" in the human mind. But that is what R. Hubert in his *Sciences sociales dans l'Encyclopédie* (Paris, 1923) has shown was the major contribution of the *Encyclopédie*, and almost in Pomeau's terms. Of course, that does not prevent Voltaire from being preoccupied with the same problem, although it does require a change in the timetable, in the sense that Professor Pomeau's surmise that the whole preoccupation grew out of the disastrous effect of the Seven Years' War is hardly acceptable if it was already apparent in the *Encyclopédie* before the beginning of that war, and in Voltaire's work by 1742. Voltaire had begun the process after his return from England with his manuscript of the *Charles XII*. He had obviously studied carefully Bayle's critical ideas upon history and those of Fontenelle. To these two he had added Lenglet-Dufresnoy's *De la Méthode* and eventually Boulanger's work. It was the latter who had been entrusted to clarify the meaning of history in the *Encyclopédie*. Attached to the critical method was a new way of regarding history as the record of the making of a civilization from the empirical analysis of "mœurs" and "esprit." It was a collective interpretation of the workings of "esprit" in bringing about a revolution in the collective human mind.

I have always thought that among the twentieth-century French critics of the past, the one who best understood Voltaire's philosophy was Lanson. Essentially, he saw this philosophy as a philosophy of history, but when it came to interpreting in what consisted this philosophy of history, Lanson seemed to veer away, definitely leaving the impression that neither philosophy nor the philosophy of history were properly in his field. Nonetheless, he saw philosophy of history as a way of looking at the world, the result of that inordinate curiosity which Voltaire perpetually expressed when he explored the phenomena around him. The upshot of this almost childish desire on Voltaire's part to understand what his century would have called "la nature des choses" was the accumulation pêle-mêle of a body of facts. Lanson was properly impressed with Voltaire's factual knowledge which was in a way rather encyclopedic, diverse, and loosely organized. Since Lanson's day, the same observation has been often made by subsequent critics of Voltaire. Professor Gay, for instance, has remarked in his introductory essay to the *Dictionnaire philosophique* that the work contains practically everything the author learned between 1719 and 1764. Professor Carr notes, in his Introduction to the *Philosophe ignorant*, Voltaire's tendency to introduce the unexpected fact as illustrative of his idea. Lanson, who went much farther than Gay and Carr, saw a desire on Voltaire's part to organize this encyclopedic knowledge in terms of history and criticism. The world of factual phenomena which Voltaire assembled was subjected by him to critical analysis and to historical control. What had been thought to have been true in the past was constantly being examined by Voltaire in the light of his experience of the present. The two tests of truth evidently became awareness of the fact and confirmation by experience. They are thus the two postulates of Voltaire's historical affirmations. What he offered was the free-play of common-sense. Voltaire actually insisted that the application of this method could easily clear up a vast number of misunderstandings in this world. Life could become less hectic, less violent, more orderly, and man would undoubtedly become happier. Lanson has noted that these aspirations of Voltaire did not work out that way, though. Naturally, the application of this method could easily produce some undesirable results as well as some desirable ones. Moreover, Voltaire's historical criticism was far from being prudently applied; he, being human, was "pétri de préjugés et de passions." He was both "amateur et journaliste." On the other hand, he had an enquiring mind, he was intelligent, he had a natural inclination to seek the truth and to select instinctively the problems to be investigated. Moreover, he had an inborn sense of criticism and readily grasped the nature of the task which fell to his lot.

The question still remains, What was the task which fell to Voltaire's lot? To get some further light on that question, we have to return to Benda's Introduction to Naves's edition of the *Dictionnaire philosophique*. While Etiemble saw primarily in the *Dictionnaire* the organic Voltaire who violently assails Christianity fundamentally (the Voltaire of Lanson, Hazard and Mornet), Benda saw him in the same work as the founder of republicanism and the father of the Third Republic in nineteenth-century France. This interpretation was essentially taken over by Gay, both in his Introduction to his translation of the Naves and Benda *Dictionnaire philosophique*. It also accounts, I suspect, for the importance which Gay attributed to the *Idées républicaines* in his *Voltaire's Politics*. Benda, however, goes so far as to insist that what prevails in Voltaire's development of this republicanism are certain mystical aspects of this creed: political egalitarianism, for instance, which consists in recognizing that despite the fact that physical, economic, social, and intellectual equality certainly do not exist, every man is equal in human dignity, that is, in his capacity as a man. This concept carries naturally two corollaries: before the law, every man has equal rights and consequently birth, heredity, and riches should confer no special privileges, and everyone is entitled to the inviolability of his person. (This is the meaning incidentally of Mably's "ownership of person" to which he attributed great importance.) This leads to a second fact. In Benda's opinion, Voltaire's republicanism is not justified by tradition but by law, and for Voltaire as for Montesquieu and a whole raft of legal experts, what supports the laws are the "mœurs." Benda claims that Voltaire, as did the Cahiers of 1789, urges that legislation should be founded upon abstract reason, upon an eternal morality.

Voltaire thus shows himself reasonably established as a republican, in Benda's (and Gay's) opinion, although he seems somewhat committed to the separation of church and state. At the same time, he appears to want to take from the priests all political power along with all spiritual actions. He envisages the establishment of a lay political system which develops in the interest of the state. He is opposed to war, of course, which in his opinion has never solved any social and political problem. He opposes likewise all metaphysics. He encourages among the thinkers a contempt for the theological controversy. Indeed, Voltaire is presented here as a deist whose departure from theology and contempt for metaphysics inevitably led to the rise of atheism, and materialism and the suppression of spiritualism. However, this breakdown in religious spirituality left open room for the optimistic faith in progress.

Benda notes here that these views of Voltaire in the *Dictionnaire* were certainly not original with him. The attack against despotism can be found in Fénelon, Boisguilbert, and Vauban; the hatred of religious fanaticism and desire for tolerance was firmly in Bayle; the contempt for metaphysics occurred in Gassendi. Consequently, after this ancestry in these ideas, Voltaire's espousal of them should occasion no particular surprise. Voltaire's function, as Benda sees the situation, in the evolution of eighteenth-century concepts was to cull ideas from all the intellectual movements of the preceding century and to organize these ideas into a coherent expression of his time. Benda concludes that since Voltaire gathered together the various currents of thought and organized this thought into dynamic action, that was assuredly his mission. The *Dictionnaire philosophique* is the storehouse of these ideas, which certainly run around in very dynamic fashion. Nonetheless, neither Benda nor Gay have made any effort to organize them in any consistent way. Lanson did not contribute much to their organization either, but he did have the great merit of trying to understand Voltaire's temperament and Voltaire's method of handling ideas. It was Lanson who insisted that the important point is that Voltaire knew how to observe, if there is any phenomena which is visible, but he was less skilled in sensing the presence of that phenomena which is more subtle. On the other hand, he was skillful in asking the right questions. Moreover, he understood that he could not always come up with the right answers. He quickly became impatient when he sensed that he was thwarted by all kinds of obstacles. One of his most unwavering convictions was that the human intelligence is strictly limited in its capacity to know. One would expect him to be resigned to these limitations, but this is practically never the case. On the other hand, those who insisted that they had the right answers baffled him completely. The realms in which he operated with the greatest difficulty were mystical religions and systematic metaphysics. He took fright whenever he was faced with anything which transcends simple human experience, and all systems of thought immediately aroused in him the deepest suspicions. Much of his reaction toward Christianity can be explained by these limitations. Lanson frankly confesses that Voltaire's treatment of Christianity is inexcusable, even to the point of bad taste, but he urges that our task here is to try and understand rather than accuse or excuse Voltaire. Voltaire achieved something of a positive nature in his reaction to Christianity—he succeeded in marking in world history what he thought was the role of the Christian church. He treated it as no different from the other religions which also played a role in the making of man's world. For reasons which we find sometimes difficult to comprehend, he bitterly opposed the cruelty, intolerance, and the persecutions of religious sects. But he was naturally closer to the religious wars and to the widespread fanaticism of the time. Lanson notes that despite all these negative reactions to the history of Christianity and all his rejections of metaphysics, Voltaire could never refrain from returning avidly to both subjects. Since Lanson's day, the whole tendency of Voltaire criticism has stressed his continual effort to understand the role of religion and the role of systematic philosophy in man's world. It might be remarked that Voltaire actually regarded both subjects in the very same way; while terribly suspicious of the phenomena, he was mysteriously drawn to reexamine both of them time and again.

Lanson interprets this constant effort to investigate the problems of religion and the basic ideas of metaphysics as Voltaire's philosophy. Indeed, he sees Voltaire as adopting some fundamental religious beliefs which are at the center of his ethics. Voltaire rejects dogma as well as all systems of philosophy, but, says Lanson, he adopts only those metaphysical elements which are necessarily inseparable from religion and morality.

This view, however, is a little tricky. Voltaire inveighed against metaphysics and dogma, and yet, he wrote an immense amount against Christianity, while acknowledging tacitly that there are five "metaphysical" problems which require very careful consideration. They are introduced at the beginning of the Cirey period (1734) in the *Traité de métaphysique* (existence of God, immortality of the soul, nature of matter and thought, free will, and the nature of good and evil). Voltaire made three attempts during his reeducation at Cirey (1734–1738) to clarify his position in regard to these five problems. He thought that what gave them authenticity was the fact that they were the five problems which had been explicitly treated by Locke, and at the same time he explained that he was strengthening Locke's position, which he judged somewhat timid. He himself stressed to his friends that he was above all presenting to himself an account of "la nature des choses." He explained that he deemed his solutions to these five problems indispensable to "la morale"—"Je ramène tout à la morale." Lanson, though, fails to stress this aspect of Voltaire's effort, but he does insist upon the way Voltaire magnified the importance of morality in his thought. It is "divine," adds Lanson, but in Voltaire's opinion, it is neither religious (that is, is not subject to religious control) nor is it revealed. God is nevertheless necessary as its sanction. The service which it renders is personal and social, that is, it contributes to the happiness of the individual and the contentment of society. Its function is to teach man his duties to his fellow man. It stands at the portal of virtue. Rightly interpreted, it is natural religion which Voltaire defined as "Adore Dieu, sois juste, et chéris ta patrie." This is what Voltaire would subscribe to as the only possible religion. Voltaire, however, was never certain that he had correctly interpreted these five metaphysical principles. Besides an endless discussion of each one of them throughout his voluminous work, he returned to them more or less in the collective format of the *Traité de métaphysique* in the *Catéchisme chinois* of the *Dictionnaire philosophique* (1764), and they also served as a nucleus of the *Philosophe ignorant* (1766).

This, if I have read Lanson's chapter on the *Philosophy of Ferney* correctly, is a bare sketch of that philosophy, along with a few cautious remarks on my part. I suppose it could be defined as the application of critical historical procedures to a natural religion which is nothing more than a social morality. The establishment of this social morality implies, however, the political and social reforms of France and, since France and England were accepted as the leaders of Europe, the reform of Enlightened Europe. This reform must not be minimized. While not total, it was conceived as extensive enough to transform all seven categories of life (religion, politics, morality, esthetics, economics, science of nature, the self as an expression of the science of man). Voltaire laid a good deal of stress upon the concept of humanity and more stress still upon the concept of fraternity. He concentrated most of all upon the concept of God, deeply convinced that if belief in that concept faltered, all was lost. But if that conviction held fast, man could work for enlightenment and progress, material, intellectual, moral, social, and esthetic (that is, he could derive great human advantages from the application of knowledge to the constant improvement of man's lot. This he conceived of not only as the increase of man's power in his world and society, but as the release of more power for his own material and spiritual fare. This chance of progress through knowledge, reform, and human power, though certainly not infinite, is the source, but more importantly the "inner" reality, of man's freedom. All Voltaire's juggling with the problem of free will, which is so exasperating to a systematic philosopher, is nonetheless a deeply human affirmation of man's power. It is true that Voltaire often gives the impression that his conviction in man's free will is as faltering as his belief in the existence of God and for the same reasons—man's human limitations. His merit, though, in the affirmation of freedom comes less from the idealization of liberty than from his common-sense, practical attitude toward possible achievements in particular aspects of freedom. He talked endlessly about these freedoms and encouraged all efforts to achieve progress in them. They are freedom of person (every man has the right to live unmolested by another so long as he does not molest another), civil liberty (every man has the right to live in his society free from harassment, persecution, and injustice), *habeas corpus* (when accused of some crime, every man must be tried by his peers, he cannot be imprisoned without a trial), freedom of conscience (each person has the privilege of believing and acting in accord with his own conscience as long as he does not molest another), and security of property (each individual has the right to possess unmolested that property which belongs to him). Needless to say, Voltaire is opposed to everything which threatens each of these freedoms in any respect: war, slavery, unjust taxation, judicial, political and social injustice, political persecution, even personal fraud. Moreover, these freedoms are not only to be defended against dangers, they are to be enhanced by all kinds of progress: agriculture, commerce, all kinds of possible advance in civilization, without neglecting the needy or the oppressed. Such comportment requires tolerance, liberty of the press, proportional taxation, equality before the laws for everyone, reform in criminal procedure, a priesthood directed and paid by the government, state-directed welfare and, in general, a liberal, prosperous administration. Lanson summarizes that Voltaire wanted his society to have all those things which could have developed, had Turgot remained in power for twenty years. That remark, though, is rather optimistic, even as an ideal. As a practical judgment, it is a total exaggeration. As everyone knows, after two hundred years, we are still trying to get somewhere with this program. The future, however, is not too bright. It is encouraging to recall that the "ideal" of freedom as conceived by Voltaire has endured in Western civilization from his time to that of Franklin D. Roosevelt, though it is somewhat discouraging to realize that we are striving so desperately to preserve it, now that we are running a grave risk of losing it forever.

To return to the problem of Voltaire's philosophy, it is now evident that the most difficult problem is to follow Voltaire as he structures his intellectual origins into his Voltaireanism and gives it its meaning, its "spirit," as we say. He obviously saw his career in such a way that the artist should become the man of thought, and the man of thought should become the man of action. He also devised a program in which the two essential activities were preparation to become an encyclopedic man and further preparation to apply the intellectual processes of the encyclopedic man to the making of a new organic way of life. These two activities, therefore, required a new epistemology and a new conception of history. Any one of his numerous enterprises could justify a life: poet, Newtonian scientist, political and economic scientist, literary critic, historian, critical deist, moralist, encyclopedist. It is evident that Voltaire wished his understanding to embrace all the categories of life, and he wished to integrate coherently and put in action the sum total of this under-standing. The thing to stress, therefore, is its scope, the necessity of organizing it into a coherent whole, and the further obligation to develop an action in accord with this apprehension of life. Because Voltaire accepted the need to structure all these preoccupations into a new conception of life, he literally had to forge a philosophy which was at the same time an art—the art of living. He was determined to give a new direction to life—life in the here and now—by chang-ing the general direction of thought and, through this modification of direction, to change the march of civilization. The procedure which he employs to achieve this is a merging process. All during the Cirey period, he talks of merging some poetic with some intel-lectual activity; poetry with science, science with history, history with "la morale." Over and over again, he refers to this merging with the expression "poétiser et philosopher." We can say it now: that is the initial movement of his Voltaireanism.

It would seem therefore to be an error to debate endlessly whether Voltaire is a poet and what kind of poet he is, or whether he is a philosopher and what kind of philosopher he is. It is, of course, pos-sible to defend any of his preoccupations as crucial. He is supremely a man of letters and a man of taste; a man of taste and a man of thought, a man of thought and a moralist; a propagandist and an artist. His constant effort toward syncretization which evokes in us a constant effort toward segmentation should now be understood. While he pushed on to the organic, we timidly remain in the realm of views, of aspects, of attitudes, and very often we formulate these attitudes upon our own individual desires. That is why Voltaire is such a superb propagandist. He suggests the idea and develops it to a certain point. He repeats the idea incessantly until it is implanted in the mind of another. Finally, he leaves the impression in that other mind that it has discovered and developed that idea and con-sequently possesses it, and therefore it is responsible to integrate it into the body of ideas and to carry it to its logical conclusion. I wouldn't wish to go too far, but I think that is what poetry is about also.

It is obvious that Voltaire prepared himself diligently to become a philosopher, a free-thinker, an encyclopedic man, a "philosophe," a propagandist, and a poet. It is clear also that in each case his preparation required him to become a critic of previous philosophers, a historian of ideas, a defender of certain particular ideas, an initiator of certain particular thoughts of great importance for the welfare of man. As a philosopher he had a method of approaching truth and he created through his method a body of truths. These truths are always derived from experience, they always possess a utility for man and his society, and they always concern relationships between man and his inner world and the outer world of nature, the forces in control of the universe, the society of which he always is a part, the institutions of that society, the things which it has created, its ways of acting and becoming. It is these relationships which are the source of human experience. Voltaire demands the right for every man to examine with his mind the validity of each experience and the utility which he can extract from it for himself and for his fellow man.

This means that despite our human limitations which frustrate us at every turn, the human mind has the ability and the right to pronounce upon the worth of human experience and to accept that experience as useful or reject it as useless. It is derived from the world of God, the world of nature, the world of man. Man, however, can not participate to any extent in the world of God, since He is infinite and man is by nature finite. It suffices that man can know valid reasons for God's existence, and that God has given him reason to conduct himself in this life. In the world of nature, which is the source of man's scientific knowledge, he can do a little better; that is, his knowledge of nature, while not limitless by any means, is respectable. It can be augmented, and it can be useful to man and to society. Man can measure, weigh, calculate, and all of this has its importance, but he can never expect to know the principles of nature. The closest he can come to a principle is the conviction that his universe of nature is an orderly, stable world in which scientific laws are immutable. The world of man, though, is the great source of man's moral experience. It is a broad world, open to all sorts of human activities, intensely interesting to the individual who will use his God-given reason to penetrate, to understand, to use it. It is a world of relationships: wherever they reach into God's world, they become obscure, uncertain, ambiguous, because of the infinity of God and man's finiteness. Whenever they reach into the world of nature, they become less obscure and ambiguous than in God's world, but they are still not terribly clear. This is especially true when man attempts to understand the meaning rather than the nature of phenomena. It is in the world of man that these relationships offer the greatest chance for understanding. He can learn a lot about his relations with his fellow man in all the human sciences: the arts, the trades, the manners and customs of the group, the analysis of the instrument for knowing, the history of man's relationships with the past and what it has produced for the good of the group, and what it has contributed to man's ways of thinking and acting, the institutions which have been created and what advantages they have given him and society. It is true that the ultimate purpose of all these relationships cannot be fully apparent to him, because of his finiteness. It is true also that in these relationships not everything is useful or desirable, and they are often terribly confusing because of the very human qualities of tension, contradiction, paradox, and irony. Nonetheless, man has the power to be good or to create good. Enlightenment in his world is a great source of human power: thought releases the human energy within every individual.

We know all this by experience. The human mind applied to the arts can create beautiful things, applied to the trades it can manufacture beautiful and useful objects, applied to society it can reproduce very useful political, economic, social, religious, and educational organizations which will be of great benefit to the human being and his group. Progress is a possibility in all of these areas. It depends upon the increase of knowledge, upon the ability to reduce evil, disharmony, ignorance, superstition, confusion. If man has the courage to act upon that knowledge, he can, granted he and his fellow citizens will unite, make a civilization which will not offer an unlimited felicity, but which can become very enjoyable through the good things it creates. Happiness, but only within the confines of the human, is possible.

The most important fact which Voltaire deduces from all this is the necessity of action which derives from conscious knowing. Life must be understood in the light of what we know about it and what we do about it. We must derive from it the "idea" of its content. This "idea" is the generating force of the new model upon which we are permitted to restructure a "new" life. It is in every sense of the word an "interior model"—a vision of things which can be, but only if man has the courage to restructure, to revise, to remake, to reorganize that which he has hitherto accepted as reality. This action naturally involves rejecting old relationships as well as establishing new ones. "Préjugés" must be crushed before new "rapports" can be adopted. Always change is king, revision is a new sort of vision, reform is another kind of form, revolution is the actualization of new kinds of possibilities. But these actions, viewed in the right human perspective are just so many steps in the creative process; they entail not only what the philosopher thinks, but what the poet feels, and insofar as each man thinks and feels, he is his own philosopher-poet, his own creator, in fact. The act of thought transformed into reflective thinking and being is as much a poetic principle as a philosophical pursuit.

What characterizes both activities is the creative process. Always the problem is how to pass from the raw product of existence through experience to an understanding of the "idea" which suffuses that raw product, to the making of an interior model which carries within itself its own inner meaning, to the restructuring of the idea and the model until they have created a new form and endowed it with the power of taking on a new and vital inner meaning. Always within the process is working that "esprit" which is the "esprit humain," always that "esprit humain" is being expressed by that "esprit" which is the "wit" of man, his response to his life, always the "human spirit" and that "wit" are creating new interpretations of the spirit of society and of the age through "mœurs, lois, civilisation."

EPILOGUE

There was a story that, at the end of Voltaire's life, he met Benjamin Franklin at the "Loge des neuf Sœurs." Franklin presented to Voltaire his nephew, a lad of six or seven and Voltaire, holding his hand over the youth's head pronounced a blessing in English with the two words "God and Liberty." Usually we conclude the story with the remark that they were in all probability the only two English words which Voltaire had retained from the English trip of 1726 to 1728.

There is possible another concluding remark of more importance. If we believe (as I do) that Voltaire never made a move of this sort, without calculating its total effect, it seems perfectly reasonable to inquire what was the effect he hoped to produce here. Obviously, what he was trying to affirm publicly was a belief in the existence of God and an adherence to political and civil freedom. I would be willing to guess that he still remembered that one of his firmest beliefs which he retained from the English sojourn was the "Dieu et mon droit" which had burned itself into the very vitals of Voltaireanism. I would surmise also that Voltaire was trying to suggest that these two ideals substantiated each other. It could be, finally, that he was suggesting in his clandestine way that all that was needed to build the good life was the acceptance of these two ideals. The Old Patriarch was speaking consciously and cautiously as a firm deist and a convinced republican. He was speaking against those who now tended toward naturalism and atheism as well as against those who now seemed to support political and social restrictions (that is, despotisms).

The point we have to consider here is whether this "God and Liberty" can be taken as his final way of summing up his philosophy and if so (at least, as a conscious attempt) whether it actually does embrace the full philosophy of Voltaireanism. If we wished to do so, we could ask whether this Voltaireanism can best be understood in the *Dictionnaire philosophique* or in that broader *Dictionnaire philosophique* which he called the *Questions sur l'Encyclopédie*. There is no doubt in my mind that Voltaire regarded the latter work as the final statement. Questions, yes; that was the way Voltaire interpreted the meaning of his age and also the meaning of life. We have to await a better moment before we can find the answers. I get the impression nonetheless that Voltaire felt that the *Encyclopédie* was going in the right direction. But the *Encyclopédie* could never have got started, had it not been aided by Voltaire's "petits chapitres."

ORGANIC UNITY IN DIDEROT

THE epigraph from the *Neveu de Rameau*, taken from Horace's *Satire* (II, 7, v. 14), *Vertumnis, quotquot sunt, natus iniquis*, has with some unanimity been attributed to Diderot himself, but to my knowledge no one has ever suggested that the constant changing which is his curse is what renders impossible a unified Diderot. Yet, implied in Horace's statement and Diderot's selection of it as suitable for the *Neveu* is the subtle suggestion that a unified Diderot is forever impossible and that the famous remark coined by Rimbaud and other poets of a later day: "Moi suis un autre" is the dead center of Diderot's activity. The person Diderot branches out from that center, as Professor Crocker once remarked about his esthetic theory, "as spokes from a wheel." Of course, all this is in the nature of a paradox; it is, in fact, the vital cause of that paradox which occurs everywhere in Diderot's life and works. It has even been suggested that in Diderot's day the word "paradox" meant "something new." For Diderot, who reveled in metaphors, it was above all "une métaphore singulière." It is what Voltaire understood "spirit" to mean when he defined it: "Ce qu'on appelle esprit est tantôt une comparaison nouvelle, tantôt une allusion fine: ici l'abus d'un mot, qu'on présente dans un sens, et qu'on laisse entendre dans un autre: là un rapport délicat entre deux idées peu communes, c'est une métaphore singulière, c'est une recherche de ce qu'un objet ne présente pas d'abord, mais de ce qui est en effet dans lui." Thus "esprit," and consequently "paradox," is an instrument for harmonizing and vitalizing thought. Voltaire explains that the function of "esprit" is to achieve something new, to sharpen and clarify the obscure, to destroy something threatening, to show the close relationship between two ideas seemingly contradictory, to bring out the meaning of something present but not easily apprehended. Voltaire continued: "C'est l'art ou de réunir deux choses éloignées, ou de diviser deux choses qui paraissent se joindre, ou de les opposer l'une à l'autre, c'est celui de ne dire qu'à moitié sa pensée pour la laisser deviner." Thus "esprit" is Voltaire's instrument for separating the true from the false, for uniting the true with the true in order to obtain "new" truths, for penetrating to the core of old truths and seeking new sources of enlightenment. It is a nimble playing of wit upon phenomena and thereby brings out unsuspected meaning. It is the dynamic force of thought, devastatingly destructive, but amazingly creative. Diderot understood these things as well as Voltaire, from whom he had learned them, but what Voltaire called "esprit," Diderot was inclined to call "paradox." It seems to me, though, that Diderot has added something which I do not perceive in Voltaire. Thought is a power for both; for both, it is a power for change. The change for Diderot, however, begins in the thinker. What one thinks changes the person thinking, he becomes literally "un autre." It is that quality of high metaphor in Diderot's thought which distinguishes it from Voltaire's "esprit." With Voltaire, "esprit" is used to carry on his everlasting debate with his public. With Diderot, on the contrary, he uses his high metaphor to carry on an everlasting debate with himself. Constant transformation threatens in the debater the unity of personality, however; one is always another *moi*, debating with another *moi* who has now become a *lui*. This metaphoric "dédoublement" which was such an important factor in Diderot's theory of artistic creation was equally crucial in the creation of himself.

Consequently, the problem of Diderot's unity is first of all Diderot's own problem, as I suspect it is the personal problem which every man has to face. The only difference is that no man has ever been as deeply conscious of how crucial it is to the becoming of a well-integrated personality, unless it be his early friend Rousseau, from whom Diderot undoubtedly learned the whole procedure. The ultimate paradox is that thought makes for unity, and at the same time destroys unity; it is the only instrument of integrity we possess, but it constantly threatens that integrity; it ought to produce a harmony and a serenity, but it is the source of eternal instability and the search for something else. It is not surprising that Diderot was constantly probing into himself in his efforts to know himself. He often reverted to the dilemma in his conversations—that is to say his *Correspondance*—with Sophie Volland, in an endless effort to explain himself to his mistress but, above all, to himself. These explanations, however, were concerned more with his temperament (see H. Dieckmann, "Zur Interpretations Diderot's," *Rom. For.*, 1939, pp. 46–84) than with the nature of his intellectual preoccupations or the central focus of his interests or the relative importance of his

varied works. What he seems to be seeking are insights within himself which could apply to any living man. For example, he notes
(*Lettres à Sophie Volland*, I, 369) that "our soul is a moving picture
from which we constantly depict ourselves. We do the best we can
to make it an authentic picture," he added, "mais il existe en entier
et tout à la fois." No fairer statement could be made of how difficult
it is to know one's self, but Diderot adds that it can only be grasped
simultaneously and as a whole. Still, he confesses that all kinds of
circumstances modify the total effect of that picture. His fellow citizens at Langres, he said, "ont de l'esprit, de la vivacité, de la gaieté,"
but they are as unpredictable as the weather vanes which turn in
every direction (*Correspondance inédite*, I, 66). As a true son of
Langres, Diderot acknowledges that what contributed in his case to
the rapid changes was the constant flow of his ideas: "Il faut que
j'occupe mes pensées ou que je sois dans un état de souffrance"
(*Œuvres complètes*, XX, 40). He pictures himself as in a perpetual
state of effervescence with his thoughts and has almost unbearable
compulsion to draw conjectures from them. He grants cheerfully
that not all his conjectures are true or useful, but he adds: "Il faut
encore mieux risquer des conjectures chimériques que d'en laisser
perdre d'utiles" (*Œuvres complètes*, XIV, 46). He approves of dis-
traction as a means of meditating, but he disapproves of being
"distrait." Meditation, however, is a specific means of extending
thought: "On trouve que c'est l'histoire de tout ce qu'on a dans la
tête et de tout ce qui y manque" (*Œuvres complètes*, I, xxxii). To
discourse intelligently about a needle, Diderot maintains, one would
need to be endowed with universal knowledge. Diderot delights in
this intellectual vagabonding. He boasts of letting his thoughts flow
from his pen in the same helter-skelter fashion that they occur to
him. He even finds in this method an advantage: "Elles ne repré-
senteront que mieux les mouvements et la marche de mon esprit"
(*Œuvres complètes*, II, 9). Diderot judges, in fact, that this is the
way the true philosopher operates: it is a combination of reflection
and experience with the outside world; he passes continually from
observation to reflection, what he called "le travail de l'abeille"
(*Œuvres complètes*, XIV, 523). He insists that the true philosopher
not only wants to meditate upon his thoughts, extend them indefinitely, and verify them in the outside world but he wants also to

share them with others. He admits that this is a sort of dissipation, but he maintains that it is also a source of unending pleasure. He rejects the notion that this constant sharing of ideas with others is a waste of time: "On ne me vole point ma vie, je la donne . . . Je n'ai jamais regretté le temps que j'ai donné aux autres" (*Œuvres complètes*, III, 332, 333). It was in fact a necessity with him: "Oh, combien mes amis me sont nécessaires: Sans eux mon cœur et mon esprit seraient muets." (*Lettres à Sophie Volland*, III, 294.) He confessed (*Œuvres complètes*, XI, 115) that they stimulated him to constant intellectual activity: "C'est pour moi et mes amis que je lis, que je réfléchis, que j'écris, que je médite, que j'entends, que je regarde, que je sens . . . Je songe sans cesse à leur bonheur." Diderot experiences in this constant activity of thought and sharing these thoughts with others a constant pleasure, and he claims it is the only means of rejoining the past with the future: "Nous existons dans le passé par la mémoire des grands hommes que nous imitons, dans le présent où nous recevons les honneurs qu'ils ont obtenus ou mérités, dans l'avenir par la certitude qu'il parlera de nous comme nous parlons d'eux." It was therefore a means of indefinitely extending thought in space and time. "Mon ami," he wrote Falconet (*Œuvres complètes*, XVIII, 224), "ne rétrécissons pas notre existence, ne circonscrivons point le sphère de nos jouissances." Diderot expresses a constant faith in survival; one would say it was as strong with him as with any true Christian: "Si je me porte à mon ouvrage avec des sentiments élevés, si j'ai une haute opinion de la chose que je tente; si j'ai une noble confiance en mes forces, si je me propose de fixer sur moi l'attention des siècles à venir; quoique la présence de ces différents motifs cesse dans mon esprit, la chaleur en reste au fond de mon cœur, elle y subsiste à mon insu, elle y agit, elle travaille . . ." (*Œuvres complètes*, XVIII, 171). To Dr. Clerc, who spoke to him of a projected Russian *Encyclopédie* while he was in the midst of making arrangements for the publication of his own works, Diderot wrote with genuine enthusiasm that he was willing to devote to the new *Encyclopédie* the last fifteen years of his life, and he added (XX, 67): "Laissons à quelque bonne âme le soin de rassembler mes guenilles, quand je serai mort." Notwithstanding this desire to be useful to others, to devote himself to their happiness, coupled with an almost childish faith in the future of his work, he confessed that he scattered his ideas upon paper "sans me soucier ni de les trier ni de les écrire. Il y en aura de vraies, il y en aura de fausses" (*Œuvres complètes*, IX, 107). It is obvious from these brief snatches of correspondence that Diderot sees himself as the director of the *Encyclopédie* and the author of a number of unpublished works. He acknowledges that his contemporaries would have to judge him as encyclopedist, whereas his successors would want to judge him in terms of his unpublished work.

There is no doubt, I suppose, that the thing, in his opinion, which welds the two Diderots together—the Diderot of the *Encyclopédie* and the Diderot of the unpublished works—is thought. In the opening page of the *Neveu de Rameau* where the author is obviously struggling to find a logical justification for his inner reality, he places it squarely upon his thought ("mes pensées, ce sont mes catins"). He even characterizes neatly the nature of that thought and the way it is brought by him into some sort of organic unity: "Je m'entretiens avec moi-même de politique, d'amour, de goût, ou de philosophie." If one may trust the authenticity of an author's self-portrait, it is obvious that Diderot saw himself as a kind of dialectician pursuing the rhythm of his ideas as they eluded him, or as they varied in almost incessantly paradoxical contradictions, or as they shifted like the weather vanes in Langres of which he spoke when he sought an appropriate metaphor for his own inner personality.

There is thus much analogy between the way he saw himself and Montaigne's discovery that man is "vain, divers, et ondoyant." One might even extend the comparison and note that Diderot, like Montaigne, is constantly "essaying" an extraordinarily nimble wit upon the phenomena of the universe. He, like Montaigne, is constantly trying to depict the rhythm of becoming rather than the nature of being. Like Montaigne, also, he has some deep apprehension of the vitalism in that becoming. Finally, if one examines carefully the statement which we have just quoted from the *Neveu*, he would have to conclude that while the esthetic goal is readily apparent, the ultimate goal, even for Diderot, is philosophical. He saw himself, just as his contemporaries saw him, as the Philosophe.

We should tarry a bit here and inquire what Diderot actually understands by the term "philosophe." Since he published Dumarsais's article "Philosophe" after abridging it, we generally assume that it contains his ideal of the man. When we scan it with care to get a glimpse of what Diderot has in mind, we always go astray either because of the complexity of the details or because we assume that we certainly know more about the meaning of the term than people who are living it as an ideal. If we could for once divest ourselves of this improbable assumption, we ought to be able to understand that the philosophe is an "honnête homme" who wants to live the intellectual life of his time: he is, and wants to be, sociable. But he honestly believes that guarantee of the good life, the life of wisdom, the social life he wants to live is a life with living ideas which are the vital sources of his being. He really believes that his existence is what his ideas are, his actions are the results of these ideas, his values are the merit and beauty he attributes to them. In short, he is an enlightened man because of them.

Despite the evident clarity in which the thinker and the artist unite in one Diderot, since he combined, just as Voltaire had done, "pensées vraies" and "expressions justes," he insisted with much persistence upon the concept of the two Diderots: the editor of the *Encyclopédie* and the writer for posterity. As a result of this insistence, there has been much misunderstanding concerning the development of Diderot which has vitiated in large measure the unity of that development. As a matter of fact, there are some serious confusions in this division, and it is compounded by the additional fact that once one begins to fragment the activities of Diderot, there are not two but five Diderots. There is the Diderot of the early *Essays: Essai sur le mérite et la vertu*, the *Pensées philosophiques*, the *Lettre sur les aveugles*, the *Lettre sur les sourds et muets*, and the *Pensées sur l'interprétation de la nature*. It can be argued cogently that the Diderot of the *Encyclopédie* differs from the Diderot of these *Essays*, although there are some reflections of the Diderot of the essays in the later Diderot of the *Encyclopédie*. The former Diderot is already committed to changing the fundamental relationships between thought and action in the fields of esthetics, ethics, and science. What is more, the unity of Diderot's essays lies in the interpenetration of these three fields by all of these essays. At first sight one might feel that due to a surface confusion, Diderot fails to distinguish between a moral problem, an esthetic problem, and a scientific problem. In reality, he has a distinct tendency even from the very first, to see each field as a metaphor of the other. It is this high power of metaphor which has led some of Diderot's excellent critics astray. Funt undoubtedly is referring to this trait when he speaks of Diderot's "unclassifiability." Jacques Barzun quotes a handful of these critics as saying that Diderot "cannot be associated with a stabilized genre . . . much less with a single recognized masterpiece." Belaval (*RSH*, 1963, p. 435) defines this early period as characterized by a "rash of inquiries which give his thought its definite orientation," but he interprets this orientation as a development, not as a metaphoric explanation of the universe. And that is why L. Venturi, so perceptive of Diderot's growth (*A History of Art Criticism*, New York, 1936) says: "He has no original esthetic ideas, and when he outlines some, they are without force."

Finally, J. Thomas (*L'Humanisme de Diderot,* Paris, 1950, p. 113) notes that "à mesure que le point de vue de l'artiste se substituera dans ses jugements au point de vue du savant et du philosophe, la définition du beau par les rapports s'estompera, puis s'effacera tout à fait." The important thing about this activity is not that it can with difficulty be reduced to some unified conception, but that there are vying within the man at this time at least three Diderots: the esthetician, the moralist, the scientist. The writer is not struggling to achieve some sort of unity but he is actually pretending to do so by the procedure of metaphors, which is doubtless a result of his own theory of rapports.

This can be seen from the very first in the early essays. Each essay begins with a central problem, the area of which can be clearly delineated. The core of the *Pensées philosophiques* is the problem of deism broadly conceived. It is contained in the "élargissez Dieu" and involves not only the Spinozistic *Deus sive Natura,* but the scientific, moral, religious, and esthetic interpenetration of nature. The *Essai sur le mérite et la vertu* combines, to be sure, both esthetics and morality. The *Lettre sur les aveugles,* which seems preeminently preoccupied with the biological consequences of blindness, quickly imposes consequences upon the metaphysical problem of final causes and even larger consequences upon the esthetic problem of the mimetic interpretation of a nature which is so elusive, so abundant, and so deceptive as to defy imitation. Likewise, the *Lettre sur les sourds et muets* not only proposes the physiological problem of communication for the deaf-mutes, but the larger interpretation of the esthetic problem of expression and communication for the artist. Taken together with the *Aveugles* the two essays embrace the three great artistic problems of seeing, saying, and hearing, that is, how one imitates nature when he sees it so imperfectly, how he expresses his apprehension of it when he is so limited in his comprehension, and how he is rightly understood by others when he is so restricted in the two senses of hearing and communicating.

These comprehensive moral, esthetic, and scientific problems metaphorically conceived were interrupted by Diderot's *Encyclopédie* between 1750 and 1765, and here the philosopher Diderot appeared. There is no doubt since Naigeon's day that Diderot's real contribution in the *Encyclopédie* was a new interpretation of the history of philosophy as a new kind of philosophy of history or rather history of ideas. But once the *Encyclopédie* had been given a structure, once the whole nexus of facts, theories, doctrines, and organic meaning had been structured into the work, Diderot immediately dissociated himself from it and returned to the preparation of the Diderot of posterity. He had, in fact, not waited until 1765. As early as 1757 and 1758, his interest in drama led to a whole new elaboration of the theatre. In 1761, he reverted to fiction with the first draft of *Le Neveu de Rameau*, and thereafter fiction, theatre, essay, dialogue, pour forth in increasing abundance, especially between 1766 and 1773. Here the essential categories are the same as in the period from 1746 to 1753, but the emphasis has shifted from the essay and the dialogue to the more formal drama and fiction. By 1773 when Diderot made his visit to Catherine, there had thus been five discreet Diderots: the moralist, the esthetician, the philosopher, the scientist, the littérateur, but the five have in some way merged into the Diderot we have always known. We shall now try to see what is organic and unified in this merging process, and what results when a creator or a critic or better still a creator-critic tries to be continuous, consistent, and coherent, in a universe which is constantly changing.

If we are looking for the key to bring together all the thought of Diderot, we will do well to ponder Professor Niklaus' introductory article in the *Diderot Studies* ("Présence de Diderot," VI, 13–28), where Diderot is fundamentally and from the beginning assumed to be the Philosophe. In that respect, Diderot differs from Voltaire who had to make the switch from poetry to philosophy. Once again, Diderot profited by following in Voltaire's footsteps. Just what is implied by the term "philosophe" in Diderot's case is not terribly clear. At one point he said "si l'on voit la chose comme elle est en nature, on est philosophe." Niklaus interprets that by this act, Diderot, like Montaigne, has succeeded in reestablishing the feeling of inner harmony which exists between the individual and his universe. However, it seems to me that there is also a difference between the two. I fail to see in the author of *Jacques le Fataliste* that serenity which appears at the end of Montaigne's essay "On Experience."

Nonetheless, the role which Diderot assigned to himself as contributor to the *Encyclopédie* was the section on philosophy. He succeeded admirably well in those articles, first in presenting a batch of articles upon the various schools of Greek, Roman, and even oriental philosophy. In addition, he covered surprisingly well the outstanding philosophers of the seventeenth century in Europe. Proust has analyzed these articles with extreme care and ventured the judgment that they are Diderot's profound contribution to his time. But he has insisted that Diderot extracted much of his basic material not from the philosophers themselves, but from Brucker's *Historia critica philosophiae*, 1742. Proust has shown that Diderot nonetheless interpreted these seventeenth-century philosophers in his own personal way. For instance, while Brucker, a Calvinist, shows liberal but nonetheless orthodox views upon philosophical matters, Diderot moved in his understanding of these philosophers from a deism, once more, characteristic of Voltaire, to a materialism which bordered on atheism.

Pomeau, in an excellent little book of Diderot extracts (see *Diderot, sa vie, ses œuvres avec un exposé de sa philosophie,* Paris, 1967) has prefaced his collection of extracts with an analysis of Diderot's life which he has characterized as "une vie au service de la philosophie." It is a succinct and clear exposition of how this service was performed. Pomeau notes that Diderot arrived at maturity around 1743, just after the departure of Fleury. It is the moment when the active living thought declares itself opposed to the official philosophy of the time with its insistence upon the divine right of kings, the supremacy of the Catholic church, and the class hierarchy of society. In place of this official view, there is now presented a critical interpretation of religion (the clandestine manuscripts) and a new interpretation of history (the *Lettres philosophiques*, the *Siècle de Louis XIV*, and the *Essai sur les mœurs*). The new philosophy is a combination of Spinoza (of the *Tractatus*), Newton (of the *Eléments de la philosophie de Newton*) and Locke (of Coste's translation). Of course the outstanding representative of that philosophy is Voltaire. The generation of Diderot and Rousseau was initiated into philosophical thought in these works of Voltaire and the political thought of Montesquieu. Indeed, when that generation came of age intellectually, all the preparation of French Enlightenment (critical deism, history and analysis of civilization, organization of scientific thought, union of French and English thought and art for the structuring of a European civilization) had been completed. What was now needed was the organization of these ideas into a coherent whole with a dynamic meaning. Diderot did not do this in a haphazard way, despite the first impression we get from any attempt to comprehend the whole activity. The ideas were to be gathered into an *Encyclopédie*, which, naturally, would be encyclopedic in scope, and propagandistic in intent. But it was not at all designed to be radical in expression nor revolutionary in purpose. Diderot insisted upon a solid organization of the thought of his time, its true mission for the future (which also was destined for posterity), but it was not to take its place necessarily in the vanguard of thought. With an uncanny understanding of the temper of the day, Diderot seemed to sense just how far he could go in the thought of his time and yet stay in the confines of what was acceptable. He had evidently calculated very carefully just how much the traffic would bear. All the evidence within the *Encyclopédie*, all the evidence around the *Encyclopédie* (even Diderot's insistence, when in its most dangerous days the world of the Old Regime was closing in upon it, that it must be completed in France) indicates that he was determined that these limits must not be exceeded. He gave every sign of being aware that the more general conclusions of all this intellectual effort would have to wait. Hence, alongside an activity which provided for the present state of the *Encyclopédie*, Diderot prepared in a whole string of clandestine works his thought for the future.

We think of Voltaire as the clandestine eighteenth-century writer par excellence. I am not so sure that isn't a mistake. It is very likely that Diderot was even more clandestine in his writing than Voltaire, who was undoubtedly more devious. Pomeau stresses the point, for instance, that Diderot masked his veritable thoughts so well that no difficulty was encountered in his parish at the time of his death. Pomeau maintains that he nonetheless pushed his philosophy as far as it would have been tolerated. I am less certain about that point. I get the impression that after the Vincennes episode, Diderot never wanted to risk another disagreeable experience of that sort. This view, to be sure, would somewhat mitigate the appeal to posterity which many of his biographers have stressed. But Diderot is often ambiguous and contradictory in his attitudes when there is no apparent reason for taking a particular stand. His early correspondence with Voltaire would be a case in point, where the problem of his real thought is not easily resolved. His criticism of both Holbach and Helvétius when he saw an earnest, if not authentic, attempt to present what his two comrades must have thought a straightforward account of his own thought is puzzling, to say the least. The curious thing about his refutations in these two cases is that his arguments are what we would expect an opponent of Diderot's ideas to offer against Diderot.

Pomeau recognizes that these contradictions can be troublesome ("son matérialisme volontiers cynique s'accorde mal avec l'idéalisme de sa morale"). Moreover, Diderot seems always to be pursuing ideas which are ever eluding him. His arguments are often based upon a hypothesis for which there is not the slightest trace of proof. All of us, carried away by the brilliance of the idea, forget all about its verification (see "sensibilité, propriété universelle de la matière . . ."). The whole of the *Rêve de d'Alembert* is pure fiction which the most down-to-earth critic will praise as thrilling science or profound philosophy or wonderful morality, when all the evidence we can muster only proves that it is great art. Pomeau has already stated that the *Encyclopédie*, which naturally requires a rigid method, "fut vécue par lui comme une aventure." The *Pensées sur l'interprétation de la nature* are almost a suite of lyrics posing as a discourse on scientific method.

At all events, Pomeau, Dieckmann, and Proust have each given very detailed accounts of the nature of that "new" philosophy that in some respects is distinguished by contradictions. Pomeau explains these contradictions in part by the attribution to Diderot in the

Assézat edition of his works *Encyclopédie* articles which he did not write. It is not, however, contradictions of this sort which cause the difficulty. It is in the larger issue of what really constitutes the nature of Diderot's philosophy. It has often been remarked, for instance, that his materialism is not at all in accord with the idealism of his morality. Moreover, in Diderot's discussion with Voltaire after the *Essai sur les aveugles,* where he clearly renounces his belief in the proof by final causes of the existence of God, he reassures Voltaire by stating that he is still a deist, and thereupon he proceeds to give further arguments (still of an atheistic nature) which Saunderson could have added to those he had already offered. This sort of open-ended attitude of Diderot toward ideas in general is rather character-istic of him, but it can at times be very disconcerting. It was what occasioned the remark, I suspect, about the authenticity of ideas to which he reverted the most often. Pomeau refers to this tendency very neatly as Diderot's adventures with thought and adds that "son esprit trouve son climat le plus favorable dans une sorte de libertin-age intellectuel." In fact, Diderot takes a childish delight, even in the *Encyclopédie*, in upsetting established beliefs.

Diderot evolved rapidly from a deist into a wavering naturalist. Did he thereby become an atheist? Often he will proclaim that he is not, whereas his comportment could easily be interpreted as tend-ing toward atheism. Certainly he excludes any explanation of the universe drawn from finalism and he counsels his companions to avoid the "pourquoi" in favor of the "comment." All of this negative skirmishing entails the establishment of a monistic conception of nature. Inherent therein is movement and an inner energy not unlike the inner energy of Leibniz's monade, and from there he advances the notion of "sensibilité, propriété universelle de la matière." Natu-rally, life and feeling exist in a portion of matter in an inert state.

Diderot agrees with Rousseau that the basis of all inquiry into the meaning of nature must always begin with the nature of man. There is parallelism between man and animal. Consequently, one can only conclude that man is a portion of organized matter. Diderot insists endlessly upon the principle of organization. Seen in this perspective, man is a colony of organs. But Diderot insists that a central control is necessary to bring these organs into harmony: one control center is situated in the brain, which controls thought, the other in the diaphragm (heart) which controls the sensibility. But both mind and heart are controlled by the phenomena of matter. Consequently, free will is an illusion. To Landois he wrote that free will is a word "vide de sens . . . Nous ne sommes que ce qui convient à l'ordre général, à l'organisation, à l'éducation et à la chaîne des événements." At this point, however, it seems that Diderot is not in accord with himself. These ideas of his regarding free will reappeared in Helvé-tius's *De l'Homme* and Diderot, writing a commentary on Helvé-tius's work, denounces them. Critics argue vehemently to prove that Diderot is not inconsequential. And yet this "âme sensible" which is called "le matérialisme du sage" (and this term, it must be re-called, originated with Rousseau, not with Diderot) does not appear althogether divorced from the spiritual side of man. Indeed, Rousseau is still there to prove that it is the spiritual side of man.

Moreover, if there is no freedom of action, there can be no vice or virtue, Diderot insisted in his letter to Landois. Virtue is "bien-faisance," that is, it is a social phenomenon, while vice is malevolence, it is the activity of a wicked individual. One is "heureusement" or "malheureusement né." Notwithstanding this conclusion, Diderot insists that man's nature may be modified by rewards and punisments (which was Voltaire's point), by example, by exhortation, and by education. Diderot even conceived of man as a creature of conscience (which was Rousseau's point). Hence, he must have some sort of way of making decisions for himself. Once again, Diderot ran upon his own ideas concerning morality in the *De l'Esprit*, and this time he rejected them too, asserting that it is possible to find an eternal foundation for justice and injustice in our needs, in our organization, in our sensibility, in the "nature originelle de l'homme."

His treatment of esthetics appears to be more consistent. In accord with his time, he defines carefully what he understands his terms to mean: the beautiful, the true, the useful. From these he turns to the capacity of the individual to use the faculties of the human mind to explore the surrounding world: memory, imagination, enthusi-asm. When he turned to painting and sculpture in the *Correspon-dance littéraire*, he avoids for the most part the "technique" in favor of the "moral," that is to say, he discourses endlessly upon the "moral": the subject-matter, the passions, movement, the characters, the "effet général." The directing force of all his criticism is derived from his interest in the theatre; that is to say, what he endeavors to achieve in the "new" theatre is a criterion for his judgment in art. It has been pointed out often that the qualities which he saw in the "drame" are those which he saw in the *Salons* he so enthusiastically depicted. And yet, critics have often debated whether his descriptions of the paintings are an art or a defect, whether his criticism is coherent or a pure "laissez-aller" without organization. We have already mentioned that Crocker asserted that Diderot's criticism is a multiplicity of theories flying out from a center like the spokes of a wheel. Belaval insists that while not absolutely contradictory, Diderot's esthetic ideas have often hesitated. Pomeau concedes that the *Paradoxe sur le comédien* in which Diderot apparently contradicts himself outright on the importance of sensibility in art is "perhaps" totally lacking in coherence.

These criticisms are certainly valid. However, they do not seem to place Diderot's real contribution to esthetics in proper perspective. Beginning with a new concept of genius, he has redefined the poet and examined the vital aspects of his art: how to grasp the phenomena of nature, how to organize the phenomena which have been selected, how to establish the "idea" of his material, how to structure the idea into a coherent work, how to transmit to the structured work the possibility of a living form, how to assure to the work the gift of interpreting itself to the public. It was, as modern critics have shown, a new concept of the poet, of the poet's imagination, of the poetic act, consisting in finding new answers to three questions always involved in artistic creation: how to see in nature that which is poetically relevant; how to give to that vision the correct expression; and how to offer to the public—as limited in its ability to comprehend as the poet is limited in his ability to see and to express what he has seen—the chance to hear. Art thus becomes a struggle between a limitless nature, a limited artist, and a very limited public. It is played out by an artist who can control only a most insignificant part of that nature, and who must devise means to give it a coherent reality. Diderot refers to the operation as lifting the veil which covers the mysteries of Saïs. The artist is nonetheless circumscribed by his expression, and he is talking to a public which is just as deficient in its capacity to hear and understand, while he is woefully restricted in his vision. Hence all art is illusion, a lie, but it is the creation by the poetic imagination of something which has never existed in that form, but now it can exist, thanks to the genius of the poet, in that form forever. What is implied, of course, is the notion that the art of living is in reality a poetic act, that to create is to live, that every living being is the genius of his existence, and that his every thought, be it ever so humble, is the guarantee of that existence. Thought thus becomes the power of creation, but this creation is the release of inner existent power.

We must stress, as Pomeau has done (p. 35), that the poetic act is involved in the creative act, but of greater importance still is the involvement of thought. In *Sur le génie*, Diderot wrote that "l'esprit d'imitation ne regarde point, il voit." It is a sort of prophetic spirit. Indeed, what is imitated is not precisely what the poet has seen, it is a sort of inspiration through the "ideal model" of what he has seen. Diderot confesses that it is an inspiration given only to a few rare geniuses. One would be forced to conclude that the "idea" is very restricted, but the idea of reality interpreted by the "enthusiasm" or by the imagination of the poet operates in the field of ethics in the same way as in that of esthetics, and there it is anything but restricted.

Thus, we may conclude that Diderot, like Voltaire, lived in a world whose outstanding trait was an abundance of ideas. One has only to glance at the titles (*Pensées philosophiques, Pensées sur l'interprétation de la nature*, and so on) to see him surrounded with ideas. The problem which he constantly faced concerned the collection of these ideas, the method of organizing them, of submitting them to some sort of general system, and of giving to them a more precise interpretation. This imperative was stressed by Diderot in the opening paragraph of the article *Encyclopédie*: "Le but d'une *Encyclopédie* est de rassembler les connaissances éparses sur la surface de la terre, d'en exposer le système général aux hommes avec qui nous vivons, et de le transmettre aux hommes qui viendront après nous." We omit for the moment the ultimate goal of this transmission: to produce better informed descendants who will become more virtuous and consequently happier. The point to stress here is that Diderot presents the full program of the way he proposes to handle ideas and his intention to prepare them for posterity.

There are, however, several remarks which we should add. In

Diderot's view, a system of knowledge is an organic something consisting in an ordered "enchaînement" which, when broken, distorts both the "fond" and the "forme." This concept implies a rigid method in the organization of knowledge and in its filiation. An item out of place or omitted "rompt l'enchaînement et nuit à la forme et au fond." Nonetheless, it is evident in the article "Encyclopédie" that Diderot is not too certain that the best method has been used or that the best order has been followed. The analogies of the orders with geographical maps show some hesitation on his part. Moreover, the order which prevails is really the alphabetical order of a dictionary rather than a systematic order of an encyclopedia. In reality, the system of references was devised to remedy in part this difficulty. One wonders, though, whether the device did not complicate rather than remedy the situation. Dieckmann has quoted a remark of Diderot which shows that he was well aware of the danger: "Plus on médite un sujet, plus il s'étend; on trouve que c'est l'histoire de tout ce qu'on a dans la tête et de tout ce qui y manque: et cela sert d'autant mieux que les idées et les connaissances y sont plus liées." What apparently astounds Diderot is the immense number of relationships which operate in any given case. Therefore, it is not strange that he suggests that "méditation" can produce a more satisfactory solution than an a priori approach. What helps is an analogy which brings ideas together by an inner attraction. Diderot adds, though: "Ce n'est qu'en méditant profondément sa matière qu'on trouve une distribution générale. C'est presque toujours la dernière idée importante qu'on rencontre; c'est une pensée unique qui se développe..." But what adds immensely in the process is the instinct of the thinker united with a "don d'observation."

Dieckmann has stressed that Diderot has been greatly conditioned in his conception of the world by the mathematical approach of Newton, by the esthetic vision of Shaftesbury, and the optimism of Pope. Once again, we must note that these were the background against which Voltaire also had developed his vision of the world. It is quite possible that these three were the origin of Diderot's initiation into his world. There was really no need to go so far afield to encounter these three approaches, though, since Diderot could have found them already united in Voltaire. I suspect, in fact, that to a large extent, he did. For the latter, the world is already one; it is subject to a set of universal laws which modern science has now deciphered. Man also has a place in that order and the moral law which directs his action has an especial significance in the harmony of this order. God essentially directs this harmony and insures its continuity. The world thereby becomes a machine which has its "roues," its "cordes," its "poulies," and its "poids."

There are nonetheless some hesitations on Diderot's part, just as there are on Voltaire's. Nature is not nearly so perfect in its manifestation. How can one be sure that what one observes in this our world can be equally found "éternellement" and "universellement"? How can one be certain that what occurs in our little corner is present everywhere and always. Voltaire had already undergone these doubts in *Micromégas*. Diderot resumed them in his *Lettre sur les aveugles*. What had taken place in the thought of the time was that the concept of the world as machine which could be handled in a mathematical and geometrical way became complicated by the notion of organic life which could only be handled, it seemed, by experience. Diderot announced in the *Pensées sur l'interprétation de la nature* the end of the geometric world, indeed, the end of mathematics, and the birth of a new science—"la physique expérimentale." It was a totally new concept of the method to be used in the pursuit of the biological sciences. In this concept, instinct, "esprit observateur," conjecture, hypotheses, which Newton had so studiously excluded from his science, now played a preponderant role. The scientists of nature who can use these faculties instead of weighing, measuring, and calculating the phenomena of nature have now become the true interpreters of nature.

The result of these two movements of thought—the one abstract, mathematical, the other biological, empirical, and to a large extent historical—have constantly brought up in Diderot's case the problem of coherence in his ideas. Many of the critics have stressed (see Mornet) that his ideas are contradictory and consequently it is impossible to establish a logical continuity in the contrasting opinions which he has proffered on any given subject. Others have insisted upon a "certain unity" which, says Dieckmann, they have tried painstakingly and ingenuously to trace in his meanderings. Dieckmann willingly grants that the person is "une." The problem, however, as he says, is whether the "Œuvre" is "une." In this respect, the commentary of Dieckmann is crucial (*Cinq leçons*, p. 67): "En tenant compte du rôle que la tradition de la systématique des idées et la tendance personnelle au système ont joué dans la pensée de Diderot, en comprenant l'opposition chez lui entre cette tradition et cette tendance, et en étudiant la fonction de l'interprétation, on rejoindra le sens de la nouvelle critique de Diderot,—la critique de Diderot doit pour ainsi dire comprendre l'échec du système pour se retrouver dans l'interprétation. Elle abandonnera également les tentatives d'expliquer Diderot dans les catégories du cartésianisme, du baconisme, du spinozism et du Leibnizianisme. La pensée de ces auteurs n'est jamais apparue à Diderot sous la forme d'un système; aussi finira-t-on toujours par admettre que les idées de Diderot ne se laissent point enfermer dans de tels cadres."

The last part of Dieckmann's statement brings forward a problem which has been discussed on several occasions, always with varying emphasis, and as practically always in any matter involving Diderot's intellectual activities, with a wide variety of opinion from the participants. It seems perfectly reasonable to expect that if there is any validity in the title Philosophe, which was ascribed to Diderot during his life by his contemporaries, he would have some well-defined qualities to his philosophy. Indeed, in the very passage which we have quoted, Dieckmann expressly discusses the role played by the previous philosophical tradition. This problem naturally renders necessary a characterization of the attitude of Diderot toward the method of philosophical thought. Dieckmann faces these matters very straightforwardly: for him Diderot has never found acceptable the systematic, formal thinking of at least four of the outstanding seventeenth-century philosophers—Descartes, Bacon, Spinoza, and Leibniz—the very four whom Diderot elected as his masters. He concedes, though, that Diderot is not at all averse to thinking systematically in his philosophical endeavors. Nonetheless, he posits as the opposite of the systematic the method of interpretation which he stresses as Diderot's preferred method. Dieckmann recognizes that the question of Diderot's unity has often been discussed in terms of logical arrangement or of coherence of ideas. He states that a large number of those who propose the question have answered it in the negative, insisting that Diderot's ideas are contradictory. A few, on the other hand, have acknowledged that he has some sort of unity, but when they attempt to describe it, it turns out to be a simple description of Diderot's meanderings in the intellectual world or an abstract concept such as the relationship between personality and thought. Dieckmann proposes that some effort be made to solve the problem of Diderot's philosophy by insisting that it is not really a philosophy or that it is predominantly one particular aspect of philosophy, such as esthetics, ethics, science, and, more recently, politics and economics. Underlying these presentations is the conviction that Diderot has no unity or that he has a unity of sorts or that he has no philosophy or that he has grasped only an aspect of philosophy. What I propose to do now is to examine carefully the finest of these presentations with the problem of his unity clearly in mind. There is certainly no lack of material.

Diderot's portrait of his inner self has been attempted often by those who have struggled with the problem of his unity, as if it is tacitly agreed that one of these things cannot be understood without the other. Sainte-Beuve, one of the first to take up the problem anew in the *Portraits littéraires* (I, 239–264), contradicts himself at every moment in his effort to get to the crux of the matter. Without producing much evidence, he declares that the eighteenth-century writer was both "philosopher and artist" and adds that he was little interested in politics, although in philosophy, he was, so to speak, "the soul and the organ of the century." Sainte-Beuve insists that Diderot is fundamentally encyclopedist, a kind of journalist. He recalls Grimm's estimate of his colleague when he compared him to nature as Diderot always thought of nature—"riche, fertile, douce, et sauvage, simple et majestueuse, bonne et sublime, mais *sans aucun principe dominant*, sans maître et sans Dieu." Before Sainte-Beuve reaches the end of his sprightly portrait, Diderot has become the *atheistic philosopher* who is so little atheistic that he is hardly more than a deist, *the biological, vitalistic, materialistic, natural* philosopher whose naturalism tends to that inevitable deism. As *artist* and *critic*, he is, insists Sainte-Beuve, "éminent," while in the *Correspondance*, he is "moraliste, peintre, critique." It must be confessed that the portrait is excellent in rendering the intellectual dispersal of the eighteenth-century encyclopedist, in whom the nineteenth-century could apparently find, to quote Grimm's remark, "no dominating principle." Despite the insufficiency of Sainte-Beuve's portrait, he has at least taught us that what we are seeking in Diderot is that dominating principle. The history of all Diderot criticism since Diderot's time has been an account of that search.

One of those in the early part of the twentieth century who did much to attribute to Diderot the importance which he deserved was Professor Jean Thomas whose *Humanisme de Diderot* (1932) has always been considered one of the fine critical analyses of the eighteenth-century author. Thomas mentions that at the time of Brunetière, critics had just about given up all hope of discovering in Diderot's opinions a unity of doctrine. Every one seemed pretty much in agreement that what united so many paradoxes was the author's own temperament, which was characterized by disorder and incoherence. Taine, for instance, remarked that Diderot did not control his ideas; they, on the contrary, controlled him. He was their slave. He was lacking, said Taine, in that solid good sense which in Voltaire and Montesquieu acts as a sort of deterrent to undue outbursts. Thomas (p. 38) concedes Diderot's innumerable contradictions, but he maintains that two principles stand out amidst them: the principle of unity and the principle of evolution, one of which concerns the intellectual method of his procedures, the other, the growth of his wisdom. Diderot's unifying quality is his humanism, which Thomas defines as "vivre, agir, fuir la banalité et l'ennui, sentir et penser fortement, voilà sa devise" (p. 76), to which he adds "aller au réel, au fait." Thomas denies that Diderot found this humanism in Descartes, Malebranche, Spinoza, or even Locke; he found it rather in the center of French humanism, Montaigne, who had dared establish his wisdom on ancient learning and assert his individualism. But Montaigne's great superiority in humanism lies in the fact that the core of this humanism is oriented toward the science of man, it is destined for man and adjusted to man's measure. Thomas states that Diderot always sang the praises of Montaigne (see also J. Schwartz, *Diderot and Montaigne*, Geneva, 1966), although he adds that among the philosophers proper, Diderot preferred Leibniz. Thomas, however, sees in Diderot a rather diminished replica of the humanist Montaigne, much overshadowed by Goethe. Thomas finds the sources of this humanism in the scientific training which Diderot gave himself and which preserved him from Utopianism. His sensualism has given him a sense of the beauty of the human body and thereby has awakened in him an enthusiasm for all the arts. His contact with artisans and artists has made him respectful of the technical arts. Thus by temperament, by his scientific training, by his artistic taste, and by his curiosity in the technical arts, Diderot's "humanism" has become the most authentic, the richest, the most concrete of all the philosophies of the century (p. 160). Thomas's presentation received very general commendation, which it richly deserved. Vernière approved his seeing in Diderot two important principles: one a principle of unity dealing with the permanent procedures of his intellectual method, the other a principle of evolution, responsible for the progress of his wisdom. He adds, though, that "dans ce champ immense qui épuise les visées humaines, la clarté des approches demeure diffuse." (P. Vernière, in *Diderot: Œuvres philosophiques*, Paris, 1956, p. xviii.)

Professor Mornet also commended the *Humanisme de Diderot*: "M. Jean Thomas a eu raison de dire, dans un livre pénétrant, que le Diderot de 1770 est assez différant du Diderot de 1746–1760, et que, de la confusion de ses premières aspirations, il a peu à peu dégagé celles qui lui étaient essentielles." However, not for that does Mornet approve either the notion of unity or that of evolution in Diderot. In his introduction to *Diderot: L'homme et l'œuvre* (Paris, 1941), one of his most penetrating eighteenth-century studies, Mornet calls the editor of the *Encyclopédie* a "homo duplex," one of the most changeable and contradictory of men, and insists that "there has not been any real evolution in Diderot" (p. 10). Mornet grants that Diderot himself wanted to be a thinker and a Philosophe, a writer and an "artist." To achieve these two ambitions, he was forced to use two faculties utterly distinct: a lucid intelligence, which was cold, logical, and conducted by experience, and sudden inspiration, which wells up from the heart, from enthusiasm, from genius. These two sources of his thought are often in opposition, which accounts for the contradictions in his principles, in his methods, and in his conclusions. Mornet notes that Diderot's conception of nature and his materialism form a unity, which finds itself in conflict with the doctrine of human freedom, one of Diderot's strongest assertions. There is a similar conflict between the simple life of the savage and the necessity of a belief in progress. Mornet concludes that always the author finds himself in disaccord with himself and that his thought and his work are directed often in two opposing directions.

Since there is so much difficulty in establishing a unity in Diderot, there has been a general tendency in Diderot criticism to seek out the area in which he was judged to have been most active and of most consequence. It has not been easy, however, to determine what that area was. Beginning with Hermand's *Morale de Diderot* (1923) and continuing down to Proust's *Diderot et l'Encyclopédie* (1962), there have been numerous attempts to make Diderot a moralist, an esthetician, an encyclopedist, a political and economic theorist, a reformer, and a formal philosopher. These presentations are not always exclusive; the critic may, on occasion, offer for study two aspects of his life, as in the case of Professor L. Crocker's *Two Diderot Studies: Ethics and Esthetics* (Baltimore, 1952).

Crocker confesses in a foreword his inability to "bend Diderot's thought to a mythical unity, rational or psychological." For him Diderot's struggle "is his real personality, his real unity." Yet, elsewhere (p. 4), he declares it an error to analyze Diderot's ethics "without reference to the evolution of his thought in general," and he does not hesitate to characterize the structure of Diderot's thought as an interplay between morals and nature. He divides the ethical thought into periods: a period of "formalistic ethics," the moralistic type of thinking; a subsequent period dominated by "scientific inquiry and positivistic naturalism"; a period of "evolutionary" morality, and so on. We must note, further, that this ethical thought is said to have progressed dialectically and yet that Diderot left "this synthesis in an undeveloped form that has concealed its true worth and significance."

In the second essay, Crocker attempts a reevaluation of Diderot's esthetic ideas. After quoting G. Boas to the effect that there is no need for unity in eighteenth-century esthetic theory, L. Venturi's remark that Diderot "has no original esthetic ideas," and F. O. Nolte's opinion that Diderot was "primarily interested in social and moral, rather than in esthetic values" (p. 51), Crocker sets out to discuss Diderot's treatment of subjectivism and objectivism as a means of obtaining a clearer understanding of the character of this esthetic thinking. He analyzes Diderot's attitudes toward basic problems which concern (1) the nature of beauty, (2) the relationship between the artist and outside reality, (3) whether the artist is merely an imitator of the beauty of the outside world or whether he creates that beauty, (4) what the role of the imagination is and (5) what the moral effect of the artist's work is. Crocker finds that, as in the case of the ethics, there is some sort of dialectical movement in Diderot's concept of art which fluctuates (or hesitates) between the subjective and the objective, and renders difficult the establishment of Diderot's ideas on taste, and the role of the imagination (p. 106). These hesitations Crocker attributes "to conflicting tendencies within himself" (p. 106). He notes that "his esthetics are not an independent growth," that there is little "systematic theory," only "fragmentary comments" which we have to piece together without imposing upon them a "unity which Diderot never gave them" (p. 109). Nonetheless, Crocker tends to emphasize "a certain unity that underlies the divergent theories, and which this discussion, he confesses, has tried to make apparent. This unity lies in the nature of his (Diderot's) approach to art, in his constant preoccupation with the artist's function of selecting and combining material according to the triple standard of beauty, truth, and morality" (p. 112). He concludes that "the simple fact is that Diderot has no definite, coherent esthetic philosophy, but a multiplicity of theories" (p. 114). Finally, he expresses a well-justified impatience with those who treat Diderot's philosophy in part (p. 108). He terminates his discussion with the remark, which agrees with Dieckmann (p. 80), that "we must consider Diderot's work in its *totality* or else falsify him."

I want now to consider three of our other distinguished Diderot scholars who have turned from a Diderot "moraliste" and Diderot "esthéticien" to espouse a Diderot "politique." The first of these is Mr. F. Venturi. Contrary to Mornet, who believes that there is no evolution in Diderot's thought, Venturi, in the Preface of *La Jeunesse de Diderot* (Paris, 1939, p. 10) distinguishes three periods. (1) During a period of preparation for the *Encyclopédie*, Diderot gathered together his energy, his forces, and his ideas. This first phase came to an end with the *Pensées sur l'interprétation de la nature* (1753). (2) It was followed by the period of the *Encyclopédie* and the theatre, two aspects, said Venturi, of the same movement. This second phase is one of propaganda, expansion, battles, and the affirmation of ideas (1750–1765). (3) When the *Encyclopédie* was completed, Diderot withdrew from the public, wrote for himself, and recounted his experiences in a series of master works, which he refused to publish. He then entered a final period in which he attempted to refine and deepen the ideas for which he became the leader of his time. Of more consequence is Venturi's insistence that Diderot was too new to his ideas and too violent in his words to be considered a "littérateur," that he was neither a philosopher "au véritable sens du mot" nor a poet "au sens profond." His masterpiece, says Venturi, is the *Encyclopédie*. His great contribution consisted in giving a political meaning to Enlightenment philosophy (p. 9). Venturi calls it the new force of the Enlightenment coming after the literary force and the religious force of the first half of the century, and it transformed France into the core of European Enlightenment by inserting the ideas and the aspirations of the philosophes into the history of France and of Europe. Diderot is largely responsible for this new political force.

Professor J. Proust (*Diderot et l'Encyclopédie*, Paris, 1962) confesses in his Preface that he has tried to seize Diderot's thought in its becoming. The dominant nature of that thought being, in his opinion, political, Proust admits that he has centered his study upon politics. "Tout article de Diderot," he writes, "quelque soit son contenu, a d'abord pour but de modifier l'opinion du lecteur pour en faire un *citoyen*, plus *éclairé*, plus utile, et faire avancer par là une Révolution nécessaire" (p. 6). That is to say, it is first and foremost a political article. Proust adds that Venturi was of the same opinion. Nonetheless, he does not apparently feel that politics constitutes, even with the broad definition he proposes, a unifying element in Diderot's thought, since he excuses himself for not treating Diderot's scientific contribution to the *Encyclopédie* on the grounds that it has been fully treated in J. Mayer's thesis. Curiously, he assures that this exclusion will not falsify our perspective on Diderot. On the other hand, he finds that, even with this exclusion, there is coherence in Diderot's ideas for the period from 1750 to 1765 when he was writing for the *Encyclopédie*, although Venturi fails to bring out just what this coherence amounts to. And his inference that there is a difference between this period from 1750 to 1765 and the later period from 1765 to 1784, which proves that "son évolution n'est achevée en

1765," certainly indicates that Diderot's unity consists of at least two things.

Professor Vernière has also returned to the importance of politics in Diderot's thought. In the four volumes (Garnier edition) of Diderot texts with their very important introductions, Vernière (responsible for three of these volumes) has undertaken to present a philosophical, an esthetic, a political, and a novelist Diderot. He has not attempted, however, a synthesis of the four aspects of the editor of the *Encyclopédie*. On the contrary, in the Introduction to the *Œuvres philosophiques*, he notes how risky it would be to give offhand an interpretation of the man and reduce his doctrines artificially to a unity (p. iii). Vernière admits that he has no ready explanation for Diderot. He sees among contemporary critics two schools of thought; those who temper Diderot's prudences and judge him an idealist and humanist whose theses are fine paradoxes, and those who enroll Diderot under their banner as a pretext for advancing a particular ideology.

Vernière, in fact, tends to avoid the problem of unity and to shift the emphasis to the problem of impact. It is as a philosopher interested in politics that Vernière stresses the present-day importance of the eighteenth-century philosopher. Vernière notes that Diderot never passed for a political thinker, and quotes Mornet: "Dans l'ordre politique, son influence est nulle." However, Vernière states that in recent years, the rediscovery of Diderot's papers has revealed a number of works that are politically oriented. Vernière notes that one idea dominates the political essays of 1770 to 1774: enlightened despotism is not the true politics of the Enlightenment. Contrary to Proust, who sees in the whole political development of Diderot in the *Encyclopédie* as a general tendency toward reform (see Proust, *Diderot et l'Encyclopédie*, "Principes d'une Politique" and "Diderot réformateur"), Vernière sees in his conclusion a Diderot with a double vocation: "révolutionnaire et réformiste, l'une qui pousse à reconstruire le monde, l'autre à l'aménager." This is tantamount to saying, I suppose, that Diderot, just as his time did, used all his ingenuity to structure a new civilization and all his intellectual powers to tear it to shreds.

I have tried to present the considered opinions of these Diderot scholars, not with any desire to combat them, but with the hope of discovering in them Diderot's dominating principle. As a matter of fact, I find them extremely interesting and, for the most part, well-substantiated opinions. It is true that they are at times self-contradictory and often the judgments of one contradict the opinions of others. Since they are dealing with a strong character who has these same characteristics, it is only reasonable that their analyses should partake of this quality. Their error, if error there is, does not consist in misinterpreting Diderot's ideas but in failing to analyze the structure of Diderot's thinking until they attain the form of his thought. They all have a tendency to justify Sainte-Beuve and Mornet when it would be, it seems to me, more advantageous for Diderot studies if they would seek means of justifying Dieckmann. No one knows better than I how difficult and even frustrating this task can become. One means of getting at this structural thinking, though, is to ask in the case of these eighteenth-century philosophes just what was the outstanding achievement of each. We have shown in our study of Voltaire that he wanted to be judged as France's superior dramatist, lyric and epic poet, metaphysician, moralist, scientist, historian, political theorist, reformer, critic, and many other things. When it comes to verifying those claims and selecting the area which was his dominant interest, it was not easy, as we have seen, to make a choice. There is no reason for surprise that the same difficulty applies to Diderot and Rousseau.

Diderot, as well as Voltaire and Rousseau, has often been judged by the variety of his achievements. Many of his critics have seen in him the scientific genius who has become the precursor of Lamarck and Darwin. Others, particularly in recent times, have selected as his outstanding trait his powers as an art critic. Some have expressed the opinion that this criticism furnishes the foundation upon which is built an entirely new esthetic and a new poetry. Still others have hailed him as the founder of a new dramatic art and have seen in him the father of modern drama. To others, he is the inventor of the realistic, philosophical dialogue novel—even a kind of antinovel. Some claim that he should be credited with the invention of the "conte philosophique," which, to be sure, differs entirely from the "conte philosophique" of his contemporary, Voltaire. He was regarded in his day as the Philosophe. Curiously, with all these claims to a place of distinction in modern times, there have been those who tend to deny the superior quality of these achievements. His hesitations, his paradoxes, his obscurities have often been subjected to adverse criticism. Niklaús, who has noted the divergence between those who praise his achievements and those who are prone to question his superiority, insists that even if one wanted to question the efficacy and stability of his thought, one could hardly question the quality of his mind. For Niklaus, the unity of Diderot must be sought in his skepticism which underlies his materialism, but underlies even more his constant search for truth. Niklaus likens this quality to that of Pascal, who in another realm also used unstructured thoughts as a means of structuring a life—the life of the spirit. Niklaus subscribes to this method of Diderot which he presents as encyclopedic (that is, it insists upon the "enchaînement des connaissances") and highly hypothetical (that is, it suggests endless possibilities). I get the impression that Niklaus is fascinated by this respect for facts which Diderot insists must be organized into suggested theories which must lead to the integration of these new theories into the "enchaînement des connaissances." It is a philosophy founded upon the material universe, highly realistic in its search for facts but a priori in its deductions which lead to questions, hypotheses, paradoxes, and to that most essential of all things, "organization." Niklaus has taken the *Rêve de d'Alembert* as the masterpiece of the genre. His commentary is characteristic of many judgments upon Diderot (*DS*, VI, 21): "Il est donc oiseux de se demander si le *Rêve* doit être tenu pour une conjecture, un beau paradoxe, ou l'expression d'une opinion définitive. Nous savons que Diderot se complaisait dans ces dialogues, sans doute parce qu'il savait qu'il avait enfin trouvé une hypothèse scientifique qui lui permettait d'expliquer le monde sans avoir recours au surnaturel." Niklaus, nonetheless, recalls that Diderot characterized his dialogue as "de la plus haute extravagance, et tout à la fois de la philosophie la plus profonde," but he refrained from publishing it.

Niklaus concedes that Diderot's determinism affected naturally Diderot's morality. If "tout est écrit là-bas," there is naturally no vice nor virtue, only "bienfaisance" and "malfaisance." Diderot nonetheless asserted continually that virtue brings with itself happiness, that he was never completely happy unless he could "jouir de [mon] âme et d'être moi tout pur." Notwithstanding this obvious ambiguity,

Crocker sees in *Jacques le Fataliste* a moral experience which leads to no conclusion, and J. Thomas asserts frankly that Diderot has no morality. Niklaus notes that free will is as ridiculous as determinism, and he suggests that Diderot declares for the human and the pragmatic, although, in the *Réfutation d'Helvétius*, he rejects these ideas as insufficient.

We come now to the second problem with which Diderot has to struggle. (See H. Dieckmann, *Cinq leçons*, "La Pensée et ses modes d'expression"; and R. Mortier, *CAIEF* 13 [1961], "Diderot et le Problème de l'expressivité: De la pensée au dialogue heuristique," pp. 283–297.) Both Dieckmann and Mortier seem to agree that Diderot disposed of numerous modes of expression: essay, dialogue, letter, paradox, "pensée," "entretien." In that, Diderot resembles Voltaire. Mortier seems inclined to regard all these genres (or should I say modes) as fundamentally a conversation, but the elements which enter into the conversation vary widely. Indeed, there are those of his contemporaries who maintained that he carries on a conversation less with other individuals than with the ideas themselves. That view, however, is probably exaggerated. It is true that Diderot wrote to Grimm (*Œuvres complètes*, VII, 320): "Je suis habitué de longue main à l'art du soliloque," and while this can be the case, there are other instances in which he converses either with a chosen friend (Grimm, for instance, in the *Salons*), or with an imaginary interlocutor who is condemned to remain silent, although he is not without importance. Sometimes, this silent friend is the imagined audience, at others he is the recipient of a letter. However, often it is a dialogue "en règle," where the interlocutor has privileges equal to those of the author in arranging and advancing his ideas and in presenting and defending them. And there is at least one case where there is a steady dialogue between the protagonists and the author or the author and his audience (*Jacques le Fataliste*). Mortier explains "dédoublement" is a constant necessity with Diderot. Moreover, underlying the constant tendency to dialogue are other characteristics: digressions, continual subjection of the interlocutor to a bombardment of questions, and the promenade, where the actual physical movement from one place to another is balanced by a mental promenade (*Promenades d'un sceptique*) which is both imaginary and emblematic. The masterpiece of the technical dialogue is *Le Neveu de Rameau* where it is neither, as Mortier has so neatly demonstrated, a thesis, nor a judgment, nor a "fantaisie." Diderot's position is not precisely that of *lui*, nor even of *moi*. The goal is clear ("il cherche la vérité, en l'occurrence la vérité morale à travers ses deux personnages, sans s'identifier avec aucun"). Hence, the dialogue this time can come to no fixed conclusion. Yet, Mortier has shown in the end that a fixed conclusion can be found in the intention of the author ("L'Intention de Diderot, c'est de montrer qu'une morale doit être vécue et en même temps jugée, que nous ne pouvons ni accepter passivement des normes ni les rejeter à priori, que l'expérience morale est à la fois risque perpétuel et constante invention").

Dieckmann distinguishes a greater diversity in the modes of expression than Mortier. There are, for instance, analogies between the *Pensées* of Pascal and his own and some analogies between himself and La Bruyère. More important, though, is the fact that Diderot also has a manner of expression which is rigorously philosophical. It is seen for the first time in the *De la Suffisance de la religion naturelle* and reappears in the articles of the *Encyclopédie* as well as in the *Introduction aux grands principes, Principes philosophiques sur la matière et le mouvement,* and all the scientific work with the exception of the *Rêve de d'Alembert.* In addition, the problem of composition is crucial with him. We particularly have noted his tendency to digress. He himself notes: "Je jette mes idées sur le papier et elles deviennent ce qu'elles peuvent" (*Œuvres complètes,* I, 406). He accords thereby full autonomy to them, free to obey their own impulsion. What he hopes to gain from this procedure is a clearer explanation of "la marche de mon esprit." Later, in the *Essai sur les règnes de Claude et de Néron* (*Œuvres complètes,* III, 10), he defines his own position as he sees it: "Je ne compose point, je ne suis point auteur; je lis ou je converse, j'interroge ou je réponds . . . et l'on ne tardera pas à s'apercevoir que c'est autant mon âme que j'écris, que celle des différents personnages qui s'offrent à mon récit."

Certainly, one other point which has to be settled is Diderot's attitude toward the seventeenth-century philosophers—indeed, Diderot's attitude toward philosophers and philosophy in general. Since he was known as the Philosophe and since he took over the section in the *Encyclopédie* upon philosophy, it would seem that nothing would be simpler than to assemble the articles which he wrote on that subject. As we have seen, there is some difficulty in getting an accurate view of his position in that matter because of some doubt concerning which specific articles were his. Also it appears not too easy to distinguish between his expressed views on each philosopher and those of the sources which he used. In addition, there is the difficulty that Diderot dared to express his own views on philosophy in a work which was being censored. Proust, who has discussed these difficulties, has concluded that we can accept as Diderot's articles in the *Encyclopédie* only those which appear with an asterisk (which was his mark) or those which were attributed to him by Naigeon who seems to have been particularly well informed about the matter. As we have noted elsewhere, Naigeon around 1770 brought together a three-volume collection of these philosophical articles without the collaboration but with the knowledge of Diderot. Somewhat later, Naigeon assembled in the *Encyclopédie méthodique* the Diderot articles along with many which were not by Diderot. In 1821, he made a third collection in the edition of Diderot's *Œuvres* under the title of *Dictionnaire encyclopédique*. These articles are reminiscent of those found in Voltaire's *Questions sur l'Encyclopédie*.

The ramifications of these problems naturally fall to Proust's study in *Diderot et l'Encyclopédie*. As far as I can judge, he has not undertaken to treat Diderot's philosophy. He has preferred to give the historical background of the writing of these articles and their assembling by Naigeon, along with some specific information, for example, Brucker's *Historia critica philosophiae* of 1742 became a source for Diderot's material along with other works of a similar nature (Deslandes, Formey, and Bayle). All of this is impeccably done and I am certainly not condemning his way of doing it. What I note is that if the eighteenth century in France is par excellence a philosophical century coming after all these brilliant seventeenth-century European philosophers, someone should inquire to what extent the people who made the eighteenth century philosophical got their basic material from those of the seventeenth. Proust has not been able to do this. On the contrary, what he has done superbly well is to show how, with his philosophical interests, Diderot moved from deism to naturalism.

Just how difficult and vexing these problems can become is seen in Professor Vartanian's book entitled *Diderot and Descartes* (Princeton, 1953). Here, the critic has taken one of those twelve seventeenth-century philosophers and studied in depth what Diderot owed to him. It is Vartanian's thesis that the naturalistic philosophy developed by Diderot and Buffon as well as by Maupertuis, La Mettrie, De Maillet, and the Montpellier doctors of medicine (Bordeu and others) derive from Descartes, not from Newton. Vartanian concedes that the Descartes-Newton quarrel was a reality. He also grants that it was a quarrel which could be broadly defined as between "philosophie rationnelle" and "philosophie expérimentale." He agrees that what distinguishes between the two methods is the inductive method of Descartes and the deductive method of Bacon and subsequently Newton. Vartanian does not deny that after 1738 Descartes's physics had been generally discredited in favor of Newton. Nevertheless, he maintains that though the vortex system was "in a moribund condition," it survived "after a fashion" until the 1770s. This survival was not "the result of any merit of its own," but was attributable to "its greater degree of conformity, when compared to attractionist theories, with the abstract ideal of science recommended by Descartes." Vartanian cites some later Cartesians, Fontenelle, Dambésieux, and Paulian, who continued to defend Descartes. What he fails to note, however, is that they are, in general, interested not in defending Descartes and attacking Newton but in affecting some sort of compromise between the two. It was the title of Paulian's work, in fact. This desire to preserve a positive value to Descartes while asserting that Newton was correct in his computations and his conclusions and that Descartes was wrong, persists among the French historians of ideas to this day. Usually it expresses itself with the statement that Newtonism was correct in its calculations and in the explanations of the system of the world, but Descartes taught all who followed him the way to use the human mind, that is to say, the correct method. I have no particular quarrel with this point of view. But to call the outcome of this merging process Cartesianism or Cartesian philosophy or Newtonianism or Newtonian philosophy doesn't seem to me to be justified. I would rather incline to the belief that when the merging process is completed in the Enlightenment, it is no longer Cartesian or Newtonian, but an Enlightenment philosophy which consists in ingredients taken from ten or twelve prime seventeenth-century philosophers. For instance, it would seem possible to state that Diderot's treatment of the formation of the world owes more to Descartes's *Monde* than to Newton's *Principia*, that La Mettrie's discussion of *L'Homme machine* is derived from Descartes's theory of *Bêtes machines* and not at all connected with Newton's *Principia*, that Buffon and Needham and Diderot have a tendency to think in hypotheses and to draw from the hypotheses conclusions which are not entirely substantiated by the facts, but to call this tendency Cartesian rather than Newtonian and to regard it as Descartes's philosophy is an exaggeration of some magnitude. I would even be a bit skeptical about the remark that Buffon is a follower of Descartes's method. It is true that Buffon's talk about the "molécules" which he invented is reminiscent of the "vortices" which Descartes claimed existed, but that hardly justifies calling Buffon a Cartesian in method. As a matter of fact, Buffon's volume on the method of pursuing natural science studies, which he outlined at length in the first three volumes of his *Histoire naturelle*, differs in many crucial respects from the *Discours de la méthode*. And we must not forget that Buffon concluded in these three volumes that the correct method of investigating natural science remains to be created.

Perhaps a word or two about the nature of Paulian's book will reveal the attitude of those who are obviously trying to restore the prestige of Descartes. Representative of this merging process, the book is entitled *Traité de paix entre Descartes et Newton précédé des vies littéraires de ces deux chefs de la physique moderne* (Avignon, 1763, 3 vols.). Paulian's tactics do not differ significantly from those of Fontenelle. I select him chiefly because his work dates from the sixties, whereas Fontenelle's dates chiefly from around the end of the seventeenth century and the opening decades of the eighteenth. Paulian admits that there is a rivalry between these two giants in modern physics, and states that he intends in these three volumes to bring them together. He notes that he owes this effort of reconciliation to the greatest philosopher that France has ever had, and he promises to rise up and smite the audacious, crazy deist and to denounce the sacrilegious philosopher or the impious materialist—I take it he means Newton. This statement, though certainly misplaced, is important, particularly when it is recalled that Voltaire actually thought that Descartes's philosophy led to materialism. Despite this seeming antagonism on the part of the Jesuit priest to Newton because of his supposed deism, Paulian announces in the preface (I, vi) that he intends to delineate "les véritables sentiments de Descartes et de Newton et faire une espèce de traité de paix" between these two leaders of modern physics. He adds that he will bring out the errors each has committed and the truths each has discovered. In the end, he promises to propose a "système mixte." He acknowledges that Privat de Molières has already undertaken, but not very successfully, the same task. In an additional preface to Volume III, the author defines his position by quoting from a passage in the *Journal de Trévoux*: "On jugera que le Père Paulian est Newtonien." He is, said the *Journal*, but not altogether Newtonian. His system is about halfway between that of Newton and that of Descartes. He accepts Newton's celestial physics and his optics, but he is much closer to Descartes's treatment of density, elasticity, fermentation, and capillary attraction. Paulian notes that Newton has defined two different methods in physics: an analytical one, which he describes as deducing the cause from a large number of phenomena, and a synthetic one, which is just the reverse. Paulian does not seem to treat of the "new" physics, which Diderot called "physique expérimentale." He does not make the distinction, therefore, between the systematic and the interpretative, which Diderot made in the very title of *Pensées sur l'interprétation de la nature*, and to which Dieckmann referred so explicitly in the *Cinq leçons*. Nonetheless, Paulian concludes his overly lengthy treatise with a list of useless questions which are being investigated in modern physics, followed by a corresponding list of pertinent problems which might be reasonably studied. These two developments strongly suggest the content of Diderot's treatment in the *Pensées sur l'interprétation de la nature*.

One hesitates to be too arbitrary about Diderot's intimate relationships with these twelve or so seventeenth-century philosophers. But that the relationships do exist cannot be questioned. J. Thomas has noted that in the *Encyclopédie* article "Logique" Diderot has astutely attributed all the progress in the art of thinking to four modern philosophers. Descartes is the restorer of the art of reasoning and the inventor of a new method of reasoning, "beaucoup plus estimable que sa philosophie même," to whom we are all greatly indebted for the precision and exactitude which dominate not only our studies in physics and metaphysics but also those concerning religion, morality, and criticism. We owe to him, Diderot added, the analytic method which his principles have taught us to exercise in weighing the meaning of words and ideas. Locke, he says in the same article, has taught us to decipher the operations of the human mind strictly in accord with the operations of nature and without getting lost in opinions distorted by systems rather than confirmed by realities. He has, moreover, taught how to distinguish the ideas of thought ("esprit") from the idea of judgment. Malebranche has the talent of extracting from an opinion all the consequences of importance which human imagination can grasp. Finally, Condillac, disciple of Locke, has enormously advanced the system of his teacher and has developed the origin of ideas "jusqu'aux limites que la nature a prescrites." (J. Thomas, *L'Humanisme*, pp. 58–59.)

The result of all this skirmishing with the preceding philosophers was the formation of a materialistic philosophy. We are not too clear about the exact nature of the materialism. Proust, for instance, gives an explanation for Diderot's materialism which differs somewhat from Vartanian's (see Vartanian, *Diderot and Descartes*, pp. 161–164), though not entirely, since both agree that in that development Maupertuis, La Mettrie, Buffon, and Needham play a role. But where Vartanian assumes that Diderot and these four are descendants of Descartes, Proust assures that Maupertuis owes more to Leibniz, and he also sees Leibniz as a source for La Mettrie and Buffon. He does not seem to have marked out the source for Needham. He is nonetheless very explicit about the filiation of Diderot with his predecessors. It began with Pierre Bayle who was distinguished by the director of the *Encyclopédie* as a historian of ideas, rather than a Cartesian. As historian, however, Bayle united in his work two currents: a critical and a historical current. The critical current was greatly preoccupied with Biblical criticism which, of course, was unthinkable in the philosophical production of Descartes. In contrast, it was certainly very strong in the *Tractatus,* where Spinoza had used it to combat Bossuet and the theologians. Diderot in Proust's opinion, actually began with Bayle and then turned to Brucker. Proust stresses that what Diderot obtained from Bayle was how to doubt that thought which he deemed the closest to truth. This entailed a critical history which submitted everything to reason and attempted to bring out, as he said, "une sorte de sobriété dans l'usage de la raison." The two currents also meet in the works of Fontenelle, in Proust's opinion. This has been thought the normal way for the progression of thought in the years preceding the Enlightenment proper. It is what is meant by regarding both Bayle and Fontenelle as equal in the Enlightenment—both of them united the "esprit historique" and the "esprit critique in a similar fashion. I would be inclined to modify this view slightly by creating a third characteristic "esprit" of the opening years of the Enlightenment— the "esprit moderne." Thus, in the sixteen-eighties and the nineties there would be three merging "esprits," not two—an "esprit historique," an "esprit critique," and an "esprit moderne." It is true that all three are present at the time and they are merging into an "esprit philosophique" which becomes the characteristic of all Enlightenment thought. However, in Bayle's thought, the "historique" and the "critique" predominate, while in Fontenelle, the "critique" and the "moderne" are outstanding. By the time we get to the 1730s, all three spirits have merged, especially in the intellectual activities of Voltaire. For this reason, it seems to me risky on Proust's part to write the following note (*Diderot et l'Encyclopédie,* p. 240, n. 31) in speaking of the predecessors of Diderot's thought: "C'est pourquoi nous ne disons rien d'auteurs comme Mme. du Châtelet, ou même Voltaire, à l'égard de qui Diderot ne semble pas avoir de dette particulière. Cela n'exclut pas, bien entendu, qu'en lisant Voltaire, Diderot se soit impregné de son esprit, comme tous ses contemporains." Proust offers as the reason for his exclusion the statement: "Seuls nous intéressent ici ceux qui à quelque titre ont pu orienter Diderot dans son travail d'historien de la philosophie." Nobody has a greater respect for Proust's study than I do. In this particular case, however, the very reason he gave ("se soit imprégné de son esprit") should have led him, it seems to me, to Voltaire. At all events, no one can quarrel with Proust's inclusion of Stanley's *Historia philo-*

sophiae (1711, 3 vols.) and Deslandes's *Histoire critique de la philo-sophie* (1756). Only a glance at Deslandes will bring out the con-vergence of interests between him and Voltaire in *Essai sur les mœurs*, where both meet on the "histoire même de l'esprit et de ses progrès." But Proust's quotation from Deslandes is the really crucial one: ". . . remonter à la source des principales pensées des hommes, . . . examiner leur variété infinie, et en même temps le rapport imper-ceptible, les liaisons délicats qu'elles ont entre elles; . . . faire valoir comment ces pensées ont pris naissance les unes après les autres, et souvent les unes des autres." This, to be sure, is the definition, not of a philosopher, but of a historian of ideas. What interests Deslandes, Voltaire, and Diderot is thought itself, rather than systems of thought. I understand from Proust that Brucker (p. 244 ff.) also began with this same preoccupation (*cf. Testamen introductionis in historia m doctrinae de ideis* and *Historiae philosophica doctrinae de ideis*, 1723). And what makes Brucker really important is his progress from an interest in ideas as such to an interest in the history of philosophy as we now understand it. The problem here is whether Diderot respected this change. Proust has discovered that he did not and, he surmises, that is what turned Formey to the writing in 1760 of the *Histoire de la philosophie*.

Proust has studied with care Brucker's place in the rationalism of his day. He finds, for instance, that Brucker's rationalism closely resembles Bayle's, but he finds also that Bayle's method is essentially Cartesian. Thereupon, he pronounces that it cannot be likened to Diderot's method, which owes most in that respect to Locke. Proust proves this point by analysis of the article *Syncrétistes*. Notwithstand-ing this remark, Proust presents Brucker as a liberal of sorts who has a deep respect for rationalism and much regard for orderly method, but who has a horror for atheism and materialism.

Proust concludes that Diderot should not be credited with having been directly influenced by the German philosopher. In his opinion, Diderot used Brucker in two different ways: first of all as a fellow historian-philosopher, using what we would call the basic material of the subject treated. Diderot was always ready, also, to use Brucker's opinions when they coincided with his own, and even to distort them when they didn't. The motive behind this tactic was to use the his-tory of philosophy as a means not an end, as a weapon in the struggle between unbelief and religion (p. 257). *La Religion vengée,* for instance, accused Diderot of attributing to Epicurus the doctrine he favored and then adopting it as acceptable.

Proust quotes a passage from Naigeon's *Mémoires* (p. 57) which indicates on Diderot's part a definite mode of operation and a specific progress of attack: "Diderot a prêté aux anciens comme aux modernes ses idées, ses réflexions, ses conjectures, ses doutes mêmes . . ." Proust even demonstrates (p. 265) how the technique was devised: "Les causeurs dans *l'Encyclopédie,*" he wrote, "ne sont que deux. Brucker, l'historien érudit et pieux, fournit la trame du récit. Diderot l'écoute, l'entend de travers, à l'occasion, lui coupe la parole quand il l'ennuie, rehausse ses propos de spirituelles saillies, ou greffe sur telles de ses réflexions ses propres rêveries." Proust explains (p. 266) that the public was not upset by this practice, because what the populace expected was not historical accuracy, but a "certain esprit." Specifically, he concludes (p. 267) that Diderot's *Histoire de la philosophie* goes far beyond the liberal intentions of *Historia critica philosophiae* and actually betrays Brucker's intentions in three respects. It does so (1) by substituting another kind of rationalism drawn from Locke for Brucker's Cartesian rationalism, (2) by using against Christianity all the material presented by Brucker against the fables and the superstitions of paganism, and (3) by changing Brucker's "déisme idéaliste" into a "matérialisme athée."

As Proust has outlined them, these moves represent a calculated determination upon Diderot's part to exploit Brucker's work to the fullest in the interest of forging an instrument which would contribute to the spread of Diderot's materialistic philosophy. The primary intention of the director of the *Encyclopédie* has been deliberately transformed from the desire to augment and organize knowledge to the urge to propagandize in the interest of a particular philosophy—materialism. That is to say, Diderot increased his attacks upon Christianity by reverting to the arguments of the clandestine deists and to those of the most radical of them to establish once for all his materialism. Proust has added: "Jusqu'à *l'Encyclopédie,* le matérialisme de Diderot ne se distingue pas de celui de maint écrivain clandestin . . . C'est un matérialisme spéculatif . . ." Now, however, Meslier's *Testament* provided the intellectual content (the eternity of the world, movement as a principle of generation and corruption, that is, change, life and death are only movements, and so on). But Proust does not assume that Meslier provided all the necessary material, since Diderot also had Buffon. There are nonetheless a few troublesome details. There were two moments which had to be pinpointed by Diderot with great precision: the moment of passage from the "inanimé" to the "animé," and the moment of the point of rupture between animal and man. More crucial still was the determination of the cause of the passage and of the rupture. It was at this point that Diderot turned to Leibniz and his theory of monads for the solution. It was not a sudden turn, since Diderot had been preparing for it ever since the *Pensées sur l'interprétation de la nature.* We must note, however, that the solution certainly does not consist in adopting the spiritually oriented monads of Leibniz, but in presenting the theory of analogy between a molecule of matter and a monad. The deeper meaning, though, goes far beyond that error. It consists essentially in applying the principles of experimental science to the history of ideas and particularly to the history of religious thought. I am not sure that was not a greater error still.

This materialism thus created has, in Proust's view, a direct bearing upon both the categories of morality and politics. Proust notes (p. 296) that "L'antiChristianisme était le dénominateur commun des principaux collaborateurs de *l'Encyclopédie.*" It is, adds Proust, the only point on which all critics of the *Encyclopédie* agree. He recalls that Vernière had already stressed that the moral thought of Diderot took its unity from its opposition to Christianity. We should add that much of this opposition from Diderot and Voltaire stemmed from the bitter intolerance of the wars of religion, but also from the Inquisition and other persecutions, not to mention the cruelty of the Crusades. In time, it appears, Diderot, like Voltaire, identified himself with all the persecution of the universe. One could find more than a modicum of fanaticism in this very attitude. Persecution finishes by spreading to the point that it has become a fact of human nature rather than a defect of Christianity, but the philosophes had no time to regard with equanimity the nature of things about which they discoursed endlessly. The misdeeds of any religious organization are undoubtedly many and one does not have to look far before encountering reasons for believing in the crimes present in all religions (that was, in fact, Meslier's main point). At all events, with the passage of time, Diderot, who was now prepared to accept the *Suffisance de la religion naturelle*, wrote that "la religion révélée ne nous a rien appris sur la morale." The question naturally arises, then, What does? Diderot attempted, as Hermand established in 1912, to build his case upon the sensualism of Locke (primacy of the passions, denial of free will, the forces of determinism which operate, the denial of vice and virtue, man cannot be held responsible for his misdeeds if they are committed through necessity, education can be a force in correcting his vices but the hardened criminal can hardly be corrected). All of these points had been debated since Locke, Collins, and especially the clandestine deists. It is hard to see much more in these arguments than in Voltaire's treatment of them almost thirty years before. As a matter of fact, a full discussion developed in a curious way on the ethical problem. Contributions to the debate were made by Condillac with his *Dissertation sur la liberté* (1754), Rousseau with his *Second Discourse* (1755) and his *Lettre sur la Providence* (1756), Voltaire with his *Loi naturelle* (1752), his *Désastre de Lisbonne* (1756), and his *Candide* (1759), and Diderot with his *Lettre à M. Landois* (1756). Proust has noted casually that only Diderot and Rousseau dominated in the argument; one stood for necessity, the other for freedom. Diderot's insistence upon "ni vice ni vertu," and the fact of "heureusement" or "malheureusement né" causes some difficulty in finding precisely where he does stand. One arrives at the point where Diderot denies all morality. Then, at the moment when it is necessary to decide that Diderot is either cynical in his morality or amoral in his interest, one learns that there is no real morality except social morality and virtue is the highest expression of sociability. It is mildly disconcerting to be brought up at that point, but the result at least proves that for Diderot there is a close unity between morality and politics.

It has been noted by Proust that because of the close relationship between man's obligations and his tendency to sociability, his morality ends by uniting almost completely with his politics. The thing which brings them together is, of course, "mœurs," so that, just as "mœurs" was involved in law, it is likewise connected with vice and virtue, particularly in social relations.

Proust maintains that Diderot has brought together a political philosophy in the *Encyclopédie,* although he concedes that it is by no means of the calibre of that of Jean-Jacques Rousseau. In fact, he grants that only after 1765 did Diderot collaborate with Galiani and Raynal in special political problems, and only after 1773 did he take an active part in the political problems of Catherine. This view is consistent with that of Vernière, who has devoted one of the Diderot volumes in the Garnier edition to political matters. It is not, however, the whole story, since R. Hubert, in his *Rousseau et l'Encyclopédie,* has analyzed very carefully the political views of Rousseau and Diderot in the period from 1743 (or perhaps 1746) to 1755, that is the period in Diderot's life when the two were close friends. It is, in fact, reasonable to distinguish three ten-year periods in Diderot's life which are marked by some interest in political matters of consequence: from 1745 to 1755 would then be the period of preparation by Rousseau and Diderot; from 1755 to 1765 would be the period when Diderot guided the fortunes of the *Encyclopédie* along the lines of political thought and action; from 1766 to 1776 would then be the post-*Encyclopédie* period when Diderot collaborated with Galiani and Raynal on political subjects and when he undertook to guide Catherine in her political reforms in Russia. Of the three periods, the first is perhaps of most consequence in the intellectual history of the Enlightenment, since it offers an occasion to compare the preparation in politics, morality, and philosophy of the two giants of the second generation of philosophes.

In his political preparation, Rousseau read with great thoroughness the natural law school of thinkers (see Derathé): Grotius, Barbeyrac, Pufendorf, and so on, while Diderot seems to have accumulated what understanding he had of these writers through Rousseau. In addition, Diderot studied a certain Heinecke, *Elementa juris naturae et gentium* which he is known to have borrowed from the Royal Library. Everyone agrees that there is no comparison between Rousseau's solid preparation in this area and Diderot's rather elementary one. On the other hand, when it comes to Hobbes, Diderot took his basic information from Brucker, to whom Rousseau does not seem to have referred. It is possible that Diderot's study of Hobbes was superior to Rousseau's. At all events, Voltaire was much impressed with Diderot's article. Diderot had the three volumes of Locke's work in 1762, by way of Sterne. It was decidedly late for an acquaintance with the two treatises on government, and we are inclined to assume, without much evidence, it is true, that Diderot must have known him much earlier. We know of his deep respect for Montesquieu from the story that he alone of the encyclopedists attended Montesquieu's funeral procession, and we have assumed that the glowing tribute to the author of *L'Esprit des lois* in Volume V of the *Encyclopédie* was paid by the director of the project. Nonetheless, Proust has stated (p. 348) that Diderot's borrowings from Montesquieu are negligible.

The combined sources of Diderot's political thought are thus rather slim. And yet, his interest in the subject was active, seeing that he reserved the article "Autorité politique" for himself and assigned the article "Economie politique" to his friend Rousseau. Although at a much later date, in the *Emile*, Rousseau wrote: "Le droit politique est encore à naître et il est à présumer qu'il ne naîtra jamais . . . Le seul moderne en état de créer cette grande et inutile science eût été l'illustre Montesquieu, mais il n'eût garde de traiter des principes du droit politique." Diderot also reserved for himself the article "Droit politique." Proust concludes that Montesquieu has certainly not been considered by Diderot as his master in political thought. After this meager collection of possible sources, it seems all the more reasonable to return to the position of R. Hubert (*Rousseau et l'Encyclopédie*) and to A. Adam's fine article on "Rousseau et Diderot" (RSH, 1949).

We have already outlined the various steps which Rousseau and Diderot took as each progressed from a general conformity of views on the present state of their society as each experienced it in contemporary France between 1746 and 1756. Each could at this moment agree that the frivolous society which surrounded them expressed the decadence from the ancient "cité" described by Montesquieu as the ideal community where each citizen gloried in his civic virtue, his love of the fatherland, and his pride in stoic renunciation. It is possible that for Diderot and Rousseau at that moment, the common opponent was Voltaire with his "mondain" and his approval of luxury. I would be more inclined to think that it was Melon and perhaps Dutot or, more probably still, the society of Paris with its post-Regency "insouciance." Certainly Diderot and Rousseau could agree upon its laxity of morals, but as each examined the reasons for that laxity and sought the answer to the more important question of the origin of society itself, there began to appear divergences of opinion. Was society rendered necessary, for instance, by man's natural sociability or by man's needs? Does each man seek the achievement of his personal interest, and does this egotism, perfectly natural, create a condition which wrecks humanity, Or does it create, on the contrary, a condition which preserves humanity from wrecking itself? Are the arts, sciences, letters, and commerce results of a political system which forces man to contribute to the happiness of others in order to preserve individual happiness? It is clear that whereas the two friends agreed to the general proposition of decadence at the beginning, they agreed less and less on the explanation of the phenomenon. The widest divergence can be seen in Rousseau's "Tout tient à la politique," or better still, between the *Apologie* for De Prades and the preface for *Narcisse*. Diderot accepted that in the beginning man was a savage with one duty, to live, and he had no conception of justice. He finally recognizes corresponding needs in others. This is the origin of the group. But the personal interest of each threatens the integrity of the group. Professor A. Adam sees in this disaccord the difference between Leibniz (Diderot) and Spinoza (Rousseau). "Il [Rousseau] est donc, entièrement, dans la ligne de Spinoza," he writes. It is more complicated than that, however. While Rousseau had absorbed the German and Swiss jurisconsults, Diderot had plunged through Brucker into Hobbes. Finally, while Rousseau insisted upon the priority of politics, Diderot gave that priority to a special kind of morality.

We ought now to be able to sketch Diderot's philosophy fairly accurately—that which justifies his title of Le Philosophe. His materialist philosophy undoubtedly shows a close affinity with Heraclitus; that is, it presents the world as one and the laws which control the movement derive from a common principle. Diderot is inclined to call this principle "la raison universelle" but, although he refers to it as common and divine, he does not regard it as transcendent but immanent, the common measure of all things. Man's place in this universe is to follow its general order, and, what is the same thing, to live according to nature. It is clear that under those conditions there is no place for moral freedom; man is free only to deceive himself about his destiny. Since there is neither good nor evil and since everything is necessary, man can forget the place he occupies of necessity. The only possible evil is ignorance. The only proper conduct is submission of his will, enlightened by reason, to nature's law. Diderot concludes with the Spinozistic concept: "tout est dans tout." In terms of politics, humanity is the combination of all societies, each of which is a collection of individuals. This does not mean that nature is a chaos, it is, as Holbach called it, a system. Proust insists that it may be regarded as a deism or an atheism. However, one must remark that the deity is not the Christian Deity, it is rather the Spinozistic Deity.

In this society, the notion of sociability is of primary importance. Diderot has three definitions of this sociability: in the early years before the *Encyclopédie*, it is conceived as a "benevolence." Later, it becomes a reciprocal feeling for utility, only to return to the concept of sociability as inherent benevolence. Diderot puts great faith in the idea of a collectivity, built on the conviction that natural inclinations of each (natural urge of man to seek his fellow man, the sexual instinct, the maternal instinct, and so on) fostered this sociability. What created some difficulty was the exact nature of this sociability. Was it disinterested or was it utilitarian? Diderot seems to have tried to justify both views: he stresses that it is the origin of "la morale," the universal law, engraved by God in the heart of every man but, he adds, "C'est le précepte éternel de la sensibilité et des besoins communs." It is obvious that Diderot's difficulty was troublesome because ultimately it involved the relative importance of personal interest and collective interest in the organization of society, thereby bringing up a possible conflict between the individual and the group. But the problem went deeper than that, because ultimately what had to be decided is whether individual sociability or natural needs render society inevitable. Diderot was inclined to glide from one to the other without understanding that the solution to the problem would explain in one way or *the opposite way* the nature of the social contract. It was precisely at this point that Rousseau, following the natural law theory, deviated from Diderot, who was more or less following Hobbes. Voltaire, who regarded society as a natural fact, did not have to face the problem of its origin. When one adds to this dilemma Diderot's conviction that the individual is driven by his passions and his endorsement of "les passions fortes," the moral problem, or rather the problem of man's immorality, becomes necessarily a problem in knowledge. Diderot wrote (*Œuvres complètes*, II, 88, n. 1): C'est l'esprit qui nous conduit mal, . . . nous ne sommes criminels que parce que nous jugeons mal. C'est la raison, et non la nature qui nous trompe." The far-reaching effects of this move are evident; the whole doctrine of political and moral virtue through enlightenment is threatened. That, however, is not the most serious consequence. The accusation against Diderot that he has established moral life on a utopian view of man appears fully justified. One would say that already he has wholly accepted Talleyrand's theory of "la douceur de vivre."

That brings us to the question of the state of nature. Is it an ideal state or is it a historical reality in the development of humanity? Diderot gives assent to both questions, but Proust stresses that Diderot is more and more inclined to view it as a historical moment. Diderot characterizes it as the moment of "equality" and "liberty." Once again, he finds himself hard pushed to justify this equality and liberty. He argues that the equality is first of all physical, derived from an identity of organization. But he concedes that racial differences occurred because of "mœurs," usages, climates. These circumstances also contribute to a moral inequality. Diderot finally conceives that it is a virtual equality. But there are difficulties. In the first place, the sum total of moral and physical equality does not add up to total equality. Thus, as things are, natural equality merely becomes an ideal among abstract individuals. The question of liberty does not fare any better. It is simply "le droit qu'a tout individu de ne pas être contraint d'agir contre son gré." The opening statement of "Autorité politique"—"Aucun homme n'a reçu de la nature le droit de commander aux autres"—is acceptable only as an ideal, abstract pronouncement.

It should be noted that Diderot certainly did not pass through the same sort of intellectual development which we have sketched in Voltaire. He really didn't have to do so, since Voltaire was there to furnish him with the material. Of the seven forces which ultimately combined to form Voltaire (free-thinking, Horatian poetry, seventeenth-century classical literature, utopian novelists, England, deism, seventeenth-century philosophers), not one was really essential to the formation of Diderot save the last. Still, all of these influences show up in one way or another in Diderot too, and often in the same way they occurred in Voltaire. There was also a difference. Voltaire had come into a world which was making a changeover from arts and letters to science, history, and philosophy, with the result that he had to reorient himself totally to that changeover. Diderot, due to the fact that he appeared on the scene some twenty years after the debut of Voltaire, was not confronted with any necessity to readjust himself; he could profit by the change which had been wrought. He had in reality fallen heir to all these changes chiefly through Voltaire's *Lettres philosophiques*, the *Eléments de la philosophie de Newton*, and the histories. If it makes any sense to divide the Enlightenment into a period of preparation and a period of philosophical expression, Diderot only appeared with Rousseau at the beginning of the period of philosophical expression. Whereas Voltaire began his career as the poet, Diderot began his as the philosophe.

He made his debut very modestly by adapting Shaftesbury's *Essay* to his needs. His *Pensées philosophiques* tackled some of the deist problems, but only at second hand. More effort was directed to the probing of final causes in the *Lettre sur les aveugles*, and problems of psychological impact in the *Essai sur les sourds et muets*. With the *Pensées sur l'interprétation de la nature*, whatever preparation Diderot had to make had been completed. These fragmentary attempts at structuring will always be characteristic of his work. Always the foundation of his activities will be his thoughts. Always the range of these thoughts will be encyclopedic in character, that is, they will fluctuate in some sort of dialectical way over a wide area of content. They seem to express always an open-ended dialectic which is distressingly incomplete. If they have any nucleus, it will be in the realm of science, chiefly in physiological science, but always with a philosophical conclusion. Diderot's interests in philosophy are both broad and deep. In a curious way, he pursues his ideas with logical consistency, but he always attributes to them analogies which are very startling. In "Philosophy of Organism and Philosophy of Consciousness in Diderot's Speculative Thought" (*Studies in Romance Philosophy and French Literature presented to John Orr*, Manchester, 1953), Alexander takes the position that if Diderot's materialism is assessed in the proper light, he will be seen to be the veritable precursor of the "philosophie de la conscience" and strikingly similar to some of Whitehead's views in his philosophy of organism. In this view, Diderot, having adopted a facile materialism, became aware that the real problem was not the nature of matter, but how to establish the right relationship between the being of the self and that global being of the external universe. That is to say, the problem is not free will and determinism, but the proper relationship between a materialistic monism and an individual endowed with consciousness, reflection, and ultimately self-consciousness. However, as Alexander sees things, Diderot does not conceive of a gulf between subject and object. For him, personal reality is a mirror wherein the universe is reflected and absorbed within the self. He insists that thought is the link between self and the world. The problem took its origin in the reaction to the mechanistic view of the universe which satisfactorily explained the physical sciences but was obviously inadequate in explaining the vital sciences. Maupertuis first proposed a Leibnizian solution to the dilemma, but Diderot, beginning with Maupertuis and others (La Mettrie, Buffon, and Needham) reintroduced Leibniz and Spinoza. From Leibniz he took the concept of the spiritual monad, the principle of continuity, and an added principle of vitalism, which is probably Lucretian. But Diderot clings to the unity of composition of Spinoza. From these sources, Diderot devises the concept of molecules endowed with energy (i.e., movement and sensibility). Thus a common sensibility, together with contiguity, suffices to explain the process. There is as a result only one energized matter subject to incessant change. "Tout change, tout passe, il n'y a que le tout qui reste." There is, however, another factor in the process—the individual who emerges. Diderot is not concerned so much with what it is (it is an existent), but how it happens to emerge. The two factors involved are the external objective data and the internal subjective form. The entity which is created has a value implying choice, selection, and therefore a subjective process of absorbing data, itself a value which creates value. The individual is a causal force; as Alexander explains, its essence is a willing activity seeking self-realization. This type of materialism had existed since the days of Descartes, Hobbes, Gassendi, and Spinoza. All of them contributed to its development. However, Diderot gives the idea a new turn. The consequences must always differ according to the vitalizing principle, the physical organization, and so on. All of this reintroduces a spiritual factor that had hitherto been eliminated. Helvétius here parts company with Diderot. An essential difference has to be made between the physical and the moral, the sensational and the reflective, between man and animal. In this debate, Helvétius is presenting the ideal conclusions ordinarily defended by all Platonically derived philosophies. That is to say, Diderot rejects innateness (as everybody else does), but he replaces it with dispositions toward inclinations and aversions, selection and self-awareness. I approve of this, of course, but I naturally find it strange that Diderot thinks he has solved the problem, since he seems to me only to have changed the terminology and redefined his terms. His change in vocabulary resembles that introduced by Rousseau. Sensation (cœur) is opposed to esprit (sentiment). Feeling (sentiment) differs from sensation in its unity and its continuity. Sensation can be transformed into sentiment by reflection. Consciousness for Diderot is always consciousness of the world. Diderot opposes analysis with synthesis based on analogical reasoning. Synthesis for him derives from intuition, hence the hypotheses, and so on.

Consciousness of self is the domination of the sense-organs by the "central organ" which is the "rapporteur" or, as Mlle. de Lespinasse explains it, the spider in its web. There is a distinction in Diderot between the consciousness of the self and the consciousness of the self's existence. This occurs in "rêverie"; the self is an activity of mind, an energy, the self's existence is a passivity.

Alexander concludes (p. 19) that Diderot as a philosopher leaves us with a final vision of a universe infused with energy in all its parts, a universe where all is effort, not consciously directed in its lower levels, but in man achieving that self-awareness which enables it to be comprehended. In this universe all is organic relation, each level rises above its determining conditions and itself becomes a cause; philosophy of organism rather than mere transformism, most of all a philosophy of consciousness which transcends materialism and idealism. Above all, it is a philosophy of never-ending analogies. For example, the two essays on the blind and the deaf-mutes have, by their nature, biological connotations, but by analogy they carry metaphysical as well as esthetic implications, since they concern the apprehension of nature, the expression of nature, and the communication of nature. Diderot, unlike Voltaire, does not reduce all science to morality. But he does try to equate the good, the true, and the beautiful; that is, he feels that esthetic values enhance moral values, and moral values augment metaphysical values. He has to be concerned not only with these analogies, but with their coherent integration. But he has to be most concerned with where he, Diderot, fits into that universe, that is, as Diderot phrased it in the *Neveu*: "La chose importante, c'est que vous et moi, nous soyons, et que nous soyons vous et moi."

The problem is very definitely one in esthetic methodology. Involved in it is (1) how to pass from the fact to the idea to the theory to the doctrine to integrated action. Voltaire faced the same problem, since he, too, had pretensions to being both encyclopedist and philosopher. (2) But the fundamental problem of passing from thought to action also entailed the necessity of having to organize completely the categories of life (religion, art, ethics, science, politics and economics, and so on) and the qualities of the structured categories into the full life. It also entailed the coherent, consistent, continuous expression of this full life in such a way that it constantly changed not only the thought but, as Cassirer has noted in his *Philosophy of the Enlightenment*, the accepted way of thinking. Diderot's thought at first glance appears fragmentary, confused, contradictory, and above all, paradoxical. We readily concur that it is ambiguous, eclectic, and self-assertive in an explosive way, and it is self-contradictory in its facile conclusions. This is so because life is that way. Consequently, encyclopedism is ultimately a way of thinking and knowing, and philosophy, which is not a subject but a way of life, draws all its energy from the freedom of the human to wander among all the other subjects of life and to constitute thereby ways of thinking and being.

All of this is clearly stated by Diderot himself in the article "Eclectisme" in the *Encyclopédie*. There he defines the eclectic as a philosopher who crushes out prejudices, tradition, antiquity, universal consent, authority, everything which enslaves the mind. He dares think by himself, to work back to clearest general principles, to examine and discuss them, to accept nothing except on the evidence of his experience or his reason. Out of all the philosophies he has examined impartially, he creates a private philosophy of his own. For the ambition of the eclectic is less to be preceptor of humankind than to be its disciple, less to reform others than to reform himself, less to know the truth than to make it known to others. He is not one to plant, but rather to harvest and to sift the wheat from the chaff. Diderot contrasts him with the sectarian. While the latter has embraced the doctrine of another philosopher, the eclectic recognizes no master.

Diderot denies that there could exist an eclectic sect, unless one designates a sect a group of people who have one principle in common. For the eclectic, this principle is to submit his thoughts for review to no one, to judge only by his own experience, and to doubt a truth rather than risk, by failing to examine things carefully, admitting a falsehood. Diderot likens them to skeptics, but he points out that they are not skeptics, because they choose those things they believe true. They do not doubt everything. They are also more jealous of freedom of thought.

Eclecticism is thus not a new philosophy. Diderot argues that practically all heads of philosophical schools (such as Plato and Pythagoras) have been eclectics.

He finds it difficult for a man of judgment acquainted with several schools of philosophy not to fall either into scepticism or eclecticism. However, eclecticism is not syncretism, which is a sect. The syncretist strengthens his sect by modifying the opinions of his masters. Diderot calls Luther, Cardano, and Bruno syncretists; Francis Bacon is an eclectic—indeed, he established modern eclecticism. Finally, syncretists are very numerous, eclectics are rare. Diderot carefully describes the way the eclectic operates with ideas. He does not gather truths according to a definite plan. If a newly discovered truth fits with a preceding proposition, he considers it true, if it does not fit, he suspends judgment; if it opposes a previous proposition, he rejects it as false.

In spite of his obvious enthusiasm for eclecticism, Diderot has contempt for the eclectic school which flourished in Alexandria from the fourth to the eighth century, calling it "le système d'extravagance le plus monstrueux qu'on puisse imaginer." He nonetheless, in discussing the group (V, 273), was led to examine the relationship between their thought and poetic genius, enthusiasm, metaphysics, and the systematic spirit. This digression is important, since Diderot approved of this relationship between poetry and philosophy.

He experienced some difficulty in bringing out these relationships, however, all the more since he approved of modern eclectics as fully as he disapproved of ancient, Alexandrian eclectics. He consequently confused the eclectic's qualities, which he admired, with the exaggeration of those qualities at Alexandria, which he deplored. For him, the typical eclectic is not an Alexandrian such as Plotinus, it is an enlightened man such as Descartes or Leibniz or Diderot himself. Consequently, there are many analogies between an eclectic of this kind and the poet, the enthusiast, the metaphysician, and the systematic philosopher. For, says Diderot, what is the genius of the poet except the talent of finding imaginary causes for real effects, or imaginary effects for real causes? What is the effect of enthusiasm in an inspired man, except the capacity to perceive relationships in far-distant objects which no one has ever seen or even imagined? What can a metaphysician not attain if he abandons himself to meditation and turns his thoughts to God, nature, space, and time? What result will a systematic philosopher not achieve if he pursues the explanation of a phenomenon through a long chain of conjectures? The conclusion to which this leads is the conviction that the eclectic is the poetic genius, the enthusiast, the metaphysician, and the systematic philosopher. He is, above all, Diderot.

Diderot attributed the movement of thought from the Renaissance to the activities of the eclectics. In a magnificent passage which is a miniature philosophy of history, a personal confession, and a blueprint for the future, the editor of the *Encyclopédie* sums up the movement of thought from the Renaissance to his day, tries to find his place in the continuation of thought, and proclaims the remaking of the world by the eclectic (V, 283). Fundamental with Diderot is the conviction that the progress of human knowledge is a predestined road, from which it is practically impossible for the human mind to stray. Every century has its ideals and its great figures, and requires its special talents. He who is born with superior aptitudes no longer desirable in the age must either adapt to that age or consent to die. In the renewal of letters in the Renaissance, what was needed at first was not new productions, but an evaluation of the previous creations. And so, the intelligent turned toward the art of grammar, erudition, criticism of literature, and the objects of antiquity. When finally the works of the past were understood, they proceeded to imitate them, and thereby appeared "discours oratoires," "vers de toute espèce," and the flowering of philosophical works. "On argumenta, on bâtit des systèmes, dont la dispute découvrit bientôt le fort et le faible." It was at that moment that it became clear that no system could be accepted or rejected in entirety. The efforts made to establish the right one gave rise to syncretism. But syncretism brought out the weakness in all philosophies:

La nécessité d'abandonner la place qui tombait en ruine de tout côté, de se jetter dans une autre qui ne tardait pas à éprouver le même sort, et de passer ensuite de celle-ci dans une troisième, que le temps détruisit encore détermina enfin d'autres entrepreneurs . . . à se transporter en rase campagne, afin d'y construire des matériaux de tant de places ruinées, auxquels on reconnaîtrait quelque solidité, une cité durable, éternelle, et capable de résister aux efforts qui avaient détruit toutes les autres; ces nouveaux entrepreneurs s'appellèrent eclectiques.

In gathering the solid pieces from the ruins of the past, they discovered that the new structure of the universe lacked some pieces. In fact, "une infinité de matériaux" was lacking. Convinced these materials are in nature, they set to work to discover them. That is what we now call "cultiver la philosophie expérimentale." It was not enough, however, to select from the stones of the past those which are still valid and to add to them the newly discovered materials in nature. "Il fallut s'assurer par la combinaison, qu'il était absolument impossible d'en former un édifice solide et régulier, sur le modèle de l'univers qu'ils avaient devant les yeux." Because, said Diderot, those eclectics proposed nothing less than to rediscover the portfolio of the "Grand Architect" and the lost blueprints of the universe. But the materials are infinite and the ways of putting them together are infinite also. Many of these ways, in fact, have been tried, but with little success. Nonetheless, the eclectics continue the quest. These are the *systematic eclectics.* Those who are convinced that nothing satisfactory can be made out of the present materials seek new materials, while those who think that the moment of reconstruction of the old and the new material has come, try to rebuild some part of the future edifice. That is the state we have now reached:

D'où l'on voit qu'il y a deux sortes d'eclectisme, l'un expérimental, qui consiste à rassembler les vérités connues et les faits donnés, et à en augmenter le nombre par l'étude de la nature; l'autre systématique qui s'occupe à comparer entr'elles les vérités connues ou à combiner les faits donnés, pour en tirer ou l'explication d'un phénomène, ou l'idée d'une expérience. L'eclectisme expérimental est le partage des hommes laborieux, l'eclestisme systématique est celui des hommes de génie; celui qui les réunira, verra son nom placé entre les noms de Démocrite, d'Aristote, et de Bacon.

Thus the human mind must always structure the inner human reality. Revision is always a new form of vision; reform is another kind of form; evolution is a different sort of revolution. Always change, not chance, is king. The blueprints of the universe have not been lost, as Diderot assumed; all the evidence we have (and it is most assuredly meager) seems to indicate that they have just never been discovered. It could be that they have not yet been made; it could even be that it is our task to attempt to make them. At least that is what Diderot assumed.

ORGANIC UNITY IN ROUSSEAU

Ils auront beau faire un Jean-Jacques à leur mode, Rousseau restera
toujours le même en dépit d'eux. *Œuvres complètes*, I, 985.

J'ai écrit sur divers sujets, mais toujours dans les mêmes principes,
toujours la même morale, la même croyance, les mêmes maximes, et
si l'on veut, les mêmes opinions. *Lettre à Christophe de Beaumont,
Œuvres complètes*, IV, 928.

T HE place of Rousseau in eighteenth-century thought has been
considerably misunderstood, not only because of arbitrary
likes and dislikes, but because of Rousseau's own intellectual mobility and a personality which we apparently find very difficult to grasp. We all insist, for instance, that it is impossible to seize
the true import of Rousseau's thought without placing it strictly
in the context of his personal experience and the incidents of his life,
probably because he tied life and thought and works tightly together
in his *Confessions*. When we attempt to do so, however (and we are
curiously prone to want to do so, at first), we experience difficulties
in interpreting the hesitations, the contradictions, the shifting attitudes in his life which seem to occur in his thought. We then quickly
attempt to dissociate life and works, stressing Rousseau's inconsistencies. When his contemporaries, for instance, pointed out that
there were serious discrepancies between what he wrote, what he
thought, and the way he acted, he often defended himself by stating
that he had been misquoted, misjudged, misinterpreted. He also had
a tendency to shore up the validity of his thought and action by
distinctions which were as hard to understand as the original remarks. The result has been that a large number of critics have
stressed his deep sincerity and an equally large number have maintained that he was nothing more than a fraud.

In spite of this dilemma, it is absolutely necessary, if one wishes
to penetrate the reality of the Enlightenment, to understand the
meaning of Rousseau. It is not exaggerating to state that in the history of French thought he has been as influential as any of France's
great thinkers. Indeed, one could argue plausibly, in my opinion,
that since the formation of Christianity, there has been in Western
Europe no man more influential upon Western civilization. The very

vigor with which that thought is still debated, the wild contradictions which its defenders and its traducers propose in these discussions are added indications of its dynamism and importance. After some two centuries of these violent debates, we have not made too much headway in understanding what is its unity, but we have arrived at a point where we should be able to regard the problem with some equanimity, or at least we could probably agree to certain principles in order to arrive at a more balanced judgment.

It is an error to consider Rousseau's works as independent of his life. It is unjust to condemn them because of his life. It is dangerous to assume that he stands apart from his century, and it is fatal to maintain that he is in harmony with it. It would be an error, though, to proceed in this way with any artist, thinker, man. We know that already and we rarely do so with others to whom we give our attention. Yet we inevitably fall into that dilemma when we undertake to interpret Rousseau. To affirm that he is a forerunner of the romantic movement is true, it is even possible that he is the fountain-head of Romanticism. Professor Derathé states that it is the custom in France to regard him as a sentimentalist, while in Germany he is generally considered "the moralist," who condemned single-handedly the philosophy of the Enlightenment and thereby broke with a long intellectualist tradition by proclaiming a new ideal in morality. These two aspects, which are certainly present in Rousseau, are traditionally regarded as the two dominant traits of Romanticism. But to insist upon them as so paramount in Rousseau's case as to be distinct from his eighteenth-century qualities obscures rather than clarifies about half of his work. To make him "the moralist" alone is to forget the whole long line of French moralists who extended from Montaigne to Rousseau. It is impossible to treat him exclusively as a novelist or as an economist or as an anthropologist or as an educationalist or even as a political theorist. It would be equally difficult to do so with any of these Enlightenment giants, his contemporaries. To consider him a radical, a revolutionist, a madman, and idiot is manifestly unfair, but to make of him a conservative is just as absurd. To attribute to him all the evil of the Revolution and the nineteenth century is as nonsensical as to credit him with all the good. Nothing so disturbs an impartial judgment of the man than love for him—unless it is hatred for him.

There seems now to be general agreement among the major critics of Rousseau that the only procedure possible is to move from the man to the work and to seek in the work some kind of organic unity. Rousseau, in his various attempts to explain the consistency and the coherence of his ideas, followed this tactic. As a matter of fact, after 1762, all his works embracing the *Lettres écrites de la montagne* (1764), the *Lettre à Christophe de Beaumont* (1763), the *Dialogues* (1772–1773), the *Rêveries* (1776–1778) and the *Confessions* (published posthumously in 1782) are constructed in such a way that they are derived from his temperament and his thought, and they are always arranged, at least in part, in such a way as to present some kind of unity. Even in the four *Lettres* to Malesherbes, regarded often as the initial impulse for the *Confessions*, Rousseau employs all his ingenuity to define his character or to establish his identity. It is a curious remark to make, but Rousseau and Diderot seem both alike in having cut short their earlier productive careers as thinkers and to have devoted themselves as creators of their own images as artists. That is probably what the Enlightenment had been trying to do all along: to discover a smooth way to move from art to thought, and then from thought back to art. The scholar who has best understood the importance of this attitude is Marcel Raymond, whose most recent work on Rousseau subtitled *La Quête de soi et la Rêverie* is startlingly apt.

There are nonetheless difficulties attendant upon this method, which requires not only a great delicacy of feeling for another but an extensive knowledge of the human heart. Professor Raymond uses it with a supreme mastery to the point where the Rousseau who emerges is delineated with a poetic precision and a human warmth which parallel Rousseau's portrait of himself. Others (Starobinski, Grimsley, and Burgelin) seem to me to have consciously followed in Marcel Raymond's footsteps, although they have naturally modified some of his procedures. I think that their combined presentation of Rousseau is one of the most important contributions to the meaning of the Enlightenment which has been made in the last sixty years.

In fact, since 1912, there has been a rather long line of scholars who devoted themselves to the problem of Rousseau's unity of thought, or the lack thereof. Lanson's article, "L'Unité de pensée

dans l'œuvre de Rousseau" (*Annales JJR*, 1912, pp. 1–30), has been
followed by a surprising number of others who have given careful
consideration to the problem: Vaughan, Hendel, Hubert, Schinz,
Cassirer, and more recently, Burgelin. Lanson, however, and those
who came immediately after him used the statement in the *Dialogues*
which treated of the unity of the works, omitting the previous
development which treated of the character and the thought. He
undoubtedly decided that it was injudicious on his part in the light
of contemporary circumstances to incorporate the unity of character
with the unity of the works. At the time when Lanson published
his article, there was a rather large body of criticism which insisted
upon the contradictions in Rousseau's thought and works. Lanson
names particularly Faguet, Espinas, and Lemaître, all three of whom
vigorously stressed Rousseau's inconsistencies. There were, however,
others whose denunciations were more deadly still: Lasserre, Brunetière, and eventually Babbitt and C.H.C. Wright in America. In the
opinion of these critics, there is no reasonable way to conciliate the
Discours sur l'inégalité with the *Contrat social* or *Nouvelle Héloïse.*
The article "Economie politique" in the *Encyclopédie* and the *Essai
sur l'origine des langues* clearly contradict the *Discours sur l'inégalité.* The *Lettre à d'Alembert*, which condemns the theatre, is between two of Rousseau's dramatic works. Moreover, the ideas which
he presents as crucial to his system just don't hang together. He is at
first an individualist, then a collectivist; he supposes man good, after
having declared him naturally a savage. He judges public education
superior to private instruction, then writes a long treatise on the
advantages of private education. Society is artificial, though natural;
it is corrupt, but beneficent. Property rights are condemned, but they
are sacred. Mr. de Wolmar is a virtuous atheist, though an atheist,
virtuous or no, must be executed. Lanson explains that some responsibility for the contradictions rests with the critics themselves who
have a tendency to reduce the presentations of Rousseau to abstract
formulae (the *Contrat social* is authoritarian socialism; the *Nouvelle
Héloïse* is the aristocratic patriarchal regime) without careful attention to Rousseau's concrete examples.

His explanations notwithstanding, Lanson hesitates to exacerbate
a situation which has been rather violent, thereby omitting one of
the aspects which has to be considered. There is no gainsaying the

fact, though, that both aspects—the unity of the man Rousseau and the unity of his works and thought—are essential and consequently of equal importance; that is what is clearly implied in the epigraph to this chapter. Indeed, the starting point should certainly be the character and the thought or, perhaps more exactly, the character of the thought. The initial document should probably be the Malesherbes *Lettres* where Rousseau begins by trying to explain his character. He stresses his "cœur trop sensible," confesses that he over-indulges his independence and his pleasures and that he has a supreme contempt for injustice and wickedness. He remarks upon his marked inclination for solitude, and states that in Paris, where he had slight occasion to follow this tendency, "une bile noire rongeait mon cœur." He also confesses to an "imagination déréglée" and to an "indomptable esprit de liberté que rien n'a pu vaincre," but he insists that the cause of this yearning for freedom is "paresse," not "orgueil." Indeed, he adds that he finds the slightest duties of civilian life unendurable. He nonetheless concludes that, in spite of the personal idiosyncrasies, "de tous le hommes que j'ai connus en ma vie, aucun ne fut meilleur que moi." It should be noted here that though he lays claim to superior goodness, which he regards as a natural disposition (good-natured), he does not insist upon his virtue which for him is a supreme trait of character (striving for perfection).

He who would know Rousseau's basic character must constantly recall that he was first of all Genevan and Calvinist. As did his fellow Genevans, he not only had a passion for his native city but a deep and abiding pessimism concerning the fall of man. Geneva was, in his early years, perhaps the only city-state in Europe where the spirit of patriotism and the sense of sin were deeply woven into the temperament of its citizens. The title "Citoyen de Genève" had a compelling—almost a mystic—meaning for the author of the *Contrat social*. Moreover, not only was Rousseau permeated with patriotism for his native city, but he was steeped in the relationship between politics, religion, and morality, and, most important of all, he had been trained to regard all three as closely integrated. He was furthermore thoroughly imbued with the ideas of his time. Much of his learning was book-learning, almost as encyclopedic as that of Voltaire, Diderot, or Montesquieu. In addition, Rousseau was by nature extraordinarily proud, excessively egotistic, and unbelievably sensitive to all constraints, both physical and moral. His first reaction is practically always explosive and negative and not very logical or consistent. The picture he gives of himself at the time of the *First Discourse* is practically always the way he responds. This emotional outburst, which is highly sentimental, is always followed by a return to a highly rational attitude. Seen as a contrast to the first response, the second usually suggests a paradox or something inconsistent. But as it is examined in the light of cold logic, it is not at all devoid of sense. What gives it added authenticity is the style, which, as Mme. de Staël once remarked, "enflamme tout." It is this style, in fact, which not only carried conviction, but stamps him as a man of supreme sincerity—or, for those who refuse absolutely to be convinced, as a fraud. Sincere or insincere, for Jean-Jacques there is no middle ground.

In his search for an awareness of himself, he was very conscious of these strong contradictions. The famous sentence in the second Malesherbes letter which Rousseau recast in the *Confessions* is indicative of the constant antithesis he found in himself: "Une âme paresseuse, qui s'effraie de tout soin, un tempérament ardent, bilieux, facile à s'affecter, et sensible à l'excès à tout ce qui l'affecte, semble ne pouvoir s'allier dans le même caractère et ces deux contraires composent pourtant le fond du mien."

As a result of this basic conflict, he explains that he has developed a contempt for his century and his contemporaries, that his heart is in constant contradiction with his intellect, that his ills are the work of nature, but his happiness belongs to him. Despite an awareness of vices, he holds himself in high esteem, he loves his fellow man in general, but hates the nobles, their estate, their harshness, pettiness, and all their vices. He concludes that insofar as possible, while working for himself he has done what he could for society. He acknowledges, finally, the power of dreams and asserts that had all his dreams turned to realities, he would have "imaginé, rêvé, désiré encore."

It has been pointed out by Professor Burgelin (*La Philosophie de l'existence de JJR*, Paris, 1952) that this dilemma of apparent and real inconsistency is not uncommon in the case of all philosophers, although it is not present customarily in so crucial a form. Burgelin explains that the philosopher is customarily faced with the dilemma that he is seeking to establish a science (that is, a body of general knowledge which is acceptable universally, although in reality it is presented in the form of a personal experience, which, being personal, can in no way be considered an authentic philosophy established within the confines of collective anonymity). Thus, while aspiring to reveal the universal truth acceptable to any reasonable living contemporary, the philosopher can only couch it within the framework of his own imagination and his intellectual habits. The result inevitably is that it is always *his* truth. While he maintains with all his intellectual energy that it is also "everybody's truth," offered now as the capstone in the everlasting debate of man in search of "his truth," he is met by his fellow philosophers with the charge that he has failed to express his thought dynamically and universally, that because of the inertia of his language he has failed to achieve either clarity or precision. We should add that this same dilemma, customary with the philosopher, is also common in the case of the poet—what is put in question in both cases is not so much the experience, but the "style."

Clearly then, every philosophy has a style, and in view of what we have just seen, this style, to paraphrase Buffon's famous remark, "est l'homme même." Incidentally, this situation explains Cassirer's remark that the eighteenth century not only submitted to the factual, but insisted that it be raised to the absolutely universal. It also explains the basic fact of the *Encyclopédie* and Diderot's insistence that "les faits sont la vraie richesse du philosophe." He must cash in on that "richesse," though, by raising it to the universal and making it "stick." Otherwise, he is accused of disorder, contradiction, ambiguity, inconsistencies, and lack of harmony with the universe in which we all have to live, at least for a time.

In short, every philosopher (and poet) accepts a role in the creation of *his* philosophy, and responsibility for its universal permanence. This role, to be sure, varies in accordance with the temperament of the individual. In general, it fluctuates between the desire for total impersonality and its extreme opposite, that of deep personal involvement. One philosopher may make strenuous efforts to efface himself, to follow scrupulously the order imposed by his deductions, "au sein d'une lumière intellectuelle toute pure," as Burgelin says. Another will demand that his *moi*, in all its richness, be central and inevitable. These two attitudes represent the extremes of the philosophical (and poetic) stance. Every philosopher thus finds himself caught up in a tension, which fluctuates from the totally impersonal to the deeply personal. He is forced to make believe that the experience is *his* and *everybody's* experience. He recognizes, though, that the dangerous areas are precisely the ultimate extremes, that is, the areas of the exaggerated, the paradoxical, the ambiguous, the contradictory. In most cases, he learns how to adjust *his* response to the apprehension and the revelation of *his* truth and to harmonize it with the absolutely universal response to *this* truth. There nonetheless remain individual cases where the tension is so unbearable and the response so explosive that it may appear to others just not true at all. Such an individual is very apt to appear not only exceedingly tense, but also self-contradictory, and even unbelievably irrational. In these cases, when he senses that this is the impression which he is making, he may attempt to shore up his credibility by assertions which will justify his impersonality more than his ardent personality. The impression he usually leaves is thus more likely to be the very opposite of what he is attempting. Others will conclude, however, that he is self-contradictory, exaggerated, too personal, not sufficiently universal.

We must now go back to Rousseau's remark, which he often made, that he was being misquoted, misunderstood, and misinterpreted. That was due, he thought, to the fact that the reader was not reading him correctly. He insisted that he must be read in a particular way: he didn't approve of any reader who attempted to judge the true aim of the author by picking out special, disconnected sentences. He maintained that a work must be read in its entirety and the reader should constantly ask himself in what state of mind (disposition de l'âme) the readings had left him, always assuming that there must be a perfect accord between his "disposition de l'âme" and that of the author. He should also keep in mind that the author's doctrine "tendait au bonheur du genre humain." Moreover, Rousseau insisted that there was a set of specific things he wanted to be seen in his works. They are not, he insists, an "aggrégation des pensées" as are found in other contemporary works but rather the "méditations d'un solitaire" and they require a consistent attention. If the reading is done consistently, the reader will find that the author has a veritable passion for virtue, freedom, and order. Rousseau confesses that in his ardor for these three things he is apt to discuss violently his attitude towards them. That is to be attributed to the strict relationship between the author and his works and between the author and his fellow man. If these things are rightly understood, the reader will see that these writings will all proceed in a certain order. The order that he will have to follow is counter to the chronological. If the reader is serious in wanting to follow this order, he will have to begin with the *Emile*, which is the final work of the series, and proceed backward to the *Discours sur les sciences et les arts*. If he does this correctly, he will see that the author has as his final goal the apprehension of true reality. To attain this goal, he must seek what is essential in order to reach the point where he may pass judgment upon this reality. He must constantly keep in mind, though, that he is dealing with an author whose "manières de sentir et de voir" distinguish him from all the other eighteenth-century authors. The dominating principle of these principles is that "La nature a fait l'homme heureux et bon, la société le déprave et le rend misérable."

It would seem, then, that what has to be examined with the greatest care at this point is the statement made by the Frenchman who is striving to interpret Rousseau's intellectual position in the third *Dialogue*. The Frenchman adds by way of conclusion: "J'y ai trouvé des manières de sentir et de voir qui le distinguent aisément de tous les écrivains de son temps et de la plupart de ceux qui l'ont précédé." This statement which is certainly crucial to our problem does not seem to have received any close attention from all who have analyzed this matter. In the past, I have judged that it merely called attention to the fact that Jean-Jacques just didn't look at things in the way others of his contemporaries regarded them. I therefore stressed in the Introduction to the Princeton eighteenth-century anthology that it is true that he was not in complete accord with his times, but he was nonetheless in agreement with them in many respects. I even gave a fair number of cases in which he agreed with the views of his contemporaries. For instance, like Condillac, he believed in the doctrine of the sensations. Like Voltaire, he yearned for liberty, but he placed equality above even liberty. Like Montesquieu, he was vitally interested in problems of political science. He united with all the encyclopedists in decrying the principles and practices of revealed religion. The logic of Condillac was his logic. The expansive sentimentality of Diderot was his sentiment. He was as interested in education as Helvétius, Diderot, and Holbach, though he saw the problem differently. In fact, there is hardly a major doctrine of the eighteenth century in which he did not interest himself. He is credited with establishing in the thought of his time four of the twelve major theories—that of the social contract, of the natural goodness of man, of liberty, and of equality. Furthermore, he expressed his views upon tolerance, sensationalism, personal interest, deism, state education, war, natural law, the nobility of primitive life, the breakdown in contemporary morality, the evolution of government, the effects of climate, and the importance of attendant circumstances. In his political theory he closely resembles Montesquieu; in his hypothetical anthropology, he is closely allied to Buffon; in his psychology, he, as was everyone, was a disciple of Condillac; and in his revolutionary reaction to contemporary society, he followed, at least for a time, Diderot.

However, despite these resemblances, Rousseau in every case succeeded in modifying the thought of his contemporary in an intensely original way. One aspect of Rousseau's originality can be attributed to his trait of using the same ideas, the same problems, and the same phenomena as others of his time, but in some inexplicable way he often offers neither similar approaches nor similar solutions nor similar conclusions. It is true that the reason for the deviations stems from his own personal way of looking at things, literally as he says, "manières de sentir et de voir." The emphasis here should be placed upon the "sentir" and the "voir," upon the penetrating of the external world and the transposition of these experiences into the internal world of Jean-Jacques. This is not the rationalization of reality, it is rather the realization of feeling. Explicitly, it is the incorporation of both processes into revery, whereas in the opinion of Rousseau, all of his contemporaries incorporate both processes into reflection. However, although Rousseau saw this distinction between himself and all his contemporaries he carefully noted that there were those in the past who also replaced reflection with revery.

Rousseau is not only vitally concerned with turning reflection into revery, he also insists upon turning revery and reflection into reality. In this, he demands most scrupulously the logical arrangement of all ideas. Seen superficially, this means that Rousseau sees his development as something which is intensely rational, and he defends it in the most argumentative way possible. This is particularly the case with his "system." Over and over, from the letters to Malesherbes to the posthumous *Confessions*, he reverts to the assertion that the core of the "system" can be found only in the *Emile*. The key statement is once more in the third *Dialogue* used by Lanson in the *Annales* article, but before taking up Lanson's interpretation, it would perhaps he better to extract here Rousseau's statement (*Œuvres complètes*, I, 932–33). It is still the Frenchman of the *Dialogues* who is talking about the works of Jean-Jacques:

> Ces livres-là ne sont pas, comme ceux d'aujourd'hui, des aggrégations de pensées détachées, sur chacune desquelles l'esprit du lecteur puisse se reposer. Ce sont les méditations d'un solitaire; elles demandent une attention suivie qui n'est pas trop du goût de notre nation . . . Je crus qu'en méditant très attentivement ses ouvrages, et comparant soigneusement l'auteur avec l'homme que vous m'aviez peint, je parviendrais à éclairer ces deux objets l'un par l'autre et à m'assurer si tout était bien d'accord et appartenait incontestablement au même individu.
>
> J'avais senti dès ma première lecture que ces écrits marchaient dans un certain ordre qu'il fallait trouver pour suivre la chaîne de leur contenu. J'avais cru voir que cet ordre était rétrograde à celui de leur publication, et que l'auteur remontant de principe en principes n'avait atteint les premiers que dans ses derniers écrits.

We should note here that there is frequently a tendency on the part of Rousseau to tie his works together. Doubtless, the most important of these occasions is the one in the *Dialogues* where he attempts to explain in systematic order the "suite" of his works. This attempt was so impressive that Lanson used it as the basis for his article upon Rousseau in the *Annales* as well as for his chapter upon Rousseau in the *Histoire de la littérature française*. Rousseau, however, did this, at least partially on other occasions. In a letter to Malesherbes of 12 January 1762, he wrote referring to the experience on the road to Vincennes: "Tout ce que j'ai pu retenir de ces foules de grandes vérités qui, dans un quart d'heure, m'illuminèrent sous cet arbre, a été bien faiblement épars dans les trois principaux de mes écrits, savoir, ce premier *Discours*, celui sur *l'Inégalité*, et le traité de *l'Education*, lesquels trois ouvrages sont inséparables et forment ensemble un même tout." (*Correspondance Générale*, edition Hachette, no. 1249.)

Lanson was really the first to make a serious attempt to follow the meanderings of Rousseau's thought, as he reacted to the society of Paris. Thus he stresses Rousseau's initial unfavorable reactions to the mundane life of Paris, which in Rousseau's opinion lacks the primitive virtues of man and gives the highest qualities to appearances rather than to existence. In his attack against these artificial virtues and the subsequent defense of his position, he retreats as he always does from the absolute condemnation while seeking at the same time the underlying causes of his objections. In the discussion which ensued from the *First Discourse*, Rousseau modified somewhat his absolute condemnation of the situation as he understood it, but he nonetheless still attributed the artificiality of Parisian life to a loss of primitive virtues. Hence, in the *Second Discourse*, he was prepared to show that the three states of nature were the history of a decline and, at the same time, that the root of the evil lay in property rights and that the basic difficulty was inequality. The net result of this attack was the enthronement of individualism. Already, though, a reaction had taken place and little by little, under necessity of organizing a defense against those who launched the attack, Rousseau began a modification of unbridled individualism. Thus, rather than countenance a return to the absolutely primitive state, Rousseau noted that "la nature humaine ne rétrograde pas," thereby annulling any doctrine of reform and encouraging an adoption of those virtues present in the simple life, with manners and customs closer to the pastoral life in Switzerland than to the sophisticated life in Paris. Rousseau then adopted two notions which in many respects are antithetical. Man is what men have made him; society is nonetheless necessary. The first notion, said Lanson, grew out of all the various discussions which took place after the *First Discourse*, the second seems to have represented a point of view more closely related to the *Second Discourse*. There is, though, some uncertainty about the origin of these two notions. Lanson is inclined to attribute the source of both to Montesquieu's *De l'Esprit des lois*. It is agreed by practically all the critics that the influence of Montesquieu upon Rousseau was very strong, but it would seem impossible that that influence was exerted as early as the two *Discourses* in this specific way, all the more since Rousseau had said that in 1743 and 1744 he had had the intention of writing a work on politics. It is not at all clear in the first place that the two notions were originally Montesquieu's nor that Montesquieu ever espoused them. It is likely that they came from the Abbé de Saint-Pierre, who died in 1743, more likely still that they were original with Rousseau, and most likely that they were worked out together by him and Diderot. At all events, in the *Lettre sur la vertu et le bonheur*, Rousseau adopted the notion that social life, bad or good, is here to stay. Hence, in the "Economie politique" written for the *Encyclopédie*, he declared that property rights are sacred and constitute the basis of the social life. Lanson, however, insists that the article derives from a current of thought which precedes the *Second Discourse*. Once more, we cannot be too sure that Lanson's surmise is correct.

It is, however, at the moment of the *Economie politique* (presumably 1754) that Rousseau seizes an opportunity to rethink the whole problem in the light of the *Two Discourses*, the *Lettre sur la vertu*, and the *Economie politique*. Lanson notes, though, that the problem has now changed: "Comment, sans retourner à l'état de nature, sans renoncer aux avantages de l'état de société, l'homme civil pourra-t-il recouvrer les bienfaits de l'homme naturelle, innocence et bonheur." His next work, though, the *Lettre à d'Alembert*, is not seen as an outgrowth of this problem; it is rather a special case of the problem of the *First Discourse*, an example of the way arts, letters, and sciences may contribute to the ruin of moral virtue. Here Rousseau inserts the idea of reform, rehabilitation, and restructuring of life.

The *Nouvelle Héloïse* and all the other great works issue from this notion. Julie reforms herself, Julie and M. de Wolmar reform the society around them. In a regime of inequality is introduced a regime of equality. The story then is designed to portray the reform of the individual in his intimate and in his family life. On the other hand, the *Emile* is a demonstration of the way the "bonté naturelle" of man may be preserved in spite of the encroachments of society. Hence, Lanson felt that the education of Emile would be, more or less, the education of humanity, as outlined in the *Second Discourse*, but not with the final disastrous outcome, since the new *Contrat social* would reform the institutions of the state. Note that for Lanson, it is more a problem of education and reform than a plan of constitution. But Lanson also adds that the *Contrat,* contrary to the *Nouvelle Héloïse* and the *Emile,* derives from the current of thought which betrays an influence of *L'Esprit des lois,* and he sees further in the substance of the *Contrat* an attempt to resolve at the political level the problem of inequality.

The strength of Lanson's demonstration of the unity in Rousseau's thought lies not, as one might easily be led to believe, in the logical development of Rousseau's ideas into an organic body of thought but in Rousseau's progressive build-up between 1749 and 1758 of a negative condemnation of civilization, followed between 1758 and 1762 by a similarly progressive development of a body of positive thought designed to restructure the "new" society, through the restructuring of the "new" individual (*L'Emile*), the "new" family (*La Nouvelle Héloïse*), and the "new" state (*Le Contrat social*). Moreover, in the development of Rousseau's doctrine, Lanson finds that there enter equal doses of morality (both personal and family) and politics. The implications are very strong in the whole of Lanson's demonstration that Rousseau is both moralist and political theorist and that what has to be brought into harmony are both of these factors. Lanson, however, did not show how this could be done. He did feel, all during this period around 1912, that the change of the greatest significance which had taken place in the early part of the eighteenth century in France was a transformation in the area of morality. He did not, though, suggest anywhere in his article on Rousseau's unity that either one of these two essential areas should be subordinated to the other in Rousseau's case.

This stand was taken by C. E. Vaughan in 1915 with the publication of his two volumes entitled *The Political Writings of Jean-Jacques Rousseau.* The underlying thought of the title suggests strongly that Vaughan has chosen as the very core of Rousseau's doctrine the area of politics rather than that of morality, with the natural implication that we are dealing primarily with a political theorist rather than with a moralist.

It seems clearly indicated in these statements that there is an avowed connection between "vie" and "œuvres" and between "vie" and "lecteurs" which amounts to a mystical affair. There is also a tightly-woven relationship between work and work, which, however, is chronological rather than psychological. Each work has a particular place in the evolution of a time-span, and insofar as it bears a relationship to the sequence of time, it has its special place in the development of a consistent corps of ideas. This development, though, does not seem to be the important thing. What is important is that each work is rounding out a corpus of principles which are a development in reverse order of the publication of the works, in such a way that the first principles can only be found in *Emile* which is the last work. Thus the body of principles can be built on the first principles established in that work by going back one by one to the *First Discourse*. All of this which could, I suppose, have some sort of hidden significance and which can only mean that Rousseau's "system" developed only by piecemeal, does not seem to make much sense when applied. What we are supposed to do, presumably, is seek carefully the principles, arrange them in reverse order, and see what light they throw upon the organic unity of the system as a whole. At all events, Jean-Jacques, in discussing the importance of his central ideas, referred on several occasions to the fact that the *Emile* contained the key to the whole situation.

If, however, we drop all attempts at arbitrariness (that is, instead of trying to establish the principles of Rousseau in the reverse chronological order of the appearance of the works and look for the first principles only in the *Emile*), we get a clue of sorts to the development of his ideas. We learn, for instance, in the third *Dialogue* that he composed the *Discours* only to destroy the "prestige d'illusion" which leads us astray. If we may give credence to Rousseau's assertion as to the real intention—in fact, the idea of the *Emile*—this should be the first time that Rousseau affirmed the natural goodness of man. In the *Emile*, he defines "un traité de la bonté originelle de l'homme, destiné à montrer comment le vice et l'erreur, étranger à sa constitution, s'y introduisent du dehors et l'altèrent insensiblement." Marcel Raymond explains that rather than a demonstration that the child is originally good, the work is a demonstration of how Rousseau makes himself and unmakes himself and remakes himself. There is no evidence, it appears, that Rousseau was designing a practical treatise on education. It is rather a utopian treatise on education, as the *Contrat social* is a utopian treatise on political right.

The author's goal is to distinguish between words and things. Words introduce the human self into a false, imaginary world, which gives free reign to all our desires. What the child must be shown is how to adjust the imaginary to the real. Marcel Raymond insists that those who see in this procedure the underlying principles of the *Morale sensitive*, which Rousseau projected but never wrote, are probably not far from the truth.

We should now turn to the *Emile* as the unifying element of Rousseau's thought. The critic who has best presented the case for this unity is P. Burgelin (see *Œuvres complètes*, vol. IV, Paris, 1969, pp. lxxxviii–cli). Burgelin recalls that Rousseau had insisted that the unity of his doctrine could be found in the two *Discourses* and the *Emile*. Burgelin also reminds us that Rousseau asserted that it was not until the *Emile* that the various threads of that doctrine were brought together. At this point Burgelin makes two remarks of importance. Not until Rousseau was established at Montmorency (1756) did he determine to devote himself to his three major projects. At the same time he determined that the *Emile* was to be the major work of his maturity—"celle qui contenait son système." On occasion, Jean-Jacques advised anyone who wished to seize his thought to read the *Emile* first. Burgelin notes that the work contains "ce qu'il (Rousseau) sait des hommes, de leur malheurs, et de leurs possibilités, et de l'espoir qu'on doit mettre dans la génération qui se fait . . ." The important factor, however, is that although the *Emile* is a treatise on education and is very much concerned with the way a child grows through his experience with this world, it is more deeply concerned with the way man goes through the same process. And just as *Emile* in the course of his learning process makes himself, unmakes himself, and remakes himself, as Marcel Raymond had already pointed out, so each individual undertakes the same creative process throughout his life. Specifically stated, seen in perspective, the *Emile* would seek some sort of answer to the question "How can one visualize the connection between knowing, saying, and doing; that is, will training the right student to be the right citizen in the right state lead to an awareness and the creation of the right civilization? Naturally, before one can get a reasonable answer to that question, one has to inquire into the sort of education required to insure this right training. Rousseau lays down two specific conditions:

it must conform to nature (that is, it must be natural) and it must conform to order and avoid disorder. It implies a thorough training in the understanding of man's nature. We should recall here that Rousseau said he wanted to make a positive contribution to the study of man's nature. This remark helps explain the doctrine of natural goodness, and it further helps explain the necessity of founding it upon a sense of order. However, the ultimate goal in applying this order is to create, as Vaughan said, "a free citizen in a free state."

It is in this way that the supreme act, for Rousseau, is a political act. He had long since made the discovery on returning from Venice: "Tout tient à la politique." That means, for Jean-Jacques, that everything is a political act, but conversely, it means also that a political act is ipso facto an ethical act or, if one prefers, despite its political aspect, every political act embraces both a religious and an ethical act, and even an esthetic act. Of these three ingredients, the ethical is the one which stands out, since he defines it "l'éthique consiste à trouver sa place, ce qui veut dire à être soi en toutes circonstances."

This theoretical development of the citizen is thus balanced by the psychological development of the individual. And both of these developments coincide in the reality of Jean-Jacques's meditation, which terminates in the assertion of the self. It all began with the experience of the 1740s in Paris, where Rousseau and Diderot were both overwhelmed with the gilded corruption of post-Regency France. Diderot ultimately made some kind of accommodation with that Parisian life; it would seem that Rousseau could never adjust to it. That was the psychological reason of the break between the two friends. But it had a great bearing upon the explosion on the road to Vincennes also. In the first *Discourse*, the cause of the corruption and the evils of civilization can ultimately be traced to bad education. Jean-Jacques undoubtedly pictured himself during those early years in Paris as being the master instructor in education. It was what he judged himself competent to do. He defines the education needed as preparation for adult life, one which establishes an upright judgment. One does not know exactly how it can be administered if one does not have a clear view of the nature of the student. Rousseau became aware that the thing which was undeveloped was the science of man. He decides that he must make a significant contribution to that science. It was while writing the notes to the second

Discourse that he ran upon the notion of "bonté naturelle." Thereby the tension between the evil of Parisian civilization and the inherent goodness of man became clear. This could be resolved, if some way could be found to train man for the citizenship which is his goal. The *Essay on Inequality* thus became a new school for the new citizenship. Rousseau dedicated it to Geneva, because he felt that his native city had trained him in true citizenship. He adopted the title of Citizen of Geneva, actually made a pilgrimage to his native city, and returned convinced that he had discovered his truth. On his return, he consummated the break with Diderot and ultimately with his philosophe friends. He wrote the *Lettre à d'Alembert*, defending the political training given in Geneva against the criticism of the philosopher. The break was made final by the withdrawal to Montmorency in 1756. Rousseau carried the three projects with him: the pedagogical project which would terminate in the *Emile*; the "matérialisme du sage," which was thought to have been abandoned eventually; and the *Institutions politiques*, which culminated in the *Contrat social*. As Burgelin sees all this, it is, just as Rousseau insisted, the *Emile* which really incorporates the three projects. Burgelin concludes (*Œuvres complètes*, IV, cvi): "Ainsi convergent, croyons-nous, les trois projets de Rousseau; ils se fondent dans le traité de l'éducation, qui parle de tout l'homme et nous donne bien la clef de son système." But a greater consequence, I would think, is the *Emile* not only embraces the education appropriate for the true citizen, but it incorporates what Rousseau deemed the role of the true religion, the true politics, the true economy, the true esthetic, the true science (which is the science of man), and the authentic representative of all this truth—individual man. But we must not anticipate. We have a fairly difficult road to travel yet.

When the *Emile* and the *Contrat social* were published, they were condemned, as every one knows, both in France and in Geneva. The two documents which carried the condemnation—the "flétrissure," as Rousseau called it—were the Censure of the Conseil de Genève and the *Lettre de Christophe de Beaumont*. Rousseau made a vigorous protest to both of these acts. The one which should be examined here is the reply to Beaumont's *Mandement* of 20 August 1762. In order to understand the import of the *Mandement* we should keep in mind that it took Rousseau completely by surprise. Not that he expected the archbishop to subscribe to the *Profession de foi*; he anticipated rather that it would be treated with silent contempt. When, on the contrary, the *Profession* was denounced for its pernicious consequences, Rousseau was nonplussed because he judged the *Emile* was perfectly consistent with his attitude of the past. Consequently, his opening remark at the very beginning of his *Lettre* is a reminder that his attitude in the *Emile* is sincerely coherent with his thought in his previous works. The statement asserts clearly that although the subject-matter may vary, his principles, his morality, his beliefs, his maxims, and his opinions remain unchanged. Further, he wrote (*Œuvres complètes*, IV, 933): "Mon *Discours sur l'inégalité* a couru votre Diocèse, et vous n'avez pas donné de *Mandement*. La *Nouvelle Héloïse* a couru votre Diocèse, et vous n'avez pas donné de *Mandement*. Cependant, tous ces livres, que vous avez lus . . . respirent les mêmes maximes, les mêmes manières de penser n'y sont pas plus déguisées: si le sujet ne les a pas rendu susceptible du même développement, elles gagnent en force ce qu'elles perdent en étendue." Later on in this letter, Rousseau acknowledges that they would certainly not be built upon the Catholic doctrine of original sin, which a Catholic bishop would be expected to uphold, but that disagreement could not possibly warrant the archbishop's cruel denunciation of his religion. Rousseau firmly asserts that, although he does not accept the doctrine of original sin, he is a Christian. This assertion is important, but for the moment the other aspect of Rousseau's consistency is what concerns us, since it involves the unity rather than the orthodoxy of his thought.

Rousseau understood that what was essential was a fundamental principle which held all the aspects together. The statement he made in conclusion (*Œuvres complètes*, IV, 935–37) was an attempt to establish that fundamental principle: "Le principe fondamental de toute morale, sur lequel j'ai raisonné dans tous mes écrits, et que j'ai développé dans ce dernier avec toute la clarté dont j'étais capable, est que l'homme est un être naturellement bon, aimant la justice et l'ordre, qu'il n'y a point de perversité originelle dans le cœur humain, et que les premiers mouvements de la nature sont toujours droits."

We should point out here that Vaughan could have used in support of his thesis the statement of Rousseau that he had discovered in Italy in 1743 that "tout tient à la politique," and that Rousseau had made precisely the same statement in the "Economie politique." But while Vaughan was well aware of the statement, for reasons which I fail to fathom, he refrained from according it any particular weight as a means of supporting his argument. Indeed, rather than pursue first what were Rousseau's views on the interrelationship between religion, politics, and morality (and science) as seen in the period 1749 and 1755 or, if one prefers, from the publication of the *First Discourse* to that of the *Second Discourse*, Vaughan switched to a different though derivative problem—whether Rousseau's politics were based upon individualism or collectivism?

In one of our very best introductions to these political writings, Vaughan has pointed out a phenomenon which, if true, renders impossible or perhaps we had better say, has thereafter been considered to have rendered impossible, any organic unity in Rousseau's thought. The fundamental thought with Vaughan is that although Rousseau started out as a moralist and fully displayed moralistic tendencies in the two early *Essays*, he switched, almost miraculously, from moralist to political theorist. In the change, he turned from an extreme individualism, which was characteristic of the *Essay on Inequality,* to a defiant statement of the collectivist ideal, of which the *Contrat social* is the highest expression. Rousseau, says Vaughan, may have taken over the concept of the state of nature and of contract from Locke and the individualists, but, if so, they both have been altered beyond recognition. The state of nature has been reduced by Rousseau to a condition of pure animalism, while the contract, far from being an instrument of freedom for the individual, demands the total surrender of all the powers the individual has possessed. Vaughan concedes that in the early part of the *Contrat social*, some traces of individualism are still apparent, but he insists that thereafter Rousseau has ruthlessly burned his former idol. Not entirely, though, Vaughan admits, because in an earlier section, he has shown that Rousseau had made an attempt to restrain the state in practice from crushing out the individualism of the citizen. Rousseau's main argument, however, is that the individual is nothing but a "stupid and limited animal, and it is only through the state that he becomes a reasoning being and a man." However, this is achieved not by any conflict between a state which is unyieldingly collectivist and the individual who concedes no right to the state. There is a moment in which the individual of his own accord makes a total surrender of all his powers to the state and thereafter the state protects these powers for the full benefit of the individual. Rousseau achieved this by placing full sovereignty in the people, and by having the expression of this full sovereignty interpreted in the general will. Accordingly, the individual will loses itself in the general will, purges itself of all selfish interests, and the individual gains the right, along with all his fellow men, of saying: "L'Etat, c'est moi." Vaughan, however, notes that though this is the ideal and despite the fact that Rousseau made all sorts of provisions to curb the power of the state, it remains virtually absolute. He argues that despite evidence that the individual citizen is all too prone to find himself helpless in its grasp, Rousseau's intention never varied, and can be formulated as "a free citizen in a free state." To comprehend this, we must understand, Vaughan reiterates, that he has given a particular interpretation to both parts of the statement. The freedom of the citizen is not a freedom from constraint. Though the constraint appears to come from the collectivity, it also comes from the individual and expresses even more accurately the individual's will than he could do. Moreover, this corporate expression releases the individual from bondage to his baser, selfish instincts and fosters not only devotion to the welfare of the group but freedom for service. It is, as Vaughan maintains, a moral freedom, whose highest expression lies in the spirit of self-sacrifice (cf. Diderot). But the state must also be free; it too must live out its own life, free from interference. In Rousseau's view, federation is the only guarantee of this kind of freedom. The state should enjoy also another kind of freedom, what Rousseau defines as the intensity of Civil life, a "consuming zeal for the welfare of the community and all its members." To this power of the state Rousseau assigns the quality which he calls "virtue," the power which lifts a man out of himself, gives him a sense of moral duties, and makes him as a free citizen understand that freedom means strife, sacrifice, and effort.

Thus, Vaughan's interpretation, essentially making of Jean-Jacques's unity a movement toward a restricted type of collectivity by crushing all tendencies toward individuality, presents a Rousseau who suddenly shifted from an individualist ideal to a collectivist position, and from a concrete analysis of man's situation in society to an abstract, utopian declaration of the only way in which a stable society can be organized. Rousseau affirms, says Vaughan, that the goal of human existence is the formation of stable, coherent, permanent government. Those other aspects, which for Lanson played a role in the development of Rousseau's thought and which in their way should have a place in the unity of that thought, are given short shrift by Vaughan.The moralist and the religious thinker are to all intents and purposes forgotten by him. In Vaughan's view, man is essentially a political animal for Rousseau. Moreover, Rousseau's conclusions lead the reader to believe that in the relationship between the body politic and the individual, the former is everything, the latter is nothing. Thus, Vaughan overlooks the fact that, in Rousseau's day, the political category enhanced both the religious and the ethical categories.

Vaughan's explanations over the early years of the twentieth century produced, or at least brought together, a corps of Rousseau critics who saw in his doctrine this extreme political despotism. Lemaître and Faguet, for instance, saw in the doctrine a kind of political imperialism, which in their opinion has been man's curse since the days of Rousseau. Vaughan does not accept this conclusion any more than Lanson does. He does, however, make some troublesome concessions. He grants that Rousseau was collectivist, heart and soul.

While conceding that Rousseau may have taken over the concept of the state of nature and the contract from Locke and other individualists, he concludes that they have been altered beyond recognition. Consequently, the accusation of an unbridled individualism on Rousseau's part is unthinkable; what is needed, if anything, according to Vaughan, are ways of bringing his collectivism within bounds. Vaughan, however, praises Jean-Jacques for being the first to assail individualism "as a speculative theory of right" and to deny the individual a true existence. All that man really is, Rousseau asserts, he owes to the state.

Among all those who insisted that Rousseau's doctrine has a consistent and coherent unity, the one who presented his case with the greatest clarity was René Hubert in *Rousseau et l'Encyclopédie* (Paris, 1928). Hubert accepted that in 1743 in Venice Rousseau discovered, as he said, that "tout tenait radicalement à la politique." Until 1749, though, he did not clearly perceive the difference which separated him from the philosophes, especially Diderot. However, the *First Discourse*, by turning him to the problem of politics, led him to recognize his own thought as separate from theirs. In this *First Discourse*, he develops the idea that both science and the arts favor the social vices by confirming the progress of political inequality. Hence, Hubert insists that the *First Discourse* is politically as well as morally oriented. He objects to that view eventually espoused by Havens, Schinz, and Hendel that "natural goodness" of primitive man furnishes the core of Rousseau's argument; he suggests that in reality Rousseau is closer to Hobbes than to Grotius in the *First Discourse*. Rousseau presents as evidence of his views the predominant wickedness of contemporary man and explains the formation of society by the needs of each individual. But even in the first outburst, he lays down the basic idea of a contract (p. 72): "Celui de la liaison de la morale et de la politique, du rapport entre la décadence morale et les progrès de l'inégalité." Moral man is already in his opinion what his government has made him. What Rousseau objects to, says Hubert, is not so much sciences and the arts, as such, but the fact that they flourish because of the vices of luxury and inequality. Rousseau thus rejects the theory of Mandeville, Melon, and above all, such ideas as are expressed in both *Le Mondain* and *La Défense du mondain* of Voltaire. He thinks man's salvation abides in a return to himself and in a search for happiness by practicing virtue. Hubert adds that underlying all of Rousseau's thought was always an effort not only to understand his time but to understand himself in his time. This is the origin of his constant assertion that no man is morally superior to him, which led to his conviction of the soundness of his morality. There is implied, as always, the conclusion that he as much as anyone else can be led astray by a bad society. Hence, of pressing concern from the very first is the nature of the social body from whence springs the necessity of political institutions. That is the reason that in 1732 (still according to Hubert), in the preface to *Narcisse*, Rousseau insists that "tous les vices n'appartiennent pas tant à l'homme qu'à l'homme mal gouverné," and that everything really depends radically upon politics. As a result of this conviction, he had already formed (1750) the project of his *Institutions politiques* because he was now convinced that the key to the problem of individual virtue is to be discovered in that government dedicated to bring out the highest virtue of moral man. In the meantime, he turned to Montesquieu; he redefined virtue as the primitive instinct for nourishment, self-perpetuation, and self-defense (that is, natural law); he carefully pondered D'Alembert's remarks addressed to him in the *Discours préliminaire* of the *Encyclopédie*. He had now begun to reject the Hobbesian idea of a primitive wickedness. But by far the greatest amount of his energy is expended in formulating his replies to those who attacked the *First Discourse*. Now clearly noticeable was a definite insistence upon "natural goodness," a more complete definition of virtue, and a clearer understanding of the origins of inequality which impedes this virtue. The preface to *Narcisse* (1752) not only recapitulates Rousseau's basic points as he developed them in his replies, but it shifts somewhat the emphasis of his stand. For instance, he wrote: "dans un état bien constitué, tous les citoyens sont si bien égaux, que nul ne peut être préféré aux autres comme le plus habile; mais tout au plus comme le meilleur." Rousseau now suggests that the prime vice is inequality; rhetoric is deemed superior to the duties of man, he laments. And not only sciences and arts are "mots vides de sens; [l'homme] n'est ni parent, ni citoyen, ni homme; il est philosophe." Rousseau insists that many have pointed out these vices, but he alone has discussed their causes. And he has concluded that science is not made for man. "Il [l'homme] est né pour agir et penser, et non pour réfléchir." Study corrupts his morals, upsets his health, destroys his good disposition, and spoils his reason. Rousseau, in addition, already subscribes to the relationship between customs, morals, laws, passions, evil, so characteristic of Montesquieu. "Le moindre changement dans les coutumes, fût-il même avantageux à certains égards, tourne toujours au préjudice des mœurs . . . Car les coutumes font la morale du peuple; et dès qu'il cesse de les respecter, il n'a plus de règle que ses passions, ni de frein, que les lois qui peuvent quelquefois contenir les méchants, mais jamais les rendre bons."

The *Narcisse* thus represents a step in advance over the *First Discourse*, and, in a way, summarizes his position up to that point. The *Institutions politiques,* of which he began a draft in 1751, represents the positive side of his activity. By 1755, when the *Second Discourse* appeared, Rousseau had, as Hubert says, a well-rounded plan for the *Institutions*. He noted that having created the "vrais principes du droit politique," he would have to establish international law, commerce, rights of war and conquest, public law, confederations, negotiations, and treatises; that is to say, the subjects discussed by Montesquieu in the *De l'Esprit des lois*. Rousseau admits that there has been an evolution in his thought and that now he is concerned with the influence which the sciences have on the "mœurs" of people. He also stresses the relationship of the political and the moral order. And he has elaborated the concept of the "bon sauvage." From all of this he concludes the relativity of political and social phenomena: "Tout ce qui facilite la communication entre les nations porte aux nues, non les vertus des autres, mais leurs crimes, et altère chez toutes les mœurs qui sont propres à leur climat et à la constitution de leur gouvernement." He still believes that societies are formed by the collective needs of individuals. He declares in summary that it is a bad mistake to regard "comme le chef-d'œuvre de la politique de notre siècle, les sciences, les arts, le luxe, le commerce, les lois et les autres liens qui resserrent entre les hommes les nœuds de la société, par l'intérêt personnel, les mettent tous dans une dépendance mutuelle, leur donnent des besoins réciproques et des intérêts communs et obligent chacun d'eux de concourir au bonheur des autres pour pouvoir faire le sien." (Preface to *Narcisse*.) He thinks that society should be attributed, not to mutually individual needs, as he thought before the *First Discourse,* but to "bienveillance mutuelle" and "intérêt personnel." To this he adds an attack against philosophers, and discusses the need for another kind of education.

It is clear that by the beginning of 1754 Rousseau was faced by a choice between his comrades, the encyclopedists, and the theories of Montesquieu. Up to that point there are some very strong analogies between Diderot and Rousseau; not so much, it is true, in the solutions which each presents to social and political problems as in the common interest which both evince in these problems. There are differences, too, as Hubert has pointed out. Diderot seeks the causes for the establishment of government while Rousseau seeks the nature of the social body. Diderot insists that it is the social instinct which brings men together in a society. Rousseau denies this social instinct and insists upon personal needs. Diderot believes that the social instinct works with the passions to form society; Rousseau believes, on the contrary, that the needs only serve to bring men together, while the passions work to separate them. He adds: "Plus nous devenons ennemis de nos semblables, moins nous pouvons nous passer d'eux." It is this conflict between needs and passions which increases the disorder of society, according to Rousseau. For Diderot, the law of sociability is "un acte de pur entendement," while Rousseau maintains that at the moment of uniting into a society this "entendement" does not yet exist. Consequently, for Rousseau, there is no social contract dictated by nature; he calls the notion a "véritable chimère." His fundamental objection to Diderot's theory is that the latter assumes a general society before primitive man is capable of comprehending its necessity, and that he assumes an extension of this general society when man, now capable of understanding its necessity, is impeded by the passions.

Hubert maintains that Diderot and Rousseau understood differently the concept of "volonté générale." For Rousseau, it was the creation and the expression of the social contract; while for Diderot it was "un acte de pur entendement" in the conscience of each individual. Finally, Hubert notes that Rousseau did not start with the concept of "natural goodness," as Schinz and others thought. Rousseau himself stated clearly that his meditation started with the observation that all human activity took its origin in politics, and that no morality would ever be better than that conditioned by the nature of the people's government. Hence, he decided that the question to be answered was what is the best government to produce the most virtuous people. What is the government which always is closest to its law? And what is law? Hubert concludes that these fundamental questions posed by Rousseau were at the origin of his system and did not represent any principle of inherent goodness of man. He further rejects the notion that there was a period strictly philosophical and encyclopedic in the evolution of Rousseau's thought, as Schinz had proposed, around 1753. Hubert argues that if such a period really existed when Rousseau and Diderot agreed to the principles of politics, it was between 1744 and 1749, before Diderot's thought matured. Even in the *First Discourse*, it is clear that Rousseau cannot subscribe to the ideas of the philosophes, and in the Preface to *Narcisse* (1752) there is a section which is a veritable attack against them. The reason for this divergence is clear. Rousseau built his fundamental political principles upon his own observations, which led to conclusions different from those of Diderot. He shored up these principles by arguments generated by the attacks against the *First Discourse*. He also sought aid from Pufendorf's *Droit de la nature et des gens,* where Pufendorf also rejected the theory of natural sociability, stressed the role of needs in the formation of society, and pointed out the necessity of positing a first convention between the contracting parties. He defined the notion of general will, insisted upon *two* contracts (one to bring the individuals together, and a second to establish a government), and made a distinction finally between an "état populaire" and an "état tyrannique." It is also true that, having thoroughly digested Pufendorf, Rousseau now addressed himself to a careful study of Barbeyrac and eventually of Grotius. It was at this time (1753) that he decided to devote himself henceforth to an *Institutions politiques.*

Then came the second question proposed by the Dijon Academy and the problem of the principles of political science requested by Diderot as an article for the *Encyclopédie*, while Diderot reserved for himself the article on "Droit politique." There is some evidence that Diderot and Rousseau consulted together on the subject-matter of the two *Encyclopédie* articles. It was even thought up to 1928 by some critics that Rousseau wrote the two articles. But there is clear evidence that the content of the two articles is not the same and even that there is a difference in thought between the two writers, a difference which can be attributed to the attitude of the *Encyclopédie* and that of Rousseau. Rousseau's attitude was strongly conditioned by the changes wrought by the reading of Pufendorf, Grotius, Barbeyrac, and the organization of the material for the *Institutions politiques.* He was actually developing a philosophy of political history which he inserted in the "Economie politique" (early 1754). He saw Diderot's "Droit politique" at the end of 1754, and pointed up the differences in his revised "Economie politique." He was now inclined to see the problem of politics through the *Esprit des lois.* In the expanded plan he gave to his *Institutions politiques* at this time there entered the general scheme of Montesquieu in treating the subject. But there is more than that to Rousseau's developed scheme. He actually looked upon the problem of politics in Montesquieu's way rather than in the way of the *Encyclopédie*. Montesquieu proposed, as Hubert states, "un gouvernement bien ordonné, libéral, et sagement tempéré." It required the wisdom of the lawgiver to establish this kind of government, which depended not upon a special concept of government or upon an ideal government but upon the nature of the people. It was, in short, a pragmatic solution of the problem. The *Encyclopédie*, on the contrary, believed in the melioration of the political order by the progress of enlightenment (especially science and philosophy) and emancipation from religious dogma. Clearly, Rousseau adopted the views of Montesquieu rather than those of the *Encyclopédie*.

They were, in Rousseau's opinion, nonetheless deficient in three very fundamental respects. Montesquieu could really assign no acceptable origin to the foundation of the state, that is, his treatment of natural law was unacceptable to Rousseau after the latter's introduction to Pufendorf and Barbeyrac. Furthermore, Montesquieu's treatment of the center of power in the state ignored the importance of the general will; that is to say, though Montesquieu's detailed analysis of the pragmatic institution of government was acceptable to Rousseau, that government lacked a logical beginning and an ideal goal. Above all, it was not necessarily in Montesquieu's mind a republican form of government as we now conceive of that form—that is, a different form of government from a monarchy—since he picked England as the model government whenever he sought a practical example of the kind of country he had in mind. Rousseau obviously thought of Geneva as his practical example. He clearly felt that a republican government was the only possible form of government conceivable, and he thought of it in the same terms as we do. He felt that only a republican form of government could be a "pure" democracy and that no monarchy could qualify. Both Montesquieu and Voltaire, with their adoption of England as their example, had to make sharper distinctions between monarchy and "pure" democracies. They did so apparently by adopting the English concept of "mixed" government as it was discussed by Bolingbroke and others. Rousseau was spared this sort of finagling because he thought the only conceivable type of government was a "true" democracy. The result of these two divergent views had very important consequences in the way Montesquieu and Voltaire, on the one hand, and Rousseau, on the other, regarded sovereignty of the people and representative government. With Rousseau, sovereignty of the people is essential and representative government is impossible, while with Voltaire and Montesquieu representative government is essential whereas popular sovereignty is inconceivable.

Hubert's analysis of the organization and sequence of Rousseau's thought has succeeded remarkably well in tracing the relationship of morality and politics and the ultimate dominance of politics as the controlling factor in Rousseau's thought through the two *Essays*, the *Narcisse*, and the "Economie politique." It gives full meaning to the "tout tient à la politique" which was launched in the "Economie politique." It also gives a profound meaning to Rousseau's conviction that "man is what his government has made him." Finally, it offers a very plausible explanation (but still a fairly limited one) of the relationship between Rousseau's political theory and Montesquieu's which, briefly put, consisted in writing the *Second Discourse* as an introduction and the *Contrat social* as a conclusion to the *De l'Esprit des lois*, while in reality transforming the body of Montesquieu's treatise into an apology for republican government rather than for a monarchy. Thus, thanks to Hubert, we have a clarification of both the chronological sequence and the thought consistency of Rousseau's political stance in the early works. Further, we can more clearly recognize the coherence of his thought, particularly as it related to that of Montesquieu, Voltaire, Diderot, and the other Encyclopedists. But, of course, it ignores both the coherence and meaning of *Emile* and the *Nouvelle Héloïse*. That, too, can be recognized, if one recalls the immense importance which Montesquieu and all his contemporary political theorists, including Rousseau, attributed to the strict relationship existing between "mœurs" and "lois."

The year after Hubert's *Rousseau et l'Encyclopédie*, Professor Schinz brought out *La Pensée de Jean-Jacques Rousseau* (Northhampton, Mass., 1929, 2 vols.). Schinz protests loudly against Rousseau's detractors, especially those who praise his style, or those who explain that the reason for his aberrations can be traced to the fact that he is not French, but Genevan, and Protestant. Schinz insists at length upon the conformity of Rousseau's literary ideas (evil of the sciences and the arts, luxury, natural man, property rights, controversy on theatre, the personal novel, sentiment, Anglomania, nature, political thought, education) with the traditional development of these ideas in France before Rousseau. Schinz's main point, however, is that while Voltaire and Montesquieu have a certain philosophical unity to their doctrines, it is impossible to achieve the same result with Rousseau: ". . . En vain les critiques divers ont longtemps essayé de tout ramener—selon leur humeur ou leur préférence à quelqu'une des théories accusées chez Rousseau, le rationalisme philosophique ou la liberté politique, le retour à la nature ou le sentimentalisme moral, ou le sentimentalisme religieux: un examen attentif des textes, écartant impitoyablement tout subjectivisme, n'autorise plus pareille tentative." Schinz cites that A. Bertrand (1891) had already noted that the *Second Discourse* is incompatible with the rest of Rousseau's work and that Morley had made a similar observation; that Chuquet had judged the ideas of the *Contrat social* in disaccord with all the rest of his work and that Faguet had written, "Les ideés politiques de Rousseau me paraissent, je le dis franchement, ne pas tenir à l'ensemble de ses ideés." Finally, P. Sakmann (in Herrig's *Archiv*, 1913), also cites as a critical problem in Rousseau precisely how to conciliate the diverse elements in his *Works*. Schinz promises at the end of his introduction that, rather than spend his energies seeking a coherent philosophical synthesis, he intends to disentangle the nature and extent of the lack of philosophical coherence, determine what interpretation should be given to that phenomenon, and "examiner si ce ne serait pas là ce qui donne à l'œuvre de Rousseau son caractère propre et essentiel."

Schinz sees a conflict in the last half of the Enlightenment between the "Christian spirit" and the "spirit of the time" which had been going on since the Renaissance. The age of Louis XIV had interposed a momentary halt to the "spirit of the time" in the name of tradition. After the Sun King's death, this reaction was replaced by innovations which, resuming the antitradition of the Renaissance, bring back the social and moral problems of that time. Rousseau appeared at that juncture when "une puissante onde romantique (ou d'affranchissement moral) succédait à une longue onde classique (ou de discipline morale)." In Rousseau himself, a struggle developed between a "Rousseau romantique" and a "Rousseau romain," both of whom are reflected in the works of Rousseau more or less alternately. Schinz believes this alternation is what lies behind his incoherences and contradictions. He refuses to see in Rousseau a "personnalité simple" or "harmonious in its complexity." Rousseau began, according to him, by plunging into romantic escapades. But the tendency in Geneva was toward the "contrainte des passions et le renoncement aux jouissances de la vie." Hence, what must be retained is this: "dès la plus tendre enfance un conflit existe virtuellement dans l'âme de Rousseau; il sera sollicité par deux tendances morales qui vont en sens exactement contraires; l'une qui l'engage à s'abandonner aux sollicitations de son *moi*, et elle créera ce que nous appellerons le Rousseau romantique; l'autre qui l'engagera à résister et créera ce que nous appellerons le Rousseau romain ou calviniste" (p. 105). Schinz states that Rousseau's romanticism had exasperated his *moi* at the beginning. When discipline followed, he naturally revolted. But Schinz tries to have it both ways: Rousseau's *moi* is exasperated by the discipline, but Rousseau is also fascinated by this "vertu romaine," which is discipline. Fortunately, we don't have to worry too much about the conflict in Rousseau's mind. Schinz notes (p. 125) that "les Charmettes sont le suprême adieu de Rousseau au romantisme."

That seems, however, only a manner of speaking. If Rousseau adopts in the *First Discourse* the "esprit romain," it was because he was now revolted by the romanticism he witnessed in the Parisians. If the *First Discourse* is a hymn to virtue, it is to "vertu romaine," which he identifies with "Christian virtue" or, I suppose, with stoic virtue. Schinz, however, stresses that Rousseau distinguishes three kinds of virtue: moral wisdom, Christian virtue, and natural virtue; that is, happiness is achieved by satisfying the desires of nature. Schinz fails to note that Rousseau carefully defined virtue as struggle and strife. He does note that there is considerable incompatibility in the four notions of virtue, but that the different kinds are all present in the *First Discourse*, although he concludes that Rousseau seems to defend the "vertu" as a source of happiness—"vertu-sagesse." Schinz, after much hesitation, believes that the virtue which predominates is the "vertu-renoncement" which he believes Rousseau opposes here to the virtue of the libertines.

All of this appears a bit too complicated, as indeed it is. One wonders whether Professor Schinz could not have simplified a little by admitting that Rousseau began by being somewhat "libertin," became shocked by the excessive "libertinage" of the Parisians, and opposed to it in the *First Discourse* a stoic virtue.

Schinz stresses that the *Second Discourse* is dominated by the concept of "bonté." However, the definition of "bonté" varies also. There is a (1) "bonté chrétienne de discipline," (2) "bonté sentimentale de désintéressement," and (3) "bonté eudaimoniste." Schinz affirms that Rousseau does not use these concepts, however. The "bonté" which he affirms is "natural goodness." (See note 1 to *Second Discourse*.) Rousseau insists that he has proved that man is naturally good (Schinz denies that he has done so) and thereupon he concludes that society has made him evil because of inequality. This, for Schinz, is enough to warrant the conclusion that the *Second Discourse* is not a logical suite of the *First*, but in radical opposition to it. To begin with, Rousseau is no longer occupied with "virtue," but with "happiness." This preoccupation is, he says, a return to an attitude "romantique" (p. 172). "Certes cette attitude vis-à-vis le bonheur est le but de l'existence et que nous définissons comme l'attitude romantique—n'a rien d'extraordinaire." Nonetheless, in Schinz's view, the three ideas which have been hitherto thought by other critics the characteristic foundation of his doctrine—the natural goodness of man, the happiness of the noble savage, the return to primitive life—do not at all express the views of Rousseau.

In this respect, the *Lettre à d'Alembert* begins in an austere tone which easily induces the readers to believe that he has returned to the stoic virtue of the *First Discourse*. Schinz, however, notes the *Lettre* is neither in accord with the *First* nor in disaccord with the *Second*. Rousseau, he insists, differs from Bossuet's condemnation of the theatre as a source of public vice as well as from the philosophes who maintain that the public well knows how to use the theatre for the good of the community. Rousseau believes for his part that mankind will use the theatre to its disadvantage. According to Schinz, Rousseau's deviation from both extremes—that is, the Christian condemnation of the theatre as vice and philosophe's approval of the theatre as an instrument which fosters moral virtue—lies in the fact that he has shifted his interpretation to two other terms—"conscience morale" and "vivre selon la nature." Moral conscience he now regards as an innate feeling for virtue, whereas in the past he regarded it as essentially a rational faculty; "to live according to nature" no longer means to live according to primitive life but to live in accordance with the nature of man. Since there are amusements other than the theatre which are more in accord with the nature of man (those especially which are practiced by the Swiss), Rousseau feels that they are advantageous to man. They can also be more easily adjusted to man's nature, and consequently they are more in accord with his rational self. Because there are two ways of defining "nature"— primitive or rational.

It is apparent now that if one adopts Schinz's innumerable distinctions, there is no satisfactory consistency or coherence in Rousseau's thought, due not only to fluctuations in his vocabulary but to very vital contradictions in definitions which he attributes to a whole key set of terms. One wonders, however, whether the inconsistency and contradictions are not attributable more to Schinz than to Rousseau. Whatever the case may be, it can certainly be argued, if one wishes, that it is moral thinking which does give a unity to Rousseau's intellectual activities. The whole body of Rousseau's thought for Schinz turns that moral thinking around. Essentially, although in a vastly different context, Schinz has adopted the same position which Hendel will choose. Schinz, however, differs greatly from Hendel in feeling that these variable key words with their ambiguous definitions are the vital elements of Jean-Jacques's thought. He now suggests that with the *Nouvelle Héloïse*, they can all be reduced to (1) reason ("raison des philosophes et raison en soi"), (2) sentiment ("moral et naturel"), and (3) nature ("morale et romantique"). What is important for Schinz is that Rousseau had reached this duality through the three concepts of virtue: "vertu romaine, renoncement et calviniste, vertu innocence, et vertu de sagesse." While it is not easy to justify all these distinctions, they nonetheless represent a moralist position.

Some six years after Hubert's *Rousseau et l'Encyclopédie*, Professor C. W. Hendel published his *Rousseau Moralist* (Oxford, 1934, 2 vols.) in which he, as did Schinz, shifted the primary emphasis from Rousseau's political to his moral thought as the possible focus of his unity. Hendel was well aware of the multiple ways in which Jean-Jacques was regarded by other contemporary critics. In the last paragraph of his book (II, 331) he notes that Rousseau's career resulted in his acquiring many names and reputes: author on education, politics, and religion. He has been called said Hendel, seditious, a rhetorician, a man of paradoxes, a hypocrite, and a madman. By some he was dubbed a sentimentalist hostile to reason. He was content to be called "Citoyen de Genève." Hendel recalls that Diderot taxed him with being a hermit. Hendel, however, refuses to find that strange, "if he does not stay from life and affairs, draws wisdom from sources other than his books and the conversation of men. He has visions of a right order of life, right in relation to other men, to Nature and to God. He makes efforts to put these true ideas into effect, and if, in doing so, he betrays weakness, he is the more severely judged because he has taught men to know what real strength is. Those friends who had insight, and those who were not too impatient with him, recognized what manner of man he was when they spoke of him as 'the moralist.' "

Hendel adopts this same view throughout his lengthy work. He defines the moralist as one "who criticizes severely the very things he loves." In reality, Rousseau is the critic, the reformer, says Hendel; he resembles such moralists as Plato, Malebranche, Bossuet, and Fénelon. Hendel expresses in an epigraph drawn from Plato's *Republic*, that the unity he would like to bring out in Rousseau is that in which "some contradiction is always combined with it in all its manifestations, making it appear the opposite of unity, quite as much as unity itself." He confessed, nonetheless, his intention to determine "what the ideas of Rousseau really were." Hendel thereupon proposed a special method which had been elaborated by him and his teacher Christian Gauss: "to scrutinize at every moment the occasions which made him write, his studies and meditations, his friendships and relations, his personal letters and his unpublished fragments." It was fundamentally the Lansonian method followed by all of us from 1905 to 1935. In this particular case it did not differ from the necessity of getting at Rousseau's thought by a rigid analysis of his sources, his experiences, and his intentions. Hendel thus states that his theme will not be "Rousseau the political scientist, nor Rousseau the religious apologist, but Rousseau the moralist."

Hendel thereupon proceeds to regard both religion and politics and all the other aspects which Rousseau developed in his ideas from the moralist point of view. I find no place, however, where he has discussed the nature of "la morale" in French thought. Likening it to Plato's thought or to Malebranche's, as he does, seems to me to be especially risky. I would be more inclined to believe that "la morale" took its origin with Rousseau in the problem of the nature of man.

From Montaigne on, it had been an area of knowledge as important as natural science, religion, or jurisprudence. One studied the nature of man in order to find out what were his duties. French letters, particularly in the seventeenth century, had been filled with "moralists"—magnificent ones such as Pascal, La Rochefoucauld, La Bruyère, to mention only a few. They found from a constant study of man's nature that his duties were normally expressed as a series of relationships: between the individual and himself, between himself and society, between himself and the Supreme Being, between himself and nature. An analysis of any of these relationships would bring up specific problems. A problem of the relationship between man and himself could concern (and did, in fact) the importance of the passions in the actions of man; the second relationship might concern the theory of sociability or the duties of the citizen or natural rights (all of which had to be considered by Rousseau); the third relationship might deal with revelation or miracles or the existence of God. These are selected here as examples, but they all had an important place in the thought of Rousseau. There are, in fact, numerous relationships of these four orders and an infinite number of moral problems which cover the whole ground from thinking, feeling, acting, passions, vice and virtue. Always they grow out of these relationships: man and nature, man and God, man and society, man and his will or his conscience; in short, all the phenomena attached to man and his existence. If, however, one accepts as the corps of Rousseau's thought the *First Discourse*, the *Second Discourse*, and the *Emile*, and if the *Emile* establishes the foundation of that thought, creates the principles upon which it rests, manifests itself in many subjects (aspects of life), and expresses itself in a body of clear maxims, then subjects, principles, ideas, maxims, and expression unite in the making of an organic, full life. That's what Rousseau claimed as the source of his consistency in the statement I have extracted from the *Lettre à Christophe de Beaumont* (IV, 928) as the epigraph of this chapter. Of course, they may collectively be envisaged as belonging to man and his institutions—church, state, education. Hendel asserts that Rousseau has organized them in the three categories of religion, society, and morality.

It would seem that those French who have been inclined to look for the origins of Rousseau's political doctrine have sought them in the French. From Lanson on there has been a general tendency to seek them in either Montesquieu or Diderot, and it is indeed true that Jean-Jacques leaned heavily upon Diderot in the early days of the formation of his political doctrine and more heavily still upon Montesquieu when the fundamentals of that doctrine were formed. One could argue, nonetheless, that the full impact of Montesquieu upon Rousseau has not yet been completely explored. Now that we have Professor Shackleton and his reconstitution in his *Montesquieu* of that author's lost *Traité des devoirs*, now that we get a glimpse of the way Hendel understands that Rousseau is a moralist, it is not difficult to see the relationship between Rousseau's morality of obligation and the earlier *Traité des devoirs* of his predecessor. Nor is there any difficulty in establishing that there is no discrepancy in having a moralist in Rousseau's day be deeply interested in politics, religion, education, or social organization. Indeed, Rousseau does not differ in this respect from his contemporaries—Voltaire, Diderot, Condillac, or any of the others—except in his personal way of interpreting this situation. The ramifications of this notion, however, extend not only to Montesquieu, they can be traced back further to Hobbes (*De cive*), Locke (*Two Treatises on Government*), and the whole natural law school of political theorists in Germany and Switzerland: Grotius, Pufendorf, Barbeyrac, and Burlamaqui. The very titles of Pufendorf's treatises need no extra commentary in this regard: *Le Droit de la nature et des gens ou système général des principes les plus importants de la morale, de la jurisprudence, et de la politique* and *Les Devoirs de l'homme et du citoyen tels qu'ils lui sont présents par la loi naturelle*. There is no way to avoid the conclusion from these titles that the matter of politics is not a simple affair of organization of people into a community, it is above all the interrelationship between morality, law, and the state. In the strictest sense of the expression, "tout tient à la politique," as Rousseau had discovered when he decided in 1743 in Venice to undertake a vast work entitled *Institutions politiques*. It was indeed true for him that "man is what his government has made him."

Once, however, Rousseau had discovered the magic formula and the magic coherence of all the aspects of life as they met in the general area of rights and duties, he could say just as simply, "tout tient à la religion," or, "tout tient à l'éducation," or any other category of man's living, so closely are they all knit into the unity of life. It was Rousseau's way of making man understand that "tout est dans le tout." What he wants to make clear is the impossibility of touching life at any point without involving the whole of life. In short, for Rousseau life is its own inner organic unity whether it is considered under the rubric of nature, of man, or of rights and obligations.

These relationships have been worked out in the excellent *Jean-Jacques Rousseau et la science politique de son temps* (Paris, 1950) and *Le Rationalisme de Rousseau* (Paris, 1948), both by Professor Robert Derathé. It is not our purpose to review these two works here. That has been done superbly well by the late Professor Cobban (*PSQ* 66, June 1951: 272–284).

It has been shown by Professor Derathé that Rousseau not only took up again the traditional preoccupations of the political theorists of his time, but he recast them in new terms. The goal of the state is the preservation of its members; the citizens are constrained to accord the state as much power as necessary for the execution of this task; such was the fundamental thinking of Rousseau's predecessors. Rousseau does not deny these two principles. He simply changes the whole problem, however, by insisting that this should never be done to the detriment of freedom. The very formula which announces the goal insists that each citizen "reste aussi libre qu'auparavant." The contract binds the contractors "without subjecting them to anyone." The safeguard of freedom becomes the real goal, because in fact men subject themselves to laws in order to become free. Thus the concept of protection becomes secondary with Rousseau, for whom the essence of the body politic resides in the accord of obedience and freedom. The guarantee of the accord lies in the general will which is the sovereignty of the people. This "volonté générale" can act only through general laws and tends toward the equality of all. Consequently, there is no way it can jeopardize the freedom of the citizens which it is designed to defend. Rousseau concludes that sovereignty is by nature "une personne morale"; it has only an abstract and collective existence. He insists that sovereignty is something totally inalienable and cannot be ceded to any other under any circumstance. This, of course, differs entirely from the opinion of those who advocated natural law in that each of them conceded that one could transfer his rights as he could any other piece of property. The alienation of a "bien" does not differ from the alienation of freedom. And if an individual can so act, a collectivity may do likewise. Rousseau definitely opposed this argument: "La liberté n'est pas susceptible d'être cédée par un pacte, car il n'y a rien au monde qui puisse pour un homme ou pour un peuple compenser la perte de cette liberté." However, both Locke and Hobbes would agree that there are rights which are inalienable. Rousseau, who deftly executes a merging of these two opposing views, agrees with Pufendorf, Grotius, and the other representatives of the school of natural law that every human authority is founded upon conventions and consequently upon consent of those who submit. At the same time, he argues that no amount of consent would make legal a pact which would deprive anyone of his liberty. To invalidate an engagement, it is not sufficient that it contain a reciprocal promise, it must contain nothing contrary to natural law. From which it may be concluded that what gives validity to the social pact is less the unanimity of the consent than what the pact must do: (1) it must unite men without enslaving them, (2) it must make possible mutual assistance without harming them, and (3) it must furnish means for furthering their noblest possibilities. This is what Rousseau calls "la liberté morale" which is, he says, "Ce qu'il y a de précieux pour l'homme." As long as he lives isolated, he knows not good nor evil, he is free of wickedness, but he has no morality in his actions. The establishment of this morality of obligation is the ideal he now proposes, not happiness, although it certainly has some relationship with happiness. The strangest thing of all, however, is that this morality of obligation really does not guarantee utility. It does lead man to know virtue, that is, to strive, to struggle, to subdue himself, to sacrifice his interest to the common good. Of the three things which Spinoza stated that God demanded of man—obedience, justice, and charity—it preserves at least two of these things and it can actually preserve all three. Its greatest quality for every man, though, is its ability not only to give freedom to every man to perform these three supreme human acts, it releases within man the power to become creatively human, it is, in short, not only freedom from (which is a critical act) but freedom to (which is a creative act).

Derathé notes that the notion of a social pact was a commonplace in Rousseau's day. What led him to modify the commonplace beyond recognition was the conviction, contrary to the opinion of his contemporaries, that "tout tenait *radicalement* à la politique." It is the little word "radicalement" which transforms everything. Contrary to Locke and Pufendorf, who insisted that the state had done its work when it had secured the safety of the citizens, Rousseau insisted that it must furnish means for the intellectual and moral development of man. We are back in the realm of man's obligation to create his civilization and at the same time to preserve his freedom. It is the point where Montesquieu, Voltaire, Diderot, and Rousseau must forever meet. Indeed, I wonder why we strayed so far from it in the first place.

Our final task is to determine how Jean-Jacques puts these things together in some sort of organic way. We shall especially use in the enquiry four relatively recent investigations: R. Derathé, *Le Rationalisme de Rousseau* (Paris, 1948); R. Grimsley, *Jean-Jacques Rousseau, A Study in Self-awareness* (Cardiff, Wales, 1961); J. Starobinski, *Jean-Jacques Rousseau, La Transparence et l'obstacle* (Paris, 1957); and Cassirer, *The Question of Jean-Jacques Rousseau*, translated by Peter Gay.

The starting-point should be located around the early years of the twentieth century when Rousseau critics were more or less equally divided between a sentimental and a rationalist Rousseau. Masson, Brunschvicg, Lasserre, and Basch opted for the "romantic" Rousseau, while Beaulavon, Höffding, Lanson, and Durkheim laid emphasis upon the rationalist Rousseau. The characteristic way of setting up the problem was proposed by V. Basch. (See R. Derathé, *Le Rationalisme*, p. 5):

Je pose comme centre, comme source du génie de Rousseau, non pas cette volonté morale, non pas cette volonté autonome, non pas cette liberté métaphysique, qu'a conçue Kant et dont l'essence est totalement étrangère à la nature sensible et sensuelle de Rousseau, mais bien ce qui est contraire à la volonté rationnelle, à savoir le sentiment opposé à l'entendement, à la raison, ce sentiment . . . qui, pour moi, est l'âme même de Rousseau homme comme de Rousseau penseur . . . Sentiment égal à individualisme, et c'est avec cela que je construis, quant à moi, tout Rousseau.

It is true that Rousseau wrote: "J'ai senti avant que de penser, c'est le sort commun de l'humanité. Je l'éprouvai plus que nul autre . . ."

and he adds: "For us, to exist is to feel," "we have experienced sentiments before acquiring ideas." Rousseau, in fact, is rather categorical with statements of this order, which are fairly abundant. "If
reason is what makes a man, feeling guides him," is somewhat contradicted by the assertion that "the best guides which upright people
can have are reason and conscience." One recalls also the apostrophe
to conscience at the end of the *Profession*. Rousseau, however, quali-
fies this remark by "les actes de la conscience ne sont pas des jugements, mais des sentiments." We must not assume, though, that he
misesteems reason. In the passage at the end of the *Profession*, he
does vaunt conscience, which he calls the driving force of a sensitive
being far above reason: "Conscience! Conscience! Instinct divin. . . .
juge infaillible du bien et du mal; . . . sans toi je ne sens rien en moi
qui m'élève au-dessus des bêtes . . . que le triste privilége de m'égarer
d'erreurs en erreurs, à l'aide d'un entendement sans règle, et d'une
raison sans principe." Rousseau adds that conscience never tricks
us, the implication being that reason and understanding do. Often,
however, Rousseau places full confidence in reason. He will lament
that far too often reason deceives us, but he will assert that "il n'y
a rien de plus incontestable que les principes de la raison" or that
"l'autorité commune est celle de la raison, je n'en reconnais point
d'autre." He protests against those who urge him to submit his
reason to faith; it is, he says, an insult to the Author of his reason.

To discover a means of weighing judiciously the relative merits
of reason, feeling, and conscience in Rousseau would seem to require
the wisdom of a Solomon. Derathé argues that Jean-Jacques accepted
that feeling was anterior to speculative thought, but that it does not
take primacy over thought. What does have primacy over the speculative life is "la vie morale." Rousseau appears to find the solution to
the moral problem in the balance of reason and feeling, what R.
Ravier called "l'équilibre du sentiment et de la raison." Derathé
goes further and adopts the stand of Beaulavon that Rousseau is
a rationalist, but has both reason and feeling. He concedes that Rousseau nonetheless rejects the rationalism of the school of natural law,
which he attempts to refute. In Derathé's opinion, he is closer to
Malebranche than to Descartes. Rousseau asserts that reason is only
virtual in the state of nature where it is not needed, but development
of social life and reason go together. This coincides with the rise of

sociability. These are the factors in Rousseau's opinion which support man's perfectibility, what in fact distinguishes him from other animals. The state of nature thus is not really the most favorable for the well-being of man.

"La morale" consists in two elements: "vertu" which means struggle, striving, sacrifice of one's self for others and "bonté," which Schinz has defined as natural goodness. Rousseau regards these two elements as complementing each other and leaves the impression that "la morale" is perfectly simple. But, as Derathé has pointed out, goodness is fragile and cannot resist the onrush of the passions. The only safeguard is to use reason to combat them. Rousseau, as all the philosophers of his time, accepted that this reason is a gift of God to man whereby he may order his life and regulate his activities. This ordering and this regulation are brought about by law. Law is thus the source of freedom which in turn is furthered by submission to law. (See Derathé, *Le Rationalisme*, pp. 122–123.) Rousseau stresses that man cannot achieve freedom through his own powers; he must submit to reason and to law. That explains why he who refuses to obey the law must be forced to do so. However, submission to reason and to law is inadequate, because this moral freedom which is the ultimate goal can only be firmly secured if the reason is working in close connection with conscience and "sentiment intérieur." Rousseau does not conceal that conscience, "sentiment intérieur," and even prejudices are unstable factors which vary constantly (p. 132): "la conscience s'altère et se modifie insensiblement dans chaque siècle, dans chaque peuple, dans chaque individu, selon l'inconstance et la variété des préjugés."

All of this would seem to indicate that each of these factors—reason, feeling, passions, conscience, sentiment intérieur, even prejudices—have a role to play in the nature of man. However, as each plays its role, one becomes aware that no item is solidly trustworthy or autonomous. The one which comes closest to being the most satisfactory is conscience, which "ne trompe jamais," is the "vraie guide de l'homme," and is to the soul what instinct is to the body. This approval of conscience by Rousseau is what has induced many critics to believe that he dethrones reason and replaces it by feeling. It is true that he says that reason is of the order of knowledge and understanding, while conscience is of the order of feeling, and that the acts of conscience are not judgments, but sentiments. Nonetheless, I know of no place where he says that the order of knowledge and understanding is reprehensible and that judgment is necessarily to be reproved. Rousseau, however, rejects the distinction of the natural law theorists between reason, which furnishes general rules of conduct, and conscience, which indicates how these rules are to be used. They thought that conscience is an act of the understanding, while Rousseau identifies it with "l'instinct moral." In the *Rêveries* he wrote: "Dans toutes les questions de morale difficile comme celle-ci, je me suis toujours bien trouvé de les résoudre par le dictamen de ma conscience plutôt que par les lumières de la raison: jamais l'instinct moral ne m'a trompé." Apparently, the "instinct moral" is a product of the heart ("Mon cœur suivait machinalement ces règles avant que ma raison les eût adoptées, et l'instinct moral en fit application"). From this statement one must conclude that conscience precedes reflection, and leads by intuition to the same result to which reason would lead—or does lead—by reflection. This moral instinct, or "sens moral," is thus a faculty of the soul which immediately discerns good or evil—"le bien et le mal moral"—independently of reasoning and reflection. That is why Rousseau can write: "Tout ce que je sens être bien est bien, tout ce que je sens être mal est mal, le meilleur de tous les casuistes est la conscience."

It is through the working of these elements that natural law leads man to his obligations. Reason does not suffice in Rousseau's opinion; conscience as well as sentiment are likewise required to constitute a well-balanced "vie morale." Rousseau thinks it is useless to expect reason to restrain the passions. It is rather the love of order which Rousseau calls "l'amour du beau" which serves to restrain them. It is a sentiment and serves as a principle to conscience. Hence at each step of the moral life, feeling is indispensable. Man does not rise, though, to justice and virtue by reason alone but by his sensitivity to goodness and beauty and by sensibility, which is the pure ingredient of "la vie morale." For Rousseau, sentiment is not pure movement of nature but consists in an innate natural urge which is spontaneous and is to be found in that acquired knowledge which is reflective. The two factors are again fused and work together: "La conscience ne se développe et n'agit qu'avec les lumières de l'homme." Indeed, there are three activities (conscience, reason, liberty) which work together and lead man to justice and virtue. Finally, Rousseau distinguishes between virtue ("lutte, combat") and goodness (to follow one's inclination). Man has to conquer his virtue; nature has given him his goodness. Rousseau notes that virtue is superior to goodness because it requires reason and can only arise in a social state. He declares that "là où il n'y a point de société, il ne peut y avoir de justice, ni clémence, ni humanité, ni générosité, ni modestie." Consequently, man in society is superior to man in nature, because he finds there the basis of all "vie morale."

Rousseau often makes an effort to bring these factors together in some sort of genetic way, as in his definition of a virtuous man (quoted by Derathé, p. 114): "Celui qui sait vaincre ses affections, car alors, il suit sa raison, sa conscience, il fait son devoir; il se tient dans l'ordre, et rien ne l'en peut écarter." At other times, he attempts to arrange them in order, as when (Derathé, p. 20) he gives the steps in the education of an individual. He asserts that the normal education of a man should begin with training the body before training the mind. For instructing the intellect, however, one starts with the senses, continues with the imagination (which, says Rousseau, is the first faculty to develop itself), and finishes with reason, because it is the most difficult to train. However, by using the imagination before reason and by exercising the senses, one prepares the enhancement of reason in stages. Rousseau carefully marks out these stages. There is first of all, (1) a prerational state in which one freely uses the senses, particularly memory. In this way, images are formed which will later lead to ideas and later still to judgment. We must remember that ideas are "notions des objets, déterminés par des rapports," and that there are two kinds of memory (one which is "sensorielle," the other which is "intellectuelle"). Apparently, the application of the two memories in subsequent order is what gives rise to a second state of reason, (2) "la raison sensitive," which in time becomes (3) "la raison intellectuelle." In this latter stage "l'homme apprend à voir des yeux de l'esprit ainsi que des yeux du corps." In the transition from stage II to stage III, there is involved a whole series of operations adopted from Condillac's theory of the sensations: two things (two ideas) must be seen simultaneously, leading to comparison. An infinite number of relationships must be observed leading to various types of ideas: "de convenance, de proportion, d'harmonie, and d'ordre." Finally, one arrives at the cultivation of a sixth sense, called by Jean-Jacques "perceptions" or "ideas." Rousseau insists that reason which is thus elaborated is very different from the abstract reason of Descartes. Derathé, in fact, finds it is the opposite of Descartes's and that it is much closer to Malebranche. Nonetheless, there is certainly a suspicion that Rousseau followed rather closely the framework of Descartes's *Discours*; so closely, in fact, that if one substitutes "sentir" for "penser" (for instance, "j'existe, et j'ai des sens par lesquels je suis affecté" in place of Descartes's "Je pense, donc je suis"), the rest follows. Moreover, the objective which Descartes had in mind (the reestablishment of religion and morality) is adopted also by Rousseau who insists the acquisition of reason is necessary to build character and is therefore all-important in religion and morality.

Masson has nonetheless tended to make of Rousseau a sentimentalist, while conceding to him a certain rationalism that sprang up belatedly without sufficient preparation. Derathé rejects this view. He insists that Rousseau proposed a religion which owes absolutely nothing to personal opinion and is based uniquely upon individual reason. Moreover, no one is under obligation to obey any one except himself. Consequently, religious liberty is established upon the same foundation as political freedom. Derathé notes that religious freedom is the only principle which Rousseau retains from Protestantism. His "culte du cœur," he suggests, does not contrast with a "culte de la raison," but with a "cult of formal ceremonies." It does not depend, as it does in Pascal, upon an antithesis between heart and reason. Rousseau wrote in his *Lettre à Christophe de Beaumont*: "Dieu, seul Maître de changer mon cœur et ma raison." Rousseau nonetheless wrote to Vernes: "J'ai donc laissé là ma raison, et j'ai consulté la nature, c'est-à-dire le sentiment intérieur qui dirige ma croyance indépendamment de la raison."

Derathé gives (*Le Rationalisme de Rousseau*, pp. 38–39) a list of quotations which shows that Rousseau generally accepts reason as criterion for religion. He concludes that Rousseau yields to the authority of reason in religion and recalls that Rousseau defined the *Profession* an "œuvre d'un homme de bonne foi qui raisonne." Reason, though, is rarely alone when he seeks to justify his beliefs. It is frequently combined with some other quality, conscience, for instance. Masson had already noted, though, that Rousseau's adoption of sentimentalism as contrary to reason is proved by the vicar's indifference to speculative problems and his appeal to "sentiment intérieur." I would be inclined to think that certain confusions of this sort occur because of our own readiness to conclude that feeling is the opposite of reason. This is induced by the whole Romantic outburst after Rousseau, but it is fostered by Jean-Jacques's admission (which does not differ in this respect from Voltaire and all the philosophes) that man has serious limitations in the activities of reason. Rousseau, however, while adopting the whole skeptical current since Montaigne in regard to reason's weakness, is not inclined to blame reason for these limitations. He feels rather that they are unimportant to our welfare. What man has to know for his well-being are "considérations d'ordre moral," not speculative matters. Man was made to act, he states, not for a contemplative life. In this respect his attitude resembles that of Voltaire. These views have been called the pragmatism of Rousseau, especially by Schinz, who explains that it is the expression of Jean-Jacques's rationalism. Derathé still likens it to Malebranche. Schinz differs from Derathé in that he feels that Rousseau underwent a pragmatic current followed by a sentimental current, but Derathé, recalling Voltaire's deep interest in Malebranche, quotes the latter's remark: "L'esprit de l'homme a sans doute fort peu de capacité et d'étendue, et cependant il n'y a rien qu'il ne souhaite de savoir; toutes les sciences humaines ne peuvent contenter ses désirs, et sa capacité est si étroite qu'il ne peut comprendre parfaitement une seule science particulière." Malebranche also said, "Il est vrai que la plupart des sciences sont fort incertaines et fort inutiles. On ne se trompe pas beaucoup de croire qu'elles ne contiennent que des vérités, de peu d'usage" (*Le Rationalisme*, p. 47).

Rousseau has detailed in the *Profession* these weaknesses in our reason: "We have no faculty for measuring this immense universe; nor can we calculate justly the relationship of its parts; we know neither its primary laws; or its final cause; nor do we know either our own nature, or our active principle."

In religion Rousseau rejects everything contrary to reason: miracles, mysteries, original sin, transubstantiation, the resurrection of the body, the Trinity. On the contrary, he admits everything which can be considered in conformity with reason, if it is not considered unreasonable: free will, immortality of the soul, existence of God. He maintains that they are proved by a "sentiment intérieur." For those things, which are beyond our reason, but are not necessarily absurd, he suspends judgment: eternal punishment, for instance, he treats with respectful doubt. This "sentiment intérieur," Rousseau defines as (1) an inner conviction added to rational conclusions, and (2) a sentiment which can affirm things inaccessible to reason. It is a feeling which is not in opposition to reason. It merely comes to Rousseau's assistance when reason is suspended. Rousseau explains that the rule to refer these things to feeling is confirmed by reason. This manner of proceeding in reality derives from Bossuet, Malebranche, and Voltaire. Malebranche defines this "sentiment intérieur" as "conscience," while Rousseau, who also equates it with "conscience," defines it as "la lumière de notre faible entendement, lorsque nous voulons aller plus loin que ce que nous pouvons concevoir." In short, it is a guide to reason when reason falters. Rousseau wrote: "La voix de la conscience ne peut pas plus être étouffée dans le cœur humain que celle de la raison dans l'entendement: et l'insensibilité morale est tout aussi peu naturelle que la folie" (*Third Dialogue*).

The net result of all these attempts to define with precision all these moral terms is to leave the impression that Jean-Jacques must be a highly mystical character, since his vocabulary is so very esoteric. To a certain extent, this is undoubtedly the case. It is possible, though, in these terms, to overplay the grounding of Rousseau's thought in his personality. Cassirer, in his *Question of Jean-Jacques Rousseau* (p. 10), acknowledges that although this thought had its origin in Rousseau's nature and individuality, it was neither circumscribed nor bound to that individual personality. It is Cassirer's contention that this thought brings forward an objective formulation of questions which are valid not only for Rousseau, and his era, but contain, as Cassirer says, "an inner, strictly objective necessity." He concedes, however, that this necessity is not formulated in any systematic, abstract way, but it emerges from the first cause of Rousseau's nature and must be liberated, so to speak, from that first cause. Once the liberation is effected, there follows a whole string of similarly deduced questions which have a similar origin and together form the content of Rousseau's thought. The primary condition of that thought is its "inner logic, and its acquired vitalism," but it cannot be articulated in any systematic, abstract way. It must be grasped, as Mornet said of Diderot's thought, *in fieri*, rather than *in esse*. Cassirer, contrary to Mornet, believes that the quality of this type of thought is not a lack of unity. He is inclined to feel that it is governed by a higher, more dynamic unity. He lays down certain specific ways whereby this dynamic unity may be discerned. He insists, for instance, that one must seek the center which will be a single point of view around which the several doctrines are so many facets. The critic, however, must sympathetically live Rousseau's world of ideas and recreate his environment. But the absolutely essential ingredient is the nature of man. For Cassirer, the single point of view is "freedom." ("For him [Rousseau], the true and the only sure basis lay rather in the consciousness of freedom and in the idea of law which is inseparably connected with this consciousness.")

For Cassirer, as for Hubert, the way to tackle the problem of unity in Rousseau is the genetic method—to regard each work as the response to a situation and each response as a logical sequence to a preceding one. The *First Discourse* is the active reply of a moralist who, trained in the Genevan environment and educated at the Charmettes in a provincial atmosphere, is suddenly thrown in the brilliant community of Paris with its artistic and scientific fermentation. He becomes suddenly aware of a tension between morality and luxury, between sincerity and sham, between the integrity of the individual and the pernicious forces of the community, between morality and politics, politics and religion, feeling and thinking, and most important of all, thinking and being. Rousseau attempted a synthesis between civilization and nature but he understood badly how to enter into such a complicated matter, and the attempt was weak and halting, what Cassirer acknowledges as far as the *First Discourse* is concerned as a rhetorical masterpiece. The attacks upon the *First Discourse* forced Rousseau in his replies to build a stronger case for his views and actually to clarify for himself these views. The key cry he raised was "back to nature"—it was not a novel suggestion, having been the conclusion of the vast travel literature of the previous two hundred years. But Rousseau clarified his present grievances against the civilization of his day. In all probability, he, like Voltaire, had just been reading Mandeville and Melon and he was prepared to see that the basic vice of his time was inequality. Besides it was a view which Diderot espoused to whomsoever would listen. Thus, when the alert Dijon Academy proposed the subject of the *Second Discourse*, Rousseau was prepared to present his case with great clarity.

Cassirer notes that subsequent to the *Discourse on Inequality* "an almost inconceivable reversal occurred in Rousseau's thinking." Instead of the individualism of the first two discourses, he places a limitless authority in the community as a whole. Each individual will is crushed by the power of the general will. Indeed, there is a total identity between the general will and the social contract. One is but the expression of the other. Cassirer mentions that Morley, Faguet, Ducros, and Mornet have all declared that the *Contrat social* "explodes the unity of Rousseau's work," despite continual protestations on the part of Rousseau concerning his unity. Cassirer notes that Rousseau preserves this unity by introducing the concept of freedom and giving to the concept a new meaning: "the submission to an inviolable law which the individual erects over himself." Thus, in obeying the general will, the individual is obeying himself. The state therefore is not an arbitrary power, coercing the citizen, it is a benevolent power protecting the individual and assuring his rights. Thereafter, freedom also meant, for Rousseau, freedom under the law. The magic source of freedom is the law, but the real magic lies in the law itself—its power to exercise legitimately authority over the individual will. Consequently, what at first appears abstract and arbitrary was really a shrewd move to conjure the necessarily ill effects of inequality by creating a reasonable state. The *Essay on Inequality*, says Cassirer, is in reality complemented by the *Contrat social*. Rousseau explained how he came to the solution of the dilemma conjured up by the inevitability of inequality and the impossibility of a return to nature. "I had realized," he wrote in the *Confessions*, "that everything was basically related to politics and that no matter how one approached it, no people would ever be anything but what the nature of the government made it." And hence the real problem was to find the best possible government fitted to shape the most virtuous, the most enlightened, the wisest, and the best people. In short, he set out to construct that government which would assure the pure rule of law.

Cassirer in a Part II of his *Question* affirms that the final result of Rousseau's thought was to free his time from the domination of intellectualism by replacing it with the force of feeling. He finds that this new quality was especially effective in the realm of poetry, which, until Rousseau, was stagnant. Without creating a single piece of what might properly be called "lyrical poetry," Cassirer wrote, "he discovered and resurrected the world of lyricism." His discovery inaugurated a new epoch in Europe, characterized by a new interest in nature and, above all, by sensibility. Derived from this sensibility is a new ethics, characterized not by passions and feeling, but by the sense of obligation. It is in this light that the ethics of obligation appears both in the *Nouvelle Héloïse* and the *Contrat social*. Rousseau regarded it as the result of law, and law as a gift from Heaven which is discovered by God-given reason. Hence, there is exaggeration in making Rousseau the apologist of the passions, or even the sponsor of an unbridled, irrational feeling. In reality, Cassirer regards this stand as "eliminating feeling from the foundation of ethics," in contrast with Diderot who insisted that society was the product of the social instinct. Rousseau, says Cassirer, constantly opposed this thesis. Hubert makes the same point.

The end of Cassirer's essay seems to me somewhat confused in this matter of feeling, sensibility, reason, and the ethical will. After establishing his view that "mere" feeling, as he calls it, is subservient to reason, and sensibility and the passions to the ethical will, he concludes that Rousseau's view is that feeling is no mere passive impression or sense perception, but a dynamic force capable of judging and evaluating. Cassirer notes that in this assertion, Rousseau has turned from Condillac to Leibniz. The validity of this view is certainly questionable. As a result, Rousseau's thought on religion and education appears in the *Question* as somewhat of a hodge-podge, lacking any consistency and possessing very little coherence. To cap the confusion, Cassirer insists that there is no contradiction between the *Emile* and the rest of Rousseau's work. There is no discrepancy, he says: "pedagogy and politics, ethics and religion, religion and philosophy fully interlock; they are but developments and application of a single principle." Just what the principle is is not made very clear. Is it a necessary "solidarity between the individual's will and the general will?" Or is it "l'amour de soi," or simply "self-awareness and self-consciousness?" Or could it be still "freedom" which is the dynamic source of "equality?" Whatever we decide, it will always be a portion of that organic entity which we can call, for want of a more comprehensive term, the nature of man. That at least fits with Jean-Jacques's assertion that he wanted to make a positive contribution to the science of man.

There is, however, another aspect of this science of man as seen by Jean-Jacques. Professor Starobinski, in the opening paragraphs of his "avant-propos" to *La Transparence et l'obstacle* (Paris, 1957) explains that Rousseau never wanted to separate his thought and his personality, his theories and his destiny. Consequently, says Starobinski, he must be taken as he presents himself in the fusion and the confusion of existence and idea. We are thus forced to analyze the literary creation of Rousseau as if it represented an imaginary activity and his conduct as if it constituted a living fiction. Professor Starobinski notes that Rousseau's career was varied; he was adventurer, author, musician, and political thinker. In spite of its variety, his life was rich enough to bring out the themes and the motives which will assist us in grasping the dispersion of his tendencies and the unity of his intentions. The critic promises, by naively listening to Rousseau, to select the images, the desires, and the yearnings which obsess him, all of which dominate his activities and give them a permanent direction. Starobinski indicates that if he can arrange these elements in some sort of human order: themes, motives, tendencies, intentions, images, desires, and yearnings, he will be able to describe the structures of Rousseau's world. He assumes that by merely reading and trying to unravel the order or the disorder of the texts under discussion, he will discover the symbols and the ideas which underlie the organization of Rousseau's thought.

There are, however, two worlds involved: the one which Rousseau finds unacceptable and the one which he would put in its place. It is the conflict of these two worlds which explains Rousseau's life. He would like "la communication et la transparence des cœurs" but, frustrated in this desire, he accepts "l'obstacle" which permits him to fall back upon a passive resignation, firmly convinced of his innocence.

Professor Burgelin, in an article entitled "L'Unité dans l'œuvre de Rousseau" (*RMM*, 1960, pp. 199–209), has attempted to put

Starobinski's presentation in proper perspective. The work of Rousseau, he notes, was extraordinarily rich and has produced a new sort of "âme sensible," open to pity, love, nature, and religion. It has also nurtured generations of reformers, given a new conception of morality and history, transformed pedagogy. For Rousseau, all these diverse tendencies have a unity, which he tried to explain in the *Dialogues* as centering upon *Emile*. But in the *Second Discourse*, Rousseau points out that the science of man does not yet exist and states he wants to make a contribution to it. In the *Contrat social*, while recognizing the importance of the *Esprit des lois*, he notes that it lacks a solid foundation in political science. Burgelin suggests that, put together, these affirmations indicate clearly Rousseau's design to coordinate these things in his philosophy.

Rousseau, however, is not satisfied to build an abstract system. He wants his structures to be intimately connected with his personality and he acknowledges freely the imperfections of this personality—difficulty in organizing and integrating his ideas, surrender always to his imagination and his passions, insistence that his doctrines satisfy his own needs. He talks constantly against coherence, condemns others for their consistency, which he attributes often to bad motives, and expresses his desire to be considered above all, a poet.

Rousseau criticism, says Burgelin, has always fluctuated between a demonstration of incoherence in Rousseau's work, while stressing the character of the man, or a presentation of an abstract coherent doctrine, while noting the inconsistencies of his character. "L'accent," says Burgelin, "est tantôt sur l'enseignement politique et social, tantôt sur le témoignage intime."

Burgelin notes that two recent interesting Rousseau studies are Starobinski's *La Transparence et l'obstacle* and Rang's *Rousseau's Lehre vom Menschen* (Göttingen, 1959). Starobinski, he explains, has approached his subject through the interpretation of Rousseau's key words, two of the most important being *transparence* and *obstacle*; through key metaphors, the two most important being *voile* and *dévoilement*. Through a rigorous study of their use, Starobinski has sought to bring out an "essential motivation," a "fundamental experience" of Rousseau's sensibility and thought. The play between these key ideas—*light* and *darkness, concealment* and *revelation*—offers a rich ground for a constant symbolization of human experience. Light and darkness can be symbols of good and evil, right and wrong, or truth and falsehood; concealment and revelation can be symbols of the mask and sincerity. As a matter of fact, the phenomenal world and the noumenal world of human experience break into an infinite dualism: reason and the senses, reason and feeling, individual and society, will and passion, general will and personal will, nature and reason, reflection and fantasy, revery and thought. One could continue indefinitely, but the curious thing about all this contradictory dualism is that it does not ultimately represent opposition, but unity.

Despite these dichotomies with which Jean-Jacques is continually obsessed and which are the substance of his world, his "self" and his thought are constantly involved in the Enlightenment's reality, too. They are not abstractions, but express concrete living phenomena, deeply human intentions and desires, and an active creative energy. If there is a unifying force in all this inchoate contradiction, then it ought to bring about a release of inner power, institute an ultimate order, and constitute a creative intention which symbolizes the motives and purposes of man's universe. Knowledge of its transaction, awareness of its being, and realization of its self coincide with freedom and justice. Henceforth nothing can stop the change, alter the goal, or even deny the vision.

Professor Starobinski has noted all this rich symbolization created by Rousseau's struggle for complete inner revelation and perfect sincerity in the presence of a public which absolutely rejects his authenticity. But the feeling of lack of authenticity of Rousseau's public should not be neglected. Rousseau attributes it to the evil which is generated by the movement from inner reality to outward appearance—what Jean-Jacques designates as "nous avons perdu l'innocence et les mœurs." The masses grovel in misery; all are the slaves of vices; we are submerged in our prejudices, in our vulgar philosophy; we nurture our passions; cultivate low, personal interests, and flatter our egos. Consequently, the integrity of the public no longer exists, and man is the slave of opinion. Science, which man yearns to embrace, was not made for him. Rousseau seems to think nonetheless that the cure for these ills is the creation of the science of man, which, Burgelin insists (p. 29), "implique non seulement les conditions géographiques et physiologiques, les formes sociales, mais aussi l'univers des valeurs, les aspirations morales, esthétiques et religieuses, où se révèlent les structures ontologiques du monde et de l'homme, enfin la complexité infinie des personnalités absolument libres."

Starobinski accepts Rousseau's statement that he has no intentions of upsetting the institutions of the monarchy in France. Still, he notes that Rousseau suggests that "le mal réside . . . dans la désintégration de l'unité sociale," not essentially in the progress of arts and sciences; although arts and sciences "favoriseront cette désintégration sociale." Starobinski argues that in implying that he is opposed to society, Rousseau admits that there must be a break between his life and his principles. In fact, he is not very consistent here since he presents a new kind of cure in education for this ill.

With all his meticulousness in bringing together the aspects of life, in the harmonization of these aspects by adjustments to a totally new psychological vocabulary, in inventing a new method of synthesizing this vocabulary by raising the values of things to a very high degree of symbolization and by attaching to this symbolization a whole new set of spiritual values, Rousseau does not at first seem to accept, as all his contemporary philosophes did, the simple statement that what one thinks is what one is, what one says is what one does. The two roots of that simple statement, though, from Descartes ("l'âme est une substance pensante") and from Malebranche ("nos idées sont l'occasion de nos mouvements") have been adopted by him. Indeed, put together, Rousseau in his special way seems to say the same thing: "N'apprendrez-vous jamais," he wrote, "qu'il faut expliquer les discours d'un homme par son caractère et non son caractère par son discours." Burgelin's commentary (p. 34) on this remark is essential for an understanding of Rousseau's own character: "De tels textes sont-ils entâchés de ce subjectivisme qui est le péché philosophique? Ils nous orientent vers l'opposition de l'artiste et du philosophe [or would it be clearer, if we said the poet?] l'un cherchant à exprimer la vérité, l'autre sa vérité . . . la philosophie ne se passe pas de l'art, le fond de la forme, la pensée d'un certain accent . . ." Burgelin adds (pp. 36–38) that when one recognizes that the thought of Rousseau is by nature "multipolaire" (as in Pascal's case also) one understands more clearly why that thought transformed art, philosophy, and politics, first of all through a type and a spirit of prophecy, and why, in addition, intimate experience prevails over argumentation and poetic expression over technics. The result is, adds Burgelin, a contradictory interpretation which makes of Jean-Jacques a scorner of reason and the whole social order, even of all discipline; or he who has restored to reason its proper place, uniting it with "la conscience morale" for the dignity of all mankind —the Newton of human nature. And thus Jean-Jacques, with much help from Cassirer, Grimsley, Derathé, Starobinski, Burgelin (and a little from me), did make his contribution to the science of man.

Professor Starobinski regards the attitude of Jean-Jacques as a veritable confrontation ending in an ultimate defeat and rejection for Rousseau. His appeal to the public is one of utter sincerity and total integrity. His "dévoilement" is complete, only to be met by the scorn of the public. Even before Rousseau has been heard, he has already been condemned. And so he has used upon his fellow men a "dévoilement." They also, conceal themselves, appear what they are not, shroud their intentions in darkness. Rousseau denounces their pettiness. There are thus two aspects, as Starobinski has shown (p. 8), to this revelation: one is "dénonciateur"—a critical act which serves to demolish an error. Rousseau confesses that he has used this denunciation to reveal the deep errors treated in the two *Discourses*. He explains that it was directed against the philosophers, especially those of the "Coterie Holbachique," who, having denounced the selfishness of religion and politics (the church and the state) try to substitute in its place an "intérêt bien entendu." Rousseau denounces the folly of proposing an "intérêt bien entendu." This metaphoric penetration is not unlike Diderot's, with the difference that in Diderot's case it is pure metaphor, whereas with Rousseau it is interpreted through allegory and symbol—what Condillac and the philosophes called "signes." Rousseau, for instance, presents "La statue de Glaucus" as "Natural Man"; he calls the "Dévoilement de Galathée" the "Morceau Allégorique sur la révélation." Of course, his Pygmalion is a dramatic presentation of the same idea.

Starobinski points out that the multipolarity of the author is evident in these activities. Initially, the procedure is used to stress the moral significance of the *Confessions*; it is a personal demonstration of self-denunciation. Since Jean-Jacques acknowledges his ineptitude in discussion and his awareness of this defect, he simultaneously asserts in this intricate stylistic way, says Starobinski, his presence and his absence. Starobinski notes that this explains some of the themes of Jean-Jacques, particularly the theme of return (or arrival) which he often uses. A case would be his arrival at Mme. de Waren's on Palm Sunday, or the return of St. Preux in *La Nouvelle Héloïse*. Rousseau adopts the Lockean theory that signs are essential to words, that one moves from thought to speech to sign. Again, there is much similarity here with Diderot's insistence that speech must be accompanied by gesture. Once more, though, there is some difference. Rousseau uses conduct to confirm language rather than language to confirm conduct ("Si quelquefois mes expressions ont un tour équivoque, je tâche de vivre de manière que ma conduite en détermine le sens"). He speaks also of "Le parti que j'ai pris d'écrire et de me cacher." Applied to his own life he wants his language interpreted by his life. That is, he denies that he is the egotistical, arrogant, suspicious person who can be read into the language. Conduct as sign, he thinks, is a truer form of communication than words. He confesses, though, that these signs are misunderstood, or misinterpreted, condemning him to solitude.

Rousseau also stresses his own ability to recognize, recall, and interpret these signs; what Jean-Jacques calls the "signe mémoratif." He explains in the *Confessions*: "Le signe extérieur est tout ce qui me frappe. Mais ensuite tout cela me revient: je me rappelle le lieu, le temps, le ton, le regard, le geste, la circonstance, rien ne m'échappe. Alors, sur ce qu'on a fait et dit, je trouve ce qu'on a pensé, et il est rare que je me trompe." Rousseau explains that this kind of sign does not herald an external reality, but rather internal images.

We must return now to the opening statement in Starobinski's analysis in which he promised to treat experience as fiction, and fiction as reality. The point to seek is the moment in which the two merge so clearly that they have become one. The core of Jean-Jacques would thus be the inner reality of his biography created by his thought. Starobinski has stressed that there is an abundance of autobiographical work in Rousseau. Usually, Jean-Jacques takes the position that he is entirely open to others. He insists, however, that they believe that his truth is hidden to them as if he constantly wears a mask. Indeed, it has often been said that the *Confessions* were written to rectify this mistaken view of others. Rousseau is forever inquiring why his transparency is not immediately recognized by others. His apology thus is not an excuse. He confesses that his transparency is inexistent so long as it is not reflected in the eyes of his interlocutor. The essential thing is to convince others of the transparency. His despair is great because he is finally persuaded that the real reason for the rejection is that he has been judged without having been heard.

We thus get the impression that an esthetic act has been performed in which the suspension of unbelief is far more important than logical conviction. Biography has attained the highest form of art by identifying itself with all human possibilities. Of course, this can be done only by adhering to the strictest methodological procedures (*La Transparence*, p. 233). "Pour bien connaître un caractère," Rousseau wrote, "il y faudrait distinguer l'acquis d'avec la nature, voir comment il s'est formé, quelles occasions l'ont développé, quel enchaînement d'affections secrètes l'a rendu tel et comment il se modifie, pour produire quelquefois les effets les plus contradictoires et les plus inattendus." Rousseau added that everyone sees himself in his own particular way and according to his fantasy. He has no fear that anyone will confront the image and the model. For how would anyone reveal this inner model, seeing that he who paints it in another could never see it in himself, and since he who sees it in himself wouldn't want to reveal it. Jean-Jacques maintains that there is no difference between knowing one's self and feeling one's self. Both phenomena occur spontaneously, just as one judges his innocence immediately. The artist must know how to pursue this genetic method step by step "suivre chronologiquement le développement de sa conscience, recomposer le tracé de son progrès, parcourir la séquence naturelle des idées et des sentiments, revivre par la mémoire l'enchaînement des causes et des effets qui ont déterminé son caractère et sa destinée." Thus it passes from the history of a life to the creation of a soul, and from the domain of truth to that of authenticity. "La grande affaire," he added (p. 248), "n'est pas de se penser ni de se juger, mais d'être soi." Starobinski calls this living the dangerous pact of the *moi* with language, "la nouvelle alliance dans laquelle l'homme se fait verbe."

We have to ask now whether Rousseau's reality is essentially the creation of a total political, religious, or esthetic act, or whether it is a unity of all these acts harmonized in the authenticity of one human being. And we must be prepared ultimately to consider whether the best way to characterize what has been going on here is to return to the Greeks and call it formally the authentic philosophical act, or add to it the poetic act, too.

Professor Burgelin has attempted to make a case for Rousseau as philosopher, even going so far as attributing to him an existential philosophy. This philosophy, he notes, is characterized by a constant effort to balance two extremes which oppose each other. Rousseau is presented as being overwhelmed by the complication of facts. He nonetheless recognizes that a unity is essential. He adopts the dialogue as the only means of resolving the complication. Eventually, the dialogue which at first is reduced to a kind of debate between himself and an interlocutor (in the *Essays*, for instance) becomes an inner debate between Rousseau and himself. There is, in fact, a tendency on his part to bring everything back to himself, to the point of identifying himself with his literary creations. Burgelin assumes that what guarantees the unity and the order is the philosophy of Rousseau. It is designed to equate work and style, style and author (in the Buffon sense that "Le style, c'est l'homme même"), and author and man and his place in the world of his creation.

Rousseau's analysis of the condition of man, however, is not very comforting. While nature is all harmony and proportion, human nature is confusion and disorder. Social, moral, and political life is full of injustice. Man's institutions foster prejudices, encourage passions, and spread egotism. He is in contradiction with himself, he lacks an organizing reason. Rousseau deplores that the world lacks legislators of the calibre of Numa and Moses. As a consequence virtue, particularly civic virtue, is now missing, and religion is being ruined by materialism and naturalism. Rousseau blames philosophers in large measure for man's unsatisfactory condition. He condemns them for the artificial character of their principles. Their metaphysical pronouncements are useless; they are expressed in an impossible jargon, introducing abstract ideas which lead to untold errors. They establish these principles upon their own limited experiences. The philosophy they build up is founded upon appearances, not upon reality, and leads to negative, destructive results. It constructs nothing and corrupts everything. Rousseau's condemnation is global and general, and does not proceed at all from a minute analysis of doctrines. In these circumstances, he is, in fact, opposed to reflection as a principle.

Still, his denunciation of man's sorry state does not conclude upon this negative note. In place of the useless metaphysics, the pseudo-science, the ruin of natural religion, the lack of true legislators: "la ruine de l'individu et la dégénérescence de l'espèce," Rousseau counsels inaugurating the science of man and he dedicates his energies to the formulation of this "new" science which he defines as embracing geographical and physiological conditions; social forms; moral values; human, religious, and esthetic aspirations; ontological structures of man's world; and the complexity of every individual. It is, as Burgelin insists, a "philosophie du dictamen," a philosophy which begins with the individual and finds within the individual the sources of all his inner reality. What it seeks is an awareness of that inner being, an awareness of what constitutes the self; and not only what constitutes it, but what enables man to draw from that self-constituted inner reality the awareness of all those possibilities which become self-determined. So that there is a search for self-identity through the effort toward self-awareness, a conversion, so to speak, of one's yearnings into a recognition that they are one's being, that they become simultaneously a moral, a political, a religious, an esthetic act, a creation of something by awareness of a desire for that thing, and a possession of that desired thing because it is immediately recognized as possible, useful, good, and therefore beautiful. Reaching for the moon creates the moon, but only when the seeker (the poet) identifies himself with the creation.

The search is, however, a very complex affair. It forever transforms politics, art, morality, and philosophy. What is the nature of this philosophy which is forever transforming the possibilities of the individual? Is it the philosophy of the dreamer, the utopian, the creator of fancies out of touch with reality? Or the poet of human values who transforms those human values? We debate endlessly where to place those values. Ever since Plato, we alternately accord them meaning and deny them reality, strive to achieve them and lament their impossibilty, identify ourselves with them and decry their insubstantiality.

Rousseau's philosophy requires so many contradictory activities that a poor human being trying to find himself becomes lost in the struggle. The procedure is to "rentrer en soi-même." That seems simple enough. To see the truth within that self, that is much more difficult. To recognize one's limits, that ought to be dreadfully simple. Moreover, here all our faculties come into play: our reason, our conscience, our passions, our feeling. How do we use them correctly? Our perplexities deepen at this point, because, as Rousseau insists, "L'Homme est un," but "L'homme modifié par les religions, par les gouvernements, par les lois, par les coutumes, par les préjugés, par les climats," is always becoming different from himself, and always he is transforming politics, art, religion, philosophy. What then is "véritable fin?" Here Rousseau inserts a whole raft of difficulties: "speculative philosophy" spoils always "the practical life, peace, moral unity." The objective is "être soi." But how? Rousseau seems to insinuate that what motivates man is a living dialectic of nature and freedom, of happiness and virtue. Man's self-awareness is really a goal, not a science, not even a substance. Hence, instead of any speculative philosophy, man should substitute a "morale sensitive," a philosophy of virtue, conscience, instinct. The search for virtue, awareness, and being, becomes one's virtue, awareness, and being. In that way, a "morale" becomes another metaphysics, politics, esthetics. This philosophy is at the point of contact of consciousness and reason. It is another morale, another esthetic, a penetration of *soi* and nature, another politics and religion. It depends greatly upon the imagination. "Je vois clairement," said Rousseau, "que chaque chose existe pour le tout et que le tout est un, et résulte d'un seul et même système." It is in this sense that Rousseau's unity is all-embracing within his *moi*. Burgelin calls it "la passion de l'unité . . . la passion philosophique." When applied to Rousseau, all the abstractions (justice, goodness, virtue, even happiness) meet in "l'être": they become alive.

If one stops and analyzes the situation concerning the organic relationship of Jean-Jacques *persona* with the organic meaning of his work, it is evident that between Lanson in 1912 and Burgelin in 1960, the attempt to achieve a synthesis of man and his work has made great strides, despite some obvious difficulties. Two notions have been debated back and forth since the Lanson article. Is it possible to integrate the existence of Jean-Jacques into the work of Rousseau in such a way that it occupies an absolutely essential place in the organic existence of that work? Is it possible to characterize the work in a specific way which will bring out the core material? Can we center that work in its totality on Rousseau's "Tout tient à la politique"? Or can we build it around Rousseau's stated intention to reconcile philosophy with religion? Or that other remark that the science of man had to be inaugurated and he wanted to make with his work a contribution to that embryo science? In short, can we be satisfied with focusing his total activity upon politics, religion, la morale, or esthetics? Would that make of Rousseau essentially a moralist, a religious thinker, or a political theorist, the maker of the science of personality, the founder of a new art, or, as Burgelin suggests, the creator of a unique philosophy which Burgelin defines as "contact with the real" and "contact with the values"? Voltaire, faced with the same problem, called it more simply "Philosopher" and "Poétiser."

At all events, we should recall that Rousseau in the *Dialogues* strongly suggested that his principles were not definitively established until the *Emile*, and he indicated that to grasp the unity of his argument one should begin with that work. We have noted other places where Rousseau insisted that the *Emile* was the center of his philosophical activities, in the letter to Malesherbes, for instance, 12 January 1762, where he asserted that the two *Discourses* and the *Traité de l'Education* "sont inséparables et forment un même tout." It would seem, therefore, reasonable to heed those assertions and to consider what would be the result if we undertook to center the whole of Jean-Jacques's work upon the *Emile*. Curiously, I know of no one who has taken this tack until Martin Rang's *Rousseau's Lehre vom Menschen* (Göttingen, 1965). Rang explains in his "Vorwort" that Rousseau's work focused resolutely upon the *Emile* but, rigidly subjected to the genetic method of analysis, it will bring out a totally unsuspected anthropological doctrine. At first, Jean-Jacques devotes his energies to the general problems of his time. To treat them adequately, he is forced to move from his own limited experience to the wider experiences of other authors. The move led to a confrontation of his ideas with the book-learning of others. Rousseau documented himself scrupulously; we have already noted his assiduity. Not that he has no originality of his own. But he plunges into the popularizers of Plato, the works of the stoics, Malebranche,

Hobbes, the rich voyage literature of his time, and eventually the philosophic school of natural law. This preparation does not differ greatly from that of his contemporary philosophes—Diderot, for instance, or Condillac or Helvétius. Though he displays an originality of his own, a creative imagination superior to many of his friends, and a depth of knowledge greater than many, he had become only another philosophe. From 1750 to 1756, he does not show too many signs of deviation from his philosophe friends. As Hubert showed, he makes some special efforts to hold them as his friends. Even the retreat to Montmorency provided peace and quiet for the elaboration of a political and moral philosophy. Rang notes that down to 1762, there was no great divergence between Rousseau and the others. He works at the history of the human heart, reflects upon justice and freedom in society, undertakes the solution of some problems in education, and establishes an anthropology.

ORGANIC UNITY IN THE ENCYCLOPÉDIE

THE rapid development in the natural sciences, in history, politics, and in psychology, that is to say, in the human sciences, during the first half of the century made a general inventory of knowledge imperative. This need became all the more urgent since the century believed implicitly in the solidarity of the sciences and the unity of knowledge. Diversity of thought, as well as of method, threatened this essential solidarity. Moreover, certain authors, in process of accumlating information had apparently lost their way, and those who held steadfastly to the paths they had chosen were continually harassed by the authorities. A situation was created in which it became imperative to seek means, not only for coordinating the new knowledge, but for organizing, classifying, and, above all, making it useful. It was just as important that a "société de gens de lettres" be organized where the persecutions could be resisted more successfully by the group and a counter-attack could be mounted. It was in answer to these needs that the *Encyclopédie* (1751–1780) was published.[1]

From the first, the work aimed to bring up to date in usable form the sum total of the achievements of the human mind. Diderot proclaimed its object in the article *"Encyclopédie"*: "Le but de l'encyclopédie," he wrote, "est de rassembler les connaissances éparses sur la surface de la terre; d'en exposer le système général aux hommes avec qui nous vivons, et de le transmettre aux hommes qui viendront après nous, afin que les travaux des siècles passés n'aient pas été des travaux inutiles pour les siècles qui succèderont; que nos neveux, devenant plus instruit, deviennent en même temps plus vertueux, et plus heureux, et que nous ne mourions pas sans avoir bien mérité

---

[1] The history of the *Encyclopédie* has been related at intervals during the last one hundred years, the most recent having appeared only in 1965. The accounts do not differ greatly, but they have been refined with the appearance of new documents, chiefly letters and reports from the Librairie. Also, interest in certain particular details has shifted along with the change of direction of eighteenth-century studies. The outstanding books which have dealt with the subject are: P. Duprat, *Les Encyclopédistes* (Paris, 1866); L. Ducros, *Les Encyclopédistes* (Paris, 1900); J. P. Belin, *Le Mouvement philosophique de 1748 à 1789* (Paris, 1913); J. Le Gras, *Diderot et l'Encyclopédie* (Amiens, 1928); J. Proust, *Diderot et l'Encyclopédie* (Paris, 1962), and J. Proust, *L'Encyclopédie* (Paris, 1965). The last two works contain excellent bibliographies as well as full and clear presentations of the subject.

du genre humain." Diderot could not have expressed more clearly that what one knows is what one is, that knowledge is the source of moral virtue, which in turn is the mainspring of human happiness, and that human happiness consequently has its origin in the human mind.

These ideas were not new, however; they had been developing since the early Renaissance, as we have already seen, and perhaps they could be traced still further back. The *Encyclopédie* was thus not, as Diderot said, without ancestors, the two early ones being Ringelbert's Latin *Kuklopaideia* (1529) and Alsted's *Encyclopedia* (1630). The greatest of these ancestors, however, which we have already treated at some length, was undoubtedly Bayle's *Dictionnaire historique et critique* (1697). Two of Bayle's contemporaries, Leibniz and Locke, had spoken of the need for some sort of depository for the developments of philosophy, one emphasizing that a collection of researches in natural sciences would be extremely useful, while the other noted that a philosophical compendium would be most useful. More specifically still, the Abbé Prévost in the *Pour et contre* (IV, 135) recommended that Chambers's and Harris's dictionaries should be translated into French. The philosophical material was eventually supplied in the *Historia critica philosophiae* of Brucker (1742, 5 vols.), but this need for a compendium in philosophy had already been heeded in France with the publication of the *Histoire critique de la philosophie* of Boureau-Deslandes (1737, 3 vols.), and for the sciences with Pluche's *Spectacle de la nature* (1732–1750, 9 vols.). In all this fermentation of science, philosophy, and history, the *Encyclopédie* was greatly aided by the widespread development of local as well as national academies. Dijon, Besançon, Châlons-sur-Marne, Bordeaux, Béziers, and Montpellier all made significant contributions to the furthering of the *Encyclopédie*. It is true that these provincial academies were strictly limited in their philosophical content and their scientific activities, but they did nonetheless serve, as Proust has stated (p. 26), to develop men of talent, to encourage the taste for knowledge, and to multiply the intellectual contacts between the amateurs and the scholars as well as between France and the other European nations.

The suggestion of a French *Encyclopédie* was made to the Parisian printer Le Breton by Sellius in January 1745. The project then consisted merely in translating and printing the *Cyclopedia* of Ephraim Chambers. A contract was drawn up by Le Breton, uniting Sellius and the Englishman Mills in an enterprise to translate the Chambers. The going was not entirely smooth, however. Mills, who started out by being enthusiastic, became involved in a violent discussion with Le Breton within the year, and the two parted company. Sellius drifted off after Le Breton quashed the contract, but Le Breton by this time had been persuaded that a French translation of Chambers was warranted. He accordingly entered into an understanding with his associates in the printing of James's *Medicinal Dictionary* to bring out a French Chambers. A new privilege was granted in January 1746. It was apparently this move which brought Diderot into the affair, since he had been engaged with Eidous and Toussaint in translating the James for Le Breton. He received some payments in February 1746, but D'Alembert's name appears as early in the accounts as December 1745. Neither, however, was entrusted with the managing of the enterprise at first. That assignment was given to Gua de Malves, an Abbé at the Sorbonne, in June 1746. Diderot and D'Alembert witnessed the document, but their job consisted in translating only. Diderot's engagement was justified because he had proved to be a competent translator; D'Alembert is thought to have been appointed because he was a mathematician of distinction and a member of the Académie des Sciences. What happened in the early months is unknown, but on 3 August 1747, the publishers broke the contract with Gua de Malves and on 16 October 1747, Diderot and D'Alembert were invited to take over the management. A third "privilège" was issued on 30 April 1748. It was not stipulated that the work was to be a translation of Chambers, Harris, Duche, and others, but it was now to have "augmentations." It had already been included in the second "privilège" that the translation of Chambers was to have "additions." The first "privilège" did not specify that it was to be a translation but merely stated the title was to be *Dictionnaire universel des sciences et des arts.* We have assumed that the original intention of translating Chambers was changed at the suggestion of Diderot and D'Alembert, but that assumption is unwarranted. At all events, the two editors worked strenuously between 1748 and 1750 to put some order into the translations and to accumulate a working library. However, with the *Lettre sur les aveugles* of 1749 and its ungenerous reference to D'Argenson's mistress, Diderot who, it appears, was being watched by the police from 1746 on, was imprisoned in Vincennes. The publishers requested his release with some urgency and on 5 November 1749, after 102 days of imprisonment, he was released. Since all progress had ceased with Diderot's confinement to Vincennes, it has been assumed that he was now the head man. This could have well been the case. At all events, it was he who brought out the "prospectus" in November 1750, in which he announced an eight-volume *Encyclopédie* with 600 cuts in two volumes. Diderot stressed the novelty of the enterprise as well as a new organization of knowledge, and played up the collective nature of the venture. The "prospectus" occasioned some discussion between Berthier of the *Journal de Trévoux* and Diderot. It probably did nothing more than publicize the work. The first volume appeared in June 1751 and the second followed before the end of the year. Meanwhile the Abbé de Prades, who was a contributor to the second volume, presented on 18 November 1751 his thesis for the doctorate in theology at the Sorbonne. The thesis was accepted and De Prades was granted his degree when a certain member of the jury named Lerouge read it. Properly scandalized, he called it to the attention of the other members of the jury who, it appears, had not been doing their homework, either. The faculty censured the work, which was found to contain ideas repeated in the *Encyclopédie*, Volume II. The archbishop of Paris issued a mandement against the thesis, the *Encyclopédie*, and other works which spread impiety in the public. The *Journal de Trévoux* attacked Diderot's article "Autorité politique," and Berthier, the director of the *Journal*, insisted upon the articles which were plagiarized. De Prades's article "Certitude" was roundly denounced. On 7 February 1752, the *Encyclopédie* was suspended, and an order was given to seize the manuscripts and the cuts assembled for subsequent volumes. In the past, the interpretation given to this act was that the government had become hostile. Now there is a tendency to justify the procedure by explaining that the government actually intervened to prevent the Jesuits from taking over the material. The Abbé de Prades fled to Potsdam, and two other abbés, Yvon and Pestré, also left. D'Alembert threatened to retire from the undertaking but finally decided to stay on. Diderot didn't exactly help matters with his *Apologie de l'Abbé de Prades* or rather a *Suite* to the Abbé's defense. Nonetheless, Volume III appeared in October 1753, and a volume per year appeared until Volume VII in 1757. There was every indication that the work was progressing satisfactorily. The contributors comprised some of the outstanding writers; Buffon announced his willingness to contribute, as did Montesquieu and Voltaire. The subscribers had increased greatly, and were now at the maximum. There was still opposition. The friends of the enterprise (Voltaire, for instance) found that not all the contributors were first-rate; even Diderot acknowledged that the work was very uneven. Fréron became an incessant and caustic critic. No one, however, could have suspected what lay in store for them when Volume VII appeared.

This volume contained an article upon Geneva written by D'Alembert. It was, by and large an innocuous performance, or so it seems to us, but D'Alembert had visited Voltaire in Les Délices as a preparation for his article. Voltaire had certainly suggested to his friend that the Calvinist ministers had become "Sociniens." Nonetheless, these Calvinists still abhorred the theatre and would not permit one within the city. We have never been able to determine whether Voltaire's act was sincere or not. It is possible that he felt sincerely that the Calvinist ministers were rationalists. He knew, in fact, some who were unduly liberal, or who talked with him—Bertrand, Vernes, or Polier de Bottens—as if they were. As for the matter of a theatre in Geneva, it is likely that Voltaire resented the Genevan authorities' criticism of his own private theatre at the Délices and he was now using some ill-timed diplomacy to express a pet peeve. The result was not totally surprising: the Genevans resented both points of view. Tronchin encouraged Rousseau, who had now become famous because of his two discourses and who had abandoned Paris for the open country, to undertake a reply to D'Alembert. The immediate result was the *Lettre à d'Alembert sur les spectacles*, which elicited from D'Alembert an equally lengthy reply. D'Alembert again became uneasy in his post. Rousseau, who since 1756 had been drifting away from Diderot and the philosophes and had entered into discussion with Voltaire by publishing his *Lettre sur la Providence*, now consummated his break with Diderot. Thus disarray entered the encyclopedic group. Worse was yet to come. Helvétius published in 1758 his *De l'Esprit* with the approval of his censors. It raised a furor and Helvétius was forced to recant on three separate occasions. It was denounced as scandalous by the authorities, while Voltaire, Rousseau, and Diderot wrote refutations. The Jesuits and the Sorbonne tied its doctrine of personal interest to the *Encyclopédie*. On 5 January 1757, Damiens had attempted the assassination of Louis XV, and Parlement began to talk about the effect of these "livres tendencieux." On 22 November 1758, the archbishop of Paris presented his "mandement" against the *De l'Esprit*. On 23 January 1759, the Parlement of Paris condemned the *Encyclopédie*, and on 8 March 1759, a decree in the Conseil du Roi revoked its "privilège." It was at this time (January 1759) that *Candide* began to roll from the European presses. We know of eighteen different editions in French dated 1759.

The suppression of the *Encyclopédie* this time continued until January 1766, when the suspension was temporarily removed and the last ten volumes were made available to the public, first in the provinces and abroad, then in Paris. From 1762 on the plates had been distributed. Some sort of understanding had been arranged between Diderot and Malesherbes, the directeur de la Librairie, in which the former was permitted to assemble his manuscripts and plates and continue his printing. When Malesherbes gave up the librairie in 1763, he was succeeded by Sartine who was a friend of Diderot. What actually saved the *Encyclopédie* after 1759 was Diderot's persistence in continuing the work in France and Malesherbes's unbelievable fairness in protecting it. What threatened its destruction from 1758 to 1762 was the absolute disarray of the encyclopedists, the bitter attack of the dauphin's party, and the constant denunciations of people like Fréron and Palissot. What worked in its favor was the decline and finally the suppression of the Jesuits after the attempted assassination on the Portuguese king in 1759, which had involved them. On 1 April 1762, Parlement, oriented toward Jansenism, closed the Jesuit schools and on 6 August 1762, a decree of Parlement condemned the whole Society. The years from 1758 to 1762 thus became the most crucial period of the Enlightenment, when the future of the European world turned upon the outcome of these struggles around the *Encyclopédie*.

The *Encyclopédie* produced three results: it definitely organized the knowledge of the eighteenth century; it created a relatively compact organization of the more liberal thinkers of the time; and, lastly, it welded the political, social, and religious doctrines and theories into a more or less organic whole.

The task of classifying the knowledge of the *Encyclopédie* fell to D'Alembert, who divided the work into two parts: an encyclopedia and a dictionary of knowledge. "Comme encyclopédie," he wrote in the *Avant-propos*, "il doit exposer autant qu'il est possible l'ordre et l'enchaînement des connaissances humaines; comme dictionnaire raisonné, il doit contenir sur chaque science et sur chaque art les principes généraux qui en sont la base, et les détails les plus essentiels qui en font le corps et la substance." In exposing the order and relationship of the various sciences which make up the body of human knowledge, he accepted as the unity of his scheme the theory of the sensations. D'Alembert asserted that all ideas, taking their origin in the sensations, are subjected to three faculties of the mind: the intellect, appealing to memory, preserves them; the faculty of reason combines them; imagination imitates them. The results of the three processes of the mind are the three major divisions of knowledge: history, philosophy, and the fine arts. Each division has three areas in which it works: religion, society, and nature. The application of each branch to each area will give various subjects for study. Philosophy, applied to religion, for instance, will give ontology; to man, logic; to nature, mathematics, and physics.

We are usually not averse to looking upon this organization of knowledge as a perfectly lifeless and uninspired attempt to bring the subject-matter of knowledge into unity or to preserve the unity which knowledge has always wanted to achieve. It would seem, on more careful examination, that D'Alembert's classification was much more vital than that. The insistence that the factor which controlled the whole development of knowledge was the human mind, while it seemed to be only a revival of aspects of stoicism and Epicureanism, was much more subtle. Moreover, the turn to rationalism, almost exclusive of other factors, guaranteed a greater importance accorded to certain subjects—psychology, for instance, for which there was not yet the word, and civilization (human science), which did not yet exist as a word either. More important still was the tendency to make knowledge more factual, more historical, and more scientific in a new sense and more philosophical in an organic way. These things are not mere rhetorical suggestions in D'Alembert's "Discours préliminaire"; they are, rather, very dynamic moves on his part.

On the other hand, the theoretical classification of D'Alembert, drawn from that of Francis Bacon, was, as all theoretical classifications tend to become, defective, but most of its defects grew out of the tendencies of the time. It nonetheless achieved two important results. It effectively coordinated all the then known fields of learning under sensations, and it established the relative importance of each field. That it was not as useless as modern criticism has attempted to affirm can be shown by the fact that Auguste Comte did not hesitate to use it as a starting-point for his system and that Taine admired it. The classification nonetheless still exists as an excellent example of the ultimate futility of establishing a unity of knowledge.

When completed, the *Encyclopédie* comprised seventeen folio volumes of text (1751–1765), eleven volumes of cuts (1762–1772), five volumes of supplementary material, which was added under the direction of Panckoucke in 1777, and two volumes of Index printed in 1780; in all, there were thirty-five folio volumes. The associated publishers (Le Breton, Briasson, David, and Durand) worked under the general direction of Le Breton, but only for the original seventeen volumes of text and the eleven volumes of plates. The first edition ultimately comprised 4100 copies, but the earlier volumes were issued in smaller numbers. As the subscriptions grew after volume I from around 1000 to the full 4100 sets, some of the earlier volumes had to be reissued. It is probably for this reason that the remark is often made that no two copies are exactly alike. But there could be other reasons also. It should be borne in mind that the full *Encyclopédie*, including plates, supplementary material, and index is not a homogeneous work, although customarily it is treated as such.

There are other folio editions.[2] Panckoucke projected a new and revised edition as early as 1768. He consulted Diderot about the revisions to be made and received some forthright remarks. He also consulted Voltaire, who was apparently more forthright still. There are letters on this subject in the Besterman *Correspondence*. An announcement appeared in 1769 in the *Journal encyclopédique* re-

[2] For these editions see J. Lough, *Essays on the Encyclopédie of Diderot and D'Alembert* (London, 1968, Chapter I, "The Different Editions," and Chapter II, "The Panckoucke-Cramer Edition)."

ferring to this edition and promising that the work would be "entièrement neuf." Notices were printed also in the *Journal des savants*, Bachaumont, and elsewhere. In general, the publishers note the serious defects in the first edition, declare their intention to rectify its weaknesses, and announce that a subscription is being opened. At the same time, a competitive edition, which would be called the *Encyclopédie d'Yverdon* was disclosed, and a kind of open war was declared between the two publishers, M. M. Rey and De Felice. By 1770, Panckoucke had abanadoned his plan for a revised edition and decided to give a reprint of the original edition plus a *Supplément*. After the first three volumes were seized and stored in the Bastille, it became evident that there would be nothing but continual harassment. Panckoucke then entered into an arrangement with Cramer, and a new subscription was opened by Cramer in 1771. Sartine attempted to block it at the instigation of Christophe de Beaumont, archbishop of Paris. Hennin, the résident at Geneva, was consulted and replied that it was impossible to stop the printing except by appealing directly to the Conseil, and even then there was not much hope. And indeed, his opinion was well justified by the events. By 1776, the edition had been issued.

In the meantime, a third folio edition (17 volumes of text, 11 volumes of plates) was begun at Lucca (the text from 1758 to 1771, the plates from 1765 to 1776). It called down upon itself the condemnation of Pope Clement XIII in 1759. The edition pretended to remove all errors both factual and of a dogmatic nature, but the Pope's condemnation pointed out that it had not succeeded. Nonetheless, the editors did correct some factual errors, some articles were added, and refutations were appended to some articles. There was a second folio Italian edition comprising 17 volumes of text (published between 1770–1775), 11 volumes of plates (1771–1781) and 5 volumes of *Supplément* (1778–1779). This edition, printed at Leghorn, seems to have used some of the extra material in the Lucca folio edition. It was dedicated to the grand duke of Tuscany, brother of Marie Antoinette, who became Léopold II, following Joseph II as emperor. As his predecessor had been, he was an enlightened despot and encouraged the publication of the edition at Leghorn.

In addition to the three folio editions which with some rapidity followed the original Paris edition, there were several quarto editions, all of them of Swiss origin. The first was published by Pellet in Geneva, in 36 volumes, embracing in one text the contents of the original edition and the *Supplément* merged together. The first volume appeared in 1777 and was marked "Nouvelle édition." The following year, Pellet announced the publication of another edition which he called "troisième édition," and for this reprinting he associated with himself the Société Typographique de Neuchâtel. A notice from Neuchâtel explained that Pellet, fearing that the first two printings of the "new" edition would be delayed, had associated the Neuchâtel group with him for the third reprinting. The feature of this edition was the reduction in price (384 compared to 980 livres for the original Paris edition) and a drastic cut in the plates. The 36 volumes of text (completed in 1779) were followed by 3 volumes of plates, and, for those who wished it, 6 volumes of index (published at Lyons in 1780 and 1781).

In addition to the four folio editions and the three quarto editions (if not, in reality, three printings of the "new" edition), there were two octavo editions announced by the Société Typographique of both Lausanne and Berne. They were offered to the public at the modest price of 195 francs, for the 36 double volumes of the text and three quarto volumes of plates. The text used was that of Pellet's quarto editions; that is, it incorporated the supplement in the original text. It was issued in both places between 1778 and 1782.

Finally, we should mention the *Esprit de l'Encyclopédie ou Choix des articles,* published at Paris in 1768 (5 vols., in–12°). The work was also brought out in Geneva in two separate editions, also in 1768. The editors explained that they could not logically stick to selections from the arts, trades, abstract sciences, grammar, astronomy, geometry, medicine, surgery, jurisprudence, theology, chemistry, and geography. They stated that they had therefore directed all their attention to philosophy, morality, criticism, gallantry, politics, and literature. The instigator of these selections was the Abbé de la Porte. Professor Lough has noted that the work proved popular, since at least four more editions appeared by 1772. There was even a supplement entitled *Supplément à l'Esprit encyclopédique* (vols. VI and VII) in 1772. Another different selection of articles was published in 1769 under the title, *Histoire générale des dogmes et opinions philosophiques* (London, 1769, 3 vols.). While it is true, as Professor Lough states, that these selections do not all come from Diderot's contributions on philosophy to the *Encyclopédie*, they do seem to contain the major articles on seventeenth-century philosophers which he composed.

There remains only a word about the *Encyclopédie d'Yverdon* which, properly speaking, is not an edition, nor a reprinting, nor a selection. De Felice, however, does acknowledge that the *Encyclopédie* served as a basis for him. The Yverdon *Encyclopédie* was published in 58 quarto volumes between 1770 and 1780 (48 volumes of text, and 10 volumes of plates, 1775-1780).

In general, all of the editions of the *Encyclopédie* and its supplements and its abridgements were completed by 1780, the year in which the Index to the original edition and the supplement was brought out by Panckoucke. However, the encyclopedic tradition was furthered by the *Encyclopédie méthodique* (see G. B. Watts, "The Encyclopédie méthodique," *PMLA* 73, 1958: 348–66). The "Prospectus" appeared in the *Mercure* of 1781 (pp. 51–156). Panckoucke estimated that more than 20,000 sets of the various editions of the *Encyclopédie* were already in the hands of the public. He judged nonetheless that a new concept of the *Encyclopédie*, arranged as a system of special dictionaries by order of subject instead of the single alphabetical order of the previous one, would meet with popular approval. He listed the subjects to be treated separately as mathematics, physics, medicine, surgery, chemistry, agriculture, natural history, botany, mineralogy, geography, history, theology, philosophy, grammar and literature, law, finances, politics, economy, commerce, marine, military science, fine arts, and arts and handicrafts plus a volume upon universal vocabulary. The basic material was composed by cutting up sections from Diderot's *Encyclopédie* and redistributing them under the proper subject. Each separate section was to have a qualified editor in charge and a group of contributors. The three volumes of philosophy were directed by Naigeon, for example, who incorporated Diderot's philosophical contributions to the original *Encyclopédie* along with that of others. Panckoucke calculated that he would complete the work in about five years. Actually, it was not finished until 1832. By that time, the *Encyclopédie méthodique* comprised 166½ volumes of text, and 51 parts of plates. No one, so far as I know, has ever dared study it for its importance in the French intellectual movement from 1780 to 1830. Professor Watts, whose article mentioned above is the best introduction to the subject, ventures the opinion that "there is much good material to be explored in these unwieldy compilations." I might add that the Naigeon volumes on *Philosophie ancienne et moderne* have been extremely useful in Diderot studies.

From 1750 to 1780, the *Encyclopédie* was an active force in the intellectual life of Europe. If Panckoucke's estimate that there were 20,000 copies which were available in Europe throughout the time from 1750 to 1789, is correct, there is no way the work could have avoided having a tremendous influence upon the thought of its time. A really significant fact of consequence is that the material was available not only to the wealthy and the frivolous, but to all classes of society, except the illiterate and the indigent. It is true that these two groups were very large, but the widespread availability of the *Encyclopédie* to those who were literate and had only modest financial means would make it an instrument of great potential power in the formation of a European climate of opinion. We should not forget to mention that periodicals, especially the *Journal encyclopédique*, would at times reproduce those articles which were thought of particular interest to its public. Finally, we must note that when that climate of public opinion faltered in the Revolution, the *Encyclopédie méthodique* did much to preserve the encyclopedic tradition over the subsequent half century.

Proust has pointed out that the *Encyclopédie* is not only a book but a group of human beings, numerous and diverse, considered from a "société de gens de lettres," which was their original title. They were characterized by their collective enthusiasm in doing a good job. Diderot bore witness to their loyalty, particularly in those moments when the going was difficult. In the "Avertissement" to Volume VIII, after the *Encyclopédie* had been suppressed for eight years, he noted that the band grew closer together under the persecution and those who had stood aside at the beginning flocked to the aid of their colleagues. Finally, in the *Factum Au Public et aux Magistrats* following the Luneau de Boisgermain affair, he insisted that "la nation entière" was interested in the perfecting of the work and that assistance was even forthcoming from far-distant lands: "Nous nous trouvâmes en un instant," he wrote, "associés à ce qu'il y avait de gens habiles en histoire naturelle, en physique, en mathématique, en théologie, en philosophie, en littérature, en arts libéraux et mécaniques." This widespread interest seems to have obtained even in the days of J. Mills who wrote to Birch of a "société" of "personnes qualifiées." He was especially impressed by the aid given by the académies and "tous les hommes de lettres." He particularly mentions Réaumur, Pluche, Jussieu, D'Alembert, and Fouchy, the secretary of the Académie Royale des Sciences. This particular reference discloses how closely together Réaumur, Pluche, Jussieu, and D'Alembert were, even before the project was undertaken. In fact, it has been pointed out that Diderot acknowledged that much of the preliminary organization of personnel had been achieved before he had taken over. He noted that Formey's papers, which had been assembled in view of composing a philosophical dictionary, had been purchased by the publishers.

Since it is manifestly difficult nowadays to command all the material in the *Encyclopédie*, it has become rather common practice to approach its content in one of three ways: through the status of the contributors, through the key articles, or through one of the key categories. In the more recent past, the tendency has been directed to the status of the contributors. It is fairly apparent that Diderot thought of them as a "société de gens de lettres et d'artistes" who individually were each busied with his own particular field and who collectively were united by a general preoccupation with the human race. He confessed, though, that the group was composed of men of unequal talents and also of uneven status. The work had not progressed very far before there was a good deal of criticism about the unequal quality of the articles contributed, especially in the fields of religion and metaphysics. Voltaire was particularly vocal in these criticisms. Diderot was apparently well aware of these imperfections, too, but he deemed the best way to handle this difficulty was to furnish to each worker a general set of instructions. Proust maintains that this gently guided freedom which was imparted to the contributors accounts for the continual dialogue which is carried on throughout the work and even in each article. He notes that the first impression is that the group was rather heterogeneous in nature. However, they are all people of property, especially parlementarians, intendants, financiers, lawyers, and merchants. There is no great distinction, however, to be made between nobles and bourgeois. D'Alembert from the first insisted that princes had the right of admission to the group only through the ability of each to make a contribution to knowledge. Despite this assertion there were differences in status among the bourgeois—Voltaire had 200,000 livres income, while Rousseau copied music to make a living. Proust maintains, though, that even this difference in financial status was secondary. What united these diverse individuals, he suggests, was a common desire to be useful, productive, and creative. I would add that they were seized with the ambition to release within man his pent-up power. But this ambition can be exaggerated, too. The encyclopédiste differs on the one hand from the aristocratic courtier and on the other from the peasant and laborer in that if they contribute to the *Encyclopédie*, they do so, in general, anonymously. Under these conditions, the contributors leave the appearance of being a middle-class rather than a burgher class. They are administrators in the government (Boulanger, Desmarets, Bourreau-Deslandes, Turgot), scientists of repute (D'Alembert, Holbach), or doctors (Bordeu, Tronchin). Some are artists (Watelet, Goussier, Blondel) and an indiscriminate number are "gens de lettres" (Voltaire, Marmontel, Rousseau, Diderot), grammarians (Beauzée, Dumarsais), and theologians (Yvon, Polier de Bottens, De Prades). It is perhaps intelligent to see in them a "bourgeoisie encyclopédique" rather than a "bourgeois d'Ancien Régime," characterized by its social activity rather than by its economic status. They could thus call to their assistance men of good will from outside the limits of Paris and, in some cases, outside the limits of France. It was because of this peculiar quality that the *Encyclopédie* could identify with itself a whole body of previous works and could claim as its own extension a long list of subsequent works. This claim, in fact, was the cause of much of its misery. But it was also the source of much of its "rayonnement."

While investigation concerning the status of contributors has proceeded in the last two decades in depth, it is still apparent that the encyclopedists are consistent in their enthusiasm to impart specific knowledge and in their confidence that this knowledge will be advantageous in criticism, reform, and artistic creation; they do not belong to a specific class, but come from all three classes. They do not represent, however, class attitudes. The nobility do not represent the court nobility, the bourgeois, who have always been thought to have dominated the attitude of the group, are not typical of the bourgeois of the Ancien Régime, and the workers are not (both farmers and factory hands) spokesmen for the working class. It would be impossible to point out a consistent doctrine for any class in the *Encyclopédie* and least of all for the proletariat. In the strictest sense, each contributor is talking for himself about a subject where he has presumably some competence, and where his personal status is not considered important. To the further question as to who read the *Encyclopédie*, we can only give a general reply. Since literacy was anything but high between 1751 and 1780, it is fairly obvious that many could not read the *Encyclopédie*, simply because they could not read. Since it was issued by subscription in all the editions we know, it is obvious that even those who could read were not always sufficiently wealthy to afford a set, although the price ranged from around 900 francs to 195. Obviously, special efforts were made to issue the text at lower prices, and to issue editions of selections from the *Encyclopédie*. Periodicals would also publish or discuss an article. It can be surmised that the *Encyclopédie* was available to a wider public than would be normally expected. But it is inconceivable that the reading public for the work belonged to a specific class. That the readers were predominantly nobles possessing well-furnished libraries or that they were well-heeled bourgeois who could afford the relatively high subscription price or even the reverse—that there would not be a number of readers among the working class—are assumptions that cannot be justified. We just don't know what was the sociological impact of the work among the three classes. We have nonetheless asserted that its "rayonnement" was large, not only in the French public, but in England, Italy, Switzerland, and Germany, without knowing too much about specific examples of this renown.

The general tendency of students of the eighteenth century in France is to still revert to a selection of key contributors or of key articles or, at times, a choice of articles in accordance with movements of ideas. Hence we have such studies as *Diderot et l'Encyclopédie* (Proust), *Voltaire et l'Encyclopédie* (Naves), and *Rousseau et l'Encyclopédie* (Hubert). Bélin's book, *Le Mouvement philosophique en France de 1748 à 1789*, attempts to give a synthesis of the philosophical ideas which developed from the *Encyclopédie* among certain of its followers. These are very good studies, and others could be mentioned. We should add, nonetheless, that this material is massive, and our control of it is limited. And yet, if we are ever to understand how the Revolution, as has often been assumed, took its origin in the *Encyclopédie* which preceded it, we have to obtain a clearer understanding first as to whether it did and, if so, how it accomplished this task. It hardly will suffice to adopt the key article method: to recall that Diderot wrote the "Prospectus"; D'Alembert, the "Discours préliminaire"; Voltaire, the article "Histoire"; D'Aubenton, the article "Nature"; Rousseau, the article "Economie politique"; Diderot, the article "Authorité politique"; Turgot, the article "Progrès"; and so on. It is certainly advisable to know these facts as well as the content of these articles. There is some further advantage in studying the various categories (religion, politics, economics, esthetics, morality) in the *Encyclopédie* along the lines practiced by R. Hubert in *Les Sciences sociales dans l'Encyclopédie*, or even the development of certain branches, such as natural science, mathematics, psychology, and the like. Ultimately we are thrown back to the problem of the formation of the "esprit encyclopédique" and the role it played in revolutionary action, where fortunately we have the very solid work of Mornet. (See *Les Origines intellectuelles*, Paris, 1932.)

Although all of us have given the technical schematization of the *Encyclopédie,* it is likely that the *Discours préliminaire* presents a point of view which has escaped us. The initial statement which D'Alembert pronounced was that there was a strict solidarity between the sciences and the arts and that they aid each other mutually. Moreover, he points out how difficult it is to reduce each science and each art to a small number of rules or general notions and to integrate them into a true system, and finally to bring together the infinitely varied branches of human science. Hence, it would seem that it was certainly D'Alembert's aim to give some sort of unity to the field of knowledge, and he had a prearranged method for doing so. It is this program of procedure which we shall try to bring out here.

Knowledge for D'Alembert is of two sorts, direct and reflective. Direct knowledge is received immediately without any intervention of our will. Reflective knowledge is produced by the intellect through its capacity to organize the direct knowledge. Direct knowledge is the product of the senses, as we have seen. D'Alembert rejects innate ideas as everybody was inclined to do in his time, and assumes that the existence of the sensations and their effects cannot be questioned. For him, there are no notions purely intellectual which precede sensations. In fact, sensations reveal to each his personal existence, the first ideas always refer to ourselves; only the second have a reference to external objects. These sensations are multiple and yet there is an accord among them. There are also shades of difference which we distinguish in them, and they produce upon us an involuntary effect. Reflective knowledge, on the contrary, produces a voluntary effect. The conjoined effects persuade us that the objects we perceive actually exist. D'Alembert concedes that the mind is virtually overwhelmed by the quantity of its perceptions. What apparently keeps it in some sort of balance is the fact that the thing which we perceive most clearly is our own body. D'Alembert suggests that it attracts our attention so vehemently because it wants to be protected against external dangers. Pain is our feeling "la plus vive," and it forces us to choose that which is the most useful and to avoid that which is most dangerous. Thus we perceive many objects just like ourselves, and we unite with them because we assume communication and understanding with them is possible. This communication is what leads to the formation of society. However, since each person cannot share equally in these privileges, inequality appears among men, and instead of advantages which are mutual, oppression occurs. This gives rise to injustice, moral good and evil, a natural law which is in every man, and all the positive laws which derive therefrom. The end of all this development is the clear notion of justice and injustice.

At this juncture, we begin to ask what is the principle which acts in us. D'Alembert defines it as "substance qui veut et qui conçoit." The "nous" which characterizes each is formed of two principles of different natures, so much so that the substance of matter has nothing to do with thinking and willing. Still, "nous" combines these two principles so tightly that there is a close correspondence between the two. And reflection upon the liaison of these two principles raises us to the conception of a Superior Being to whom we owe all that we are. His existence is proven by a "sentiment intérieur," by a universal consensus, and by the testimony of nature. D'Alembert concludes this development with a sentence which is a perfect summary of Voltaire's *Traité de métaphysique*: "Il est donc évident que les notions purement intellectuelles du vice et de la vertu, le principe de la nécessité des lois, la spiritualité de l'âme, l'existence de Dieu et nos devoirs envers Lui, en un mot les vérités, dont nous avons le besoin le plus prompt et le plus indispensable sont le fruit des premières idées réfléchies que nos sensations occasionnent." He notes, however, that through these "vérités" and realities, the body has needs which make themselves felt. Science exists to gratify these needs of the body. It is this state of affairs which gave rise to agriculture, medicine, and "les arts les plus absolument nécessaires." It is at this point that D'Alembert attempts a short account of the organization and development of primitive life. He argues that the search for accommodating our needs leads us to an infinite number of discoveries which do not actually relieve our needs, but do contribute to our pleasures, and to our curiosity—two of our strong passions. Hence we conclude, he says, that these discoveries may one day be useful to us. With this expectation, we continue to notice other properties in bodies: movement, impenetrability, extent. D'Alembert derives from these properties the various kinds of mathematics: geometry, arithmetic, and algebra. He then deduces the idea that mathematics, being abstract, is not in itself useful except insofar as it applies to the objects in nature which are. This is the origin of mechanics, which is useful, as well as all mathematical-physical sciences, astronomy, and physics, both general and experimental. All knowledge in the *Encyclopédie*, as D'Alembert sees it, starts with two limiting influences: (1) the idea we have of ourselves which leads to God and to our duties, and (2) mathematics and its use in defining bodies and thereby establishing science. Between these two limits there is an immense interval which attracts our curiosity, but it is in reality hidden from us. Even the nature of man is "un mystère impénétrable à l'homme même." We are ignorant of our existence both present and future, the essence of the Suprême Being, and what He demands of us. We live in a world in which the Deity is a hidden God, nature is a hidden Nature, Man is an enigma to himself, and the Universe is masked in its past and its future. It is for this reason that we must have a revealed religion to tell us how to act. It, too, is strictly limited, telling us what it is absolutely necessary to know and concealing the rest. In fact, all it furnishes us is "quelques vérités à croire" and "quelques préceptes à pratiquer." D'Alembert nonetheless maintains that the common man understands these things better than the philosopher.

Mathematics is equally restricted in furnishing useful knowledge, although it is true that increased knowledge in the sciences tends to simplify our knowledge: "L'univers, pour qui saurait l'embrasser d'un seul point de vue, ne serait, s'il est permis de le dire, qu'un fait unique, et une grande vérité." Unfortunately, nobody can embrace it "d'un seul point de vue," or rather nobody has yet succeeded in doing so.

D'Alembert now takes up the growth of human sciences as they develop along with the natural sciences, but he hardly does more than define them. Logic is the art of putting thoughts in order and finding ways to communicate them. It leads to the invention of language, which develops grammar, eloquence, and eventually history, geography, and chronology. History confines itself to the study of how societies have been formed, the different kinds of government, the different kinds of laws. And thus it leads to politics which is "une espèce de morale d'un genre particulier et supérieur, à laquelle les principes de la morale ordinaire ne peuvent quelquefois s'accommoder qu'avec beaucoup de finesse." The objective of this study is to penetrate the workings of the state and to untangle what preserves it from what weakens or destroys it. This is the most difficult of studies, because it requires a profound knowledge of peoples and men. Philosophy, for its part, is concerned with "idées directes" and their combination and comparison.

D'Alembert now turns to "reflective ideas"—those which "nous nous formons à nous-mêmes en composant des êtres semblables à ceux qui sont l'objet de nos idées directes." This leads to the problem of imitation in art, Dubos's attenuated emotions in imitation, and thence to the fine arts themselves. D'Alembert concludes this part with the statement that all knowledge can be designated as being speculative or practical. These two terms serve to distinguish between sciences and arts, but there are other distinctions, because with much knowledge, he says, speculation and practice go together. He defines art as "tout système de connaissances qu'il est possible de réduire à des règles positives." There are two kinds of rules, those for the mind as well as those for the body, which give rise to liberal arts and mechanical arts. From this knowledge, which consists in imitation, are derived all the arts: printing, sculpture, architecture, poetry, and music, which bespeaks both the imagination and the senses.

This completes the enumeration of those subjects which embrace the total of our knowledge. It can easily be seen that they are either practical, speculative, or imitative; practical in the sense that they have as aim the execution of something human, and speculative in the sense that they are restricted to the examination of their goal and the contemplation of their properties. Speculation and practice are the two factors which distinguish between sciences and arts. However, in the arts, our ideas are not especially clear as to their designation, in the first place because it is possible to define arts as "tout système de connaissances qu'il est permis de réduire à des règles positives, invariables et indépendantes du caprice." This definition would permit us to incorporate some of the sciences into the arts. It is this situation which has occasioned the division of "arts libéraux" and "arts méchaniques." D'Alembert, as all the encyclopédistes, protests our tendency to consider the "libéraux" superior to the "méchaniques."

When Volume III of the *Encyclopédie* was issued, following the incident of the Abbé de Prades, Diderot added an "Avertissement" in which he gave further details of the encyclopedists' intentions in the matters treated and the people to whom the work is directed. Diderot stressed that knowledge is of two sorts. The first encompasses those things which men acquire through reading and ordinary communication in society. Diderot calls this kind "science des faits" and he notes that it is very extensive and often very useless. The second kind consists in those ideas which men produce for themselves through their own reflections. This kind, he says, is very necessary but very limited. However, he expresses the opinion that if a way could be found to put the two kinds together intelligently in the *Encyclopédie*, it should be both useful and not too large. One of his ways of cutting down on size, he states, is to omit many important names while keeping intact articles on history and mythology because they are essential to sects of philosophy, different religions, ancient and modern manners and customs, all of which contribute much to philosophical reflection. Here Diderot interjects that in his opinion philosophy is more important than the Church Fathers.

However, in the presentation of philosophy, he notes that he has treated biographies only scantily, and devoted the space to the history of thought. Implied in these remarks is the firm intention to make of the *Encyclopédie* a history of ideas. That is what philosophy has now become.

The *Encyclopédie* has also wanted to give the genealogy of the sciences, not the genealogy of saints and great geniuses who have enlightened man, and certainly not of conquerors who have destroyed him. It thus aims to be the history of the human mind "et non de la vanité des hommes." It is rather remarkable how these explanations coincide with Voltaire's remarks upon the meaning of history.

Diderot next reiterated more or less what he had tried to convey in the *Prospectus*: an *Encyclopédie* is at the same time a dictionary and a treatise of everything which the human mind may wish to know. As a dictionary, it uses the alphabetical order, is composed of separate parts, and gives careful definitions. This insistence upon definitions is one of the strong points of the work, and it will show up again in the article "Encyclopédie." As a treatise, the work shows the relationships which objects have with each other, brings together separate parts into a synthesis, and enters into the details of a problem.

Diderot used the remainder of the "Avertissement" to add some indiscriminate views concerning his work. He confesses, for instance, that it has too much a tendency to follow closely Chambers, especially in history. This he deplores. As for the manner of presentation, he advises moving from simple facts to things, from ideas to reflections. He adds that a dictionary can be rich in physics and chemistry, but should be circumspect in matters concerning causation. He promises, for his part, to raise problems in useful matters—in medicine, for instance. He would also like to stress the metaphysics of science. As for metaphysics itself, he feels that the two earlier volumes have been too generous in their treatment of it, and promises to present in the following volumes only what is obviously true and useful: "c'est-à-dire, à très peu de choses," which was precisely the phrase coined by Voltaire. On the contrary, Diderot, for his part, promises to lay much stress upon articles in the arts. It is not difficult to see in these remarks a forecast of his own intellectual life as well as a policy for the *Encyclopédie*.

As far as the readers are concerned, Diderot confesses that he has attempted to avoid being too specialist or too erudite, and particularly he has wanted to be brief. In his opinion, the *Encyclopédie* is written for those who already know the elements of a subject. Consequently, he states that he will try to lay emphasis upon new material. He promises, though, that the work will carry fairly full extracts of the best works in each field. He expresses his conviction that a work of this sort ought to be in part an "ouvrage recueilli des meilleurs auteurs." This is rather important, because one of the constant criticisms offered was that it endlessly plagiarized the works of others. Diderot concedes that too much has been borrowed from previous dictionaries, but he offers no apology for using Brucker extensively. He admits that he has made no effort to correct the mistakes of his contributors, and insists that "chaque auteur est ici garant de son ouvrage." He insists that this is not exclusively a dictionary of sciences and arts, but a "dictionnaire économique, des métiers," scholastic philosophy, blazonry, and rhetoric. Finally, he notes that much criticism has been made of the work. He announces that all criticisms of a literary order are welcome, whether good or bad, provided they are not personal.

Volume VIII, the first of the last ten volumes of the *Encyclopédie* which appeared together in 1765, also carried an "Avertissement" by Diderot. The work has now been completed, and although he complains bitterly about the persecutions, the ignorance and fanaticism, and the envy and falsehoods which have dogged their efforts, he is a more mellow man, inclined to summarize what the ultimate aim has been, rather than the particular intentions. He asserts now that "le monde a beau vieillir, il ne change pas," a statement which contradicts completely his profoundest belief. He is still willing to concede that the individual is capable of perfecting himself, but he tends to believe now that the mass of the human race is neither better nor worse.

He confesses that the thought had often occurred that the *Encyclopédie* would have to be moved to a foreign land, but that he stayed in France through patriotism. He has nothing but praise for his colleagues "qui se sont empressés à nous seconder," while others have, under the persecution, joined the band. He speaks with particular warmth of the Chevalier de Jaucourt. He boasts now that one of the great novelties of the work lies in the plates and their descriptions, and he maintains there is an infinite number of articles on all the sciences. He then restates his policy:

Notre principal objet était de rassembler les découvertes des siècles précé-dens; sans avoir négligé cette première vue, nous n'exagérerons point en appréciant à plusieurs volumes in-folio ce que nous avons porté de richesses nouvelles au dépôt des connaissances anciennes. Qu'une révo-lution dont le germe se forme peut-être dans quelque canton ignoré de la terre, ou se couve secrètement au centre même des contrées policées, éclate avec le temps, renverse les villes, disperse de nouveau les peuples, et ramène l'ignorance et les ténèbres; s'il se conserve un seul exemplaire entier de cet ouvrage, tout ne sera pas perdu.

This is a very important statement. Diderot often uses the word "révolution" in the course of his work. It occurs with relative fre-quency, in fact, in the article "Encyclopédie." Very often, it means "change," but in this particular case, it clearly means what we under-stand by revolution; that is, something which tears civilization to pieces. But Diderot tacitly affirms that he does not believe that his work will produce that revolution. His work will preserve what is left of civilization after revolution has laid waste "our world." But it has greater capabilities, he now thinks. "L'homme le plus éclairé" he writes, "y trouvera des idées qui lui sont inconnues, et des faits qu'il ignore." Diderot expresses the pious hope that within twenty years, every line of the work will be popular. He adds: "C'est aux maîtres du monde à hâter cette heureuse révolution." This revolution is clearly not the destructive kind, it is, on the contrary, constructive, a change for the better. Diderot interjects that the security of the rulers depends upon the enlightenment of the subjects. He actually expects his work to "affoiblir cet esprit de vertige si contraire au repos des sociétées, et d'avoir amené nos semblables à s'aimer, à se tolérer, et à reconnaître enfin la supériorité de la morale universelle sur toutes les morales particulières qui inspirent la haine et la troublent, et qui rompent ou relâchent le lien général et commun." And in a sort of chant of victory, he proclaims,

Tel a été partout notre but,

convinced that the two things which make the happiness of societies are virtue and truth. But what if in "our world" it is really change and revolution which guarantee this happiness, and what if we really don't give a damn about virtue, which we always reject, and about truth, which we can never know?

Diderot's article "Encyclopédie" also goes into the matter of intention and structure in a very practical manner. He insists that a work of this kind cannot be performed by one man, or by an existing literary or scientific academy. He lists, to prove his point, the existing académies in Paris and the subject-matter each exploits. Française offers the French language, inscriptions, history, chronology, geography, and literature. Sorbonne offers theology, sciences, mathematics, natural history, physics, chemistry, medicine, and anatomy. Chirurgie offers surgery. Peinture offers painting, engraving, sculpture, architecture, and design. The University offers humanities, philosophy, jurisprudence, and typography. It would be manifestly impossible for one man to embrace all these subjects, which would normally make up a part of an *Encyclopédie*. Nor is it conceivable that any one academy would be competent to take over all these matters which, taken together, constitute the science of man. The only way it could be executed would be by a group of experts, each of whom would undertake articles in the field of his competence. Diderot refers to the composite task as "cultivating the sciences." He points out that there are two ways in which this can be done: by increasing the fund of knowledge through new discoveries, and by bringing into some sort of unified order the discoveries which have been made. He asserts that although academies cannot do the job, a "Société de gens de lettres et d'artistes" can. But the "Société" would have to be composed of men "liés par l'intérêt général du genre humain" and by a "sentiment de bienveillance réciproque." Government must stay out of the affair and the "Société" should work on a tight and limited schedule within which the task has to be completed. Otherwise the material will become obsolete before it is published. However, he observes, the change could be less severe and less noticeable in sciences and the liberal arts than in the mechanical arts.

Diderot next undertakes to discuss how things are discovered. He notes that observation and experimental physics multiply our knowledge of the phenomena, and that rational philosophy compares and organizes them. The whole operation produces additional knowledge, making necessary a new vocabulary which replaces the old obsolete vocabulary. While this is going on, a "revolution" occurs in the mind of man and in the national character. A new philosophy progresses by leaps and bounds; there is a tendency to shake off the yoke of authority; people begin to put their faith in reason; one now questions even Plato and Aristotle. "Certains genres de littérature qui, faute d'une vie réelle et de mœurs subsistantes qui leur servent de modèles . . . seront négligés." Others will be renewed. Diderot points out that Bayle, for instance, has lost ground in criticism and controversy, but gained ground in other areas, while the "philosophical spirit," or doubt, has made rapid progress with La Mothe, Boindin, Terrasson, and Fontenelle. He adds, though, that he who knows man's heart will always succeed. Diderot seems to identify that individual with the genius: "le génie ne connaît point les règles; cependant, il ne s'en écarte jamais dans ses succès." On the contrary, the philosopher knows only the rules founded on the nature of things which are immutable and eternal. He notes that the most uncommon knowledge of the previous century becomes more and more common from day to day, and man's mind is driven in a general movement toward natural history, anatomy, chemistry, and experimental physics. To produce the *Encyclopédie* which he envisages, one must begin by viewing his objectives in every possible angle; he must transcend the general movement of contemporary thought, be sure to work for future generations, and shorten rather than lengthen the time for completing the job. He must recognize, however, that knowledge can never become common save within limits. Diderot confesses that we do not know what these limits are, but he insists that he does know that "les révolutions sont nécessaires." They have always been, will always be. He subscribes to the principle of collective effort, and acknowledges that it can be very productive, while urging that "la masse générale de l'espèce n'est faite ni pour suivre, ni pour connaître cette marche de l'esprit humain." In his view, the *Encyclopédie* can never become on the whole a popular work, although the common man as well as the scholar can find therein things of interest. In fact, he adds, a real *Encyclopédie* will be particularly useful in moments of utter destruction. Diderot seems haunted by the inevitability of these moments of "utter destruction."

The one thing essential to the success of the *Encyclopédie*, he insists, is careful attention to the development of language which is needed to augment, invent, and communicate ideas. While it is true that philosophy is concerned primarily with the comparison of phenomena, the philosopher actually begins a general poetics which starts with language and embraces painting ("l'art de transmettre les idées par la peinture") which Diderot compares with language (in general the comparison of poetry and painting). This yearning for a poetic interpretation of philosophy, inaugurated by Voltaire, is also significant in Diderot's thought.

There now follows a whole body of instructions for the contributors. They must, for instance, define everything. They must recall that they, too, are "hommes créateurs" and as poets "portent ce caractère particulier." It is not in turning the pages of the productions of their contemporaries that they will discover the ideas that they have to use in their writings, but rather by profoundly descending into themselves, even bursting outside themselves and examining with care and penetration the nature which surrounds them. They are forced, especially in the early stages of language, to invent signs to render with precision and with force what they first discover. It is by means of the warmth of the imagination and profound meditation that a language is enriched with new expressions. The syntax is perfected by the precision of thought and the severity of the argument, and it is the ease of the organs of speech which softens it, and the sensitiveness of the ear which renders it harmonious. Diderot affirms that "on ne sait pas encore, ce me semble, combien la langue est une image rigoureuse et fidèle de l'exercise de la raison." He suggests that putting together families of words will avoid repetition.

There is a very long section given up to the problem of order, especially the best order ("enchaînement") one can give to knowledge. Diderot distinguishes several. There is, for instance, a general order, such as relating all our knowledge to the different faculties of our understanding. This was the Baconian order which was adopted by D'Alembert in the *Discours préliminaire*. Diderot concedes that there are many other ways of arranging an *Encyclopédie*, most of them being dialectical in nature. They all more or less conform to curiosity, to necessity, or to luxury. Knowledge may thus be organized according to the science of things and the science of signs, according to the science of abstracts and the science of concretes, or of art and nature, of the physical and the moral, of the existential and the possible, of the material or the spiritual, and of the real and the intelligible. All of this gets nowhere schematically, but it is an exceedingly important statement, since it marks not what the *Encyclopédie* was capable of achieving at the beginning, but what the Enlightenment actually did achieve before it reached its goal. Diderot, realizing that it was unrealistic to strive initially for an organic order composed of all the possible human orders, offers to look for an order which is simple and brings together objects quickly and easily. "C'est la présence de l'homme qui rend l'existence des êtres intéressante." Consequently, Diderot proposes placing man in the center of things: "Voilà ce qui nous a déterminé à chercher dans les facultés principales de l'homme, la division générale à laquelle nous avons subordonné notre travail." Thus, man is the focus from which all things take their start and the goal to which all things tend.

There are other problems of order, however, which have to be examined, the most important being the length of the articles and the division of the work. Diderot suggests that length of the articles might be assigned according to the subject treated: morality, mathematics, theology, jurisprudence, history, and natural history, but he seems loath to lay down any fixed and fast rules upon the matter, or even to insist that these are the essential categories of human existence. His observation is reduced to the practical statement that the contributors themselves have vague notions about the appropriate length of their subject, and must be left as free as possible to discover reasonable lengths. He nevertheless complains that he has far too many dissertations, far too few articles. Incidentally, this defect is apparent in this very article. The problem is not only crucial in the key articles, it occurs especially in those articles which deal with different parts of a subject, or sometimes with the distribution of articles in the same category. Diderot suggests that this order can be used schematically in passing from grammar to logic to metaphysics, to theology, to morality, and to jurisprudence. But even here he pleads for freedom to construct as one deems best. Nonetheless, there are a number of key concepts which each writer should consider: genre, specific difference, qualities, causes, uses, and so on. He also counsels "une énumération méthodique et rationelle des qualités." These suggestions have no great importance, however, since they are really possible ways of structuring the articles and the work as a whole, and the eighteenth century was not yet sufficiently experienced to undertake this task. What Diderot demands is some kind of order which will enable the reader to derive benefit from the article. It is much more modest. "D'ailleurs," he wrote, "un Dictionnaire est fait pour être consulté, et le point essentiel c'est que le lecteur remporte nettement dans sa mémoire le résultat de sa lecture." Of still more importance to him is the fact that every field of knowledge has a metaphoric bearing upon all other fields of knowledge. The contributor should be sufficiently alert to produce these transitions by the metaphoric route. Diderot sums up his thought:

Il est de la dernière importance de bien exposer la métaphysique des choses, ou leurs raisons premières et générales." He has given a succinct statement of all these things in a final paragraph: "Il faut donc s'attacher à donner les raisons des choses, quand il y en a; à assigner les causes quand on les connaît, à indiquer les effets, lorsqu'ils sont certains; à résoudre les nœuds par une application directe des principes; à démontrer les vérités, à dévoiler les erreurs; à décréditer adroitement les préjugés; à apprendre aux hommes à douter et à attendre, à dissiper l'ignorance; à apprécier la valeur des connaissances humaines; à distinguer le vrai du faux, le vrai du vraisemblable; le vraisemblable du merveilleux et de l'incroyable, les phénomènes communs des phénomènes extraordinaires, les faits certains des douteux, ceux-ci des faits absurdes et contraires à l'ordre de la nature, à connaître le cours général des événements, et à prendre chaque chose pour ce qu'elle est, et par conséquent à inspirer le goût de la science, l'horreur du mensonge, et du vice, et l'amour de la vertu; car tout ce qui n'a pas le bonheur et la vertu pour fin dernière n'est rien [p. 642^v].

For the moment, the ultimate goals of all structure as well as all content are happiness, utility, and virtue. But the only possible chance we poor mortals have of ever attaining that final goal is through the cultivation of a sound judgment, as can be seen in this lengthy statement.

We must speak of the references, what Diderot calls "partie de l'ordre encyclopédique la plus importante." Diderot distinguishes two kinds: "choses" and "mots," but he is not very explicit as to the result he hopes to obtain from this division. He does state, however, that they will always have the double function of either confirming or refuting, of conciliating or contrasting. They are, in short, a device, purely artificial, I think, to establish organic unity in the *Encyclopédie*, but Diderot has assigned to them a role of supreme importance. The goal which every encyclopedia must have is "changer la façon commune de penser," the remark which Cassirer adopted as the characteristic goal of the whole Enlightenment movement. The references thus become a kind of metaphor, too. Diderot says that they can be used intelligently by the man of genius: He explains very carefully what he has in mind (p. 643ᵛ): "Par le moyen de l'ordre encyclopédique, de l'universalité des connaissances, et de la fréquence des renvois, les rapports augmentent, les liaisons se portent en tous sens, la force de la démonstration s'accroît, la nomenclature se complète, les connaissances se rapprochent et se fortifient."

The remainder of Diderot's long article contains general exhortations and observations. He insists that everything must be examined, everything must be shaken up without exception. We must dare observe things, now that we see the necessity of doing so, recognize that certain genres of literature are like compilations of laws or the first foundations of towns. They owe their existence to some peculiar chance, to some strange circumstance, sometimes to a flash of genius. We must crush out all trivial things, overturn all obstacles which reason has not presented, and return to sciences and the arts the freedom which is so essential to them. Thereupon, Diderot examines his own *Encyclopédie* and passes judgment upon it. He finds that it is impossible for the first edition to have too many contributors, even if some of them are not first-rate. The second edition, he concedes, could dispense with many of them. It is perfectly natural, he concludes, for the first edition to be shapeless and incomplete. Notwithstanding, Diderot pronounces that there are some good qualities in the work: the introduction of the mechanical arts is wise, and there is a good collection of plates, as well as an excellent corps of writers and critics. Diderot acknowledges that he has found the library catalogues extremely useful, since they bring out those works which are essential for the advancement of the *Encyclopédie*. He urges that all remember that a universal dictionary exists for the instruction of mankind. Consequently, we must extract from the authors their systems, special ideas, observations, and experiences, their views, their maxims, and their facts. Since the objective is to make mankind better as well as more enlightened, we must include all things. But satire must not be used, what is wanted are more portraits, and many reflections.

Having seen in very explicit terms from the *Discours préliminaire*, the two "Avertissements" and the article "Encyclopédie" the ways the two leaders D'Alembert and Diderot understood the organization and the tendencies of encyclopedic thought and its relationship with the "pensée philosophique," we must turn now to certain particular articles which establish some methodological principles of approach. We shall examine two of these articles: "Evidence" and "Certitude." The article "Evidence" is central to the problem of the self as well as to the problem of truth, and above all to the problem of faith. As a matter of fact, the article begins by noting that there are two kinds of certainty: faith, which is closely related to evidence, and evidence which is "bornée aux connaissances naturelles." The author states that faith is taught to us by means of the senses; its dogmas cannot be demonstrated except by means of natural knowledge. It would be impossible to have any idea of the mysteries of faith without ideas of the objects of our senses; it would even be impossible to have any comprehension of what certainty, truth, and faith are without evidence. Without the lights of reason, revealed truths would be inaccessible to man. Hence, the only conclusion possible is that evidence must come from the personal observation of our own sensations. The definition of evidence is thus "une certitude à laquelle il nous est impossible de nous refuser, qu'il nous est impossible d'ignorer nos sensations actuelles." Hence all forms of pyrrhonism are expressions of bad faith.

How all this works in human nature has been detailed by the author in a step-by-step operation. It is certain he declares, that (1) our sensations disclose to us an existence which has the property of feeling, because it is evident that our sensations cannot exist except in a subject which has the property of feeling. (2) This property of feeling is entirely passive, through which our being feels itself. (3) This passive property is fundamental and essential to the feeling being; it is itself which is this property. (4) However, the particular sensations themselves are not essential to the feeling being because they are variable. (5) They exist in the feeling individual only insofar as they affect him immediately and consciously. (6) Only our sensations are known in themselves. All other knowledge is procured by essential relationships of sensations with external objects or with ourselves. (7) The sensitive being cannot cause any sensation to itself. These sensations are caused by a power which acts upon this sensitive being and which is really distinct from it. (8) The sensitive being is thus dependent upon the power which acts upon it, and is in reality subjected to it. (9) Without memory, there is no intelligence, no combination of ideas of the present and the past. It is this memory which gives the flow of ideas. (10) In the natural order of things, there is no way to attribute to the sensitive being permanent, customary, or innate ideas. (11) What we call bodies or matter are physical causes of all representative ideas of different affections of happiness, misfortunes, willing, passions, and all determinations of the sensitive being. Hence, these objects and these laws are the necessary causes of our feelings, our knowledge, and our will. (12) The sensitive being cannot change of itself the sensations it receives through the senses. (13) The representative sensations are different from each other essentially and constantly, and the sensitive being distinguishes these differences. (14) Judgment proceeds in the same way: "Juger n'est autre chose qu'apercevoir et reconnaître les rapports, les quantités et qualités." From which fact, one may conclude that sensations produce the judgments. But affirmations, negations, argumentations "manquent de l'action dans l'esprit." Sensations make us perceive two kinds of truth: (1) real truths and (2) speculative truths. Only real truths lead to certainty. Speculative truths have to be brought back to real truths in order to have any certainty.

One can only conclude that the evidence that our sensations produce in ourselves, which is proof of the existence of our being, and the evidence that reveals to us external bodies, which is proof of the existence of external bodies, is the same evidence. We are led to give credence to the fact that these sensations themselves and all the effects and all the changes which happen in bodies are produced by a First Cause, that it is the action of this First Cause which gives life to all living bodies, which constitute essentially all active, sensitive, intellectual forms; that the active and essential form of man, insofar as he is a reasonable animal, does not depend upon the relationship of body and soul of which he is composed, because these two substances cannot act upon each other by themselves. Consequently, it is useless to seek in the body or in the soul or in the two together the constitutive form of moral man, that is to say, the active principle of his intelligence, of his will, of his freedom, of his moral determinations, all those things, in fact, which distinguish men from brutes. These attributes result from the act of the first principle of all intelligence and of all activity, that is to say, the Supreme Being manifesting himself through the sensations. He "exécute ses volontés décisives, et élève l'homme à un degré d'intelligence et de force d'intention, par lesquelles il peut suspendre ses décisions, et dans lesquelles consiste sa liberté."

The final statement is extraordinarily important: "Les formes intellectuelles dans lesquelles consistent les liaisons, les rapports et les combinaisons des idées et par lesquelles nous pouvons déduire de nos idées actuelles d'autres idées ou d'autres connaissances, consistent, essentiellement aussi dans des actes de puissance, d'intelligence, et de volonté décisive; puisque ces actes sont eux-mêmes la cause constitutive, efficiente, et directrice de nos connaissances, de notre raison, de nos intentions, de notre conduite, de nos décisions." This is the clearcut statement, so evident everywhere in the Enlightenment, that what one thinks is what he says, what he wills to do, what he is. It goes much further than that, though. Everything which man knows, says, and does comes from God, who thus decides all human actions. This was Voltaire's conclusion, also.

"Certitude," which was written by De Prades, endeavors to draw a distinction between certainty and evidence. The author tries in the article to distinguish between intuition and logical development of thought. Evidence concerns ideas whose liaison is immediately perceived by the mind. It is a type of spontaneous understanding. Certainty, on the contrary, can be attributed only to those ideas whose liaison can be understood through the aid of a number of intermediary ideas. It is consequently more geometrical in its reasoning and far less spontaneous. Curiously, the author examines the method of arriving at certainty, not in mathematics, but in history. The real purpose of this article, in fact, is to lay down rules for proving the authenticity of historical phenomena. De Prades thinks there are four kinds of witnesses to the authenticity of a historical event: the witness presented by the contemporary of the event, that assembled in the oral tradition, history itself (by which he means the written tradition), and the monuments. The author takes pains to give some rules for proving the authenticity of a book. Notwithstanding these special considerations, the whole article adds up to a discussion of the critical procedures which will guarantee the authenticity of a past event; while the whole argument tends to incline to a defense of its authenticity, the effective result could well be the establishment of a critical method which could serve to prove its lack of authenticity. Diderot, for instance, had written in the *Pensées philosophiques* that if all Paris asserted that a dead man had come back to life, he would not believe it. The author of "Certitude" argues that it is not likely that everybody would be in error or in collusion to deceive. While the article seems perfectly orthodox, the attribution of error to this particular event or the suggestion of collusion certainly leads to the suspicion that the willful confusion between a historical event and a miracle must not have been an accident.

There were several articles in the *Encyclopédie* on "économie": one by Rousseau, which occurs under the title "Économie politique"; "Œconomie" attributed to the Chevalier de Jaucourt; and "Œconomie politique," which was rather long, taken from Boulanger.

Rousseau's definition of the term is more or less in accord with that given by De Jaucourt. Rousseau defines it as "sage gouvernement de la maison," which has been developed to mean "of the state." When so used, it is called "économie générale" or "public economy" and is equivalent to the term "government." But "government" does not mean "sovereignty." Nor is it precisely correct to consider that the ruler of the state is analogous to the head of the family. Rousseau grants that there is some similarity between the two, but he insists that there are also serious differences. The difference between government and sovereignty, he states immediately, is a distinction between right and power; right is concerned with legislation, power is concerned with execution. The legislator is preoccupied with making rules which justify right action; the sovereign has the task to see to it that the proper execution of these rules leads to the correct community response. Rousseau insists further that the body politic is analogous to the human body; it is "un être moral" which has a will of its own tending to the preservation and the welfare of the whole; it is the source of laws and the rules which discriminate between justice and injustice. Law is, as we have seen, a magic force which at the same time establishes, justifies, creates, and enforces laws. Laws, being precepts for right action, are both prescriptive rules and definitions of limits. Law, therefore, subjects men in order to insure their freedom, it uses all the power of the individual for the benefit of the group. It requires obedience but releases power, creates justice, secures freedom, and reestablishes in right the natural basis of equality of each individual. Law, therefore, makes no exception and gives no exemption. It speaks the general, common will of all. Rousseau understands in the "Economie politique" that it speaks through the legislator whose first duty is to see that the announced precepts (the laws) are in conformity with the general will and whose second duty is to see that the administration of the state is in conformity with the precepts. Consequently, only that government is legitimate which is sovereign because it expresses the general will and because it insists that the particular wills concur with the general will ("faire régner la vertu," he says); it establishes what is right action between the individual and the community by putting individual interest in correct relationship with the interest of the body politic. Specifically, the government provides for the preservation of each individual, it prevents extreme inequality of wealth, it maintains freedom which guarantees political virtue, and it trains each individual in the duties of citizenship. Nonetheless, the right of property is a sacred right, no taxation can be imposed without the consent of the citizen, and all taxation should be proportionate to the ability to pay and should fall on luxury articles, not necessities.

The article "Œconomie" defines economy as a "conduite sage que tient une personne en gouvernant son propre bien ou celui d'un autre." At first glance that doesn't seem to differ greatly from Rousseau's definition. On second glance, however, it is clear that the emphasis has been taken off the political and placed upon the "conduite," from the way we live in society to the way each acts as an individual. What the author tries to do is to show man, who seeks to penetrate into himself and to turn the torch of philosophy upon the well-springs of life and upon the mechanics of existence how to proceed in his investigation. De Jaucourt analyzes the functions of life and hopes thereby to explain man's manner of action and the effects of the passions. For him, it is clear that the problem is essentially moral.

The "Œconomie politique" is defined in Boulanger's article as "l'art et la science de maintenir les hommes en société et de les y rendre heureux." Three kinds of government are discussed: (1) the despotism, where authority resides in the will of one man, (2) the monarchy, where the sovereignty rest in one ruler tempered by laws and customs, and (3) the republic, where the people—or the highest class of people—reign. The author adds the theocratic government, which he presents as the earliest form of government from which the other three are derived. They are all bound by a continual chain of circumstances which include practically all the great revolutions that have taken place in the political and moral world. Boulanger distinguishes between the Mosaic theocracy and this much more primitive brand. In Boulanger's view, man adopted the theocratic state when he came out of the gigantic cataclysms of nature. Boulanger claims to have treated this matter "en historien," that is to say, he has tried to ascertain the state of mind of the primitives coming out of the age of the great cataclysms. He has sought the impressions these misfortunes have made upon their minds, their hearts, and their characters. In short, he has sought the "idées uniformes," the "sentiments communs," "la conscience commune," "la conséquente suite des actions," "la police et les lois" of these primitives, "leur culte et leur gouvernement." We should note that this is precisely the way all writers of travel literature proceeded. From this analysis, one can see that the theocratic government was the first with its good and evil, followed by the golden age, savage life, superstition and slavery, idolatry and despotism, the Jewish reformation, republics and finally monarchies. He judges monarchy the best, because it suppresses all prejudices.

An agricultural state led to a public economy and a domestic economy with a unity of principle, of goal, and action. Domestic laws were the model for public laws. Boulanger paints these societies ideally: "l'égalité brilloit, l'équité régnait; plus de tien, de mien," everything belongs to the community. He accepts the golden age as a reality. The primitives lived an innocent life in the midst of a desert. These are, he says, "les heureux effets des malheurs du monde."

But they could not last. The state was a religious community. Laws were made to preserve the golden age. A ruler was chosen, the "Dieu monarque." Fear for the end of the world arose. Boulanger's description of these activities, though, is made in terms, not of the Old Testament or Christianity, but in terms of paganism. Human sacrifice became general. God became the Conqueror, the Cruel God. In fact, this is, after all, a treatise on the rise of superstition, the creation of prejudices (XI, 373): "L'unité fut donc rompue; la religion, étant éteinte ou méconnue, une superstition générale en prit la place, et dans chaque contrée elle eut son étendart particulier, chacun regardant son roi et son dieu comme le seul et le véritable, détesta le roi et let dieu de ses voisins." This situation is what led to God's election of the Hebrews, and the "divine legation of Moses." As a result, the picture of a heavenly bliss gave rise to a false idea of freedom, equality and independence. God became so all-powerful that man was reduced to nothingness. There followed the formation of convents and monasteries. They injure the civil state and cause the enslavement of the masses but, above all, they gave rise to oriental despotism.

In due time, the despotic theocracy passed into a royalty. But "le passage of la théocratie à la royauté se cache." The king was regarded as the representative of "le Dieu monarque." That is the reason why the principle of oriental despotism is fear. One passes from the concept of the unity of God to the unity of one individual ruler.

The despotic government gave way to republican government and "republican spirit" thus grew from the ruins of the oriental despots. It was presented by the Greeks and Romans as taking its origin in the perfecting of reason. However, this explanation was a delusion. The republics were constituted upon the reestablishment of the principle of the "Roi monarque." The author nonetheless shows that the republic awaited the arrival or the return of the "Dieu monarque," the Messiah. The great vice of the republics was that "[elles] se disoient libres, et la liberté fuyoit devant elles; elles vouloient être tranquilles, elles ne le furent jamais; chacun s'y prétendoit égal, et il n'y eut point d'égalité." In reality, the republican government was never anything more than a theocracy with the people always divided into factions.

Democracy had the same vices and lacked unity. In fact, the numerous republics led to anarchy rather than to unity. Boulanger gives a violent condemnation of democracy: "Législateur, sujet, et monarque à la fois, tantôt tout, et tantôt rien, le peuple souverain ne fut jamais qu'un tyran soupçonneux, et qu'un sujet indocile, qui entretint dans la société des troubles et des dissentions perpétuelles qui la firent à la fin succomber sous ses ennemis du dedans, et sous ceux qu'on lui avait faits au dehors." Boulanger admits nonetheless that democracies had some admirable virtues.

In conclusion, though, his picture of universal history is anything but cheerful. The excesses of the despotism, the dangers of the republics, the falsity of these two types of government, both issued from a chimerical theocracy which will teach us, he says, a bit enigmatically, what we ought to think of a monarchy. It is, certainly, the type which, in his opinion, insures the greatest unity. Its principles are founded on man's nature, and made for this world. "L'honneur et la raison," which have given birth to it, are the true ideals of man. It is the only kind of government which guarantees human happiness: the "chef-d'œuvre" of human reason. And Boulanger adds a remark which doesn't exactly conform to reality but it appears that it does mark a growing tendency among the French people: "C'est là qu'il a trouvé des rois qui n'affichent plus la divinité." Boulanger concludes that this kind of monarchy is alone capable of fulfilling the goal of political science, which is to bring together men into a society and to provide for the happiness of the world.

The article "droit des gens" is important for the information it contains about a kind of law which was attempting at the time to become scientific. One of the great contributions to the political thought of the Enlightenment has been shown by Professor Derathé to have been made by those thinkers known as the school of natural law of politics who exercised their influence in a major way through the work of Rousseau. This article analyzes the work of three of the important members of this school: Grotius, Pufendorf, and Burlamaqui, leaving out only Barbeyrac and Christian Wolff. The author defines this "droit des gens" as a jurisprudence which natural reason has established on certain specific matters among all men and which is observed by all nations. He notes that it is distinct from natural law, but for man as distinct from animals, it deals with the same things founded on the natural light of reason. He compliments Grotius for the excellent things on this "droit des gens" which are to be found in his work, but he concedes that it is impossible to regard his treatise as a methodical presentation of this aspect of law. That's what induced Pufendorf, he says, to write his *De iure naturae et gentium*, which has been translated by Barbeyrac with some very useful notes of his own. It is at this point that the writer gives an analysis of Pufendorf, "rien n'étant plus propre à donner une juste idée des matières qu'embrace le droit des gens." The analysis is a good one. The author notes in conclusion that it involves good ("bienfaisance," which was St.-Pierre's great contribution) and evil ("mal"), the necessity of repairing any damage inflicted on another, the equality of all men, and a set of moral duties for all men. He adds (what we often forget) that the seventh book of Pufendorf "traite motifs qui ont porté les hommes à former des sociétés civiles, de la constitution intérieure des états, des diverses formes de gouvernement, des caractères propres et des modifications de la souveraineté, des différentes manières de l'acquérir, enfin, des droits et devoirs du souverain." This discussion is followed by an analysis of Burlamaqui.

The article "Droit des gens" is derived from the concepts contained in the subsequent article upon "droit naturel" defined as the principles which nature alone inspires and which are common to man as well as to animal. They are named, these principles: the union of male and female, the procreation of children, the education of the young, the love of freedom, self-preservation, and the methods of self-defense used against an enemy. The author adds to these "certaines règles de justice et d'équité, que la seule raison naturelle a établies entre tous les hommes" or that God has engraved in the heart of each. This law is presented as invariable and eternal. The author adds this important statement: "De ces idées générales que l'on vient de donner sur le droit naturel, il résulte que ce droit n'est proprement autre chose que la science de mœurs qu'on appelle morale." He maintains that this "science des mœurs" was known imperfectly by the ancients. In his opinion, Pythagoras, Socrates,

Plato, and Aristotle were all weak in "la morale," and Cicero, who was certainly the best moralist among the writers of antiquity, was not very good either. Among the moderns, he states, Grotius was the first to establish a system of natural law, followed by Selden, Hobbes, "un des plus grands génies de son siècle" (but he rejects Hobbism), Spinoza (whom also he rejects), and finally Pufendorf. The all-important relationship between "mœurs et lois," which was developed by Montesquieu and his followers, was a creation of the school of natural law and was fundamentally a moral problem essential to the science of man before it became the political problem essential to the science of politics.

The key article on history was written by Voltaire. We have discussed in another work the way in which history was developed from Bossuet, Bayle, and Fontenelle to Lenglet-Dufresnoy to Voltaire and Montesquieu. We have already shown that the subject comprised not only the manner of studying history, but the utility which the study of history can have for man. This advantage, Voltaire wrote, consists chiefly in the comparisons which a statesman or a citizen can make of the laws and manners of a foreign society with those of his own country. We have gone to great lengths to show that this was the calculated utility of the *Lettres philosophiques* where a liberal country was compared with one considered very conservative; where the author worked out in careful detail what aspects of a society are to be compared, and how the comparison is to be constantly pursued in each. Voltaire gave as an example the comparison of laws and manners of England with laws and manners of France. It was a new sort of history which he envisaged, but though he himself practiced it with great success, it became, with the development of the century, the accepted method of procedure (see Vol. I, Part II, " 'Mœurs,' 'Lois,' and Economics").

Voltaire discussed the problem of certainty in history, as did De Prades and Diderot. It had arisen with Bayle and Fontenelle long before Voltaire, De Prades, and Diderot returned to it, couching it in De Prades's terms. To what extent does one lend credence to an event not totally verifiable? Does he do so according to the number and quality of the witnesses who bear witness to its authenticity? In general, Voltaire is inclined to be rather skeptical about the authenticity of related events and totally suspicious of so-called recorded speeches or conjectural motives. He does think, however, that if a judicious amount of control can be exercised, some understanding of history is possible and that it is even possible to record some progress in the development of the human mind. One aspect of this development can be seen in two points he made continually in his *Essai sur les mœurs*; it is possible to depict "le génie des nations" by explaining the laws and, conversely, to explain the laws by the manners.

In his article "Histoire" of the *Encyclopédie*, Voltaire defines history as "le récit des faits donnés pour vrais; au contraire de la fable, qui est le récit des faits donnés pour faux." He notes that it is wise to distinguish among the several kinds of history; history of opinions, which is a kind of delineation of human errors, and specially history of the arts, which he states is the most useful of all history "quand elle joint à la connaissance de l'invention et du progrès des arts, la déscription de leur mécanisme." There are also a natural history, which is a section of physics, and history of events both sacred and profane. In the beginning, history was originally transmitted from father to son. These events are only hearsay at the beginning and lose probability with time, becoming fables (this was Fontenelle's point in the *Origine des fables*). Consequently, all origins of peoples are absurd. This can be seen in early history of the Egyptians, Phoenicians, Greeks, and Romans. Indeed, the first annals of all modern nations are fables. They should be related, but only as examples of human credulity. They really are a part of history of opinions. The only test of their authenticity is to examine carefully the earliest monuments. Voltaire names three of these written monuments: (1) the astronomical tables at Babylon. They prove the existence of the Babylonians as a coherent society several centuries previous to their composition 2234 years before the Christian era. (2) The second is the record of the sun's eclipse observed in China 2155 years before the Christian era. But this observation could not have been made until the Chinese had spent many centuries forming themselves into a civilized society. Voltaire notes that the Chinese laws, manners, and language have not changed for 4000 years, and argues that the Chinese are the oldest people who still exist as a people. He also states that they form the largest nation, occupy a vast and beautiful country, and have invented practically all the arts. He deplores that in the past they were never given their rightful place in the universal histories. (3) The third written monument is the Arundel Marbles. They are much more recent than the other two, going back to the third century before Christ. Voltaire argues that the other two so-called written documents appearing before the fourteenth and the fifteenth centuries are untrustworthy. He insists that previous to them, only a few could write. He calculates that of a hundred different races, only two, at best, used written characters. He concedes, however, that there are other documents; the Pyramids, for example. Since they could not have been built until the Egyptians had become a civilized nation, and since they could have required a prodigious length of time to build, it is evident that those who constructed the Pyramids go far back in antiquity. Voltaire deplores that before the early historians there was undoubtedly an early history, which we can only surmise. Even the early historians are submerged in obscurity. Heroditus, for example, is filled with legends when he relates the stories he heard, but he is more scrupulous in describing what he saw. "A mesure qu'il se rapproche de son temps, il est mieux instruit et plus vrai." History thus begins only with the Persians in Greece. There Heroditus becomes the model historian; he had, said Voltaire, "le même mérite qu'Homère: il fut le premier historien comme Homère le premier poète épique; et tous deux saisirent les beautés propres d'un art inconnu avant eux." Voltaire glories in the Greek defense against Xerxes and his horde. "Cette supériorité d'un petit peuple généreux et libre, sur toute l'Asie esclave, est peut-être ce qu'il y a de plus glorieux chez les hommes." Voltaire passes to Thucydides and the Peloponnesian Wars. He notes that civil war, the most horrible of all wars, "a produit des hommes en tout genre dignes d'une réputation immortelle," and added "un nouveau feu et de nouveaux ressorts à l'esprit humain." Precisely at this moment, all the arts flourished in Greece. Voltaire recalls that the same thing happened in Rome following the civil wars of Caesar and, in more modern times, in the fifteenth and sixteenth centuries "parmi les troubles de l'Italie."

Voltaire follows the march of civilization as it passes from Greece to Carthage to Rome when all other nations of Europe are "buried in barbarism." He notes that "l'histoire de l'empire romain est ce qui mérite le plus notre attention, parce que les Romains ont été nos maîtres et nos législateurs." Their laws exist still, their language is still spoken throughout Europe long after their decline. By contrast, Voltaire is woefully deficient in his treatment of the Middle Ages, calling it a "histoire barbare des peuples barbares," and giving it exactly five lines of text. Only after the fall of Constantinople and the discovery of the New World, in his opinion, did politics and the arts take on a new form, and thanks to printing and the revival of learning, history became a more faithful portrayal of life and historians became abundant. He added wryly, though, that "on est accablé sous le poids des minuties." He thereupon counsels a judicious separation of the wheat ("les grands événements") from the chaff ("les petits faits particuliers"): "Un homme," he wrote, "qui veut s'instruire est obligé de s'en tenir au fil des grands événements, et d'écarter tous les petits faits particuliers qui viennent à la traverse, il saisit dans la multitude des révolutions, l'esprit des temps et les mœurs des peuples." Voltaire advises a careful, minute study of one's own country: "L'étudier, la posséder, réserver pour elle les détails et jetter une vue plus générale sur les autres nations." He finds that their history is important only in its relationship to our history, or, rather, in the great things which each nation has achieved.

He has no doubt that history can be very useful, since in the first place, it encourages emulation; it also teaches by example. The most useful, however, is modern history. Certainty can be achieved, or rather a reasonable certainty. Voltaire condemns, however, the use of satire. He concludes with the remark that, in his day, more is expected of the historian: more details, facts better authenticated, more precise dates, a better use of the documents, more attention given to the customs of the people, their laws, their manners, their commerce, finance, and their agriculture, and especially to the problems of population. That is to say, the special subjects which the historian now has to consider are all those factors which tend to the creation of a new science which deals with economics rather than with politics.

The article "Gouvernement" by De Jaucourt will make a good summary of all these political articles. De Jaucourt defines government as the manner in which sovereignty is exercised in each state. He consequently begins his treatise by examining the origin, the different kinds of government, and the causes which contribute to their downfall. He derives the ruler from the "père de famille," who was responsible for executing in his family the laws of nature. Children submitted, he says, because they wanted security, peace, freedom and happiness. Similarly, the first government must have been patriarchal. However, with time, families united to select the ruler as it is now done, said De Jaucourt, among the American Indians. "Il est donc vraisemblable que tout peuple, quelque nombreux qu'il soit devenu, quelque vaste pays qu'il occupe, doit son commencement à une organization à plusieurs familles associées." These governments eventually were founded upon deliberation, consent, and consultation among the individual members of the group, and when they were forced by circumstances to modify them, they deliberated, consulted, and contracted for the changes. Finally, the individuals made a set of laws along with stated penalties for violations. Among the principal laws were the following: each was assured of his possessions; failure to obey one's officer was punishable with death. Three forms of government became possible: democracy, where sovereignty was placed in councils of heads of families assembled; aristocracy, where sovereignty was placed in heads of principal families; and monarchy, where sovereignty was attributed to one man. There was also a mixed government, which was an organization in which the government was divided among the different groups in a republic. Sovereignty thus is determined according to the way powers (legislative and executive) are divided.

Everyone has a right to abandon a government which he finds intolerable, but nothing can downgrade a government save an open and violent revolt. The real question is what is the best one? Each has its good and bad points. De Jaucourt adds pessimistically: "Il sera toujours accompagné d'instabilité, de révolutions, et de vicissitudes." He is inclined to define the best government as one which suppresses science but does not oppress it. He agrees with Montesquieu that England comes nearest to being the ideal government. He asserts, however, that no government is suitable to all peoples. Its suitability depends upon geography, climate, spirit of the people, genius, size of nation, and character of the nation. De Jaucourt insists that the best government is the one which makes the largest number of people happy. In fact, he says, the supreme law of all good governments is "le bien public." He next asks what would be the "ideal" government, and he answers: "Dans tous les cas il nous doit être avantageux de connaître ce qu'il y a de plus parfait dans l'espèce. La succession des siècles a réussi à perfectionner plusieurs arts et plusieurs sciences, pourquoi ne serviroit-elle pas à perfectionner les différentes sortes de gouvernements et à leur donner la meilleure forme?"

The remainder of the article seems designed to suggest certain guidelines for achieving this purpose. The author has detailed in order the advice which he offers: (1) Avoid all the evident defects of the present government. (2) Laws and customs should be in accord with character of the people. (3) Laws should be devised so as to be advantageous to all classes. (4) Laws should expedite government, rather than slow it down. (5) Laws should not be justified by the religious condition of the country. (6) Laws should not be contrary to the incontrovertible maxims of good government. (7) The most important factor, is "le bien du peuple." The greatest good, De Jaucourt declares, is freedom. (8) Finally, the rules should work to eliminate all the things which weaken a government. De Jaucourt enumerates these things: (a) when the legislative power is altered, (b) when the supreme executive fails to exercise his duty, (c) when the executive or legislative uses force, (d) when those in power threaten life, liberty, and the possessions of the citizen, (e) when the country is invaded by a foreign foe.

Whenever these things occur, decline can be avoided only by bringing the state back to the principles upon which it is founded. It is unnecessary to stress how much these precepts are grounded upon the thought of Montesquieu. The key concept, of course, is that the institution of government is determined by the manners of man and the relationship between those manners and the laws which are made for his welfare. The whole argument is naturally referred to the article on "Man." To solve that problem, the author of "Homme" has reduced his article to a set of key words: perception, attention, reminiscence, imagination, all of which are of a psychological order; passions, pride, superstition, fear, desire, all of which are still of a psychological order but refer rather specifically to man's action; and finally, needs and prejudices, both of which are of a deterministic order. Le Roi, who wrote this article on "Man" has been content to give a series of observations upon man while keeping the key words in mind.

The first of these observations is that we are not aware of our existence except through immediate sensations or through our ideas. The happiness which we pursue of necessity never happens without a keen feeling of our existence. We are, therefore, forced, in order to be happy, either to change continually our objects or to readjust our sensations. We seek with interest everything which awakens in us a lot of ideas; even our physical tastes are determined that way. Man is thus the plaything of an intelligence which renews itself only to betray him. The interests of all dominate the interest of each; it is, indeed, this situation which has given rise to laws. Hence, human society must be a federation of wicked people whom a common interest has bound together; all it takes is the suppression of this common interest to arm each against his fellow-man. Notwithstanding this possibility of revolt, man has a gentle feeling which interests him in the fate of his fellow-creatures, whenever he is at peace with his own fate. The majority of men, when personal passions do not separate them from the natural inclinations of nature, will yield to a precious sensibility which is the source of all virtues and which may become the source of a constant happiness. Love of humanity in those moments counters personal egotism. But self-respect is really the surest principle underlying all strong, generous action. Education also has its role to play in all these relationships. It cannot be regarded as a matter of precepts; only examples can modify man, with the exception of certain privileged beings who judge of the essence of things because they feel that the others are carried away by imitation. We can only conclude from all this complexity of the human being that society is composed of men modified by each other, and public opinion gives to all those of the same society an air of resemblance which displays itself despite the differences of character. Each century has traits which distinguish it from another. It follows, therefore, that men make themselves and that it is very possible to give them the form which a society wishes. Consequently, in every government, opinions and morals depend absolutely upon its present situation.

If we have not been too arbitrary in bringing together these articles on economics, politics, and the nature of man, it is clear that there was a latent political doctrine in the *Encyclopédie* in which the various aspects of political thought and action have been drawn together by insisting forcefully upon the relationship between natural law and positive law, as well as between law and the nature of man, between man's nature and the nature of society, between a society and other societies. A moment's reflection will show how closely the "rapports" are all presented in Montesquieu's *De l'Esprit des lois.* However, the numerous articles are not only based upon Montesquieu, they lead in Le Roi's statements straight to Helvétius and Holbach. This ought not to be too surprising, since all three, along with Diderot, were what we have come to designate, following Rousseau's denunciation in the *Confessions,* as the "Coterie Holbachique." It appears now that there is no "coterie," but there is still an *Encyclopédie.*

We are, however, not quite at the end of our key articles. Otherwise, we would have to conclude with Proust that every article in the *Encyclopédie* is a "political" article, once having conceded that every article produced with the intention of directing public opinion is necessarily a political article. I must confess I would not be too opposed to this final judgment of Proust, if I were not persuaded that the encyclopedists' perspective was broader than the "merely" political, and embraced, insofar as possible, all aspects of life. I imagine Proust would not be too opposed to this point of view either.

One of these critical articles in the *Encyclopédie* is "Société." The editor notes that man is made to live in society, since without it, he could not preserve his life, develop his talents, or achieve a solid happiness. His faculties (speech, for instance) appear to be made particularly for living in a community. The social instinct which we possess so strongly is an additional indication that we are made for social living. Indeed, only in society can man find the remedies for his needs. The author explains that the whole social economy is built upon the desire of each member to be happy. He insists that man's two outstanding virtues given him by the Deity are "l'amour de nous-mêmes" and "la bienveillance de nos semblables." From them are derived all moral laws: (1) the common welfare is the supreme rule of all our relationships, (2) sociability is universal, (3) natural equality is a principle which we should never lose sight of, since it is established both upon religion and philosophy. The author recognizes that there is an inequality of conditions but it only serves in all its manifestations to push mankind to an equality of happiness, and sociability thereby becomes a reciprocal obligation among men. That is the reason why society is built upon the concept of justice and upon sincerity. Recognition of an order in society in which each, despite his rank, has an obligation to serve others is the true basis of the social contract. The whole system is built therefore upon reason which is the determining factor in regulating the action of each. Furthermore, no society can fully prosper without religion, which exercises a type of constraint upon the individuals. All vices on the part of individuals harm society, he concludes. These ideas are an important contribution to the understanding of the relationship of man and society in the last half of the century and they represent an accurate synthesis of the combined views of Voltaire, Rousseau, and Diderot on the problem. Further, they offered a working basis to Helvétius and Holbach upon which to build their more radical assumptions on the same problem. We should add that this one case, which is fairly characteristic of the development from Voltaire, Rousseau, and Diderot to Helvétius, Holbach, and others of the new science of sociology in that period, will help to throw some light upon the actual movement in these ideas.

"Idées" (VIII, 489^b), therefore, is another of these crucial articles, this time based on Locke's *Essay on Human Understanding* and Condillac's *Traité des sensations*, thereby throwing some light upon the way the Englishman's and Frenchman's ideas upon the new science of psychology are fused in the *Encyclopédie*. There are two aspects to this article in fact. One is the purely descriptive aspect, which tries to analyze the mechanics of a sensation becoming an idea. The other concerns the spiritual, vital qualities of an idea; that is, the relationship between what we think and what we do. The concept of idea is here united with the concept "motion" and the concept "esprit," and all of these concepts combined have an important bearing on the concept of a "self."

The article "Idées" endeavors to develop first the mechanical aspect of thought. The author notes at the beginning that we have within ourselves the faculty of receiving ideas, of perceiving things, and of representing them to ourselves. The "idée" or the "perception" is "le sentiment qu'a l'âme de l'état où elle se trouve." Ideas themselves are the first steps of our knowledge; all our faculties depend upon them. Our logic, our judgments, our reasoning, and the method we use have nothing to work with except ideas. They come from the sensation an object makes upon an organ. Perception is an awareness of the presence or the absence of a sensation. If it is absent, we call the faculty "imagination." If the perception is divorced from the object which occasioned the sensation, we call it an "intellectual idea."

With this series of definitions, the author promises to treat (1) the origin of ideas, (2) the objects which ideas represent, (3) the way ideas represent these objects. The author here makes an important remark: the "soul" has the ability to perceive within itself ideas which come from the faculty of thought or from its way of existing. Ideas can also be drawn from the ability to compare ideas. Presumably, although the author does not explicitly say so, two or more ideas acting together can generate in the human mind additional ideas merely by comparing themselves the one with the other. This faculty of the human mind to compare ideas is usually designated in the Enlightenment as "reflection" and the operation is normally called "association of ideas." The *Encyclopédie* article, however, does not use these terms here. It does make allowance, though, for this internal operation of the sensation.

The author notes that it is very difficult to explain how the impression of the object upon the sensation produces an idea. He insists that there is no innate faculty in the human understanding and he rejects likewise the "tout en Dieu" explanation of Malebranche, just as Locke did. Voltaire, however, was inclined to accept it both at the beginning and the end of his career. The author of the *Encyclopédie* article rather favors Leibniz's explanation of the monads, which he discusses. He concludes that we are trying to explain something which will always be a mystery. Locke's point of view he nonetheless finds wholly unacceptable. The author then draws a totally negative conclusion: "Nous ne pouvons savoir ce qu'est une idée considérée dans l'âme, ni comment elle s'y produit; c'est un fait, le comment est encore dans l'obscurité, et sera sans doute toujours livré aux conjectures."

We can state, he thinks, that the objects of our ideas exist outside ourselves, and sometimes within ourselves; they can also be objects we think about or don't think about, such as bodies, spirits, or God. They may be beings which exist only in our ideas. They may be at times "des êtres de raison" such as relations ("rapports"), signs, universal ideas, or "des êtres d'imagination," such as simple ideas compared ("chimères"). Other ideas, such as mathematical ideas, have only a verbal existence. The author tries to draw a distinction between primary and secondary qualities of ideas and concludes with a final category of ideas which he calls "des êtres de raison" because they are only ways of thinking.

The important point is that we live with ideas or they live with us. We perceive them, adopt them, compare them, organize them, and establish all our activity upon them. The result of transforming ideas into action inevitably ends in moulding us into our ideas. We structure the idea into a form, but the idea also structures the individual into a form. This mutual copenetration of person and thought can be exercized effectively if the person or thought can organize things precisely as they are. This procedure we call criticism.

"Critique," one of the essential articles, was written by Marmontel, who begins by differentiating between various kinds of critics: (1) literary critics, (2) historians, (3) érudits (Bollandists, Benedictins), (4) bibliographers, (5) commentators of ancient writers, (6) those who write about philology under all sorts of names.

Marmontel finds that there are two kinds of criticism in literature: (1) there is a type which is concerned with the restitution of ancient literature and carried on, for the most part, by those who made a philological penetration of particular pieces of literature (more or less, it appears, those whom we call today the textual critics). Marmontel explains that these ancient works had to be reinterpreted because there was a break between ancient "mœurs" and our contemporary "ideas." There is also (2) a kind consisting in "un examen éclairé et un jugement équitable des productions humaines": (a) sciences, (b) liberal arts, (c) mechanical arts. Criticism in the sciences concerns the ancient verities, order of presentation, new discoveries. It applies to both historical sciences ("la morale," he calls it) and the natural sciences. In sacred history, he has nothing to add to the theology of the time. In profane history on the other hand, he has a whole new program to propose. The critic, he says, examines "les mœurs, la nature des peuples, leurs intérêts respectifs, leur richesse et leurs forces domestiques, leurs ressources étrangères, leur éducation, leurs lois, leurs préjugés et leurs principes, leur politique au-dedans, leur discipline au-dehors, leur manière de s'exercer, de se nourrir, de s'armer et de combattre, les talents, les passions, les vices, les vertus de ceux qui ont présidé aux affaires publiques, les sources des projets, des troubles, des révolutions, des succès et des revers, la connaissance des hommes, des lieux, et des temps; enfin, tout ce qui en morale et en physique peut concourir à former, à entretenir, à changer, à détruire, et à rétablir l'ordre des choses humaines, doit entrer dans le plan, d'après lequel le savant discute l'histoire." I surmise from this lengthy, detailed program in the criticism of civilization as it is broken down here that the historical sciences are concerned more with ideas than with facts. On the other hand, Marmontel states explicitly that in natural history, the critic starts with facts, *not with ideas*. His task in this area consists in finding out how these facts occur. His job is here to prevent them from becoming too abstract: "ramener les idées aux choses" is Marmontel's explanation here: "la métaphysique et la géométrie à la morale et à la physique; de les empêcher de se répandre dans le vuide des abstractions." Bayle and Fontenelle are given as models of this kind of critic. Bayle, however, is criticized for being too diffuse.

The critic in the liberal arts must know a body of masterpieces, and must know how to compare them. What he needs is precision of judgment, energy, a broad and varied intelligence, a keen sensibility, and a very active imagination. He must know how to deduce moral truths from his material, combat prejudices, in short, how to qualify as a critic of civilization: "Ainsi, le critique jugerait non-seulement chaque homme en particulier suivant les mœurs de son pays et les lois de son pays, mais encore les lois et les mœurs de tous les pays et de tous les siècles, suivant les principes invariables de l'équité naturelle." The philosophe has finally become the universal critic as well as the encyclopedic man and he is now prepared to become the poet, that is, the artist of the future. Curiously, he is Everyman, a sort of modern Everyman. Marmontel concludes with two or three observations which are very important. His model critic, he says, is Montesquieu, but unfortunately there are very few good citizens. He even adds pessimistically that the more exacting taste becomes, the more timid imagination is. That, however, is really not his final thought. That was "on naît critique comme on naît poète." I suppose that it is nothing but a vitalized "innate" idea. (Although there are supposedly no such things as innate ideas in the Enlightenment!)

If "inexistent" innate ideas are still lurking around in the *Encyclopédie*, I should take a few moments to see if it has a "spirit," *L'Esprit de l'Encyclopédie*. Fortunately, we don't have to use much time on this enterprise. The thing to note is that the key article system of sampling the content of the *Encyclopédie*, though certainly not perfect in the results obtained, gives a modest insight into the nature of the articles and the general intellectual tendencies of the work as a whole. It cannot, however, tell us a lot about the popular appeal of the work. Since we are convinced that the policy of the editors, the contributors, and the publishers was largely determined by a desire to reach the largest and most typical audience possible, it would seem worthwhile to look for some edition which presented an anthology of the articles incorporated in the seventeen volumes of the text.

The simplest way of proceeding would be to make at least a preliminary investigation into an eighteenth-century collection of articles which is fairly widespread in its selection and substantial in its content. We have such a work in *L'Esprit de l'Encyclopédie, ou choix des articles les plus curieux, les plus agréables, les plus piquans, les plus philosophiques de ce grand Dictionnaire* (Geneva and Paris, 1768, 5 vols.). There was a little announcement on the title page, which reads: "On ne s'est attaché qu'aux morceaux qui peuvent plaire universellement, et fournir à toutes sortes de lecteurs, et surtout aux gens du monde, la matière d'une lecture intéressante." It must be confessed that the "curieux, agréables et piquants" give some pause, but the addition of "philosophiques" reassures a little. One could ask whether the assertion that some effort has been expended to select what is most interesting reading for the nobility is not what we would entirely insist upon as a criterion, but once more it is reassuring to see "fournir à toutes sortes de lecteurs," which is precisely what we would like to have as a controlling factor in this enterprise. The clearest statement of all was made in the Introduction (p. viii): "On s'en est tenu uniquement aux articles de philosophie, de morale, de critique, de galanterie, de politique et de littérature." One could perhaps dispense with the "galanterie" at this late date, but a quick look at the list of articles does not display an excessive amount on that subject.

The list of articles with the authors to whom they are ascribed are as follows:

I

Académiciens (Yvon), Académie (Mallet), Adultère (Toussaint), Alcoran (Mallet), Amitié, Amour, Amulette (Mallet), Anges (Mallet), Antidiluvienne, Aréopage (Diderot), Astrologie (Mallet), Aveugle (D'Alembert), Bêtes (Yvon), Bibliothèque, Cabale, Calomnie (Diderot et D'Alembert), Canadiens, Canonisation (Mallet), Caractère (D'Alembert), Cardan, Descartes (Diderot), Cartesianisme (D'Alembert).

II

Ceinture (Diderot), Célibat (Diderot), Censeurs de livres (Diderot), Chanson (Rousseau), Charlatan (Jaucourt), Civilité (Jaucourt), Colère (Jaucourt), Comédien (Mallet et Diderot), Conards (Mallet), Concert spirituel (Jaucourt), Conversation (D'Alembert), Cour (Diderot), Courage (Jaucourt), Courier (Mallet), Couronne (Chambers), Courtisan (D'Alembert), Courtisane (D'Alembert), Crainte (Jaucourt), Cri, Clameur (D'Alembert), Critique (Marmontel), Cruauté (Jaucourt), Cinisme, Cyrénaïque (Diderot), Dégât (Jaucourt), Divination (Diderot), Duché (Boucher d'Argis), Duel, Ecole militaire (Paris), Elégance (Voltaire), Eloge (D'Alembert), Eloquence (Voltaire), Encyclopédie (Diderot), Ennui (Jaucourt), Epicure (D'Alembert), Enseigne (Mallet), Envie (Jaucourt), Esprit (Voltaire), Esséniens (Mallet), Estime (Jaucourt).

III

Facile (Voltaire), Faction (Voltaire), Fat (Desmahis), Faveur (Voltaire), Faveurs (Margency), Favori, Favorite (Voltaire), Femme (Desmahis), Flaterie, Flateur (Jaucourt), Fleuret (Voltaire), Fortuit (D'Alembert), Fragilité, François (Voltaire), Frivolité, Gaieté, Genève (D'Alembert), Génie (Diderot), Gens de lettres (Voltaire), Gens du Roi (Boucher d'Argis), Géomètre (D'Alembert), Gloire (Marmontel), Gourmandise (Jaucourt), Goût (Voltaire), Gouvernante d'enfans (Lefèvre), Grâce (Voltaire et Watelet), Grands (Marmontel), Grandeur (Marmontel), Grasseyement (Cahusac), Guèbres (Boulanger), Habeas corpus, Herxularum (Jaucourt), Hermaphrodite, Heureux (Voltaire), Histoire (Voltaire), Honnête (Jaucourt), Honneur.

IV

Ignorance, Imagination (Voltaire), Importance, Indécent (Diderot), Indépendance, Philosophie des Indiens, Indiscret (Diderot), Infidélité, Inquisition (Jaucourt), Insensibilité, Insinuant (Diderot), Insolent (Diderot), Instinct, Intérêt, Joli, Jouissance, Journaliste (Diderot), Législateur, Lettres, Lettres de cachet (Boucher d'Argis), Littérature (Jaucourt), Louange, Luxe, Magie, Maléfice, Manières, Maraudeurs, Déserteurs (Marnésia), Mariage (Boucher d'Argis), Noblesse (Boucher d'Argis).

V

Opinion, Ouvriers étrangers (Collot), Philosophie, Plaisir, Politesse, Politique, Probité, Providence, Raison, Raisonnement, Réflexion, Société, Somnambulisme (Malouis), Sorciers et Sorcières (Jaucourt), Spartiates (Jaucourt), Tirade, Tolérance (Romilly), Volupté.

Additions

Affabilité (Millot), Entêtement (Millot), Glorieux, Grave, Gravité, Grondeur, Idolâtrie, Invalides (Collot).

The first comment which might be made is that the articles are selected more abundantly from the first part of the alphabet than from the last part. It should be noted also that among the leading philosophes, Rousseau practically does not show up at all (one article only). This reflects not only his early abandonment of the *Encyclopédie* but his limited connection with the enterprise. Diderot, on the other hand, appears with some of his very important articles "Encyclopédie," "Descartes," "Jouissance" and "Génie," while "Besoins," "Droit naturel," "Représentants," and "Eclectisme" do not appear. For Voltaire "Histoire," "Esprit," and "Idolâtrie," were included, along with what seems at first glance to be a disproportionate number of articles of lesser renown, but none by Polier de Bottens which he sponsored. D'Alembert shows up often in the first part, but the *Discours préliminaire* is missing. Finally, De Jaucourt and, surprisingly, Mallet appear very frequently. A disproportionate number of the articles are unassigned, in many cases when the article was evidently considered to be questionable or dangerous. Also, the assignments of author are not always correct.

I have tried to envisage what general impression an ordinary reader would get from perusing these selections. "Académiciens" stresses the skepticism of the group and states that all Greek philosophy was derived from it. Its founders were Aristotle, Plato, and Socrates. The five successive academies and their transformations are traced with Arcesilas, Carneades, Philo, and so on. "Académie" is defined as the meeting-place in Athens of the academicians. "Adultère" condemns the practice, especially because of the evil effect it has upon children. The ways it is punished are detailed. "Alcoran" is a mere description of the book. "Amitié" is defined as "commerce honnête et agréable" which is attributed to man's solitude. It is contrasted with charity. "Amour" states that character is what attracts the parties involved, but they are attracted by the senses also. In friendship, one is attracted by the intellect. "Amulette" is defined as an image which has the power to turn away evil. "Ange" means messenger. "Anti-diluvienne" discusses the state of philosophy before the flood. The author proposes the problem whether angels interposed between God and man were great philosophers, and assumes they were not. He gives a good definition of present-day understanding of philosophy: "Cette philosophie que produisent la curiosité et l'admiration filles de l'ignorance, qui ne s'acquiert que par le pénible travail des réflexions, et qui ne se perfectionne que par le conflit des opinions." The author gives a long quotation from Diderot's *Essai sur le mérite et la vertu*. He argues that it is to chance that we owe the greater part of the arts useful to society: "Ce qui fait la philosophie, c'est de raisonner sur le génie qu'elle (la société) y remarque, après qu'ils (les arts) ont été découverts." He concludes that the early ancestors of man were farmers, shepherds, and not at all philosophers. "Astrologie" originally meant astronomy. The author accepts natural astrology—the art "de prédire les effets naturels." "Astrologie judiciaire" is, however, a "préjugé." "Aveugle" is a series of reflections on blindness. This article, attributed to D'Alembert, is a very good summary of Diderot's *Essai sur les aveugles*. "Bêtes" quickly becomes a discussion of "l'âme des bêtes." "Bibliothèque" gives an outline of the Bible and its reconstitution by Ezra. It is followed by a description of the great libraries of Egypt, Chaldaea, and Europe, ending with the Royal Library. It is a very good, informative article. "Cabale" by D'Alembert, concludes with the remark: "Voilà bien des chimères, c'est-à-dire des extravagances d'un grand nombre de savants. Cela entre dans le plan de notre ouvrage . . . On peut dire qu'il n'y a point de folies qui n'aient passé par la tête des hommes." A second section of "Cabale" defines it as "tradition orale" given to Moses at the same time as the written law. The author discusses here the existence of two kinds of philosophy: one for the initiate, the other for the vulgar mob. "Canadiens, philosophie des" is a sketch taken from La Hontan. The author is favorable, but he finds some defects too. There are no conclusions. "Canonisation" gives a short account of the ceremony. "Caractère" begins with different manner of noting things, passing to printing type, and concludes with a modest dissertation upon moral character: "Disposition habituelle de l'âme, par laquelle on est plus porté à faire, et l'on fait en effet plus souvent des actions d'un certain genre que des actions du genre opposé." Author quotes Duclos: *Considérations sur les mœurs.* He notes also that the character of a nation "consiste dans une certaine disposition habituelle de l'âme qui est plus commune chez une nation que chez une autre." It confirms Espiard (who is not named), who said "chaque nation a un fond de caractère," which has not changed. "Cardan" is an abridged biography, with a short sketch of his philosophy copied from Bayle.

"Cartésianisme" is one of the major articles, as thorough as any of the philosophical articles attributed to Diderot. "Ceinture" is a purely descriptive article describing the use of the belt in antiquity. "Célibat" begins with the history of the concept when the practice was first forbidden, then tolerated, then approved, then preached; eventually, it became an essential requirement for most of those who served in Christian ritual. The author then states that having presented what history tells us about celibacy, he now intends to examine it with the eyes of a philosopher and discuss what writers have presented about celibacy. He now proceeds to present objections that have been raised against it, because it is an unnatural state, injurious to society. He states that it is not at all essential to Catholicism. At this point he quotes both the Abbé de Saint-Pierre and Melon. "Censeurs de livres" is a purely informative article on the way the system works. The author offers no strong personal opinion. He does state, though, that discussion of who is to censure books caused much confusion. "Charlatan" is discussed in connection with medicine and compared with the "empirique"—he who without university studies pretends to have special secrets in medicine and surgery. The article is a short history of "quacks." "Civilité" (and "politesse") use a "certaine convention" in manners and speech tending to please and to bring out the regard one person has for another. "Colère" is defined from Locke as an uneasiness of the soul which we feel after having been treated discourteously. It is a passion with unfortunate aftereffects. The author assures that it can be combated with proper advice from friends. "Comédien" pleads for respect for actors, as is the case in England. The author gives laws referring to them at various times. "Conards" is defined as a club which aimed to correct manners by ridicule and laughter. "Concerto" is defined as a symphonic piece composed to be performed by a full orchestra. The author also gives the modern definition of concerto where one instrument sometimes plays solo and at other times is accompanied by the orchestra. "Conversation-Entretien" is defined as "Discours entre deux ou plusieurs personnes." The author considers "entretien" the more important word. One has an "entretien" with a king. "Dialogue" and "colloque" are also defined. In "Cour" the author states that it pretends to be perfection in manners, but it is in reality a fraud. The second part of this article is a fairly lengthy description of the law courts ("cour des aides," for example). This article, which is lengthy, is a fair example of a purely informative political article. "Courier" gives a history of couriers in antiquity, from Chambers. It has been enlarged to a description of the "messageries" in France. "Couronne" is solely informative. "Courtisan" tries to distinguish between the man of the court and this individual who stands between the ruler and his subjects. "Courtisane" is a "femme livrée à la débauche publique." "Crainte" is a superstitious passion which uses the instability of future events to upset the mind. It not only threatens the happiness of man, it is always useless. The author adds: "Il faut rectifier ces malheureuses sources par de fortes réflexions sur la nature des biens et des maux." "Cruauté" presents a pessimistic view of human nature and gives examples of cruel deeds taken from history. "Cri" is an interesting article describing the cries of Paris. It should be compared with Proust's *Recherche* and Charpentier's *Louise*. "Cynisme" concludes that no philosophical sect had a more consistent appearance than the cynics: "On se faisait Académicien, éclectique, Cyrénaïque, Pyrhonnien, sceptique, mais il fallait naître cynique." The common trait of all members of the sect was to be "enthousiastes de la vertu."

"Cyrénaïque" was also originally from Brucker. The author mentions that although founded by Aristippus, it really derived from Socrates. Aristippus was a philosopher who was "très voluptueux." His partisans were the "mondains" of antiquity. He himself cultivated "la morale." He held in high regard particularly "la dialectique," especially when it is applied to moral philosophy. Diderot, the author of this article, details points (as he did in his treatment on Hobbes) which he calls principles: a philosophy founded on sensations tending toward happiness, "qu'il n'y a rien en soi de juste et d'injuste, d'honnête et de deshonnête."

"Défense de soi-même" comes from the term "amour de soimême." Natural law, which has as its goal the preservation of ourselves, does not require of us a limitless patience; otherwise the whole human race would be wiped out. Natural law orders us to defend ourselves. But in a civil society, this right is naturally limited. "Dégâts" refers to the spoils of war. It is, says the author, a "mal nécessaire." International law tries, notwithstanding, to remedy this situation by pleading for the preservation of sacred and profane things. The author quotes from Grotius and gives an extract from the *Siècle de Louis XIV* which condemns Louis's activities in the Palatinate. "Divination–Prophecy," the author suggests, was created by the Jews who gave it to the Egyptians, who passed it to the Greeks and the Romans. He quotes from Pluche *Histoire du ciel* and Condillac. He then gives their principal ideas with some of his own. This article belongs to a group which traces the beginnings of "préjugés." The author concludes: "N'y a-t-il pas aujourd'hui, au milieu du XVIIIᵉ siècle, à Paris, beaucoup de courage et de mérite à fouler aux pieds les extravagances du paganisme?" He suggests that was what the early Christians were doing during the reign of Nero. "Duché" gives a description of jurisprudence concerning organization and administration of a dukedom.

If we now sense the fluidity with which this encyclopedic material flows, we can proceed to an analysis of the total of the impressions which this fluidity engenders. We are at least in a position to modestly propose another way of penetrating the *Encyclopédie* through an organization of the social sciences. (See R. Hubert, R., *Les Sciences sociales dans l'Encyclopédie*, Paris, 1923.)

The rationale of the *Encyclopédie* was developed from two different conceptions of science. For the encyclopedist, there are fundamentally two sciences: the science of nature and the science of man. The key which opens the science of nature is mathematics; the key which performs the same function in the science of man is history. Mathematics and history, however, operate very differently. The former, for instance, requires a certain amount of empirical data, from which are deduced calculations, measuring, weighing; the latter requires a knowledge of origins and developments from which are deduced changes, tendencies, and goals. The science of nature encourages the view that its laws are abstract, absolute, immutable, while the science of man insists that he is motivated by concrete matters which are relativistic and subject to change. Nonetheless, this is true only if one accepts that initially man is conditioned by needs and that he tries to satisfy these needs by identifying himself with the needs of all men. The encyclopedists (and to a considerable extent, almost everyone else) accepted that the fundamental quality of each man was his sociability. Indeed, man's needs, his sociability, and a desire for happiness were judged at the root of all human activity. In the science of man, history can thus only be genetic, not static; one must obtain his perspective by seeking origins, developments, and goals.

Up to the opening years of the eighteenth century, the answers to these problems had been tied to the Biblical tradition which had been thought to have contained the history of man and the development of his institutions from the creation to the present. It was also thought to offer the goals which humanity would be expected to set. Bossuet best represented the dependence of all history upon that tradition, both in his *Politique tirée de l'Ecriture Sainte* and the *Discours sur l'Histoire universelle*. It is true that the continuity of tradition had been seriously put in question long before the dawn of the Enlightenment proper by the free-thinkers of the sixteenth and seventeenth centuries, but it still offered much comfort, despite its obscurities. Man had been granted innate ideas upon which to build his awareness of the universe; he had been guided in the formation of his institutions, directed in the unfolding of his powers. The Biblical tradition appeared to offer a satisfactory explanation both for the origin and nature of man and for the rise and development of societies, a code for the conduct of peoples, and a justification for man's relationship with God, actually an alliance between the Deity and man.

Still, many things which had happened among the philosophers and free-thinkers of the seventeenth century put in question more and more the validity of that tradition. Specifically, the philosophy of the time overshadowed the theology of the past. The development of natural science throughout the century from Galileo and Descartes to Huyhgens and Newton had questioned the old cosmology; Locke with the destruction of innate ideas changed completely the notion of man's nature and the importance of ideas. The problem arose how to replace innate ideas, which by definition were alive, with ideas which could become living ideas. Spinoza, however, was the force who almost single-handedly among the philosophers (though he had a massive following among the encyclopedists) questioned the historical tradition of the Bible. Hubert has remarked that the *Encyclopédie* merely carried on the philosophy of the previous century. We should not forget, though, that both the long line of English and French Deists were for the most part followers of Spinoza's Biblical criticism in the *Tractatus*. Nor should we overlook that there was a relatively large number among these followers and that (as far as the French are concerned) these followers gave some evidence of being organized against the teachings of the Scriptures. We should recall finally that the technique followed in these clandestine manuscripts had been to conclude in favor of natural religion or natural morality or natural law, that is to say, it is not enough to leave the matter with a rejection of Biblical tradition. These clandestine writers conclude in favor of revising religion, politics, and morality along more positive lines.

This stand is characterized by a constant critical attack against the teachings of the Church, much of it polemical: rejection of dogma, criticism of morality, assertion of the primacy of reason over revelation. Whatever point of attack each chooses, it is clear that all are becoming opposed to the Biblical tradition. This opposition entails, however, a total reconstruction: new explanations must be given for the formation of society, for religious, and moral beliefs, political and social institutions, languages, and science. Most of all, the encyclopedists agree in rejecting the notion that the Jews are the center of civilization or the fountain-head of all subsequent civilizations. There

cannot be, as they expressed it, a Jewish miracle. The consequences of
the rejection has been succinctly summed up by Hubert (*Les Sciences
sociales*, p. 40):

Ainsi, quelque soit le problème particulier, quelque soit l'institution sociale
qu'on considère, l'opinion commune des Encyclopédistes ne varie pas:
leur naturalisme s'oppose et le plus souvent en termes explicites, à la tradition biblique et les explications diverses qu'ils ont proposées de la formation de la société, des croyances religieuses ou morales, des institutions
politiques, du langage ou des sciences ont toutes ceci de commun, qu'elles
tendent à éliminer au premier moment de l'histoire l'intervention de la
volonté divine.

Once the crucial step had been taken, the *Encyclopédie* had to face
the necessity of a total reconstruction of universal history, which involved an adequate replacement for the Biblical tradition. If the
Jewish race was not the earliest race, the encyclopedists had to meet
the problem what was the earliest race. To get at some sort of answer,
they had to reconstruct the chronology of history, undertake the problem of the associations of races, ponder the question of the influences
of one group upon another, and inquire what actually constitutes
the social fact. Is it need, as Rousseau said; or sociability, as Diderot
and many others affirmed? Moreover, where did man acquire his
religion, his morality, his political sense and how did these senses
organize themselves in the group? Can one assume as a fact that
every man is naturally endowed with these senses and, if so, are they
innate and, if innate, how can one justify the innate moral sense and
reject an innate idea? Are there people who preceded Adam on the
earth? Are they primitive, uncivilized, living in a "state of nature"?
What would transform it into a social state?

The *Encyclopédie*, in an effort to reach reasonable answers, had to
simplify horribly. The chronology which was ultimately adopted
justified the belief that from one race derived all races of men. They
stuck as closely as possible to the concept of one species man which
was a unity. They admitted nonetheless that these multiple peoples
gathered around the eastern Mediterranean and that from them
developed ancient times. The group which preceded all others, if one
had to precede, was Egypt. Hebrew customs, as well as Greek, seem
to derive from those of the Egyptians. But if the Egyptians stand at

the origin of European civilization, there is evidence that the Hindus and the Chinese are older cultures still.

Ultimately, the writers of the *Encyclopédie* take the position that human civilization is a unified phenomenon; it is unified in its genetic development thanks to the organic quality generated by religion, morality, and the political and social institutions of all the primitive civilizations around the eastern Mediterranean. Everywhere the same natural development of knowledge and doctrines can be found which makes each appear to conform to a specific pattern of civilization. The encyclopedists conclude that this conformity renders impossible a chosen people to become the fountainhead of the races of the earth. The real miracle is not the dominance of a race, though, it is the development of man. Hence, despite many serious efforts to attribute intellectual advance in one particular people, and even to distribute these advances among the nations around the eastern Mediterranean (Egypt, Chaldea, Persia, Palestine, Phoenicia, Greece), despite the decided tendency to withdraw primacy from the Jewish race and ascribe it to the Egyptians, what the encyclopedists really stressed was the unity of historical human civilization in its origin and a consequent unity of its development, a "volonté d'expliquer par des causes exclusivement naturelles l'extension des connaissances et l'évolution des doctrines," as Hubert explains.

They followed a similar tendency to play down the Greek miracle also. Here, however, a distinction has to be drawn between the intellectual qualities and the artistic aptitudes of the Greeks on the one hand, and their political, religious, and social conditions on the other. The encyclopedists were far too classical to even think of denying them the superiority which they undoubtedly held over the others in philosophy and art. They attributed this superiority not to a spontaneous genius of the race, however, but rather to geographical and climatic causes. Moreover, they seemed disposed to prove that artistic excellence can be accompanied by religious, political, and social chaos. Hence, while admitting the esthetic grandeur of Greek poetry and its ability to dress in poetic allegories, historical traditions, scientific hypotheses and philosophic thought, while praising the Greek tendency to tolerate philosophical sects and personal opinions, the encyclopedists point out also the abstract, metaphysical nature of that thought and the constant proliferation of sects. A great exception was made by Diderot, however, to all this critical niggling when he traced in "philosophie politique des Grecs" the union of political and religious thought. Nor did D'Alembert refuse them great merit in the domain of the sciences. Nonetheless, Hubert tends to play down this admiration for Greek merit by insisting upon negative personal criticism on the part of some philosophers (De Jaucourt wrote, "Le seul but de Lacédémone étoit la liberté, le seul avantage de la liberté c'étoit la gloire"; Rousseau remarked that Athens was no democracy, but a very tyrannical aristocracy, governed by wise men and orators).

The encyclopedists also regarded Roman civilization with considerable suspicion. In the first place, since they knew but little about the Etruscans, they were inclined to feel that the Romans had borrowed heavily from the Greeks, which, indeed, they had. The encyclopedists agree that Greek institutions are at the origin of Roman beliefs and note that these beliefs in the field of religion are almost entirely Greek. Some actually coined the expression: "Rome était une ville Grecque." Indeed, everything proves the Hellenic origin of Roman civilization: the language, the art forms, philosophy, and religion. However, they concede, because of their respect for Montesquieu, that Roman merit lies in the area of politics and jurisprudence. Its civilizing influence was very restricted, nonetheless, its economic role almost nil, its scientific activity very modest indeed.

As could be readily expected, some familiarity with early universal history led to the establishment of a new, but relatively elementary, philosophy of history, the main trait being a denial of revelation and a rejection of the continuity of tradition and the affirmation of the unity of the elements of a civilization. This knowledge of universal history was supplemented by the rich body of travel literature which had circulated during the sixteenth and seventeenth centuries. The encyclopedists deduced from these accounts the superiority of the primitives over the artificialities of present-day societies or, on occasion, they noted that the tendency to idealize the living conditions of the savages had given a false view of primitive life. The Abbé Pestré (the article "Canadiens") notes that they believe in the Diety, in the immortality of the soul, in reason granted to man in order to discern between good and evil. By and large, it was the view given by La Hontan. De Jaucourt (article on "Scythes") praises the austerity of their morals. Both Rousseau and Diderot ended by according much enthusiasm to the theory of the noble savage (article on "Economie politique" and *Supplément au Voyage de Bougainville*). Indeed, many of the special accounts concerned with the North American primitives stressed the idealistic side, as we have seen elsewhere. Nonetheless, De Jaucourt regretted that the travellers have not examined with sufficient care the government, the manners and the religion of these people. There is the feeling that what is lacking is the application of a serious comparative method which would explain these manners by physical causes (article on "Espèce humaine"). Besides the accounts are far from being favorable. The Tartars have neither "mœurs" nor religion; the primitives of the North are a degenerate race, the Chinese themselves are "mols, pacifiques, indolents, superstitieux, soumis, esclaves et cérémonieux." The Hottentots "n'ont ni temples, ni idoles, ni cultes." De Jaucourt, in fact, seems to express the normal view in the article "Sauvages," when he states that "la plupart sont encore féroces et se nourrissent de chair humaine." Where there was a clear gain in all these descriptions was in the area of theory, particularly in the relationship between "mœurs" and "lois," the theory of climate, and the possibility of a society of atheists.

We should not forget those countries situated beyond the confines of the Mediterranean, particularly India and China. The encyclopedists adopted the point of view of the seventeenth century concerning these two countries. They were in the first place ancient societies which derived from Egypt or, rather, India served in their opinion as intermediary between Egypt and China. However, opinion concerning China was not unified; Voltaire, for instance (article on "Histoire"), felt that China is the oldest of the nations now in existence. It is the vastest, the most beautiful country, the one which invented all the arts before Europeans had any. Diderot accords them an important place in moral philosophy; D'Alembert acknowledges their interest in astronomy. Diderot sums up their importance: "ces peuples qui sont, d'un consentement unanime, supérieurs à toutes les nations de l'Asie, par leur ancienneté, leur esprit, leur progrès dans les arts, leur sagesse, leur politique, leur goût pour la philosophie, le disputent même, dans tous ces points, au jugement de quelques auteurs, aux contrées de l'Europe les plus éclairées."

The encyclopedists give much attention to the origin of French society. It was a preoccupation of their idol, Montesquieu, much discussed before Montesquieu by Boulainvilliers and the Abbé Dubos (*Histoire critique de l'établissement de la monarchie dans les Gaules,* 1734, 3 vols.). In general, there were two theories: one which traced the conception of the monarchy back to Rome, the other which traced it back to the Francs, tempered by "lois fondamentales" and intermediary powers with some traces of popular representation. It was this latter theory which received the support of the encyclopedists. However, in the matter of German (Frankish) origins, the most active discussion centered around the problem of the nature of the monarchy (absolute or aristocratic). It was at this point that the notion of a contract was interjected (article on "Authorité politique") between the monarch and the nobility. This notion, as is well-known, was destined to play an important role in the thinking of Rousseau and a dangerous one in Mably's *Observations sur l'histoire de France.* The supreme problem was, Who had inherited the right to represent the nation? Boucher d'Argis argued (articles on "Enregistrement" and "Parlement") that Parlement and especially the Parlement of Paris retains that right. When, however, the encyclopedists sought to justify that right historically, they discovered that Parlement did not originally exercise it, the ancient assemblies did. It could therefore be argued that the whole political system had consequently long since been vitiated.

While the encyclopedists concentrated their intellectual energies on the origins of history, they also turned their attention to the genetic development of historical phenomena. Their interest in the beginnings of history was keen, but they also entered upon serious study of the development of history during the Middle Ages and the subsequent Renaissance. Both epochs raised difficulties to any theory which attempted to explain history as development of the theory of progress or progress as a continuous movement forward in history. The Enlightenment, with its anti-Catholic prejudices, had a tendency to regard the Middle Ages as a period of decline and intellectual stagnation. The writers insist in general that the age was characterized by a total decline in letters, art, and science, and an almost total regression to barbarity. Politically, Europe tended away from liberalism toward absolutism. The great vice of the time was intolerance, which fed upon superstition. The cause for this breakdown was attributed to the Church. Grimm sounded the alarm in his *Corre-spondance*: "Il faut convenir," he wrote, "que l'esprit de l'Evangile n'a jamais pu s'allier avec les principes d'un bon gouvernement" (it was also Rousseau's point in the *Emile*). And while he conceded that some damage had been wrought by the invasions of the bar-barians, he finally concluded that the decline had set in before the invasions and that paganism had been replaced by two cults (Cathol-icism and Protestantism) which run counter to the progress of the human mind. There is no need to dwell upon their condemnation of Christianity; its dogma is mingled with earlier pagan beliefs, even its rites come often from pagan ritual, its morality is antisocial. Its actions, the Crusades, for instance, are motivated by hatred, greed, ignorance, and the desire to divert the public from its own internal disorders.

Needless to say, this condemnation appears total but is not so; the encyclopedists don't fail to balance their disapproval of Christianity against a respect for specific activities: the constitution of French public law, transformation of the function of the nobility, separation of the different orders of the state, preeminence of the clergy, rise of the third estate, progressive division of labor, the slow development of the bourgeoisie, and consolidation of royal power, all of which reached its climax in the epoch of Henry IV. Their admiration for Henry IV almost equals Voltaire's. What they read into these activi-ties is the build-up in civil, moral, political and juridical matters, which counterbalanced in a way the ill effects of religious decadence. Their portrait of the advance in jurisprudence (especially as pre-sented by Boucher d'Argis and De Jaucourt) partially redeems the dark picture of religious fanaticism. Despite these brighter spots the *Encyclopédie* understands that the decline is a threat to all concep-tions of historical progress; only Turgot undertook to strike some balance between the disorders he recognized and a continual pro-gression which he noted in the mechanical arts. "Aussi, voyons-nous que dans l'ignorance qui a régné en Europe et en Grèce depuis le Ve siècle, les arts ont été enrichis de mille découvertes nouvelles, sans qu'aucune un peu importante se soit perdue." Turgot seems to be tire-less in enumerating those aspects which, properly speaking, are economic rather than political: "La marine s'est perfectionnée, et même l'art du commerce. On doit à ces siècles les lettres de change, le papier de coton ... celui du chiffon ..., le verre à vitres, les grandes glaces, les lunettes, la boussole, la poudre à canon, les moulins à vent, et à eau, les horloges, et une infinité d'autres arts ignorés de l'antiquité" (Hubert, p. 129).

Moreover, with some ingenuity, the encyclopedists succeeded in stressing that the break in continuity occasioned by the Middle Ages was only a temporary disarrangement, since the Renaissance immediately resumed the continuity of antiquity. But the central activity for the encyclopedists was the intellecual development of civilization, what they called the "philosophical" movement. In this movement, politics will now occupy a central position and the concept of fundamental laws as the expression of the great historical traditions of the nation will be basic. De Jaucourt (article on "Lois fondamentales") presents them as veritable conventions, which passed between the people and sovereign power. De Jaucourt sees them as varying according to the type of government; they weaken none. They reduce the sovereign to a respect for the public welfare, and the public to obedience; moreover, they fix the constitution of the state. Diderot (article on "Autorité politique") saw them as justifying natural freedom and the equality of each individual. Seen collectively, though, they are the source of popular sovereignty. Diderot concludes that there is no authority without laws and no law which gives limitless authority. "Le gouvernement en effet est un bien public, qui par conséquent ne peut jamais être enlevé, à qui seul il appartient essentiellement et en pleine propriété." This presentation of the government as a combination of prince and people gives a broader meaning to the people. No longer do they think in terms of ruler and nobility, but rather in terms of nobles, bourgeois, laborers, artisans, and workers. Ways consequently have to be devised to obtain a better representation (article on "Représentation") of the people at large, to the extent that the nobility, the clergy, the magistracy, commerce, industry, the landowners, and the laborers should be heard equally in the council of the nation. The political theories of the encyclopedists are neither vague nor unsubstantiated; they are both conservative and traditional and founded upon a clearcut interpretation of history.

The characteristics of this modern period for the encyclopedists are clearly given by D'Alembert in the "Discours préliminaire" (I,

20). It was first of all a period of classical regeneration in the sciences, that is, simple erudition (article on "*Erudition*"). D'Alembert notes that this erudition has permitted a new acquaintance with antiquity, has developed a sense of criticism, and has established a body of knowledge. Moreover, it has led to the philosophical works of Bacon, Descartes, and Locke and ultimately to a philosophy of experience, based on firm principles of rationalism and a clear understanding of the workings of the human mind. It was in this way that the encyclopedists, gathering together the scattered materials of the social sciences which they found in travel literature, the writers of antiquity, the "erudits contemporains," the critics, historians, and jurists of the time, pieced together a philosophy of history, a body of coherent knowledge on society, and a method.

Having addressed themselves to assembling the facts concerning the origin and development of civilization from antiquity to the present, they endeavored to pursue the study of the origins of these elements which entered into the making of a civilization: religion, economy, politics, morality. What was sought now was not so much the facts as a genetic interpretation of the theories underlying the nature and development of those elements. The assumption was quietly made that if the nature and contribution of these could be understood ultimately, the nature of society and its destiny could be penetrated. In this way, history became the instrument for the explanation of the making of a civilization but also a key for the analysis of a civilization and, in due time, the categories of a civilization became focal points which, united, were to provide the theories for understanding society. The extent to which this was an innovation in the 1750s can be seen in Boulanger's article "Economie politique," where he refused to treat the problem as metaphysician or religious moralist, but only as a simple historian seeking psychological reactions to physical phenomena. In brief, the nature of society can be understood only through a study of human nature, what René Hubert calls "chercher dans la constitution naturelle de l'homme le principe d'explication de l'existence sociale."

At this point, we would be well advised to sum up the direction we have been following. We have assumed that the *Encyclopédie*, just like any living person of the time such as Diderot, Rousseau, Voltaire, or anybody else, has an intellectual biography. To get inside that biography, we have to concern ourselves with certain historical facts and also with a certain amount of ideological content. But we have had to remember scrupulously that behind the living history and the living ideas of the *Encyclopédie* are a relatively large number of individuals, each subjected to a personal historical development and each bringing to the work a personal ideological content. From the "esprit" of each individual we have selected, added to the "esprit" of his co-encyclopedists, we have assumed that it would be possible to forge the "esprit" of the Enlightenment. But we can do this only if we can find the intent of the group seen collectively and only if we can trace in some sort of consistent way (preferably by controlling the data of the *Encyclopédie* itself) that intent. We have therefore made our choices in the massive content of the work in accordance with two criteria. What did the public judge to be outstanding, and what was its applicability to the basic categories which every man has to live? Only after analyzing as carefully as possible the stated intent of the directors of the *Encyclopédie* and the recognized leaders in the thought of the time have we dared seek these relationships. We have tried hard to maintain some sort of coherence between that stated intent of the work and the historical content of the time. To be sure that we are not unwittingly deviating from that coherence, we have used four works as guides: L. Ducros, *Les Encyclopédistes*; Belin, *Le Mouvement philosophiques en France de 1748 à 1789*; R. Hubert, *Les Sciences sociales dans l'Encyclopédie*; and J. Proust, *Diderot et l'Encyclopédie*. We would have wished more assistance in the relationship of the encyclopedists as philosophers with the seventeenth-century European philosophers, but we do not know any reliable work in that area. We do know, however, or rather we strongly suspect, that the crucial spot is there. At all events, if we assemble certain fundamental principles current at the time ("mœurs et lois, liberté, égalité, fraternité, esprit, civilisation," and so on) and if we scrupulously examine the meaning of these principles in the development of historical thought, the organization of the social sciences and the doctrines of reforms, and all the esthetic possibilities of creation, we ought to be able to discern the same coherence in the *Encyclopédie* as a living force, as we glimpsed in Montesquieu, Voltaire, Diderot, Rousseau and the other encyclopedists.

PART IV

From "Esprit Philosophique" to "Esprit Révolutionnaire"

MORELLY AND THE DAWN OF
TOTALITARIAN DEMOCRACY

PRACTICALLY nothing is known about the author of the *Code de la nature* (1755) which the Marquis d'Argenson called "le livre des livres" and which Professor Chinard in his edition of 1950 dubbed "le chef-d'œuvre d'un inconnu." (See Morelly, *Code de la nature, ou le véritable esprit de ses lois, Abbéville, 1755,* ed. Chinard, Paris 1950.) Professor Chinard attributes to the "Mysterious Morelly," as he calls him, seven works: *L'Essai sur l'esprit humain,* 1743; *L'Essai sur le cœur humain,* 1743; *La Physique de la beauté,* 1748; *Le Prince,* 1751; *La Basiliade,* 1753; *Le Code de la nature,* 1755; and, finally, *L'Hymen vengé,* 1778. Chinard notes that the *France littéraire* of 1756 mentions a Morelly "ci-devant Régent de Vitry-le-François" who was the author of three of these works. However, in 1769, the same *France littéraire* attributes the *Code de la nature* to Diderot, and the three other works to the son of Morelly. Chinard does not contest this attribution; he merely states that it is logically possible to assign all seven works to one Morelly. However, A. Lichtenberger adopts the theory of two Morellys.

Morelly's first work is a derivative from Locke via Pope and may announce, as Chinard affirms, both Condillac and Helvétius. I would suspect that both Condillac and Helvétius knew both Locke and Pope before 1743. All have a similarity of tone and all of their works seek some sort of causal connection between the way objects in the outside world make impressions on our thought within and the way this thought within is at the origin of our moral composition. It is, in short, a procedure for studying the influences which condition self-awareness. Morelly has given a lengthy list of these conditioning factors: poverty, riches, honors, arms, law, commerce, land, sea, country-side, customs, religion, climate, and so on. The originality of Morelly in the analysis consists in showing how some of these factors work upon the "esprit"; others, upon the "cœur."

From this mechanical explanation of the origin of man's ideas and their function in the creation of character and personality, Morelly deduces that man is neither good nor evil by nature; he is merely malleable to his experiences and his education. This conclusion does not at all differ from that of Condillac, Helvétius, and Holbach.

Morelly, however, extends this interpretation to the idea that there exists among all men, if not an equality of condition, at least an equality of nature. Stressing, as everybody did, that "l'homme est crée pour le bonheur," he adds that from Descartes's "je pense, donc je suis" man has learned to derive "je sens, donc je suis." The proposed motive for this changeover from "esprit" to "cœur," from "penser" to "sentir" is the "amour de soi," but the actual motive, as Diderot had already asserted, is derived from the needs which transform man into a social creature. Morelly was willing to accept at this stage that man's needs may be found in his religion, while Diderot was already inclined to find them in the social instinct. Morelly, however, stressed the role of education in the process more than Diderot did, at first.

It is, in fact, the role of education in the process which binds the *Essai sur l'esprit humain* with Morelly's second book, *Essai sur le cœur humain*, since the subtitle of both volumes is "principes naturels de l'éducation." That is to say, both essays are respectively Parts I and II of the same treatise on education. Both aim to establish those principles, drawn from nature's laws, which condition self-awareness. Those principles are to be found in the outside world; they enter into the world of man's awareness through the media of the senses to the "organ" of the mind ("esprit") or to the "organ" of the heart (cœur); and consequently each of these operations nurtures reason and intuition, which are, properly speaking, the "rapporteurs" of man's nature as it has been created by nature's nature.

Professor Chinard has extracted, in his Introduction (pp. 12–13) to the *Code de la nature*, the pertinent passages which trace the steps from a passive blank soul to an active human awareness and a coherent, though constantly changing, expression of a self:

Pour le premier instant de sa vie, ces organes n'ont point d'autres mouvements que ceux qui sont communs à toute machine; ce qui est hors de lui fait à peine impression sur ses sens; l'âme n'en a donc encore reçu aucune par leur moyen . . . elle n'a donc pas encore formé d'idées . . . Je suppose donc l'âme comme une table d'attente sur laquelle le pinceau n'a encore tracé aucun trait . . . Les impressions qui se font dans l'âme et les différentes idees auxquelles elle fait attention, ou qui s'introduisent chez elle, dépendent ou toutes ou en partie, des mouvements organiques occasionnés par les objets qui nous environnent, et des degrés plus ou moins intenses de ces mouvements. Cette variété des esprits produite par celle des organes, . . . je veux dire les humeurs ou liqueurs qui les font mouvoir ou qui les nourrissent, qui, suivant leur différentes qualités, apporteront divers changements ou dans leur mécanique, ou dans leur substance . . .

Morelly adds that the "esprit" is defined by the objects of the external world which awaken our intellect, stir our imagination, excite our memory, engender our reflection and give birth to our judgment. On the other hand, the "cœur" is determined by the agreeable or disagreeable impressions these same objects make and the way they act upon the will. The passions are stirred by the vigorous action of the will and the desires are nurtured by the imagination.

In the subsequent work, entitled *La Physique de la beauté ou pouvoir naturel de ses charmes* (Amsterdam, 1748), Morelly moved from the realm of psychology and morality through education into the region of esthetics. Chinard who finds the work somewhat insipid and even, at times, in bad taste, nonetheless records that it is just about the first attempt to approach esthetics through the use of sensualist philosophy. I am not sure that that statement can be justified under closer scrutiny. It is nonetheless true that Morelly has produced a theory in which there is a mixture of the role of both "esprit" and "cœur" in the field of art. Coming after the first two volumes which dealt with the role of "esprit" and "cœur" in the education of perception and awareness, the *Physique de la beauté*, it seems to me, is a continuation of the series in which the findings of the first two volumes are applied to the new category of esthetics. In a curious way, Morelly has placed himself in the forefront of those concerned with the application of the new psychology to the new esthetics. In addition, Morelly has made some attempt, though not always with success, to demonstrate that his principles of esthetics can be applied as readily to painting and music as to literature. It is interesting that he asserts that the concept of the beautiful can be applied to thought and philosophy and even to morality and psychology. These novel suggestions are certainly not developed with any great consistency and coherence, but it is worthy of note that while the term "esthetics" had not yet been introduced into the language, Morelly has a fairly clear idea of what he understands it to be and actually uses the concept as a means of introducing the concept of unity in various aspects of life.

In the next three works, he turns away from the problem of psychology, morality, character-building, and esthetics (two of these areas—psychology and esthetics—having not yet entered into the usage of the day), to the more problematic subject of politics and economics. Morelly shows much hesitation in the treatment of these two subjects, although they will turn out to be the area in which he is said to have exerted his greatest influence.

In the *Prince*, he conceives of the best government as a "vrai despotisme." Chinard pronounces that Morelly's *Prince* is the very opposite of the *Déclaration des droits de l'homme*, and it must be admitted that by definition a despotism does not accord too much to the rights. The prince does have more resemblance to an enlightened despot (such as Frederick the Great or Joseph II) who is willing for the "bonheur des gens," and the "bonté de l'homme," to forget all about "droits de l'homme." That does not prevent the *Prince* from having some affinity with the utopian fiction in France and England from 1650 to 1750. This affinity is more clearly visible in *La Basiliade*, however. The subsequent work of Morelly, this time an epic poem (1753), is firmly connected with the legend of the floating island, possibly suggested by Swift, and dedicated to the "Sultane Reine, suprême Aseki (La Favorite)," possibly Mme. de Pompadour. The hero of the *Basiliade* is still a prince and the supposed author is said to be Pilpai. This work likewise grows out of the utopian literature of the preceding hundred years. The inhabitants of this floating island, similar to the inhabitants of Sevarambia in the *Histoire des Sévarambes*, regard the land as "une nourrice commune." But though they do not observe the principle of property ownership, they make no pretense at being equal. There must be, the author assumes, some sort of authority which, to be sure, is neither despotic nor arbitrary. Morelly seems to believe that it is derived from paternal authority which is regulated by mutual respect. The implication is that the prince is entitled to this same respect. The emphasis is nonetheless placed on the common use of the land (Chinard text, Introduction, p. 57): "Les travaux se font naturellement en commun, labour, moisson, etc., comme les Péruviens," and "la récolte est commune." And further on: "Tous ensemble cultivent les terres, ramassent, serrent les moissons et les fruits dans un même magasin." Otherwise, each has a profession, to which he returns once the cultivation and gathering of the crops are completed. The author has noted the obvious advantages of this system. There is a reciprocity of aid which can be extended from one province to another when and where it is needed. All the citizens are thus encouraged to be useful. The provisions are stacked as they accumulate, and the work required can be reduced proportionately as they increase. They are consumed with care and prudence, and nothing is wasted. The superfluous produce can thus be sold abroad. Morelly's conception of the "grand homme" as he who does some good for his fellow man does not differ from that of Saint-Pierre and his doctrine of "bienfaisance"; he is, first of all, the one who has made a useful discovery, that is, useful to society.

Morelly's epic proposed innovations; despite this fact, though, it caused no great stir in the public, neither in France nor in England. The reviews are not without interest, though, particularly that in the *Bibliothèque impartiale* (see *La Basiliade*, ed. Chinard, p. 80): "Le but de cette prétendue traduction est de montrer quel seroit l'état heureux d'une société formée selon les principes de la loi naturelle, et de faire sentir les méprises de la plupart des législateurs qui ont voulu réformer le genre humain." In this respect, we must recall that the basis of the totalitarian democracy which took its origin in the later part of the century was the belief that the human sciences had fundamental laws, just as the physical sciences did, and that the primitive law of all human sciences was the natural law supported by God-given reason.

If the *Bibliothèque impartiale* succeeded in pointing out a profound conviction on the part of the century, the *Critical Review* for March 1761 brought out one of its profoundest aspirations. Curiously, this was done without seeming to recognize its importance: "nothing besides numbers are wanting to gain the *Basiliade* a place among the best poetical productions of the age; yet the author would seem to prefer the reputation of philosopher, to which he may likewise form a claim, if peculiarity of opinion, and depth of meditation upon the most important topics of natural religion, morality, and politics, constitute the philosophers."

In the *Basiliade*, the author now conceives of the ideal state as a utopia. "Mille hommes," he wrote (Chinard, p. 58), "ou tel nombre qu'on voudra, de tous métiers et de toutes professions, se trouvent habitans d'une terre suffisante pour les nourrir. Ils conviennent entre eux que tout sera commun; et pour qu'il n'y ait point de confusion dans cette communauté, et que chacun y puisse contribuer pour sa part au nécessaire . . . ils s'arrangent ainsi." Morelly stresses two points: (1) they are farmers and workers at trades as well as trained professional men and the products of their common labors are held in common and distributed among the members; (2) in this community labor, there results a complete reciprocity of assistance. This ideal country is contrasted with a contemporary society based on a foundation absolutely false, whose guiding motive is personal egotism, and whose vice is property, and whose dominant quality is "préjugé." Morelly proposed in their place a love of one's fellow man, and a perfect equality. The conclusion is clear: every government should bend every effort "de rétablir et de faire régner entre les hommes cette égalité originelle dont les a doués leur Créateur."

Morelly's *Code de la nature* appeared in January 1755 and was heralded by Raynal in the *Nouvelles littéraires* of that month: "Il est répandu dans Paris quelques exemplaires d'un ouvrage nouveau intitulé *Le Code de la nature*, ouvrage qui fait du bruit et qui n'est que hardi." Raynal tore it to shreds finding it full of "des déclamations vagues," "des suppositions de principes," "des sophismes grossiers et mal soutenus," and "beaucoup de bavardages sans objet." Grimm also wrote a review of the work which was anything but favorable: "il n'y a ni principes, ni raison, ni lumière dans son livre." On the other hand, we have already mentioned that D'Argenson in his *Mémoires* (1756) was very enthusiastic about it, declaring it as far superior to the *Esprit des lois* as La Bruyère was to the Abbé Trublet.

Morelly gave a fair statement of his intentions (Chinard, p. 87): "Dans l'ordre moral, la nature est une, constante, invariable, que ses lois ne changent point, et que ces lois sont en général tout ce qui produit dans les créatures animées des inclinaisons paisibles, et tout ce qui en détermine les mouvements, et qu'au contraire, tout ce qui éloigne de ces deux penchans, est dénaturé." The work is divided into four parts: (1) "Défauts principaux de la politique et de la morale"; (2) "Défauts particuliers de la politique"; (3) "Défauts

particuliers de la morale vulgaire"; while (4) is an attempt to write
a code in the categories of living and should be regarded, I suppose,
as a first rough draft of the Rights of Man. Morelly finds the common vices of both politics and morality are avarice and property
rights which are favored by legislators, moralists, and priests.

The excellent presentation by Professor Chinard confirms that the
general tendency of Morelly's thought demonstrates that man is always what his thought has made him; that, in fact, what he thinks
is what he is, and what he is, is what he says and does. In short, this
conditioning process is first of all a mechanical affair brought about
by the impressions made by the world of nature upon the mind,
heart, and soul of man. His action is his will, his imagination, his
memory, his judgment, his nature; his education can mold his
nature in conformity with the will, desires, and aims of his society.
Indeed one would say that the educator has the same responsibility
in the making of the citizen as the legislator has, in Montesquieu's
view, in the making of the state. Both are seeking to shape an
"esprit"; one, an "esprit humain," the other, an "esprit social."

Involved in this construct of society is the problem of the relationship of thought and action, of thought and feeling, but most of all
the problem of the relationship of the individual and society, which
led to the search for the best government possible. Morelly tackled
this problem in his volume on the prince, one of whose subtitles was
Système général d'un sage gouvernement. Professor Chinard hazards
the remark that this work seems to be open criticism of Montesquieu's *Esprit des lois,* but its basic point is certainly that all governments are a struggle between the individual and the government of
the society. This, of course, was the fundamental idea of Helvétius,
and Chinard surmises that it could have been transmitted to Morelly
by way of Helvétius himself. Professor Chinard thus deduces the
hypothesis that Morelly came under the protection of Helvétius. This
could well be the case. The more striking resemblance, however, is
with Rousseau: "Alors, l'homme est hors de sa situation naturelle,
et pour l'y faire rentrer, ou, du moins, pour l'en rapprocher, la Providence permet qu'il se voie forcé par ses propres erreurs, à subir les
loix qu'il s'impose lui-même, et se soumettre à une puissance dont il
est l'artisan, le protecteur et le sujet" (*Le Prince,* p. 5). Morelly adds
(p. 8) that a consequence of this pact is that all divest themselves

of the greater part of their natural rights and place these in the hands of the state. All consent to obey whatever the sovereign orders by virtue of the power which has been given him. All agree to unite their physical strength in order to sustain his authority, and to aid him as mechanical instruments in everything he does for the common good. This is obviously a draft of J. J. Rousseau's social contract. Nonetheless, we must note that whereas Rousseau insisted that a republican government never lasts and yields inevitably to anarchy, Morelly concludes that every democracy inevitably becomes an elective or hereditary monarchy. The best government is therefore the one in which the largest number of people are happy and in which the government is most constantly the same: "Il y règne une parfaite uniformité, une parfaite unité, une intime liaison entre toutes les parties, sans être trop multipliées; toutes s'entr'aident, toutes se soutiennent mutuellement, rien de déplacé dans l'une qui rentre dans une autre; la police, le commerce, y sont arrangés de façon à demeurer constamment dans un bon ordre, et à faciliter à la justice le moyen de le maintenir."

Morelly asserts that to achieve this goal, a single system is possible, "le vrai despotisme." This affirmation is important, since it leads to the general impression that communism by its very nature must be arbitrary, absolute, and despotic. It must therefore, as Rousseau suggested, force man to be free, which, of course, is the expression of an inner contradiction.

It is relatively easy to mark out the importance of Morelly as one of the founders of communism, as A. Frank has done in his *Le Communisme jugé par l'histoire* (Paris, 1845). Professor Chinard has extracted from that work a section which endeavors to designate the role played by Mably and Morelly. In brief, Frank states that Mably deserves the credit for having completed the theory of communism and having given it its precise and most logical form, but two things remained to be done. Someone had to give to the theory the imperative character of law, that is to say, it had to be clearly presented in the form of a code, and interpreted in terms of action. As Frank sees things, Morelly performed the first task, Babeuf the second. Frank continues: "Morelly, dans son *Code de la nature*, admettant avec Rousseau et Mably, que tout est bien dans la nature de l'homme, que tous ses penchants sont bons, que tous ses mouvements le portent au bonheur et à l'amour de ses semblables, mais qu'il a été corrompu par la société, comme si les institutions n'étaient pas son œuvre, se propose le problème . . . Trouver une situation . . . où il soit impossible que l'homme soit dépravé ou méchant." This last statement is precisely what Morelly stated to be his purpose (p. 287). But, strictly speaking, this is a moral, not a political, problem. Indeed, it is well to recall that Morelly begins his *Code* by discussing the morality of the *Basiliade*. In this discussion he notes that in antiquity (155) "chaque poète s'est contenté de renfermer son sujet dans les limites d'un trait d'histoire, ou de fable qui intéressât les mœurs, la religion, ou la gloire d'une nation." At this point he states that his aim is "faire voir que le véritable héros est l'homme même formé par les leçons de la nature." Chinard calls this "l'Epopée philosophique de l'humanité." The point to stress in Chinard's remark is that this morality, which involves politics, religion, and mœurs, is really a new philosophy. Indeed, Morelly stops to record that his predecessors were Bacon, Hobbes, Locke, Pope, and Montesquieu. They all have noted, he states, that the most imperfect part of philosophy was "la morale, due to the infinite complexity of its ideas." Chinard interprets this as Morelly saying that the knowledge of man has remained static while natural science has had a prodigious progress. I think that Morelly in his rambling way is trying to state that whatever concerns religion, politics, manners and customs, is conjointly moral and philosophical. He immediately accuses morality "de débiter des absurdités, sous le nom de principes et de maximes incontestables." For instance, present-day moralists assert that man is born vicious and wicked, while others deny this but maintain that man becomes wicked through his situation.

The *Code* begins with the statement that man at birth has neither innate ideas nor inclinations. By degrees his needs make themselves felt, and he begins to consider means for his preservation. Morelly stresses once again the physical inequality in human creatures. The needs of which each becomes aware force him to seek out his human companions. Morelly is convinced that the isolated individual left to himself cannot answer to his needs or satisfy his desires. Moreover, one becomes quickly aware that each must relinquish his rights and yield to another. This combination of individual rights adjusted to the rights of others forms a natural society. This natural society should work smoothly like a machine, but in fact all these societies are subject to a vice—avarice. All the other so-called vices are derivatives of avarice. The author concludes this section with the statement that where there is no property, there will be none of these pernicious consequences. Nonetheless, there are other conditions which have to be met. Every society takes its origin in a single or several associated families. Inevitably, property becomes a factor in the development of these families. This property is the sole cause of disorder in morality and politics. Veritable political liberty consists in enjoying, without hindrance or fear, everything which can satisfy our natural desires. But since everyone is dependent upon others, there is no such thing as master or slave. There is, however, personal interest, and not chance or blind fate, which governs all men. These are the things which derive from property; they should be eradicated from the social order. When a people consents to really obey nature's laws, the result is always a democracy. There is in the eyes of God no "mal physique." Finally "bienfaisance" is the first of our moral laws. But the first principle is that in the moral order, nature is one; it is constant, invariable; its laws are unchanging. Morelly identifies the natural society with the early Christian society, but he laments that it degenerated quickly. What caused the difficulty is a negative rather than a positive Golden Rule: "Do unto others" rather than "Do not do unto others." Morelly asserts that what could preserve that society and guarantee that happiness which everyone desires would be to return to that "amour de soi" which is our natural guide. He admits that the problem for the legislator is "trouver une situation dans laquelle l'homme soit aussi heureux et aussi bienfaisant qu'il peut l'être dans cette vie." That can be achieved, he insists, only by attacking evil at the roots, by permitting all the philosophers to destroy all errors and prejudices, and by establishing the best education possible. Only then will it be possible to adopt a code which is in conformity with nature's laws. However, it is well to recall that in Morelly's opinion, nature's code is no longer adaptable to the corruption of present-day society. Consequently, the laws he proposes presuppose a radical reform, a return to that innocence which characterizes man in the state of nature. It therefore constitutes a goal to which mankind can tend, not a violent revolution. Nonetheless, the *Code* itself presupposes three sacred fundamental laws. (1) Nothing in society can belong to anyone save those things he actually is using to supply his needs, his pleasures, or his work. (2) Every citizen must become a public servant, maintained by the state. (3) Every citizen will contribute to the public welfare, in accordance with his strength, his talents, and his age. All other laws are derived from these fundamental concepts.

We ought to be able now to make some kind of summary. (See A. Lichtenberger, *Le Socialisme au XVIIIe siècle*, Paris, 1895, pp. 126–127.) For Morelly, man is unhappy and wicked. However, nature is not to blame for this state of affairs. Nature in fact made man innocent and good. The present state of morality and politics are responsible for making him wicked. Morelly subscribes wholly to Rousseau's remark that man is what men have made him. They have turned him from the way cut out for him by nature. They have created property rights, thereby giving rise to both physical and moral evils. So far Morelly and Rousseau are in agreement. Morelly accepts, however, that the situation is by no means hopeless and can be remedied. To be made happy again, man has to be led back to his natural feelings. Whereas Rousseau insisted that "la nature humaine ne rétrograde pas," Morelly affirms that man can be saved by giving to him a good set of laws, inspired by reason and nature, in a community where peace and quiet reign. Morelly points out that the existing vices, rather than man's sufferings, have provoked a sincere desire for reform. What he craves is a new system of morality founded upon nature's code. His doctrine, in many respects so similar to Rousseau's, expresses a firm confidence in the goodness of man, an aversion for individual property, and a hostility toward modern constitutions and modern morals. Rousseau, however, is more deeply pessimistic in the *Second Discourse* than Morelly in the *Code de la nature*. The latter is willing to accept arts and sciences, provided the regime is communist. Whereas Rousseau judges a good system of government impossible in the future, Morelly thinks that man enlightened by science, and conscious of his real nature, can expect to achieve an ideal state more perfect even than the state of nature.

HELVÉTIUS AND EVERYBODY'S SECRET

I T is not easy to describe in detail the formation and development of the French Enlightenment. What causes a certain embarrassment is the problem of coherence and consistency and, to some extent, of continuity. We can see quite clearly the Regency as the revival of a diminished classicism, and even as a reform. It is also possible to understand how, at the same time that there is a revival and a reform, there is a vast expansion in the field of science—a consistent growth in logical order of the physical and biological sciences, on the one hand, and of political, social, and moral sciences on the other. It is evident that this scientific activity created the necessity of keeping some sort of unity in the field of knowledge, if for no other reason than to preserve the integrity of the scientific method and to protect the scientists. It is not hard to comprehend that the dynamism of the movement produced some anxiety on the part of more traditional, conservative persons who sensed a danger to established institutions, especially religion and morality, politics, and education. It is more difficult to grasp that the movement, having arrived at some sort of intellectual plateau around 1748, remained rather static during the following decade, during which the four great philosophes asserted themselves as leaders and actually created an organ for the coherent assembling of all their intellectual activity. At the end of this decade, however, there arose a crisis which was so violent during the four following years that the destiny of the whole Enlightenment was played out therein.

The year 1757 started off with much uneasiness and with a bad defeat, Rossbach. During the twelve-month period, other events occurred which led to more confusion, the attempted assassination of the king being one of the most troublesome. Similarly, the *Encyclopédie*, which had been developing with more or less consistency since the suppression of 1752, also ran into difficulties which eventually led to the suppression of its privilege. Some dissension arose among the encyclopedists, occasioned to a large extent by the article "Genève" of the *Encyclopédie*, but more still by the defection of Rousseau, who found it impossible to conform to the views of his fellow philosophes. The *Lettre sur la Providence* addressed to Voltaire (1756), the *Lettre sur les spectacles* addressed to D'Alembert

(1758), the complete break which now took place (1757–1758) with Diderot brought about situations in which coherence of philosophic thought became more and more impossible.

Dissension was not rampant only among the philosophes. It was much more evident in the court where the Pompadour group was backing the colonial war (which was the Seven Years' War) and the Queen's group was assailing the rise of libertinage in all its forms. In religion, the fighting between the Jansenists and Jesuits now became a public scandal, the Jansenists supporting the integrity of Parlement, the Jesuits infiltrating more and more the royal group. There was consequently a fierce struggle in full swing between the defenders of royal power and those who asserted the power of Parlement. But the royal power was also attacked by the princes.

It was in the midst of all this confusion that Helvétius saw fit to bring out his *De l'Esprit*, which threatened to wreck the whole enlightenment movement.

The family of Helvétius came originally from the Palatinate somewhere around Heidelberg, the name apparently having been Latinized from Schweitzer. The great-great-grandfather was, it is believed, a doctor. In the reform, the persecution led to settlement in Holland. After several generations, the grandfather moved to Paris where he practiced medicine. His son, Helvétius's father, became the Queen's doctor in 1728. He had received his education in Paris. His son, Claude Adrien, born in 1715, was educated at Louis-le-Grand. It appears that he was not at all a model student. He did study with Porée, Voltaire's old teacher. It was said that it was his father who turned him to finance. In order to prepare for his duties, he was sent to Caen to an uncle who was "directeur des fermes." On the recommendation of the queen, Helvétius was given an appointment of "fermier-général" in 1738. Keim attributes to his career the origin of his interest in the reform in justice and his preoccupation with social and economic problems. It is possible, but much of it could have come from Montesquieu in whose *Esprit des lois* he was at first deeply interested. Indeed, Montesquieu, Fontenelle, Hobbes, Locke, and Buffon seem to have supplied him with the subject-matter of his two works. One should not overlook the more direct influence, however, of Condillac and Diderot, as we shall attempt to demonstrate. And, of course, Voltaire's influence became preponderant. Helvétius turned to him around 1738 for instruction in poetry, and even around 1770, he was still being instructed by the Master in the writing of clandestine literature. In 1751, he married a niece of Mme. de Graffigny. Mme. d'Helvétius became in time a very famous "salonnière" and was later much admired by Benjamin Franklin.

The thing to keep in mind in dealing with Helvétius is that he is not by profession a writer but he seems always to have wanted to become one. When we first hear of him he is being trained by Voltaire, during the first part of the Cirey period, in the art of poetry. We still have some of his poetry in manuscript with Voltaire's corrections and there are other bits which found their way into the Moland edition. Characteristically, the one poem which we habitually recall was entitled "Le Bonheur," published in a posthumous edition of his *De l'Homme*. We do not have too clear an idea how he moved from poetry, all of which seems to have been undistinguished and of a didactic order, to philosophy. Nonetheless, it is evident that he, like Voltaire, did make the shift. We should note that the early friendship which was struck between the two men during the Cirey years endured to the Ferney years, when the old Patriarch dubbed the "Sage de Voré," as he now called Helvétius, a representative philosophe. In the correspondence between the two, the seigneur de Ferney, properly scandalized by Helvétius's naivety in publishing a work as daring as the *De l'Esprit*, had the audacity to sign his name to it and request not only Tiercier as a censor, but an additional censor.[1] Moreover, Voltaire, around 1760, was not only training his friend in the art of clandestinity but was urging him to do much good by henceforth publishing his works on a private, clandestine printing-press. Consequently, it comes as no particular surprise that Helvétius's ideas are often echoes of Voltaire's. Voltaire, for instance, was calling his *Discours en vers sur l'homme*, "Essais sur le bonheur." However, if the short preface and the first two discourses of *De*

[1] It should be noted that *De l'Esprit* was published by Durand, one of the publishers of the *Encyclopédie*. Rousseau related in the *Confessions* that when Condillac had his manuscript of *L'Essai sur l'origine des connaissances humaines*, Diderot recommended it to Durand, who published it. From Malesherbes's activity in connection with the condemnation of the *De l'Esprit*, it appears (see Belin, *Le Commerce des livres prohibés*, Paris, 1913, Chapter V) that the directeur was favorably disposed to Durand. In fact, the book appeared unsigned, but the request for the censor gave the name of the author.

l'Esprit are perused carefully, they will be seen to have much in common also with Condillac's *Essai sur l'origine des connaissances humaines* and the *Traité des sensations*, as well as with Diderot's early philosophical works, to the point where one can hardly escape the conclusion that the *De l'Esprit* was built not only from a strong reaction to Montesquieu's *De l'Esprit des lois* but a strong response (this time favorable) to Condillac, Diderot, and Rousseau. Indeed, so strong is this impression that we can understand better how the official opinion must have been well informed to connect the central ideas of Helvétius's book with the philosophic ideas of the first seven volumes (that is, the "advanced" ideas) of the *Encyclopédie*. It could well be that the Sage de Voré did understand the "advanced" philosophical ideas of 1758 very well and that he was, as Voltaire said, a "vrai" philosophe.

Since Helvétius's *De l'Esprit* caused such a stir even among the leading philosophes as well as among those who opposed the liberal movement in ideas which had been developed during the previous decade, it is necessary to understand the import of his thought and the nature of the discussion which it aroused. In the preface to his first work, Helvétius locates the subject-matter in the area between the knowledge of ideas and the knowledge of the passions, what he calls that "morale" common to all men and which has the public welfare as its goal. Helvétius presents it as a science and insists that it can only be treated as a science. His announced objective is "faire une morale comme une physique expérimentale." He affirms that he has diligently sought the truth because he is convinced that only the true is useful, but he concedes that he could have been induced into error either because his subject is too vast and consequently beyond his intellectual powers or because his conclusions may be judged false by the reader, who is startled by the daring which he shows. Hence he avows only the purity of his intentions rather than an absolute certainty of truth.

His opening principles are precisely those of Diderot, as we have seen them in the latter's annotations to Hemsterhuis. Man has, as is generally recognized, two basic faculties: the first is the faculty of receiving impressions which external objects make upon him. Helvétius, like Diderot, calls it the "sensibilité physique." The second is the faculty of preserving those impressions; it is generally called the memory. It is nothing more than a series of prolonged sensations. The combination of "sensibilité" and "memory" at the instigation of continuing sensations produces our ideas which, says Helvétius, would be limited were we not endowed with a "certaine organization extérieure." By this organization Helvétius obviously means that human ideas are formed in the same way as ideas are formed in other animals. They are, however, very small in number in other animals because of the configuration of the body (they do not have hands and fingers, for example). All that means, however, is that we have a richer supply of ideas because of our physical condition than those less endowed in that respect. In other terms, we profit from sensibility, memory, continuing sensations, and "certaine organisation extérieure."

The fundamental activity is above all "sentir." What aids our comprehension of these feelings is our capacity for speech. Unfortunately, Helvétius points out, much misery is caused by our misunderstanding of the meaning of words, and much more is caused by our passions. The trouble with the passions is that they push us to consider external objects only from certain particular points of view and they even often lead us into error. But we should also remember that they are the source of an infinite amount of true information, and they are at the origin of our activity. As for the misunderstanding of language, Helvétius cites the word "amour-propre" which was used so abundantly in the *Maximes* of La Rochefoucauld, and was mistakenly taken for "orgueil" and "vanité" when the seventeenth-century moralist meant undoubtedly, said Helvétius, by "amour-propre" nothing more than "amour de soi," a sentiment "gravé en nous par la nature" and which originally was presumably a virtue. It could, as La Rochefoucauld showed, be transformed into vice or virtue, according to the passions, and become either "orgueil" (a vice), or "modestie" (a virtue). Helvétius concludes from his demonstration that "esprit" is the "faculté productrice" of our thought; it is merely a combination of "sensibilité" and "mémoire," and in this sense it is only "un assemblage de pensées."

The ideas of one man always exist in a community of men. The first problem to be considered, therefore, is how the community makes its selection of "interesting" ideas. This activity is guided, says Helvétius, by passions, by coordinated ideas, by prejudices, by sentiments, in short, by interest. This interest, in whatever way it may be motivated and however it may be formed, leads to action. By convention, actions which are useful are considered worthy. We must remember, though, that we never clearly know the motives of our actions in relation to our ideas. Helvétius spends much thought on these relations between ideas and actions, ideas and passions. He concedes that there are men who are so wrapped up with their own ideas which they have accepted as guides to their actions that they can follow only their own "intérêt" in those passions, and finally there are those who are capable of understanding the conflict which may occur between a "personal" interest and a "general" interest. Helvétius does not seem to think that there are many of those who are willing and eager to sacrifice this personal interest to the general interest. His observation is that "en fait de mœurs, d'opinions et d'idées, il parâit donc que c'est toujours soi qu'on estime dans les autres." But the reverse is also true. The public esteems that utility is a mark of virtue, and consequently it condones the most absurd customs, provided their usefulness is apparent. Helvétius concludes that virtue is nothing but man's desire for happiness and probity, which he defines as virtue in action, is useful action in all governments.

Helvétius adds that if there were any virtues which do not add to the happiness of society, they would be "vertus de préjugé" for that society. Contrasting with these two kinds of virtues there would be two kinds of corruption of morals: (1) religious corruption and (2) political corruption. The author hastens to add that he is only considering human virtues. The two best examples of these corruptions would be, in religion, all kinds of immoral relations, particularly between the sexes; and in politics, failure on the part of the citizens to identify their interests with the general interest. Of the two types of corruption, he declares the political by far the most dangerous. At this point, Helvétius urges that great care be exercized by all in meeting this situation. A change in mœurs can not be made until a change has been made in the legislation. Further, it would be idle to attempt to turn the people from their natural tendency to achieve their happiness in accordance with each man's desires. Consequently, the only chance of making them virtuous is to unite the interest of each with the interest of all. It is thus evident that morality is a useless science if it is not tempered with legislation and politics. A moralist, to be serviceable to his country, must sever from his considerations all personal interests. The traditional laws should be weakened, particularly laws concerned with the traditional religions. Finally, the legislator should see to it that there is a consistency and dependency in the whole corps of laws and that they are organized under a simple principle, such as utility. Helvétius disapproved of the ambitious, the fanatics, and those whom he calls the "demi-politiques"—those whom he defines as opposed to all novelty. The whole secret, he maintains, of overcoming these obstacles is a collection of good laws: "C'est uniquement par de bonnes lois qu'on peut former des hommes vertueux. Tout l'art du législateur consiste donc à forcer les hommes, par le sentiment de l'amour d'eux-mêmes, d'être toujours justes les uns envers les autres. Pour composer de pareilles lois, il faut connaître le cœur humain." The author insists that man is normally neither good nor evil, "mais prêt à être l'un ou l'autre, selon qu'un intérêt commun les réunit ou les divise; que le sentiment de préférence que chacun éprouve pour soi, sentiment auquel est attachée la conservation de l'espèce, est gravé par la nature d'une manière ineffaçable; que la sensibilité physique a produit en nous l'amour du plaisir et la haine de la douleur; que le plaisir et la douleur ont ensuite déposé et fait éclore dans tous les cœurs le germe de l'amour de soi, dont la développement a donné naissance aux passions, d'où sont sortis tous nos vices et toutes nos vertus." Helvétius concludes that the nations will each have to learn how to sacrifice national interest to an international interest which is more universal.

Such, as succinctly as I could make it, is what has been called Helvétius's doctrine of personal interest. Looked at in this general way, long after Mills and Bentham, Comte and John Dewey, the Idéologues and the Positivists, it still affirms that its general objective is "the greatest good for the greatest number," that is, universal happiness. But it recognizes two things about this happiness: in the first place it begins with the individual person, but it can only be acquired by the individual on condition that what each desires is in harmonious combination with the happiness of everybody. Unfortunately, there are some very great obstacles to attainment of this goal: the limitations of each man, for instance, both in moral virtue and knowledge. Ignorance and moral evil are great and important handicaps, and the passions are not always an unmitigated good either, although they are certainly necessary for action. It all comes down to thinking, knowing, being, doing, living. It is thus a simple matter of how one knows, what one knows, how feelings and ideas are formed, how thoughts and emotions are created, organized, incorporated into the self, how they are expressed in action, how actions and reactions are combined, reconciled, organized, expressed in community laws (lois) and transposed into group action (mœurs), how the process always goes forward, that is, progresses throughout the world, how the obstacles which are limitless can eventually be overcome, how man can see himself in a universe of man—of his fellow men.

All of this presupposes an intellectual capability of rather gigantic proportions. The formula is easily enough expressed: what one knows is what one says, what one says is what one does, what he does is what he is, what he is has to be integrated into what others are, and the process begins anew. It is a matter of science, political and social organization, and religious, political and social institutions, art and morality, jurisprudence and education. That is not a simple matter after all, and it is complicated by the antagonisms between the individual and the group, between the intelligent and the simple-minded, between tradition and modernity. It nonetheless implies that whether man accepts the challenge or not, the process goes on. Pascal is dead right, one is "lancé," at least for the time being. And whether one accepts to play or not to play is of small concern to the universe. He cannot even resign from the human race without seeing himself in it.

Keim designates as the outstanding quality of the work that it is a "cruel, implacable satire" of the vices of the contemporary political system. I would be more inclined to see in it a halting but very interesting attempt to move from the acquired enlightened view of the nature of man to a new synthesis of morality, education, and statecraft. As Keim says elsewhere, for Helvétius the transformation of society in which the happiness of humanity is guaranteed cannot be brought about without an exact knowledge of man's nature. Chastellux seems best to have grasped that intention when he wrote: "Il (Helvétius) pense qu'avant d'examiner les législations et de les comparer entre elles, il fallait étudier l'homme lui-même et fonder sur sa propre nature l'édifice auquel il doit être soumis." Hence the fundamental thought of Helvétius is that the science of man is the preliminary, indispensable chapter to political and social science. It is precisely the way Rousseau worked out his philosophy from the "tout tient à la politique" to the absolute necessity of a new "science de l'homme."

The *De L'Esprit* is a combination of four discourses of which the first is entitled "De L'Esprit en lui-même." Helvétius recognizes that it can mean several things: the result of thinking, the collections of a man's thoughts or the faculty of thinking, that is to say, the instrument. He is prepared to grant that it is an important faculty. But there are others, "sensibilité physique," for instance, through which we receive impressions from external objects; memory, which is a continued sensation, attenuated, which preserves past sensations. These faculties can furnish a limited number of ideas. What is needed in addition is a certain external organization which, properly analyzed, will bring out the difference between man and animal. Animals with a different (and more simple) organization have a smaller number of needs. Keim has stated that these remarks have scandalized a large number of readers. One wonders why, since the terminology had been used by Condillac and Diderot at least four years before Helvétius took the same stand and only a few took umbrage. Moreover, Helvétius asks, just as did Condillac, whether the two faculties are spiritual or physical, but he does not give a reply. He merely affirms that sensibility produces all our ideas. In addition, all the operations of the mind—comparing, judging, and so on—are derived therefrom. The essential is that they should be natural and correct, but, says Helvétius, they are often neither because of our ignorance or because of our passions. These passions, though, which are the cause of our error, are often the cause of our knowledge.

Helvétius notes that failure to understand the meaning of words can also lead to error. The two passions which he discusses particularly are "amour-propre" and "liberté," since they hold a central place in his philosophy. We have already noted the explanation he gave "amour-propre" attributing to it the meaning "amour de soi," which is precisely the sense which Rousseau attached to it in the *Profession de foi*. As for the term "liberté," Helvétius was as interested in getting a suitable meaning for it as Voltaire. He actually adopts one of Voltaire's definitions: "l'homme libre est celui qui n'est chargé de fers, ni détenu dans les prisons, ni intimidé comme l'esclave." But he goes beyond Voltaire in admitting that "libre" can be synonymous with "éclairé." He adopts, however, Voltaire's position in the relationship between freedom and the will, with the same tendency also to accept a kind of intellectual determinism.

The second Discourse examines "l'esprit" in relation to society. Here the author moves from the crucial problems concerning the nature of man to those concerning the relationship between the individual and the group. The underlying concept is that each individual judges of things and other individuals by the agreeable or disagreeable impressions which he receives from them, while the public accepts utility as the standard of its judgment. From this concept, Helvétius derives the rule of individual and collective activity. Personal interest presides over our individual judgments. Helvétius explains that this personal interest is not necessarily a sordid desire for material gain. In general it is a desire for those things which give pleasure or those which shield us from pain. Behind the individual's interests is a set of needs which when satisfied produces pleasure. This pleasure plays the same role in the individual's activity as utility plays in the activity of the group. We must remember, though, that Helvétius has not adopted the dichotomy of the individual and the group in discussing the moral relationships of man. In this second discourse, he accepts the general distinction of personal interest and general interest. Helvétius summed up his intention (I, 622) in the table of contents: "On se propose de prouver dans ce discours que le même intérêt qui préside au jugement que nous portons sur les actions, et nous les fait regarder comme vertueuses, vicieuses ou permises, selon qu'elles sont utiles, nuisibles, ou indifférentes au public, préside pareillement au jugement que nous portons aux idées, et qu'ainsi, tant en matière de morale, que d'esprit, c'est l'intérêt seul qui dicte tous nos jugements: vérité dont on ne peut apercevoir toute l'étendue qu'en considérant la probité et l'esprit relativement (1) à un particulier, (2) à une petite société, (3) à une nation, (4) aux différents siècles et aux différents pays, (5) à l'univers." The implications from this statement, and more still from their development in Discours II, are astounding. The basic law in morality is *intérêt*, called *utility*. It explains *all* human *actions* and insofar as these actions are useful, harmful, or indifferent (that is, of no consequence morally), we call them virtuous, vicious, or permissive. But our moral judgments vary, depending upon whether the one making the judgment is one individual, a small group (such as a family), a nation, a nation at a particular period of its history, different nations, or the universe. It would seem, then, that for Helvétius, the one universal moral law is happiness (satisfy that need, seek that pleasure, be useful, obey that interest). Looked at in cursory fashion, the conclusion doesn't seem to be too far removed from Voltaire's *Discours en vers sur l'homme* and *La Loi naturelle*. But examined with more scrupulous care, there are derived from this seemingly bland conclusion some very disturbing statements. In Chapter X, entitled "Pourquoi l'homme admiré du public n'est pas estimé des gens du monde," Helvétius summarizes: "Here we prove that the difference between public opinion in this respect and that of more particular groups in the public stems from difference of their interests." Chapter XI entitled "De la Probité par rapport au public," Helvétius sums up: "As a consequence of the principles hitherto established, we show here that general interest determines the judgment which the public pronounces over man's actions." Chapter XIV is entitled "Des vertus de préjugé et des vraies vertus." Here we learn that what distinguishes between the two "virtues" is that the former do not contribute to public happiness whereas the latter do. But we learn further that the "vertus de préjugé" lead actually to the corruption of morals both in religion and politics. In Chapter XV, we are told that the state can remedy the situation by legislation, but we must recognize that so-called moralists who delve in this practice are more motivated by personal interest or private hatred than by the public good. From which we eventually are urged to conclude, that "la science de la morale n'est autre chose que la science même de la législation." In Chapter XXII, lest we become unduly optimistic about this state morality by legislation, we are warned that "la morale, encore au berceau, semble n'avoir jusqu'à présent été d'aucune utilité à l'univers." These are, to be sure, rather disconcerting conclusions and one may be excused for being scandalized by their frankness. Mme. du Deffand was reported to have exclaimed that Helvétius had revealed everybody's secret. In the three retractions which he made after the publication of the work, the author protested so vigorously the purity of his intentions and the earnestness of his desire to contribute to the welfare of his fellow men that critics have had difficulty in deciding whether he adopted his point of view because of the cynicism of his nature or his naivety, or whether he had been drawn into it by Hobbes's philosophy, or whether he had masked his real thought by casting over it a veil of beneficence.

More, however, was to come. Up to this point, it was possible to read some sense into the doctrine of personal interest, despite the pessimistic principles concerning the nature of man upon which it had been built. It was even possible to reduce it to a doctrine of the greatest good for the largest number, and to justify that the good was in reality what satisfied best the individual and collective needs of all. It was a little disturbing to be told that conflict was always possible because of individual needs, passion, actions—in short, *interests*—and those same things which occurred in social groupings from the smallest to the largest. Realizing that these conflicts could be everywhere frequent and sometimes very violent would not foster an unbridled optimism, but the fact that social and political legislation could allay much of the conflict might carry much reassurance, especially if some understanding could be had that education is a positive factor in conciliating private and public interests. There could even be some consolation in knowing once and for all that public and individual morality are in their infancy, if a healthy determination could be called forth to bring to maturity a solid morality.

The third part of Helvétius's *De l'Esprit* was devoted to a discussion of the power of education. After the startling conclusion of the second discourse: "C'est que l'intérêt ainsi qu'on s'étoit proposé de le prouver, est l'unique dispensateur de l'estime et du mépris attachés aux *actions* et aux *idées* des hommes," the author turns now to the problem of the utility of education in morality. He places the problem, however, in a very specific context: "Si nature a doué les hommes d'une égale aptitude à l'esprit, ou si elle a plus favorisé les uns que les autres, et l'on examine si tous les hommes communément bien organisés, n'auroient pas la puissance physique de s'élever aux plus hautes idées, lorsqu'ils ont des motifs suffisants pour surmonter la peine de l'application." The first question he answers succinctly:

nature has endowed each individual with sufficient intellectual powers to take care of the situation, but for many these intellectual activities can be a bore and, if they are not heightened by strong passions or a dread of boredom, the individual can fall into a disturbing lethargy. The remedy lies in finding some way to avoid the menace of this boredom by the strength of the passions. Obviously, the thing to do is to seek the origin of strong passions and here Helvétius returns to the analysis of man's nature. Clearly, the strong passions come from our love of pleasure or our fear of pain; the strongest are avarice, ambition, pride, and friendship, all of which take their source in the "sensibilité physique." Consequently, Helvétius deduces that legislators can manipulate this search for pleasure in a way to produce these strong passions. However, they may not be too successful in the operation because there are people who constitutionally are indifferent to strong passions. Helvétius, however, concludes that this lack of "vertu" can be traced back to the legislators themselves or to the nature of the government. The worst form of government, he finds, in this respect, is despotism. Nonetheless, Helvétius states in Chapter XXVI that, although all men are capable of sufficiently strong passions to overcome their laziness, they often are not subjected to that type of education which guarantees a superiority of intellect necessary to great actions. Hence the inequality of intelligence in man can be traced back to the faulty education which they have received. This explains for him the rarity of geniuses. Moreover, this fault occurs not in the physical aspects of man, but in his moral condition. Hence, each nation shows traits of superiority absent in others and examples of defects not present in others. "Telles sont les conquêtes des peuples du nord, l'esclavage des orientaux, le génie allégorique de ces mêmes peuples, et enfin la supériorité de certaines nations dans certains genres de science, et d'arts." Helvétius concludes that all men, ordinarily well organized, possess the physical power to rise to the highest ideas, and that the difference in intelligence depends upon the diverse circumstances to which they are subjected and the education which they have received.

The fourth Discourse of De l'Esprit has been devoted to clarifying the meaning the author assigned to the term Esprit. It should be compared eventually to the article "Esprit" in the Dictionnaire philosophique. (See Wade, Voltaire and Candide, Princeton, 1959, pp.

271–277.) What we must do here is follow the development Helvétius gave to a definition of "esprit." He began with "génie," for the
simple reason that he believes that "génie" is one of the names given
to "esprit." "Génie" he defines as the term attributed to a whole
long line of superior men who have in common the art of "invention." These discoveries can be of two sorts: those which are picked
up by chance and those which we owe to genius. They are the discoveries which we make in bringing about a new combination of
things which, put together, produce a grand ensemble, are fertile in
truths and interesting for humanity. Helvétius describes the activity
as begun by an inventor, an "esprit" who is followed by another and
yet another until the thing invented has progressed far beyond its
original discovery. Thereafter, the one who brings it to the peak of
perfection is considered the "genius." For example, the French the-
ater was discovered (invented) by a number of "esprits." Corneille
then arrives and gives it its perfection. Corneille is a "genius." Kepler
discovers the laws which bear his name. Newton raises them to perfection in the theory of attraction. Newton is a genius. There is a long
line of moralists: Aristotle, Montaigne, and Gassendi discover the
importance of the sensations as a source of ideas. Locke brings them
all together; Locke is a genius. Chance plays a role in the making
of the genius, but so does the desire for glory. Imagination is a faculty
of discovery in ideas. It gives clarity to philosophy, it embellishes the
works of feeling. Feeling (sentiment) occurs at the moment the
passions are at their peak. Consequently, feeling is the soul of poetry,
and above all, of drama; Helvétius observed (after Diderot) that the
artist never depicts passions and feelings well if he is overwhelmed
by them.

"L'Esprit," for its part, is nothing but a collection of ideas and
new combinations. It, therefore, combines, condenses, concentrates,
and draws the essence of things. It always presupposes invention. The
difference between the "homme d'esprit" and the "homme de génie"
is one of degree only. Machiavelli and Montesquieu are men of
genius, while La Rochefoucauld and La Bruyere are men of wit.
The former treat more serious subjects more profoundly than the
latter. However, there are several kinds of "esprit" identified by the
epithet we attribute to it: "l'esprit fin, fort, etc." "L'esprit de lumière
est la sorte d'esprit qui rend nos idées visibles au commun des lec-

teurs." It is the talent of bringing together thoughts, of combining ideas already known to those less well known and expressing them clearly and with precision. Finally, there is "taste," which, insofar as literary works are concerned, is the knowledge of what merits the esteem of everybody. Taste is founded upon habits (based on a day-to-day study of things capable of pleasing the public) and a "reasoned taste" (established upon a profound knowledge of mankind and the "spirit" of the time). Only those who are capable of "reasoned taste" can judge originality. This latter kind of taste can only be acquired by long study.

There remains finally the "esprit du siècle." Before presenting Helvétius's views upon it, we would perhaps do well to quote a passage which describes what is the "esprit de son temps" (*De l'Esprit*, II, 80–81). Helvétius notes that there are in his day two kinds of writers—those who have earned the title "beaux esprits" and the philosophes. In general, what distinguishes each group is the importance each attributes to the art of writing or to the art of thinking. Helvétius notes that the "beaux esprits" have a tendency to misesteem works "de pur raisonnement," while the philosophes show a certain scorn for the works of the "beaux esprits." Each, in fact, accuses the other of a marked defect: the "bel esprit" finds intolerable the "sécheresse et aridité du genre instructif." They maintain that ideas which are not happily expressed can not be very important. They fall into the defect, says Helvétius, of forgetting that the art of artistic expression presupposes that the writer have something to express. The scholars and the philosophes, on the contrary, entirely taken up with facts and ideas, often neglect the "beautés et les difficultés" of the art of writing. Helvétius seems to argue that despite these accusations, what is desirable in both the "beaux esprits" and the philosophes is a constant attention to both the expression and to the content of the ideas expressed. However, he concedes that the "goût du siècle" for philosophy has filled the literature with "dissertateurs qui, lourds, communs et fatigants, sont cependant pleins d'admiration pour la profondeur de leurs jugements." The result of these antagonisms is to discredit both the "beaux esprits" and the "dry" philosophes. Nonetheless, this "goût" for philosophy has been taken by the "homme du monde" who has learned to express himself clearly and with elegance as well as to think with precision and accuracy. He could do much, Helvétius thinks, to further the taste for philosophy. However, the society of the day leads both the "bel esprit" and "l'homme du monde," who resemble the former closely, to devote themselves to "médire agréablement" of others, all the more so that the art of satirizing others is the accepted way of praising one's self. "Ce n'est que par le mal qu'on dit d'autrui qu'il est maintenant permis de faire son éloge." However, since the ambition of everyone is to be thought brilliant and agreeable, they are easily pardoned for having but little profundity and praised for having an overabundance of raillery. This is not an unintelligent presentation of the intellectual conditions of his day.

What Helvétius seeks in his discussion on education in the fourth Discourse of the De l'Esprit is the technique of training each individual human mind employs to unite its interests with its talents, and those things with the individual's passions. What he really hopes to achieve is to transform the "esprit" into "génie." If the technique succeeds for the individual, Helvétius feels that it can assure progress in society. This progress, well understood, could guarantee that happiness which every government should have as its authentic goal. It comes down really to being the right kind of training for the right kind of people, and it fully involves the problem of education. Helvétius utters here, however, a word of caution. If this type of education could be discovered, it is evident that in the present state of manners and customs, it would be practically impossible to put these means into practice (II, 206).

He nonetheless lays down certain principles concerning this education. It is, for instance, closely united with the art of government, even to the point that any considerable change in public education will inevitably bring about modification in the constitution of the state. The education Helvétius is thinking about is the knowledge of means for forming healthy, strong bodies, more enlightened intellects, and more virtuous souls. To achieve these goals, Helvétius recommends a study of Greek method for making healthy bodies, and the formation of a special plan which will produce "well-developed" memory, strong passions, and a devotion to the general good. Helvétius even introduces certain very specific suggestions. (1) The national language should be well taught, rather than having a long period devoted to a "dead" language. Helvétius does not condemn the argument that the teaching of Latin inculcates in the student good habits of study; he merely suggests that these habits can be taught in more useful studies: history, physics, ethics, and poetry. To the argument that these subjects can be taught in the classics, he replies that it could be done with greatest speed in translation, but he argues that it is not worth all the time spent to control the originals. Moreover, the same training could be given in the native tongue. And even granting that the study of Latin is not at all sterile, can one justify the eight or ten years spent in studying "words" when one should be studying "things"?

Further, the education should be adjusted to the needs of the student. While a certain knowledge should be imparted to every citizen (principles of morality and the laws of the country, for instance) other matters should vary in accordance with the formation of the student. It is idle to force each student to follow the same prescribed course. Helvétius urges the type of course which will assure superior men, but he admits that in large empires this does not appear to be thought desirable. In despotism (or even in arbitrary governments) the interest of the rulers is so far removed from the general interest that the establishment of a system of courses so favorable to public utility is not thought advisable. This contradiction between the goal of virtue and the practice of perpetuating ignorance is too common in these empires to expect a great change in education. Helvétius concludes that while a liberal education is practically impossible in any despotism, it might be possible in a monarchy, provided the monarchy was not becoming despotic and provided the corruption of morals was not too advanced.

It should be recalled that Helvétius retained his interest in education to the end of his life. The title of the work which was published posthumously was really *De l'Homme, de ses facultés intellectuelles, et de son éducation*. In the Preface, he explains why he decided to put the publication off to a later date. He protests that love of his fellow man and regard for truth led him to compose it. He assures us that if men only knew each other and retained clear ideas upon morality, they would be happy and virtuous. He admits that the *De l'Homme* is but an extension of the *De l'Esprit*, but he insists he has been more careful to prepare proofs of his position. He declares his "bonne foi" with himself and affirms that he has only said what he believes true and has written nothing which he has not adopted for himself. He concludes, though, that he is convinced that France has become a despotism, eager to stifle thought and virtue, that its period of glory has now ended, and that he despairs of finding a remedy for a malady which seems to him incurable.

The body of the work, nonetheless, seems to express the same intensity of design which we have pointed out in the *De l'Esprit*. Helvétius is still seeking man's happiness, which he is convinced depends upon the perfection of laws, upon knowledge of the heart of man and of the human mind, and of those obstacles which impede progress in the sciences, morality, politics, and education. He promises to investigate whether the talents and virtue of a people assure its power and its happiness. This can only be determined by an inquiry as to whether man's talents and his virtues are the result of his physical makeup (organization) or of his education. But before these problems can be approached, one has to seek the true principles of education. However, he acknowledges that there are difficulties. The good book is practically always forbidden. The common man, who best profits from this research, is practically always incapable of concentration.

Helvétius affirms that each man has a particular education which perhaps accounts for the inequality of intellectual ability. He insists that two men nurtured in the same country, exposed to the same customs and the same manners, and raised in the same surroundings will have nevertheless a different outlook. Some of this difference, he argues, is due to chance. But some can be traced to the contradictions in the precepts taught. Helvétius now believes that much of this contradiction comes from the false precepts of religion. He states bluntly that, in his view, Catholicism is a pure idolatry. Its greatest defect is its intolerance. He concludes (p. 66): "Une morale fondée sur des principes vrais, est la seule vraie religion."

Section II lays down his fundamental principle. All men ordinarily well organized have an equal aptitude for intelligence. Helvétius concedes that all our ideas come from the senses, but he does not grant that there is a variability in the senses which justifies the difference in intellectual ability. He notes that there are two explanations for this phenomenon: the first is that the intellect is the result of a certain kind of temperament and an internal organization, but he points out that no one has presented proofs to substantiate this view. A second view which he himself supports is that the inequality is the result of education. He therefore starts with "toutes les opérations de l'esprit se réduisent à sentir . . ." and "nous devons nos idées à nos sens . . ." But he adds that experience proves that the "extrême perfection de ces mêmes sens" does not produce "le plus ou moins grande étendue de notre esprit."

Helvétius's *De l'Esprit* was criticized so severely that he is reputed to have said to Diderot that he would rather die than write another line. (See P. Keim, *Helvétius*, p. 506.) All the evidence we have however, indicates that sometime between 1759 and 1769, he composed *De l'Homme*. On 15 August 1769, he wrote to Lefèbvre-Larouche indicating that he now had the completed manuscript. In reality, though, it was only the first volume of a projected two-volume work. The published text was actually marked: "Fin du premier volume." Keim judges that after 1759, Helvétius became more and more aware that the public in general was more favorably disposed to his work than at first. As a matter of fact, Helvétius actually mentions the favorable response of the public in the above-mentioned letter. He reflected that some of the unfavorable comment had perhaps been occasioned by his own failure to express clearly or forcefully enough his own point of view. At all events, he explained in the Preface (p. viii) that the principles discussed in the *Esprit* have been treated more profoundly and more extensively in the *Homme*. Underlying the change in his determination to continue his task was the perfectly human trait of wanting to justify the severely censured principles of *De l'Esprit* by writing his apology in *De l'Homme*. He says as much in Part II, Chapter IX, which is entitled "Justification de principes admis dans le livre de l'esprit," but it is in the following Chapter X that he most explicitly reaffirms his view (p. 177):

Qu'on ne regarde pas cette discussion sur la sensibilité physique comme étrangère à mon sujet. Que me suis-je proposé? De faire voir que tous les hommes communément bien organizés, ont une égale aptitude à l'esprit. Qu'ai-je fait pour y parvenir? J'ai distingué l'esprit de l'âme. J'ai prouvé que l'âme n'est en nous que la faculté de sentir; que l'esprit en est l'effet; que dans l'homme tout est sensation; que la sensibilité physique est par conséquent le principe de ses besoins, de ses passions, de sa sociabilité, de ses idées, de ses jugements, de ses volontés, de ses actions, et qu'enfin si tout est explicable par la sensibilité physique, il est inutile d'admettre en nous d'autre faculté.

Added to this apology, there was in Helvétius (as in Voltaire, Diderot, Rousseau, and Montesquieu) an altruistic streak which prompted him to resume his task—"I would like to enlighten the common man." The very opening sentence of the Preface asserts that the love for his fellow men and a deep regard for truth have driven him to compose this work. It is true that, despite this altruistic note, he adds that he finds the sickness which has overtaken his society is practically incurable. One should point out also a certain amount of bitter satire in *De l'Homme* which certainly stems from the severe treatment he received in 1758 and 1759 and which is not too apparent in *De l'Esprit*. Helvétius explains that the work will be printed only after his death, since there is no advantage in being subjected to the same unjust treatment he has already undergone. In addition, he now openly declares his opposition to the Christian religion. In several places, in fact, he reverts to Biblical criticism as violent as anything in the critical manuscripts of the first half of the century in a tone which resembles d'Holbach. He expressed a particular animus against the Jesuits.

What is of more concern, however, than his animosity towards Jesuits is his rigid system, which he resumes tirelessly but with a certain number of variations. Philosophy seeks the happiness of man. Happiness depends upon laws and instruction which man receives. Good laws depend upon a philosopher's knowledge of the heart, of the human mind, of the working of heart and mind, of the obstacles which impede the progress of science, morality, politics, and education. A very serious obstacle in education is the teaching of a false science. Man is a product of his education. Helvétius insists that the science of man is a part of the science of government. The minister should therefore join to the science of man the science of government and the affairs of the time, thus insuring a set of good laws.

All of this apparently indiscriminate assertion of unorganized system somewhat masks the objective of his research. The central problem which he has posed is the question: "La différence des esprits est-elle l'effet de la différence, ou de l'organisation, ou de l'éducation?" Helvétius concedes that each student receives a different instruction. What contributes to inequality of intelligence is due to different impressions made by similar objects. Chance plays a role in offering opportunity for developing talents. Helvétius states (p. 41) that the moral education of man is practically entirely abandoned to chance. He indicates that this moral instruction is motivated by a desire to destroy the passions. This he considers a mistake: "Vouloir détruire les passions dans l'homme, c'est vouloir y détruire l'action." He is particularly opposed to the morality of religion and most opposed to the Jesuit view of morality. He much prefers some sort of code of natural laws. The most sacred of these laws, he avers, is the one which guarantees to each the possession of his property, his life, and his freedom. This, he thinks, never appears in a despotic state; consequently, he declares himself inutterably opposed to all forms of political despotism. But he does accept the union of church and state, that is to say, the unity of political and religious power.

Involved in all this discussion are "esprit," "âme," the objects of the external world, and the way "esprit" reacts as it passes from perception to attention, comparison, and judgment. Also involved is the way in which all of this mechanical operation of "esprit" derives from "sensibilité physique" and leads through the passions to facts and ideas and thence to the formation of a particular character and action. Thus, for Helvétius, as for Condillac, and Diderot, the problem is simultaneously psychological, moral, political and religious. He is thus forced to make distinctions, such as his insistence that there is a difference between the mind and the soul. In the first place, the soul exists in an adolescent entirely developed, while the mind is only in a state of development. Moreover, the soul does not abandon the body during life, while the intelligence may do so in certain circumstances. Finally, ideas are necessary to the mind, as Locke has shown, while thoughts are not at all necessary to the soul. The proper business of the mind is to be the observer of relationships of objects among themselves, and the relationship of these objects with themselves. Helvétius believes that an idea can always be reduced to facts or to physical sensations. It is, in fact, this reduction which produces physical sensibility. But this cannot occur, according to him, without a complicated series of mechanical operations. Physical sensibility, for instance, leads to interest, which in turn leads to attention, and thence to comparison and finally to judgment. Physical sensibility, furthermore, is the sole cause of one's actions, thoughts, passions, and sociability, but the principle of all sociability stems from "intérêt" and "besoins." The general conclusion of all this complicated rigmarole is given in Section II, Chapter VIII (p. 167): "C'est que les principes de la morale et de la politique, comme tous les principes des autres sciences doivent s'établir sur un grand nombre de faits et d'observations. Or, que résulte-t-il des observations faites jusqu'à présent, sur la morale? C'est que l'amour des hommes pour leurs semblables est un effet de la nécessité de s'entre-secourir, et d'une infinité de besoins dépendants de cette même sensibilité physique, que je regarde comme le principe de nos actions, de nos vices et de nos vertus."

Helvétius again makes an attempt to define exactly what he means by certain terms: virtuous or vicious behavior is what is useful or harmful to society. He also returns for a third time to examine the causes for the inequality of the human mind (p. 318): it can be traced, he assumes now, to the different sequence of events, circumstances, and positions of each individual; to the keen desire everyone has to be enlightened. And there will always be the effect of chance, but it will always be limited. *Esprit*, which presupposes comparison of objects, our personal interest, is now the knowledge of the true relationships between objects and ourselves. He complains that almost everybody is without passions, without love of glory, but almost in the next moment he asserts that to declaim against passions forever is crazy, since without them there can be no great artist, general, minister, poet, or philosopher. He inveighs against those who are indifferent to truth or falsehood, and who give themselves a philosophical repose, which holds the soul in inactivity and impedes its march to truth. His views on character are not without interest. The original character of every man is only the result of his initial habits. "Si l'on naît sans passions, on naît aussi sans caractère." There is also such a thing as a national character which differs from nation to nation, and is accordingly peculiar to each nation. Helvétius defines its manner of seeing things. This particular character changes little by little with alteration in the form of government, that is to say with public education. The changes, however, are greatest in moments of revolution when people pass from freedom to slavery.

Helvétius never tires of insisting that men are the product of their education, and that this education modifies the character. Each man changes his character also according to a change in position: "C'est donc à ce sentiment diversement modifié selon l'éducation qu'on reçoit, selon le gouvernement, sous lequel l'on vit, et les positions différentes où l'on se trouve, qu'on doit attribuer l'étonnante diversité des passions et des caractères." But the predominant factor in all this change is love of ourselves.

He now enters upon a realistic view of our ideals. Law, for instance, is what determines justice and injustice; before law, in fact, there is no such thing as justice. Indeed, justice presupposes established laws, just as it also presupposes a balance of power among the citizens. The truth of the matter is that man's respect for justice itself, about which we often boast, is nothing more than a respect for force. Nations act in the same way as the individual; everything indicates that they constantly rely on their force in all their enterprises. It is a fact evident in all history. The individual does not differ from his society. He, too, esteems in justice the power and happiness it produces: "L'homme uniquement occupé de lui-même, ne cherche que son bonheur." Helvétius, like Voltaire, denies Montesquieu's principles of the various types of government. Fear is not the characteristic of despotism, nor are honor and virtue the marks of monarchy or republics. What motivates every kind of government, is love of power. The citizen, for his part, wants to please the supreme power to get some portion of its authority for himself. Helvétius concludes here whatever the type of government, it is always a despotism (of one, of several, of all). However, the government where the nation is the despot, seeks "le bien du plus grand nombre." Consequently, every nation in conformity with the interest of the majority is virtuous. Each citizen, therefore, by love of power, is led to practice justice and utilize his talents for all. The goal of each is "la félicité publique." With all his tendency to denigrate all kinds of government or to attribute to them motives which are certainly not altruistic, Helvétius nonetheless praises the republic: "Cette forme de gouvernement a toujours été citée comme la meilleure. Les citoyens libres et heureux n'y obéissent qu'à la législation qu'eux-mêmes se sont donné; ils ne voyent au-dessus d'eux que la justice et la loi; ils vivent en paix, parce qu'au moral comme au physique, c'est l'équilibre des forces qui produit le repos." Helvétius maintains, nonetheless, that if Montesquieu had reflected more profoundly upon the facts, he would have realized that all men are united by the love for power. This power is secured by different means according to the type of government. However, the important thing is that all men owe their vices and their virtues to the way this power is secured, and thus they do not love justice for justice's sake.

Furthermore, Helvétius, following Hobbes, states that virtue derives from force, and implies prudence, courage, and charity, which is vague in meaning but always refers to a useful social quality. Each person pretends to love charity for itself. But he certainly does not do so. Pain and pleasure are always the determinants of virtue (p. 384): "L'hommage rendu à la vertu est passager, celui qu'on rend à la force est éternel." Helvétius asks: What attitude do Europeans hold toward virtue? He answers that they pay it honor in their speculation because of their education, but they hold it in contempt in practice because of the form of their government.

He finds that intolerance takes its source in the love of power (p. 392). In this section, Helvétius defends the freedom of the press: "La liberté de la presse n'a rien de contraire à l'intérêt" (p. 398). But rulers, as everybody, prefer to be flattered, not criticized. In fact, he concludes, it is because of our profound knowledge of the motives of our love for flattery and for our dislike for all forms of contradiction that one owes the solution of an infinite number of moral problems, totally unexplainable without this knowledge. Helvétius adds wistfully that the genius is always persecuted because he is apt to contradict beliefs now held. But he also asserts (p. 424): "Les hommes sont de leur nature intolérants," although he concedes that freedom of thought must be a natural right.

Grossman (*The Philosophy of Helvétius*, p. 77) finds that the significance of Helvétius's whole work lies in its being an epitome of current tendencies. We don't have to repeat in detail the analogy between his ideas and those of Montesquieu (the relationship between government and education, education and character), those of Voltaire (the necessity for pleasure, the search for happiness, the inordinate number of contradictions in human nature), those of Condillac (the role of the sensations, attention, comparison, judgment), those of Diderot (sensibilité, physique, dominance of the passions, self-love), and those of Rousseau (natural law, theory of virtue and vice, education). In imitation of all these, he too has a desire to be useful to society, to contribute to its happiness. As do all of them, he finds faith in progress inextricably mixed with the problem of virtue. Helvétius seems to divine in some vague way that man cannot achieve his happiness unless he commits himself to some sort of egotism, which can never be selfishness or some kind of sentimental charity. He seems utterly convinced that everyone is determined by his passions, his thoughts, his legislation, by his environment, and by some sort of chance which nullifies every effort to organize a life intellectually. Still, he leaves the impression that it is necessary to understand the nature of man if one would comprehend the nature of matter, the nature of human energy, and the nature of human character. One never quite knows, though, what is the focus of all this: is it that man is the product of his culture, or a result of his legislation, or is he a person who is the result of both legislation and character? Is the character, as he says, a manner of seeing things and feeling? Is national character a product of institutions and education? Are passions the wherewithall to form character, to organize a way of life, to build a moral, to produce progress? Helvétius seems to assert that all these things are realities. Then why comes the insistence that primacy among the passions must be attributed to self-love; that the quality of this self-love is justice; that all the so-called virtues as well as the vices derive from self-love; that the community spends its time devising means to combat self-love and individual interest, turning the individual to the "intérêt général"? Is "sensibilité physique" a chance something which produces this self-love, this desire for happiness, this desire for power, all these passions? And where does the human mind enter into all this? Is it, to begin with, an instrument for thought or is it a body of thoughts? And if it is the instrument which Helvétius envisages, why does he waste so much time about the materialism of the universe? Why does he spend so much energy in inveighing against Jesuitism and Christianity? Why talk so endlessly about determinism without ever asking just what is being determined?

Perhaps some headway could be made if we could comprehend just what he is about. Lacking really any definite assertion from himself, one would think that at least his retractions would give some clue to his goal. But, though lengthy, they do not give much inkling of what he is trying to do or hardly any defense of his intentions. They were undoubtedly a humiliating experience and they left Helvétius bitter, discouraged, and resentful, but his resentment doesn't seem to be more than a stereotype affair. Even his second book as an apology for the first does not seem to do more than repeat (though perhaps with greater clarity) what was said in the first. Voltaire once wrote that both were but a rehashing of La Rochefoucauld. But further than the bare statement that our vices are often our virtues, and although one may often pick an echo of La Rochefoucauld, the impression is gained that Helvétius is far too disorganized to be a true descendent of La Rochefoucauld. The supreme question must be put, silly though it seems to be. Has this disorganization which has struck Helvétius not struck rather the human mind? Call it "l'esprit," or "l'homme," or what you will. Has the human mind not collapsed completely in the *light* of the evidence?

Voltaire seems to have passed all these indiscriminate judgments upon the author of *De l'Esprit*. He reiterates time and again his affection for the author, but he asserts loudly that he has never approved of Helvétius's errors or the trivial truths (but can a truth be trivial?) which are dispersed in his works. One thing which he finds disagreeable is the "air d'emphase" which Helvétius constantly uses (M. XIX, 375). He nonetheless insists that when the author of the *De l'Esprit* was condemned for his work, he, Voltaire, took his side vigorously. Moreover, he declares that Mr. Helvétius "a du génie, de l'esprit, et un cœur charmant." He protests that he is one of the most zealous of Helvétius's supporters. In his *Correspondance*, he seems fairly consistently to have taken this attitude, expressed very succinctly, as in the letter to Condorcet, in 1772, on the occasion of Helvétius's death: "Je n'aimais pas son livre, mais j'aimais sa personne." He repeated the remark to Saurin: "Vous savez que j'aimais l'auteur . . . Mais vous savez aussi que je n'approuvai point cet ouvrage." Voltaire confessed to Saurin that there were brilliant passages in the *De l'Esprit*, some extraordinary statements, expressed with imagination. However, he confesses also that he was scandalized by Helvétius's treatment of friendship, repelled by his referring to Marcel in a work on human understanding, and amazed to read that

Ninon and Mlle. de Lecouvreur have as much intelligence as Solon and Aristotle. He condemns utterly Helvétius's idea that all men are born with the same talents and objected particularly to the chapter, "De la Probité par le rapport à l'univers." Besides, he said, the work is crammed with an infinite number of quotations "puériles et fausses" and bursting with a pretentiousness which he found terribly unpleasant. To Condorcet, Voltaire confesses that the work is the product of a "bon enfant qui court à tort et à travers sans savoir où." In general, he calls it rubbish, as in a letter to D'Alembert (M. XLVIII, 399): "Ce livre m'a paru du fatras, et j'en suis fâché." Voltaire nonetheless holds to his view that, although it requires much effort to read, "il y a de beaux éclairs." He pronounces it daring, curious in some places, "et en général ennuyeux." He fears that the opponents of the philosophes will use it as a characteristic philosophical work and thereby do the cause harm. To Saint Lambert he wrote: "Il n'y a pas le sens commun." He continues to dub it "du fatras" to Frederick, to the Président de Brosses. His fullest opinion of Helvétius was sent to Prince Gallitzin who in 1775 was preparing to bring out an edition of the *De l'Homme*. Voltaire compliments the prince upon the service he is rendering reason, but he adds that the work will arouse much opposition. Nobody will dare approve that all minds are equally adapted to the sciences and differ only according to their education. Voltaire still objects to Helvétius's treatment of friendship. He feels certain that the author has allowed himself to be carried away by the "esprit systématique." Moreover, the work is lacking in method, it contains too many trivial stories. He nonetheless approves Helvétius's attack against "superstition," his assault upon intolerance, and in general his treatment upon freedom, tyranny, and man's unhappiness. These sections represented Voltaire's own attitude and after the appearance of *De l'Esprit*, he advised Helvétius to concentrate upon them. They were emphasized more in *De l'Homme*, but apparently not enough to satisfy Voltaire.

Rousseau, for his part, related in his *Lettre à Christophe de Beaumont* how he had been scandalized by the *De l'Esprit* and since he had judged its ideas dangerous (but, of course, the real question is, Are they true?), he had prepared a refutation. On hearing, however, that the author of the *De l'Esprit* was being persecuted, he had thrown the refutation in the fire. Nonetheless, we do have in the *Œuvres complètes* (XII, 298–304) a few pages devoted to particular comment upon Discourses I and II. Rousseau took exception to Helvétius's use of the "sensibilité physique," but the rest of his comments dealt with more particular details concerning the memory and judgment and, most of all, with precise definitions. These notes were written by Rousseau in the copy of the *De l'Esprit* which the author had presented to him. His notes on the copy and a few allusions in the correspondence show that he, as well as Voltaire and Diderot, esteemed the author as a man, though all three regarded his views as dangerous. Rousseau felt that the danger stemmed from Helvétius's materialist tendencies.

Voltaire's criticism of Helvétius had been, as practically all his criticism, balanced, measured, and not particularly explicit. The curious thing about it, however, was that in many respects, it coincided with Diderot's. The latter, however, was very careful to organize his criticism, but he, like Rousseau, refrained from publishing it during his lifetime. He wrote it during two different periods. Just after the appearance of the *De l'Esprit* he wrote the *Réflexions sur le livre de l'Esprit*. After Helvétius's death in 1771, Prince Gallitzin, Catherine's ambassador to The Hague, undertook to bring out the *De l'Homme*. Diderot, who was staying with Gallitzin, saw the work on the way to visit Catherine. While waiting for his escort, he perused it with care, making a set of notes. On his return from St. Petersburg, he stopped again at The Hague, took out his notes upon *De l'Homme*, and corrected them scrupulously. At some later date, he revised them a second time, kept them in his library in Paris, and after his death, they were sent to Catherine. It was this version which Naigeon knew, and which eventually was published in the *Œuvres complètes* (II, 275–456). Naigeon attributed to them a great importance which, all told, can be fully justified. Having furnished Helvétius with a good deal of his thought and some specific theories which were crucial with Naigeon as well as with Helvétius he had the opportunity to examine them as they appeared in the work of another. Vernière, in his edition of *Œuvres politiques* has given them a greater importance still. Diderot held many views in common with Helvétius, but particularly the theory of the "sensibilité physique." In this theory, Diderot not only wrote a *Réfutation suivi de l'œuvre d'Helvétius intitulé l'Homme* but also gave a critique of those ideas which in a way were absolutely fundamental to his own thinking.

His review of *De l'Esprit*, though marked *Réflexions*, is a thoroughgoing affair, which begins with the objective of the work ("considérer l'esprit humain sous différentes faces, et s'appuyer partout de faits"). Diderot notes that Helvétius seems to attribute sensibility to all matter and to reduce all intellectual functions to sensibility. To perceive, to feel, to judge, all represent the same thing. Moreover, there is no difference between man and animal except in organization. There is no false intelligence; errors are attributable to ignorance, passions, or to an abuse of terms. After these general considerations, Helvétius studies, says Diderot, the relationships of probity to itself, to an individual, to a little group, to a nation, to different centuries, to different countries, to the whole universe. In all these cases, personal interest is the measure of our regard for it; in fact, this interest is what gives it its identity. Hence, there is no absolute justice or injustice. Diderot stops to assert that this point is a paradox, difficult to prove, dangerous to morals, and therefore false, because it is possible to detect in our needs, in our organization, and in our sensibilities, an infinite basis for justice. Diderot maintains that Helvétius's difficulty comes from not understanding that probity is simple charity toward one's fellow man. Hence probity is "un sentiment de bienfaisance qui embrasse l'espèce humain en général." Diderot concedes that though his main point is false and a paradox, the author has treated other matters of importance: true and false virtues, moralists, hypocritical moralists, the importance of morality, and the ways in which it can be perfected. Helvétius's third discourse, said Diderot, is devoted to showing that the difference between men is not due to the physical organization of each, but to difference in education. Succinctly expressed: "il n'y a point d'homme en qui la passion, l'éducation, l'intérêt et de certains hasards n'eussent pu surmonter les obstacles de la nature, et en faire un grand homme, dont le défaut de passion, d'intérêt, d'éducation, et de certains hasards n'eussent pu faire un stupide" (II, 270). This likewise, says Diderot, is a paradox. The difficulty, as Diderot sees it, is that Helvétius fails to understand the slow working of causes over long periods of time, and he fails to distinguish between different temperaments, different ages, and periods, and different conditions. After showing that all the differences between man and animal is in the organization, Helvétius fails to note that this same organization is what may distinguish the genius and the imbecile. Diderot concedes that this third Discourse— which is crammed with excellent details on the origin of the passions, on their force, on friendship, ambition, and pride—is nonetheless false "dans le fond." In the meantime, Helvétius has suggested an additional paradox: physical pleasure is the ultimate pleasure which all passions envisage. Diderot denies this paradox also. He now sums up the four paradoxes presented by Helvétius. (1) Sensibility is a general property of matter: "apercevoir, raisonner, juger, c'est sentir." (2) There is no such thing as absolute justice and injustice: "l'intérêt général est la mesure de l'estime des talents, et l'essence de la vertu." (3) Education and not physical organization is what differentiates between men: "Les hommes sortent des mains de la nature, tous presque également propres à tout." (4) All passions tend to the satisfaction of bodily desires. Add to these four paradoxes, which Diderot denies, an unbelievable number of other dissertations on religion, morals, and government; on man, legislation, and educa- tion, and you will have the whole book. Contrary to Voltaire, who found it systematic but unmethodical, Diderot finds it methodical but not very systematic. It is above all, says Diderot, highly para- doxical. But, he concludes, the "esprit de méthode" is its greatest defect: "L'esprit de méthode arrange, ordonne, et suppose que tout est trouvé. Voilà le défaut principal de cet ouvrage." Nonetheless, Diderot stated that the *De l'Esprit* is really a fitting preface to the *Esprit des lois*. It was a remarkable statement to make, all the more so because he adds that Helvétius is not of Montesquieu's opinion. Moreover, what puzzled Diderot above everything was that the book was "fait exprès pour la nation"; it possesses the qualities (clarity, amusement, and charm) which the French would demand, it was written especially to please women and, at the moment when a revolt on the part of subordinates against their superiors was in full swing— "paraissant dans un temps où tous les ordres foulés sont assez mécon- tens, où l'esprit de fronde est plus à la mode que jamais, ou le gou- vernement n'est excessivement aimé ni prodigieusement estimé"—it has revolted practically everybody. Diderot suggests that its principles are false, but its details are true. He predicts that the work will ultimately be useful to mankind and, although it has not the genius of Montesquieu and Buffon, "il sera pourtant compté parmi les grands livres du siècle."

Diderot's *Réfutation suivie de l'œuvre d'Helvétius intitulée l'Homme* is a lengthy work of 175 large octavo pages. It is not easy to read, since Diderot gives the passage from Helvétius, which he follows with a denial, a commentary, or a reflection—sometimes with an anecdote to accentuate the error and frequently with personal debates with the author, in a modest but active dialogue. Each of these little vignettes can be interesting for itself, but when an attempt is made to bring them into some meaningful unity, it is very difficult to do so. It can be clearly seen that Diderot was scandalized by the position of Helvétius. Often he protests that the Helvétius he knew and respected ought not to be expected to take this attitude. Diderot seems nonplussed by remarks which he deems more or less out of character. He obviously finds it difficult to excuse them; his most charitable excuse is that Helvétius's unfair persecution distorted his judgment. But he also suggests fairly often that Helvétius's love of paradox carried him away. One general remark which Diderot made very frequently throughout the refutation was that many of Helvétius's observations are exaggerated rather than erroneous. He points out in innumerable cases that if the author had used more modest and consequently less dogmatic statements, the remark would be accepted as ingenious. His most striking criticism of the author is contained in the following comment (p. 356): "Dans presque tous les raisonnements de l'auteur, les premisses sont vraies, et les conséquences sont fausses, mais les prémisses sont pleines de finesse et de sagacité. Il est difficile de trouver ses raisonnements satisfaisants, mais il est facile de rectifier ses inductions et de substituer la conclusion légitime à la conclusion erronée qui ne pèche communément que par trop de généralité." Diderot repeated this kind of criticism almost as a refrain after condemnation of some aspect of the *Homme*, while protesting his great respect for the work. There are, he says (p. 315) "cent belles, très-belles pages; il fourmille d'observations fines et vraies." Moreover, those things he finds impossible, can be rectified without difficulty by toning down the statements. It is true that Helvétius's logic is not rigorous and the conclusions are too generalized, but he is, Diderot kept affirming, a great moralist, a subtle observer of human nature, a great thinker, an excellent writer, and a fine genius.

Diderot compares him with Rousseau, whose principles, he says, are false while his consequences are true. Helvétius, on the contrary, holds principles which are true while his consequences are false. Helvétius is sincere at the beginning; Rousseau is sincere at the end. Rousseau believes that society is only fit to deprave the nature of man; Helvétius believes that only good social laws can correct the original vices of nature. Rousseau's philosophy is in bits and pieces; Helvétius's is well unified. But Diderot adds significantly that he would rather be Jean-Jacques than Helvétius, although he would have preferred to have written Helvétius's works rather than Rousseau's. He did, to all intents and purposes; that is precisely the trouble.

Nonetheless, Diderot notes that there is a great difference between Helvétius and himself. Helvétius pessimistically despairs of man, particularly of the French, while Diderot, who is ready enough to see that humankind is rarely admirable, is nonetheless inclined to treat the subject more cheerfully. Where Helvétius, for instance, wrote that the French nation is now held in contempt by all Europe, Diderot objected: "L'expérience actuelle prouve le contraire. Que les honnêtes gens qui occupent à présent les premières places de l'Etat les conservent seulement pendant dix ans, et tous nos malheurs seront réparés." The objections of Diderot to these arbitrary statements are legion. Where Helvétius wrote (p. 300): "Sentir, c'est juger," Diderot commented that the remark is not really true unless, along with feeling, there is not also memory and comparison and judgment. Diderot's objection to these generalizations is taken explicitly here: "passer brusquement de la sensibilité physique . . . à l'amour du bonheur, de l'amour du bonheur à l'intérêt, de l'intérêt à l'attention, de l'attention à la comparaison des idées; je ne saurais m'accommoder de ces généralités-là: je suis homme, et il me faut des causes propres à l'homme." But even Diderot confesses that although he can understand in these terms the passage from feeling to judgment, and although he clearly sees in the development of the egg and other phenomena in nature, inert but organized matter which passes in a purely physical way from the state of inertia to the state of sensibility and of life, he fails to grasp the necessary liaison of this passage.

Diderot surmises that some of the difficulty springs from the fact that we understand imperfectly what we mean by matter, movement, sensibility, and organization. Furthermore, he suggests that the mainsprings of our desires and aversions lie elsewhere. Consequently, when Helvétius dares assert that physical sensibility is the sole cause of actions, thoughts, passions, and even our sociability, Diderot protests vigorously. The point he tries to make is that beyond the physical there is involved in all this the moral, which has a whole set of values not known to the physical. It is not that Diderot denies the physical aspect of sensibility, but he urges that it exists as a condition, not a cause, a goal, or even a motive. For instance, there is certainly a happiness circumscribed within the limits of the individual which does not transcend the physical, but there is also an expanding happiness, which goes from the present to the future and which "repaît de jouissances morales et physiques, de réalités et de chimères, entassant pêle-mêle" money, praises, pictures, statues, and kisses.

Diderot does not always reject Helvétius's observations, however. When the latter states, for instance, that pleasure and pain are the sole motives of man's actions, Diderot agrees, and he adds that this work is filled with an infinity of maxims with which he is in accord. Nonetheless, though he admits the principle, he denies the consequence. In this particular case, for example, Helvétius admits only corporal pleasure and pain, and Diderot insists that he has often experienced others. When Leibniz shut himself in his world to develop his preestablished harmony, he was pursuing a pleasure, but it was remote from bodily pleasures. Diderot insists that Helvétius has overlooked an important principle, which is that man's reason is an instrument which corresponds to all the variety of animal instinct. Diderot concedes that man combines ideas as instinctively as birds fly and fish swim, but he insists that each man is carried on by his organization, his character, his temperament, his natural aptitude, and his inclinations. Chance and needs play a role, too. This, Diderot maintains, is the real explanation of life, and not the sophisticated suppositions of Helvétius, proposed with much sagacity but no verity, charming details but absurd consequences.

The important Chapter XII, on the senses, is discussed at considerable length by Diderot. He accepts the doctrine of the sensations without debate, of course, but he maintains that Helvétius has forgotten the "juge ou le rapporteur." One must feel, to be sure, to be an orator, poet, or philosopher, but one is not philosopher, poet, orator, or scholar because one feels. There is a particular organ—the mind—to which the five senses must make their report. Helvétius has forgotten its organizing function. An individual whose senses are excellent but whose head is ill-organized is naturally in a bad way. The witnesses are faithful, but the judge is corrupted. That individual will always be a fool. The mind will vary, too, because of climate. Diderot states that with only a bit more attention, the author would have realized that he had neglected the most important element of them all—the mind. It is the instrument par excellence for organic unity of the senses. Whereas in an animal, one sense may predominate and actually dominate the reason if he has one, not so in man: "Il est entre ses sens une telle harmonie qu'aucun ne prédomine assez sur les autres pour donner la loi à son entendement; c'est son entendement, au contraire, ou l'organe de sa raison, qui est le plus fort." And so the man of genius and the animal "se touchent" because both have a dominant element. But the important point to stress here is that Helvétius has neglected the examination of an organ without which the perfect condition of the others is meaningless. It is this organ which is responsible for all the astonishing differences of man in all intellectual matters. In fact, it renders practically useless all discussions about chance, personal interest, attention, even physical sensibility. In addition, it transforms the moral problem by negating sensual pleasures as the principle of all action. Diderot insists that if the human mind were not in control of the senses, first one sense and then another would dominate temporarily, and this would insure a momentary consciousness, but there would certainly not be a harmonious consciousness of the entire being. Diderot concedes that this harmonizing intellectual force may be the guarantee of the "sensibilité physique." He attempts to apportion out these faculties: "La tête fait les hommes sages; le diaphragme les hommes compatissants et moraux" (p. 338). They are the two "grands ressorts de la machine." It is these two, working in harmony, which give some insight into the genius, the poet, the painter, the moralist. But we must remember that man is limited, the genius is rare. Moreover, Diderot denies that every man is born with an "esprit juste." Everybody is, in fact, born "sans esprit." It is neither "faux" nor "juste." It very likely becomes "faux" if he uses his senses ill, if he thinks he knows everything, if he is precipitate in his judgment on a matter he is incompetent to judge, if he is filled with prejudices. Which, says Diderot, is merely another way of stating that all personal interests, all prejudices, all passions, all vices, all virtues are capable of upsetting the mind and preventing an "esprit juste." In fact, Diderot wrote: "Un esprit juste de tout point est un être de raison" (p. 344). Diderot confesses that he has sought the truth, but he has never found it, from whence he has surmised (p. 345): "On n'a rien de mieux à faire pour son bonheur que d'être un homme de bien." Diderot concludes (p. 346): "Chacun est poète à sa manière, éloquent à sa manière, fait de la peinture, de la sculpture, de la gravure, même de la géométrie, de la mécanique, de l'astronomie comme soi et non comme un autre." It was the conclusion of the *Neveu de Rameau* also, which we often fail to grasp.

Diderot undertakes to correct (pp. 357-367) a number of Helvétius's statements. After a number of these modifications, he sums up: "Et ainsi de toutes ses assertions, aucune qui soit absolument vraie ou absolument fausse." He expresses astonishment that Helvétius has not realized that systematic correcting of these exaggerated statements would have transformed his *Homme* into a well-received work. Diderot insists that every impartial reader will grant that, even with its defects, it is excellent. It will, however, be decried because Helvétius has attacked many important people. Diderot adds that he himself had judged it too severely when he had read it in manuscript. "Cela ne me parut qu'une paraphrase assez insipide de quelques mauvaises lignes du livre *De l'Esprit*. He confesses that he has now changed his mind: "Je fais cas et très-grand cas de ce traité." He recommends it to his fellow citizens, particularly to those in public office, who may learn the importance of good legislation and the necessity for a satisfactory educational system. He affirms that there are nonetheless places where Helvétius wavers, others where contradictions are all too evident. Diderot seems genuinely puzzled as to Helvétius's motives, since Helvétius must have recognized these contradictions. He laments ultimately, though, that the author has not given the full measure of the keenness of his mind and the penetration of his intellect. He persists in being an "homme à paradoxe," but, Diderot adds, there is always something to be learned from these paradoxical writers.

Despite the terrible length of this analysis, we must add a few concluding remarks of our own. By way of summary, we must repeat that Helvétius was regarded during his day as the extreme radical thinker of his time. We must not forget also that he was not a writer by profession, but that he wanted to be one. He started out by wanting to be a poet, as Voltaire did, and he ended by being a philosopher, as Voltaire did. He was indeed trained by Voltaire; he followed Voltaire in many of his poetic subjects and some of his clandestine writing. But he had absorbed philosophical ideas from both Rousseau and Diderot. His composite production was oriented by a conscious and willful attempt to merge into some organic way the thought of Voltaire, Rousseau, and Diderot. All the evidence seems to indicate that he encountered obstacles in successfully executing his plan. His work, consequently, met with strong disapproval by those who disapproved of Voltaire, Rousseau, or Diderot, who in many respects did not approve of each other. There must be some importance attached to an interpretation assigned to these facts. All three were the source of Helvétius's work and all three wrote criticisms. Those of Diderot were lengthy, full, carefully prepared and even judiciously presented, but they represented a very serious critique of his own philosophical position, a sort of auto-critique, so to speak. With this in mind, we must ultimately inquire whether it is possible to obtain an organic view of an enlightenment which is compounded of the philosophical stances of Montesquieu, Voltaire, Rousseau, and Diderot. But that is not the most serious difficulty. When one recalls what the ideas presented in the *De l'Esprit* and the *De l'Homme* meant to John Stuart Mill and Jeremy Bentham, after playing a role of some importance in the formation of the Physiocrats and the Idéologues, one is justified in being a bit uneasy about the quality of our Enlightenment criticism or the authenticity of our Enlightenment thought. However, when we realize that this particular thought of Helvétius has been acknowledged, that the secret vice of mankind is now revealed to all, we are more or less prepared to understand that this is indeed, morally speaking at least, "le moment de la crise."

HOLBACH, VOLTAIRE, AND THE DEBATE ON ATHEISM

PAUL-HENRY THIRY, later to become the baron d'Holbach, and called by Rousseau in the *Confessions* a "parvenu," was born at Edesheim on 8 December 1723. The title came from an uncle who had been successful in his affairs in Paris and had procured a title of nobility. The family was apparently rather solidly middle class. The uncle took the young nephew with him to Paris and accepted responsibility for his education. In 1744, the nephew undertook his university studies at Leyden, where in 1746 he knew John Wilkes. His studies seem to have been in the area of chemistry as well as in arts and letters. The chevalier de Jaucourt was also at Leyden, but we do not know whether the two actually knew each other at that time. In 1750, Holbach married a cousin who died in 1754 and, in 1756, he married his sister-in-law, Charlotte-Suzanne D'Aine, whose mother was the life of the famous dinners at Grandval and the great joy of Diderot in his correspondence with Sophie Volland. The parties were rendered famous also by Rousseau who sealed the idea of a "coterie" organized to destroy religion.

How and when the baron came in contact with the encyclopedists is none too clear, however. Since D'Holbach wrote many articles in the area of chemistry, it has been assumed that Diderot brought him into the group precisely to look after that area. To judge by Rousseau's references and by those of others in Morellet's *Mémoires*, the reputation of Holbach among the group far exceeded the field of chemistry. Around 1935, Mornet, especially in his *Origines intellectuelles*, did much to show D'Holbach's role in publishing a number of clandestine manuscripts which circulated in France during the first half of the century, and Professor Lough, only recently, has done much to clarify the Baron's contributions to the *Encyclopédie*, which have turned out to be varied, more important, and far more numerous than had been thought in the past. (See J. Lough, *Essays on the Encyclopédie of Diderot and D'Alembert*, London, 1968, Chapter III, "D'Holbach's Contribution," pp. 111-251.) It should be added that D'Holbach also took some part in the quarrel on music which Grimm, D'Holbach, Diderot and Rousseau pursued very vigorously. In very recent times, the baron's role in all these enterprises has been subjected to a very rigid examination in an effort to ascertain whether there ever was a "coterie Holbachique," as Jean-Jacques insisted, or whether the whole denunciation has not been greatly exaggerated. We should not neglect in this respect Morellet's *Mémoires*, which we have mentioned above. Morellet wrote that "sa maison rassemblait dès lors les plus marquants des hommes de lettres français: Diderot, J. J. Rousseau, Helvétius, Barthes, Venelle, Rouelle, Carcet, Rous, Duclos, Saurin, Raynal, Suard, Boullanger, Marmontel, St. Lambert, La Condamine et le Chevallier de Chastellux." (See A. C. Kors, *D'Holbach's Coterie*, Princeton, 1976.)

J. P. Belin, in *Le Mouvement philosophique de 1748 à 1789* (Paris, 1913, pp. 267–288), nonetheless accepts the tradition of a "secte Holbachique" which flourished from 1767 to 1773, at least. Belin names as members of the group Diderot, Lagrange; a mathematician, Leroy, author of *Examen du livre intitulé de l'Esprit*, and a treatise on animals; the Abbé Morellet, whose *Mémoires* contained some information on the activities of the group; Raynal, and Naigeon. As depicted by Morellet, it had all the earmarks of a secret society, organized to prepare numerous of the clandestine manuscripts of the first part of the century for the printer and to expedite transmission to Marc-Michel Rey at Amsterdam, Rousseau's regular publisher, and on occasion, Voltaire's, Diderot's, and Holbach's. The Morellet account says a chain of collaborators was organized, and the secret was guarded so closely that not even Holbach, the "âme damnée" of the enterprise, knew all the devious manipulations whereby the manuscripts were copied and transmitted to Rey. Belin seems to assume that Voltaire, too, was in the party. Indeed, we know from Voltaire's *Correspondance* that he did prepare and transmit to Rey a certain number of these manuscripts through Jean-Jacques's erstwhile friend at Neuchâtel, Dupeyrou. There are some letters between Dupeyrou and Rey which leave no doubt that a commerce of this sort actually took place between Ferney and Amsterdam. Belin indicates that there was some collusion between Holbach and Voltaire which continued from the early 1760s to 1770, but this is none too certain. Voltaire was well aware of Holbach's activities in this field, since he wrote to friends recommending to them some of the titles Holbach is supposed to have published, along with others in whose publication Voltaire is known to have had a hand. As a consequence of all this scurrying around, we are none too sure just who did what. Mornet, in his *Origines intellectuelles*, noted that particular incidents in this area are obscure, and much needs to be done before we can be reasonably certain how the project was effected. While he himself was convinced of these difficulties and while he himself made some effort to clear up some details, he admitted that he had not succeeded any too well. There is, however, a work being prepared for publication at the present time which presumably will solve this matter. It is not the least strange that the baron's catalogue of his library does not mention a single title among the 106 clandestine manuscripts which we know. He could have prepared some of them and sent them directly to Rey, but then the story about having copies for the printer would not fit any too well.

Mornet makes the point that it really does not make much difference who carried on the enterprise of publishing a quantity of these clandestine manuscripts. Looked at from the angle of influence upon the thought of the eighteenth century, that statement is reasonable enough. Naville, however, who was interested in the formation of Holbach's materialistic philosophy, had to preoccupy himself with the specific problem of the extent of Holbach's acquaintance with these manuscripts. (See P. Naville, *D'Holbach et la philosophie scientifique au XVIIIe siècle*, Paris, 1967, pp. 139–224.) He has consequently studied a number of them for similar interests, similar ideas, and similar expression. That is not an easy task if one requires specific resemblances. Naville has been forced to bring together and review a certain number of the presumed authors of these manuscripts, particularly those who had tendencies toward materialism and atheism rather than those who were fundamentally deistic. It is difficult, however, to make this distinction except in certain particular cases, that of Jean Meslier, for instance. In general, our best and only approach is to show that in attitude, there is much in common between the writers of these treatises and Holbach and this has been done fully by M. Naville, who has grouped this material under the concept of "Matrices" in a very intelligent way. He has explained in a foreword to the second part of his book his intention of dividing into four groups these influences, which he attempts to elucidate: (1) that of a group of deists and materialists of the first part of the eighteenth century (Boulainvilliers, Fréret, Dumarsais, Mirabaud,

Meslier, etc., to whom he has added Boullanger; (2) La Mettrie; (3) the English deists and materialists (Toland and Collins, along with Hobbes, Locke, and Hume); and (4) the chemists and mineralogists in Germany. Naville adds that these works found their place in a wide range of previous works which embrace in antiquity Lucretius, Democritus, and Epicurus; in the late Renaissance and early seventeenth century, Bruno, Gassendi, Vanini, "et bien d'autres." M. Naville adds that Descartes, Spinoza, and Leibniz must have had a considerable influence upon the German baron, but he insists that Holbach always assumes a very critical attitude toward them. The critic sums up in one potent sentence his method in general: "Nous ne groupons là que les œuvres de la première moitié du XVIIIe siècle, dont d'Holbach a directement retenu quelque chose, qui jouèrent dans l'élaboration de sa philosophie un rôle particulier, qui en constituent les vraies matrices" (p. 140).

Holbach seems to have had in his publication a definite plan of proceeding. He began in 1766, just after the completion of the full *Encyclopédie*, to bring out *l'Antiquité dévoilée* in three volumes, attributed to M. Boulanger. Boulanger was a young engineer who in 1762 had published *Essai sur le despotisme oriental*, which had created a stir. Belin assumes that Holbach borrowed his name (he was now dead) in connection with the *Antiquité*. We are not quite sure that this was the way things were. At all events, Holbach brought out in the following year (1767) *Le Christianisme dévoilé*. Belin further assumes that there was some conniving between Voltaire and Holbach in connection with the clandestine deistic manuscripts which Rey brought out at this time. However, he states that in 1770, Holbach produced his *Système de la nature* and that Voltaire, properly scandalized, would henceforth have none of it. We are not exactly sure that this was the situation either. We have to draw our conclusions from Voltaire's published reaction to what Holbach said, and we do not exactly know whether they express an expedient point of view or his own personal opinion.

The author of the *Système de la nature* states in the preface (p. 13) that the aim of the work is to bring man back to nature, to restore reason to its position of primacy, to show how virtue should be adored, and to dissipate the darkness which conceals the only way suitable to lead him to the happiness which he desires. Holbach insists that he is sincere in these aims, that he is presenting in good faith to the reader only those ideas which after a serious and long period of reflection have appeared useful for the repose and welfare of man and favorable to the progress of the human mind. Holbach urged the reader to discuss these principles. He maintained that, far from wishing to break the sacred bonds of morality, he desires to tighten them, and to replace virtue on the altars which hitherto imposture, enthusiasm, and fear have raised to dangerous spirits. The wordy, pretentious, and bombastic tone of this statement is characteristic of the two-volume book which Holbach presented. He repeats over and over in the same sort of language the main points of his diatribe throughout nine hundred pages. One can imagine Voltaire's distaste at having to read this pseudo-eloquence. The ideas gave him pause, the style must have threatened something resembling a nervous breakdown. Still, the story persists that Holbach boasted that he wrote better than Voltaire, since his material had been previously corrected by Diderot. We can probably safely dispose of both the legend and his assertion. However, it will be difficult to do away with the ideas he presented.

Curiously, there is not yet a satisfactory summary of these ideas. Everyone recalls that the author is a materialist, an atheist, but no one seems anxious to plow through these nine hundred pages and cull out these ideas in some coherent way. Few would question that Holbach played a significant role in the development of materialism but nobody seems to want to study how significant this role was. Only Naville has come to grips with this problem in any intelligent way.

The ideas at least can be detailed clearly if one can exercise patience in organizing them. Holbach insists that man is a purely physical being and that moral man is nothing but this physical being considered from a particular point of view. His manner of acting is derived exclusively from his organization. This concept of organization was fundamental with Helvétius and also with Diderot. D'Holbach expressed it clearly enough in the following statement: "Ses actions visibles ainsi que les mouvements invisibles . . . qui viennent de sa volonté et de sa pensée sont . . . des suites nécessaires de son méchanisme propre, et des impulsions qu'il reçoit des êtres dont il est entouré." This seems much like the widespread notion that man is what he thinks, says, and does, but there is a great difference in the addition of the "nécessaire" and the "méchanisme." Otherwise, man's goal, as D'Holbach sees the situation, does not differ from that advocated by his previous philosophe friends: "Toutes nos institutions, nos réflexions, nos connaissances n'ont pour objet que de nous procurer un bonheur vers lequel notre propre nature nous force de tendre sans cesse." That notion, also often expressed by Diderot, was accepted by Voltaire, Rousseau, and everybody else, as Mauzi has so well shown. (See *L'Idée du bonheur au XVIIIᵉ siècle*.) However, D'Holbach gives it a slant which was not very prevalent in 1770. To achieve this happiness, man should consult physical laws and experience (that is to say, he should use in matters pertaining to himself and his problems the method of the natural sciences) in all matters pertaining to religion, morality, legislation, political organization, sciences and arts, pleasures and pain. The one fundamental law which explains the phenomena of the universe both physical and moral is motion, because "le tout" which had been discussed so widely since Spinoza's time meant nature and the great discovery in nature was the law of inertia, or the laws of movement, or the Newtonian Law. It operates in moral matters as clearly as in physical matters, simply because moral matters, as we have seen above, are merely particular ways of regarding physical matters. The all-embracing term is "nature." She is, as D'Holbach asserts "dépourvue de bonté, comme de malice." He adds: "Elle suit des lois nécessaires et immuables en produisant et détruisant des Etres."

Man in his ignorance has been enslaved. He has failed to know his duties to others. He has failed to understand his true interests. He has completely misunderstood morality. Moreover, his government would have prevented him from practicing this proper morality even if he had known it. Man has a stupid respect for antiquity, for the institutions of the past. It is this inertia which prevents medicine, physics, and agriculture from developing. The remedy for this situation is to follow reason, avoid ignorance and prejudices, practice a healthy suspicion of imagination, and accept only experience as guide. The universe everywhere offers matter and movement. It is ruled everywhere by cause and effect. Different properties of matter, different movements, different combinations, the varied ways of acting "qui en sont des suites nécessaires"—all this constitutes the essence of things, what we call Nature. It is "un grand tout," and man is an "arrangement de matières—organization."

The clarity of this exposition carries with it a certain conviction. Nonetheless, one cannot resist the impression that the *Système de la nature* is more eloquent than profound; it is, above all, verbose and terribly repetitive. On the other hand, one must grant that despite these tedious impressions, D'Holbach's arguments seem well reasoned, clearly presented, and, were it not for some serious contradictions, rather convincingly put. Its reduction of the universe to matter and movement, undoubtedly invented by Diderot as the focal point around which the whole materialism and atheism were built, was a stroke of genius. The identification of physical with moral movement had the result of uniting the science of nature with the science of man. At the same time, it tiresomely works over all the old theories of knowledge which had long since been put in question. The long discussion against the existence of innate ideas seems totally unjustified. The author proscribed such terms as "sentiment moral," and "instinct moral." He repeated (I, 198): "Ainsi, on ne peut trop le répéter, toutes les idées, les notions, les façons d'être et de penser des hommes sont acquises." Finally, despite his protestations of altruism and his desire to aid mankind, it is perfectly obvious that the author lacks any confidence in man or any faith in his institutions. As a result of these inconsistencies, we get the curious impression that the work, though highly logical and deeply rational, is flawed by a rabid dislike of certain aspects of life, which amounts to an unreasoning condemnation that is both irrational and paradoxical. When he writes, for instance, that "la diversité des tempéraments des hommes est la source naturelle et nécessaire de la diversité de leurs passions, de leurs goûts, de leurs idées de bonheur, de leurs opinions en tout genre," we cannot resist feeling that he really has no solid foundation upon which to build a *système de la nature*.

He presents a long and involved argument against the doctrine of free will. As a matter of fact, he introduces three arguments. (1) For it to be free, it would be necessary that all other beings lose their essences in his favor . . . he could no longer have physical sensibility, he could never know either good or evil, pain or pleasure. He sums up this argument with the laconic remark "Nous agissons toujours suivant des loix nécessaires." (2) A choice of an action does not at all prove free will in man, because this choice is necessitated by motives which drive him. But the third argument is the telling one. (3) Our ways of thinking are necessarily determined by our manner of existing; they depend on our organic nature. The mistake of those who accept free will comes from believing that the will is the first cause for action. The author concludes (I, 226): "En un mot les actions des hommes ne sont jamais libres; elles sont toujours des suites nécessaires de leur tempérament, de leurs idées reçues, des notions vraies ou fausses qu'ils se font du bonheur, enfin de leurs opinions fortifiées par l'exemple, par l'éducation, par l'expérience journalière." To be sure, this does not mean that man is subject to some impulsive cause. "Il renferme en lui-même des causes inhérentes à son être." He is moved by an internal organ (the human mind) which has its own laws, and which is determined necessarily by virtue of the ideas, perceptions, and sensations which he receives from external objects. The author explains that what leads to belief that we are free is the great complexity of our movements, the immense variety of our actions, and the multiplicity of the causes which drive us. Finally, we see, or at any rate we think we do, in physical matters the necessary reason for things rather than in things pertaining to the human heart.

In the moral world, as in the physical, a cause is necessarily followed by an effect. Presumably, then, a reasonable education, established on truth and wise laws, good principles, a reward granted to virtue and a punishment accorded to vice, ought to determine almost everybody to pursue virtue. But that is not so, because religion, politics, and public opinion tend to make most people wicked. Even education induces vices, prejudices, and false and dangerous opinions. D'Holbach, in a note (I, 236–237), remarks that many authors have stressed the need of a good education, but they have failed to see that a good education is totally incompatible with the superstitions of men, with arbitrary government, with laws which very often are contrary to justice, with customs which are contrary to commonsense, with public opinion which denigrates virtue, and with teachers who are incompetent.

He condemns that attitude so prevalent in his time that insists upon the corruption of man, which he attributes to the theologians. His views upon man, though, are hardly more cheerful, since he finds that the situation of man is miserable, that religion, the state, laws, and education have driven man to his low estate (I, 242):

Mais dans l'état malheureux où des erreurs universelles ont plongé l'espèce humaine, les hommes, pour la plupart, sont forcés d'être méchants ou de nuire à leurs semblables, tous les motifs qu'on leur fournit les invitent à mal faire. La religion les rend inutiles, abjects et tremblans, ou bien, elle en fait des fanatiques, cruels, inhumains, intolérans. Le pouvoir suprême les écrase et les force d'être rampans et vicieux.

After this jeremiad, D'Holbach concludes that man is not free in any moment of his existence. He is not master of his general makeup (conformation) which he has inherited from nature. Nor is he master of his ideas, which are due to causes constantly working upon him. Nor is he master to love or desire what he thinks lovable or desirable, nor even to choose what he deems the most advantageous to himself. One would think that man just is not free. But we cannot be too certain, for in the next moment we read: "Ce que l'homme va faire est toujours une suite de ce qu'il a été, de ce qu'il est, de ce qu'il a fait jusqu'au moment de l'action." That means, the author says, "to live is to exist under the law of necessity." Then he adds, "to be free is to yield to necessary motives which we carry within ourselves. Then comes the constant refrain: "Tout ce qui se passe en nous est dû à des causes nécessaires. Dans l'homme la liberté n'est que la nécessité renfermée au-dedans de lui-même." D'Holbach really offers the system of nature as a choice. The former systems have been in error, he says, because they have produced all sorts of ills. His system is, he thinks, more useful. He acknowledges that many oppose this system of fatalism because it is dangerous; it disrupts public order, gives free rein to passions, and confuses ideas concerning vice and virtue.

The things which modify society are education, law, public opinion, example, custom, and fear. These things make man contribute to the common good and regulate his passions. D'Holbach argues that society has the right to defend itself against unsociable individuals. That is the function of laws. But he maintains that the justice now dispensed is absurd. The punishment against crimes is cruel. Man is led to evil by circumstances. His education is totally inconsequential. He is driven by his needs to steal. "Il se venge par des vols."

Consequently, society often punishes the inclinations which it has fostered. The author concedes, however, that society has to defend itself. "D'où l'on voit que les injustices d'une société aveugle et mal constituée sont aussi nécessaires que les crimes de ceux qui la troublent et la déchirent." He denies, however, that this attitude tends to destroy the distinction of just and unjust, good and evil. He argues that one may accept materialism and atheism without endangering morality. And thereupon he builds up a code: All men's actions are necessary; those useful to society will always be called virtuous; every man acts and judges according to his manner of being and according to his way of regarding happiness. The only difference between "l'homme de bien" and "le méchant" is in organization. D'Holbach resumes (I, 264): "Ainsi le système de la nécessité est non-seulement véritable et fondé sur des expériences certaines, mais encore il établit la morale sur une base inébranlable." He insists that the fact that everything is necessary produces tolerance. On the other hand, he accuses the Christian religion of discouraging man with its dogma of future punishment. He rejects the argument that the doctrine of rewards and punishments acts as a restraint upon the passions. The doctrine of a future life turns people away from a consideration of their present life, since it makes many turn from their normal duties to society.

On the other hand, D'Holbach insists that education, morality, and laws suffice to restrain mankind, education being particularly effective in this respect. It will, he says, always form true citizens. A good government, he declares, enlightened, virtuous, and vigilant, has no need for fictions or falsehoods in order to govern reasonable subjects. He now finds, after conceding that mankind is wicked, evil, and miserable, that man is evil, not because he was born evil, but because circumstances have made him evil. Moreover, men are everywhere so evil and so corrupt, only because they are not governed in conformity with their nature or instructed in the necessary laws. Sovereigns are unjust and incompetent, softened by luxuries, corrupted by flattery, depraved by license. They are not occupied with the welfare of the subjects, and they engage in useless wars: "L'état de société est un état de guerre du souverain contre tous, et de chacun des membres les uns contre les autres" (I, 321). In every country, the morals of the people are totally neglected, and man is almost everywhere a slave. D'Holbach insists that if the state would give to its citizens the education and the aid they deserve, society would not be overrun with wretched criminals. He finds nonetheless that the craving for immortality is a normal desire, and he approves reverence for the great. Finally, he judges that suicide is reasonable.

D'Holbach explains that when he says that interest is the sole motive for human actions, he wishes to bring out in that statement that each man works in his own way for his own happiness. He endeavors to be more explicit than that, however. Virtue, he maintains, is the art of making one's self happy through the felicity of others, and it is the foundation of all morality. But we must keep in mind also that virtue and merit are established on the nature of man and on his needs. "Etre vertueux," he elaborates, "c'est donc placer son intérêt dans ce qui s'accorde avec l'intérêt des autres." He admits, though, that virtue is in disgrace everywhere. Still, despite the injustice which reigns in this world, there are nonetheless some virtuous men. He believes that it is perfectly natural, even necessary and reasonable, to desire the things which can contribute to our felicity. Pleasures, riches, and power are all objects worthy of our ambition and of our efforts. It would be idle to blame one for desiring them. Hence, he would encourage everyone to seek power, grandeur, and credit, but at the same time learn to use them for oneself *and* society.

D'Holbach's book is simply bursting with platitudes ("La raison ne défend point à l'homme de former de vastes désirs: l'ambition est une passion utile au genre humain, quand elle a son bonheur pour objet") and inconsistencies. Specifically, he finds that two things are wrong (I, 374): "La religion qui n'eut jamais que l'ignorance pour base et l'imagination pour guide, ne fonda point la morale sur la nature de l'homme, sur ses rapports avec les hommes, sur les devoirs qui découlent nécessairement de ces rapports" (I, 376). "C'est ainsi que la somme des malheurs du genre humain ne fut point diminuée, mais s'accrut au contraire, par ses religions, par ses gouvernements, par son éducation, par ses opinions, en un mot par toutes les institutions qu'on lui fit adopter."

D'Holbach accepts Diderot's analysis in the *Réfutation* which tended to make the mind the center of the total nervous system. The former objected, however, to the whole philosophical tendency of Descartes and the post-Cartesians to separate the soul from the body.

They seem, he said, to be distinguishing the mind from itself. "En effet," he wrote, "le cerveau est le centre commun où viennent aboutir et se confondre tous les nerfs répandus dans toute les parties du corps humain" (Naville, *Paul Thiry d'Holbach*, p. 270). D'Holbach explains that the function of this organ is to produce all the operations commonly attributed to the soul: the impressions, the changes, and the movements communicated to the brain modify it. It, in turn, reacts and starts up the other organs of the body, or it sets upon itself and becomes capable, within its own range, of a great variety of movements which we call "intellectual faculties." For D'Holbach, as for Diderot, the mind has to be the center of operations within man as well as without. It undergoes movements which we designate as sensations and feeling; it, in turn, produces responses which we call ideas and reactions. In addition, it gives orders not only to the senses but to the organs of the body. It is, as Diderot called it, "le rapporteur"—what we would call "the coordinator." But this means that it is the clearing-house for human activity and necessarily the storehouse for human energy. It also brings together the physical and that other thing hitherto called the "spiritual," but D'Holbach, as did Helvétius and even Diderot on occasion, called it "sentiment" or "sensibility." It is, to be sure, similar to what Haller had called "irritabilité." D'Holbach now defines it explicitly: "Cette façon particulière d'être remué, propre à certains organes des corps animés, occasionnée par la présence d'un objet matériel qui agit sur ces organes, dont les mouvements ou les ébranlements se transmettent au cerveau." D'Holbach actually used Diderot's metaphor of the spider in his web as a means of explaining the operation.

As regards the power of nature which was one of the major points of D'Holbach, he remarks over and over that nothing occurs by chance and that nature does nothing except what is absolutely necessary. All the works of nature, in fact, are produced in accordance with a body of laws, uniform and invariable, whether our mind can follow the chain of successive causes which nature puts in action or not. He confesses, though, that the way nature goes about putting these laws in operation is totally unknown to us. D'Holbach also follows Diderot in stating that matter arranged and combined differently will result in different organs, minds, temperaments, tastes, properties, and talents. Helvétius, it will be recalled, did not accept this. As for D'Holbach, he did not admit that nature has a specific goal. It exists necessarily, its ways of action are fixed by laws which are derived from the constitutive properties of the varied beings which it embraces and the circumstances which the continuous movement will bring about. It is we who have a goal; it is to preserve ourselves. As for nature, its only goal is to act, to exist, to preserve its totality. If we are asked to what purpose does nature exist, we have to reply that she exists necessarily. D'Holbach states that the failure to give a positive answer in the case of nature would occur also in the case where God replaced nature. Hence, this modifies the *Deus sive natura* of Spinoza. D'Holbach proposes, indeed, that the words "God" and "create" be abolished. After these remarks which are radical, it seems ridiculous to read this sentence (II, 197): "L'homme est un être matériel. Il ne peut avoir des idées quelconques que de ce qui est matériel comme lui; c'est-à-dire, de ce qui peut agir sur ses organes, ou de ce qui a du moins des qualités analogues aux siennes." And yet, he concedes that we know nature and its ways in a totally incomplete way, and we have only superficial and imperfect ideas concerning matter. It was a point which all the philosophes made. Therefore, since we cannot rise to first causes, let us be content with secondary causes and with the effects of experience.

One can only remark that D'Holbach is really fanatical against the idea of God. He returns to it over and over, and with the same trite arguments, but with a vehemence which betrays a kind of obsession. It is, however, the obsession of a lucid person, who has apparently been exasperated by the arguments of those who are obsessed in exactly the opposite way. Take the idea that religion, whether true or not, is nonetheless useful to society. D'Holbach had already argued in Volume I that the system of nature is a doctrine which is useful to society, because it establishes some order in a highly disorderly world and thereby contributes to the happiness which everyone seeks. He now rejects this kind of argument when used by his opponents. He argues (II, 219) that the utility of an opinion doesn't make it any truer. He thereupon condemns the statement of Clarke, who asked if it would not be desirable for a Being "bon, sage, intelligent, et juste" to exist? D'Holbach replies that the question does not represent the true condition of the world. Actually disorder and order, evil and goodness, justice and injustice, folly and wisdom exist side by side. Consequently the author of this state of affairs can be no more characterized as good, wise, intelligent, and just than as evil, perverted, foolish, and unjust. Moreover, the expediency of adopting a particular point of view doesn't make it any more possible. All of this certainly is logically correct, but it would be just as correct about nature, if one adopted the view that the system of nature is the true doctrine. D'Holbach actually concedes that the same condition obtains in the system of nature as in the Christian system (II, 223): "Ne voyons-nous pas en effet dans la nature un mélange constant de biens et de maux? S'obstiner à n'y voir que du bien serait aussi insensé que de vouloir n'y apercevoir que du mal." D'Holbach even insists that our way of judging will always be founded on our way of feeling and seeing, and our way of feeling will always depend upon our disposition, our organization, and particular circumstances.

These concessions are not made to excuse the existence of God; they are made to justify a theory of optimism. What d'Holbach holds against this theory is that it protects the theory of Providence, which maintains that the evil of the part is always less than the good of the whole. He maintains that the whole has no aim in itself. We should add, though, that despite its one-sidedness, it could have exercized some salutary effect upon the one-sidedness of the opposing view. It would be normally expected, I suppose, that a debate of this kind would lead to a skepticism which could be healthy. But in this case, although during the whole of the seventeenth and eighteenth centuries, this did happen over and over again, that was not the final result. Let us not anticipate, however.

D'Holbach rejects that optimism which he equates with deism, theism, and natural religion, which, he says, is anything but natural. His main objection to it is that it reintroduces the notion of a future life to compensate for the evils of this one. When we get to Voltaire's protest against D'Holbach, we will have to recall that in the discussion of optimism, his point of view is not unlike D'Holbach's. He thinks, as D'Holbach does, that the optimists are not a very cheerful bunch, that they incline to fatalism, and that they negate initiative in this life. He does not equate optimism, though, with deism. He has a tendency to separate deism from theism and he talks more and more about the virtues of theism. The one remark of D'Holbach which upset him the most was (II, 234): "Il n'y aura jamais qu'un pas du théisme à la superstition." And he would resent bitterly the subsequent remark: "La moindre révolution dans la machine, une infirmité légère, une affliction imprévue suffisent pour altérer les humeurs, pour vicier le tempérament, pour renverser le système des opinions du Theiste ou du dévot heureux . . ."

D'Holbach takes the straight rationalist attitude toward evil. Needs are the causes of passions, desires, and bodily and intellectual functions. Our need forces us to think, to will, to act. Therefore, "le mal est nécessaire à l'homme." No evil, no good. It was, according to D'Holbach, this idea of evil which led to the notion of divinity. Man is subject to a pack of ills. The more ignorant he is, the more fearful he is. He was terrified by natural phenomena. Hence, calamities were regarded as responsible for the inexplicable phenomena of nature. God then took on the meaning of that power which produced what we cannot explain. Mankind became persuaded that all nature existed for man. Consequently, one came to believe that "le bien" is natural, and "le mal" is an injustice. The author blames man for not recalling that he is only a feeble portion of nature. A moment's reflection will do away with this prejudice. We will understand that we are forced to undergo good and evil naturally. Everything being necessary, evil is as normal as good. Prayers are thus useless. The natural result is also that "chaque homme veut un Dieu pour lui tout seul." Each person demands miracles. And thereby was raised "le Colosse imaginaire de la Divinité." D'Holbach reasons that if ignorance of nature led to the creation of gods, knowledge of nature will lead to their destruction: "En un mot ses terreurs se dissipent dans la même proportion que son esprit s'éclaire."

Still, certain communities developed under the influence of those few who studied nature and imparted their "connaissances supérieures" upon the "hommes sauvages, grossiers, dispersés, dans les bois." Nations became civilized, and from these civilized societies came those individuals who brought sociability, agriculture, arts, laws, gods, cults, and religious opinions to the uncivilized hordes. They "adoucirent leurs mœurs," brought them into an organized society, taught them to aid each other, and gave them their own opinions. But D'Holbach, following Boulanger, accepts that the great cataclysms of the universe caused numerous dispersals. He does not insist, though, upon this notion. He does maintain that we can trace the origins of several existing nations, organized by the legislators and instructed by the poets. And so we have the rise of mythology and the spread of theogonies (II, 43): "Tout nous prouve que la nature et ses parties diverses ont été partout les premières divinités des hommes." They were spread in the public by the physicians, poets, sculptors, and the priests.

D'Holbach, however, senses a difficulty. The poets and the physicians were transformed into metaphysicians, and they made an "être abstrait et métaphysique" and the powers of nature were transferred to the "être métaphysique." These forces became endowed with incomprehensible qualities. Intelligible words (matter, nature, mobility, necessity) were replaced by obscure words (spirit, incorporeal substance, divinity). The concept of God became anthropomorphic, gods began to proliferate, polytheism replaced monism. All these gods were subject to the Fatum, which, said D'Holbach, is apparently nature acting by rigorous, necessary laws. Eventually, monism was restored, but there was invented the theory of the rebellious angels. D'Holbach repeats that mankind in every country has adored gods who are bizarre, unjust, bloodthirsty, and implacable, and whose rights they have never dared call into question. Hence, the portrait of a cruel, evil, fearsome god became more important than that of a beneficent god. This is not true, of course: there is the portrait of a cruel god, but there is also the portrait of the Christ. D'Holbach ignores this aspect of Christianity, and falls into the absolute which he condemned in others: "Tous les systèmes religieux," he wrote, "des hommes avec leurs sacrifices, leurs prières, leurs pratiques et leurs cérémonies n'ont eu jamais pour objet que de détourner la fureur de la divinité, de prévenir ses caprices et d'exciter en elle le sentiment de la bonté dont on la voyait se départir à tout moment."

D'Holbach complains that man has never been able to conceive of a Supreme Power endowed with other than his own qualities. Besides, men have exaggerated the portrait of divinity until He became an impenetrable mystery, and so unlike human beings, said D'Holbach, who had just said the opposite, that theology became utterly senseless. The result is that the theological attributes of God are pure negations of those qualities which occur in man—"infini, immuable, immatériel." Theology, however, has tried to bring man closer to God's qualities by the establishment of a Christian morality —*bonté* (but from whence come the floods, earthquakes, sicknesses?), justice (but from whence comes all the injustice in the world?). These qualities embrace a whole group of contradictions. Future life was invented to protect the concept of justice in God, and the system of free will was invented to prevent the Deity from being responsible for evil.

D'Holbach rejected universal consent as a proof of God's existence. To begin with, there is no such thing as universal consent in this respect. The views of everybody vary according to time and place. To show how complicated the matter is, D'Holbach analyzes Clarke's *Traité* (II, 112–151), which had been one of the mainstays of Voltaire's arguments for the existence of God in his *Traité de métaphysique*. D'Holbach stresses that several theologians do not accept Clarke's proofs; nor do they accept his a priori method, which Voltaire used also.

D'Holbach gives a number of Clarke's propositions: something has existed for all eternity; a Being independent and immutable has existed for all eternity; this immutable and independent Being exists by himself. There are twelve of the propositions which D'Holbach refutes by rational argument. He denies particularly (II, 145) that there is any such thing as a "sens intime," or an "instinct naturel," whereby we may discover the existence of God, or the verities of religion. What we call "sens intime" is merely the effects of habit, enthusiasm, uneasiness, or prejudice. D'Holbach concludes the chapter by summarizing the replies to Clarke's treatise. There are twelve of these points. (1) There is no way of conceiving how matter has existed for eternity. (2) Matter is independent since there is nothing outside matter, it is unchanging, since it can never change its nature, although it can change its form. (3) It exists of and by itself, it has neither beginning nor end. (4) Its essence is unknown to us, although we know some of its properties. (5) Point 3 is repeated. (6) This matter is infinite, and cannot be circumscribed by anything. (7) It is unique, although its parts are infinitely varied. (8) Modified, arranged, and combined in a certain way it produces intelligence. (9) Matter is not a free agent since it acts only in accord with Nature's laws. (10) The power of matter has no other limits than its own nature. (11) Wisdom, justice, and goodness are qualities common to matter as organized in human nature. (12) Matter is the principle of movement which it incorporates in itself.

The author now turns to proofs of the existence of God offered by Descartes, Malebranche, and Newton. He rejects Descartes's ontological proofs on the score that everything we conceive of (in this case, perfection) does not necessarily exist. One may think of a sphinx, for example. This seems to me to twist Descartes's thought. D'Holbach argues that a finite creature cannot conceive of an infinite being, and that a man can have no positive idea of perfection or of other abstract qualities attributed to the Deity. He concludes with the remark that Descartes's conception of God is a "Spinozisme pur." Besides, he has been accused of being a theist. D'Holbach condemns Malebranche because he falls into Spinozism also. Moreover, his doctrine destroys free will in man. "Il est évident que d'après le système de Malebranche, Dieu fait tout et que ses créatures ne sont que des instruments passifs dans ses mains. Leurs péchés ainsi que leurs vertus sont à lui." It should be recalled that this point had been made early by Voltaire. As for Newton, he, too, had gone astray just as soon as he lost sight of nature and its laws: "En un mot le sublime Newton n'est plus qu'un enfant quand il quitte la physique et l'évidence pour se perdre dans les régions imaginaires."

D'Holbach's attitude toward the existence of a God is absolutely intransigent in the *Système*. He declares openly that all religions in the world are founded upon manifest contradictions. "Un Dieu," he wrote, "tel que la théologie le dépeint, est totalement impossible." D'Holbach's strong point is the charge that the concept of the Deity proposed by religion is that of a God, who, being the master of all, distributes both good and ill, who is as often unjust, filled with malice, imprudence and unreason as with goodness, wisdom, and justice. The author, who rejects the concept of a God responsible for good and evil, preaches the acceptance of a nature which is a "mélange constant de biens et de maux," and, in the case of nature, he frankly confesses that "s'obstiner à n'y voir que du bien serait aussi insensé que de vouloir n'y apercevoir que du mal." He maintains further that each individual is a necessary mixture of good and bad qualities, while all nations are composed of vices and virtues.

All beings are engaged in a perpetual war, each living at the expense of the other, and profiting by the misfortunes "qui les désolent et les détruisent reciproquement" (II, 224).

D'Holbach points out, however, that there may be human beings who have enjoyed the benefits of the good and have not suffered from the evil. These individuals could be expected to shut their eyes on the disorders of the universe. They would be the partisans of that optimism who assert that whatever is is right. D'Holbach insists that there is little essential difference between the deist, the theist, the enthusiast, the optimist, and the superstitious. He states: "Il n'y aura jamais qu'un pas du théisme à la superstition." He condemns very specifically this theism which Voltaire had come to adopt after *Candide* as a "prétendue religion naturelle," and asserts that it can never have firm principles. He notes that philosophers have wished to substitute theism for superstition, not realizing that the weakness of theism is its tendency to be corrupted. D'Holbach gives a definition of the theist: "ceux qui détrompés d'un grand nombre d'erreurs grossières dont les superstitions vulgaires se sentent successivement remplies, s'en tiennent purement à la notion vague de la Divinité." They are of all kinds, particularly those who humanize their notion of Divinity. Thus it is obvious to the author of the *Système* that the deist God is useless, and the theist God derived therefrom is full of contradictions. He adds that, despite the opinion of his opponents, nature is not a cruel mother, and man is not dependent upon an inexorable fate. But even if nature is blind, inert, and inanimate, it would be better to depend upon her than upon a cruel, capricious God.

The author now passes to the problem of the interrelationship of religion, morality, politics, science, and the happiness of nations and man, which he places in the context of utility. He asks point-blank if one can find in revealed religion our ideas of virtue. If religion announces a despotic, vindictive, capricious Deity, would mankind be moral in imitating such a model? He insists that all the Gods (pagan, Jewish, Christian) present a portrait of cruelty, and consequently none can be models of virtue. Nor can one find in their representatives on this earth models of virtue; they are, rather, "enhardis au crime, intrépides dans l'iniquité." It would be idle also to expect that the notion of an avenging and rewarding God would have a salutary effect upon the rulers of the world. The author maintains that it is because the priesthood has encouraged by flattery the rulers that despotism, tyranny, corruption, and unbridled license thrive in the state. He inveighs against these monarchs "qui arrachent le pain des mains des peuples affamés, pour fournir au luxe de leurs courtisans." In fact, history offers a long list of "vicieux et malfaisants potentates," many of whom were superstitious, totally indifferent to virtue, and insensitive to the ills of their subjects. Although they are practically all religious, very few know what morality is or practice useful virtue. Consequently, it should be expected that such depraved rulers would corrupt the state, and thus nations, deprived of intelligent administration, are lacking in just laws, useful instruction, and reasonable education; they are kept in ignorance and in bonds. D'Holbach's condemnation of society is almost as all-embracing as Meslier's: "Les vertus sociales furent inconnues, l'amour de la patrie devint une chimère, les hommes associés n'eurent intérêt qu'à se nuire les uns les autres." The only remedy for this situation is universal enlightenment. But religion has done nothing, maintains D'Holbach, to advance enlightenment. D'Holbach's conceptions of morality (p. 288) and what man is are described (II, 289): "Voilà comment la religion et la politique ne font que réunir leurs efforts pour pervertir, avilir, empoisonner le cœur de l'homme, toutes les institutions humaines semblent ne se proposer que de les rendre vils et méchants." All this could be remedied if man's morality could be based on his nature. The thing D'Holbach stresses, however, is that ideas of divinity are harmful to morality, politics, to happiness of society, to progress of human knowledge.

The author now emphasizes the impossibility of giving a clear notion of God. Proofs of His existence are weak and obscure; those advancing them fall into all sorts of contradictions. Since only a few people are capable of meditating upon a problem of this kind, very few have ever stopped to consider what is understood by the term God (two in one hundred thousand). As a consequence, belief in the Deity is founded solely on authority. The whole vocabulary of theology is in fact incomprehensible (spirit, immateriality, creation, predestination, grace). Instead of debating endlessly the meaning of these words, one would do better to perfect the sciences, morality, law, and education. Holbach, as did Voltaire in the *Epître à Uranie*, stresses that there are two contradictory portraits of God: (1) "colère, jaloux, vindicatif, et méchant; (2) bon, intelligent, équitable et sage. In reality, every man has his own idea of God, and this personal idea varies according to conditions. We should note that the author does not at all suggest that this may be a good thing. He remarks rather that all the divergences of opinion are responsible for the different cults, sects, dogmas, and rituals. He concludes, as Lucretius did long before him, that "La crainte a fait les dieux," and from his statement, he deduces that man is ruled by prejudices. The author despairs of curing these prejudices, but he urges that each recall that he is a man, not a wild beast, and that the advantages which accrue to society from truth, justice, good laws, an intelligent education, and a peaceful morality are more solid than anything given by divinities. He counsels, therefore: seek truth and perfect morals, learn the art of being happy, improve government and laws, busy yourselves with education, agriculture, useful sciences, work with zest. "Jouissez des biens attachés à votre existence présente; augmentez-en le nombre... Si vous voulez des Dieux; que votre imagination les enfante; mais ne souffrez point que ces êtres imaginaires vous enivrent au point de reconnaître ce que vous devez aux êtres réels avec qui vous vivez." This injunction doesn't differ greatly, if at all, from fundamental Voltaireanism. It is not too surprising, seeing that the work was composed to convert Voltaire.

Its presentation at this point is explained in Chapter XI which is an apology for the rantings of the rest of the book. There is no way, says Holbach, to destroy error which has been formed over the ages and is now supported by common consent, fostered by education, upheld by authority, and nurtured by people's fears. The author concedes that anyone who sets out to change this situation for the good of mankind must expect fierce opposition. He is, says Holbach, the *Athée*, he who destroys the fancies harmful to the human race in order to lead mankind back to nature, experience, and reason. He is accused of acting in bad faith, of attributing everything to chance. It is they, he exclaims, who are the atheists, who wield importance, spread ignorance and fear and fanaticism. On the other hand, real piety consists in serving the fatherland, in being useful to one's fellow man, and in working for the welfare of all.

D'Holbach's final point is that atheism is compatible with moral-

ity. An atheist, he maintains, in rebuttal to Abbadie, is a person who
knows nature and nature's laws, who knows his own nature, who
understands that vice is harmful, who recognizes that society is useful
for his happiness, who is devoted to his country, and who realizes
that justice is essential to society. He is the opposite of the "Enthou-
siaste." Moreover, never have the writings of the atheists caused
discord in the public, but, he adds, the principles of atheism are not
made for the common people. They are not made either for frivolous
people, for the ambitious, nor even for a large number of educated
people who lack the courage to divest themselves of prejudices.
Moreover, he asserts that the country in which superstition reigns
is where one finds the lack of morals. "La vertu est incompatible
avec l'ignorance, la superstition, l'esclavage." He combats the notion
that religion is needed to restrain the common people—Voltaire's
firmest belief. Holbach rejects it because no error can be useful for
the public. He adds the very significant point: "Il n'est point à
craindre qu'elle ne produise ni troubles, ni révolutions . . ." The
unbelievers and reformers only prune a "poisoned tree," rather than
pull it up root and all. Holbach makes an earnest plea to the unbelievers and the deists who flourish in those countries where freedom of
thought now prevails. The author concludes that there can be no
morality, without consulting the nature of man and his relationships
with his fellow man, there can be no fixed principles of conduct by
basing it upon unjust, capricious, wicked Gods, no firm politics without consulting the nature of man, living in society in order to insure
his happiness and to satisfy his needs. No good government can be
established on the notion of a despotic Deity. No laws will ever be
just without consulting the nature and goals of society. No jurisprudence can ever benefit nations if it is founded on the passions
of tyrants. No education will be reasonable unless it is established
on reasonableness rather than on prejudices. The author concedes
that atheism cannot be made for the common people, nor even for
the majority of men. "Ce n'est donc pas pour le commun des hommes
que le philosophe doit se proposer d'écrire ou de méditer."

The *Système de la nature* is affiliated in a curious way with one of
the most important intellectual movements of the time and two of
its outstanding figures. It grows out of the clandestine deistic movements of the first half of the century which itself had grown out of

Spinoza's *Tractatus*. The movement had been embraced by Voltaire who, with Mme. du Châtelet, had made Cirey its center, and we know now that both had dabbled in this clandestinity. But it had also been embraced by Diderot and Rousseau. How it was taken over by these two is still not very clear, but we do know that each used it differently: while Rousseau used some of these clandestine works to enlarge the area of religion in the life of man and developed the deism into a pantheism, the other extended the deism of the clandestine manuscripts into a naturalism. Curiously, Voltaire who was most responsible for having these clandestine manuscripts published in the second half of the century had also shifted his position from deism to theism. Just what was the significance of this shift we don't exactly know. We do know that he defined it (M. XII, 321) as the only religion on this earth which has never had an assembly; the one on which the least has been written, which has been the most peaceful, and which has spread everywhere without any special means of communication. That sounds very much as if he is speaking only of a religion which exists everywhere in the hearts of men. Theism he defines as the only sect which has not upset society by religious disputes and which has always been without fanaticism. Voltaire writes their *Profession de foi*. They recognize in God the Father of all men, condemn superstition, have never persecuted anybody. "La religion consiste . . . dans l'adoration et dans la justice." To that extent it is represented by natural law, although it no longer has the third requirement of natural law: "et cheris ta patrie." Its cult is "faire le bien," its doctrine, "être soumis à Dieu." Once more, we must note that it differs little from Spinoza's admonition: "What God requires of man is obedience, charity, and justice."

Voltaire's theism, Rousseau's pantheism, and Diderot's naturalism reached Holbach while he was propagating the printing of the clandestine deistic manuscripts with Marc-Michel Rey in Amsterdam. It is clear that there had to be (1) some very fundamental similarities between Diderot, Rousseau, and Voltaire in religious thinking and (2) some very fundamental divergences in their conclusions. Holbach's atheism in the *Système de la nature* may not be terribly impressive, but Diderot's and Holbach's thought is so close together that one can with difficulty escape the impression that the *Système* actually represented the combined efforts of these two to shake the position of Voltaire in religion. The work also gives the impression that Voltaire, having sensed the weakness and instability of the deistic position had already made moves to give it a firmer basis in theism. Indeed, there are passages where Holbach, discussing free will, innate ideas, and the soul's immortality seems actually to be addressing his arguments to Voltaire. At all events, this time Diderot despite some reservations in which he excused Holbach's bizarrerie kept silent, while Voltaire in the pamphlet entitled *Dieu* accepted the challenge of the author of the *Système*. But, although "Dieu" attempted to present his side of the case, the final seven years of his life were colored by his discussion of Holbach's book. It should be noted that nothing shows the difference between Voltaire and Holbach as beautifully as the way that Holbach had to expand his work to gigantic proportions to reach Voltaire, while the latter, who had now adopted the "petit chapitre" as the instrument of his polemics, wrote a reply which was under fifty pages.

Professor Pomeau (see *La Religion de Voltaire*, pp. 385–390, the chapter entitled "Une Réforme manquée") has undertaken to read into the Patriarch's mind explanations for his attitude at this moment in 1770. Indeed, he sees clearly from 1768 on a renewed preoccupation with the metaphysics of religion. Voltaire, he believes, has again begun to ponder the problem of the soul's immortality— particularly, now that he has gotten old and weary, the immortality of Voltaire's soul. He has turned his thoughts once again to the problem of man's happiness and the complicated affair of why, even when the chances for happiness are very high, man deliberately destroys it with his own wickedness. He now reflects with puzzlement at the inordinate brutality of human beings, and the disorders which are injected into society by this human brutality. In the midst of these doubts, which are perfectly human, and the tribulations of age, which are very natural, there came the move to "convert" Voltaire. The old Patriarch was apparently not unaware of the move. Damilaville, in fact, is said to have gone to Ferney in 1765 charged with the mission—but we don't know precisely to what Voltaire was to be converted. We do know, though, that the *Système* is in three places an argument *ad hominem* for atheism, materialism, and naturalism and a defense against the charge that atheism leads to immorality, endangers the state, or menaces the progress of that education which produces enlightenment.

Voltaire, however, was not convinced by these arguments. He rightly saw that the basic position of Holbach is that attributed to Spinoza, but in a much better style, he says, than that of the philosopher. Often the former is clear, sometimes even eloquent, although he is very repetitious, declamatory, and contradictory, just as everybody else in these matters. Voltaire concedes that Holbach has been extensively read by the scholars, the ignorant, and women. However, he insists that "pour le fond des choses," one has to be very prudent when dealing with science and morality. In this particular case, what is at stake is the interest of the human race. One must examine carefully whether the doctrine is true and useful.

Voltaire questions whether Holbach can say that neither order nor disorder exists when there is a child born with a blocked windpipe, or murder of one's friend occurs, or even slander is pronounced by one's adversaries. History is filled with great massacres, the world is filled with evil. One can say that much of it is caused by the passions, but it is a horrible disaster, and it's ever present. Voltaire questions also whether matter can give itself intelligence and life when it is combined in a certain way. It would be necessary to know precisely how matter can give itself life and that we don't know. But we can define what we understand by life; some say it is "organization with feeling," but whether this comes from movement in matter is very problematical, since there is nowhere to be found a proof that such is the case. Why, then, assert so loudly that we "know"? Holbach pompously asks: What is man? Voltaire remarks that the forthcoming answer is certainly no clearer than Spinoza's most obscure remarks, "et bien des lecteurs s'indignent de ce ton si décisif." Voltaire questions further how one can say that "matter is eternal and necessary" and with no free agent existing, its form and its combination are contingent. "C'est là où l'on se trouve encore plongé dans un labyrinthe où l'on ne voit point d'issue."

Voltaire now takes up the crucial points. When one states that there is no God, and that matter acts in and of itself, one has to prove it as one proves a proposition in Euclid. When one dares affirm that if vice produces happiness, we must love vice, one must realize that a rule of this sort would be the ruin of society. Besides, how does the author know that one cannot be happy without having vices? Has it not been proved by experience that the satisfaction of having conquered one's vices is a hundredfold greater than the pleasure of having yielded to them. Finally, Voltaire, though perfectly willing to reject innate ideas, questions that this rejection proved the impossibilty of God's existence. Is there any contradiction in saying that God gives us our ideas through the senses? Would it not be more reasonable to assume that if God gives man life, He also gives him senses and ideas? The only way to prove this point would be for Holbach to prove that God does not exist, and this he has not done. Voltaire adds that Holbach and his friends have been carried away by Needham's presumed discoveries in spontaneous generation, which he, Voltaire, rejected. He argues that even if authentic, rigorously speaking, they would not prove that God does not exist. He finds it bizarre that men, while denying a Creator, have assumed they have the power to create eels. To Holbach's statement that final causes are risible, Voltaire replies that they are accepted by people as intelligent as Cicero and Newton and many other scholars. Voltaire insists that Holbach affirms rather than proves. "Il ne prouve jamais rien, et il affirme tout ce qu'il avance." Voltaire concludes that Spinoza at least confessed that there was an Intelligence who directed this whole universe and that was truly philosophical.

Voltaire grants that matter has certain qualities, but he insists that no one has ever seen a rock with feeling or thought. He insists that since matter does not give itself these things, and since he, Voltaire, possesses them, he must owe them to a greater power than himself. On the problem of evil, he confesses that he is completely baffled, though he still believes that it is necessary to believe in a Supreme Being.

Voltaire now comes to the main point. He still maintains that there is no great virtue in metaphysical arguments; it is important, though, to weigh whether it is advantageous for poor, human creatures to admit the existence of a punishing and rewarding God who will serve as a consolation in time of trouble and as a restraint in time of weakness, or whether it would be better to reject this notion and abandon ourselves to our misfortunes without hope and to our crimes without remorse. Voltaire grants that philosophy gives no assurance of a future bliss after this life. There is no way, however, to prove that it is impossible. It is true that reason cannot prove its certainty either. Common sense shows nonetheless that the notion is useful. Voltaire's fundamental argument comes down really to the notion that those who have believed in a future life have been more trustworthy citizens. Voltaire reduces his belief solely to the injunction that we must cultivate virtue, be kind to our fellow men, look upon superstition with horror or pity, adore the design manifest in nature and the author of this divine plan, and hope that eventually we may be happy by God's will. Voltaire grants that neither he nor Holbach can achieve certainty in these things, but he argues that in these matters it is better to cling to some hope than to give way to despair. Voltaire reaffirms that he believes Holbach in error, but he is convinced that he is acting as he deems best, although he does say that if vice assures happiness, then we must follow vice. On the other hand, Voltaire points out that there are innumerable cases where wicked priests have increased the world's misery, where wicked kings have sacrificed without remorse their friends, their family, their people. Voltaire proclaims loudly his opposition to all this human sacrifice. At the same time, he proclaims loudly his opposition to those who claim to "know" what life is about. Strange fellow, this chap Arouet. The best he can settle for is Spinoza's remark: "All God requires of man is obedience, charity, and justice." Having almost modestly uttered his "obiter dictu," Voltaire, now a curious King Lear, a sort of "foolish, fond old man" wrapped himself in that silence which permeated the universe—*our* universe—and waited.

RAYNAL

RAYNAL's massive work was *Histoire philosophique et politique des établissements du commerce des Européans dans les deux Indes* (Geneva, 1780). In a general way, it is treated disparagingly by eighteenth-century critics, although it is far from being unimportant. Raynal at least had the courage and the intelligence to recognize that the world must be one. He selected foreign commerce as the controlling force in the world, and he hoped that it would eventually bring the world all together and justify its existence.

First of all, it should be noted that the *Histoire* is a continuation and, so to speak, the culmination of the long line of travel literature which had exploded in the previous two centuries. We have already noted the common procedures of that literature. Raynal is inclined to pursue those same procedures. When, for instance, he takes up Hindustan, he has a chapter (I, VIII) entitled "Religion, gouvernement, jurisprudence, mœurs, usages de l'Indostan." He took up China in Chapter XXI, entitled "Etat de la Chine." Japan is introduced in an initial chapter entitled "Arrivée des Portugais au Japon: Religion, mœurs, gouvernement de ces isles." The discovery of the New World is heralded (I, i) as follows: "Alors a commencé une révolution dans le commerce, dans la puissance des nations, dans les mœurs, l'industrie et le gouvernement de tous les peuples." Raynal presents the movement as a sort of crusade (I, 2): "Les productions des climats placés sous l'équateur, se consomment dans les climats voisins du Pôle, l'industrie du Nord est transportée au Sud, les étoffes de l'Orient sont devenues le luxe des Occidentaux, et partout les hommes ont fait un échange mutuel de leurs opinions, de leurs loix, de leurs usages, de leurs maladies, de leurs remèdes, de leurs vertus et de leurs vices."

Raynal adds that everything has changed and is destined to change still. He asks whether the new things derived from the revolutions will be useful to the men of the time; whether they will produce more tranquillity, pleasure, and happiness.

His history is a veritable hymn to commerce. He presents it as the great civilizing force of the universe. He notes that the Phoenicians, the earliest traders, were the model of all merchants, colonists. He asks why modern Europeans haven't a great superiority over the Greeks and the Phoenicians. His answer is startling (I, 7–8): "Dans la Grèce le commerce trouva des hommes; en Europe, il trouva des esclaves. A mesure que nous avons ouvert les yeux sur les absurdités et nos institutions, nous nous sommes occupés à les corriger; mais sans oser jamais renverser entièrement l'édifice. Nous avons remédié à des abus par des abus nouveaux, et à force d'étayer, de réformer, de pallier, nous avons mis dans nos mœurs plus de contradictions qu'il n'y en a chez les peuples les plus barbares." Raynal is sweeping in his condemnation of Roman civilization. Their government, which was a military despotism, oppressed the people, suppressed the genius, and degraded human nature. Moreover, this government fell apart, due to two laws of Constantine: (1) a law freeing the Christian slaves and (2) a law suppressing paganism throughout the Empire. Raynal's disapproval of the spread of Christianity is total (I, 10): "La superstition dominante épaississait les ténèbres. Avec des sophismes et de la subtilité, elle fondait cette fausse science qu'on appelle théologie, dont elle occupait les hommes aux dépens des vraies connaissances." He records that this state of affairs was changed by the invasions of the Scandinavians and the Arabs, but he condemns the Crusades as a kind of counter-invasion. His opposition to the Christian religion is unremitting. Where Montesquieu had credited it with the abolition of slavery, Raynal explains that this abolition was brought about by the revival of trade which always encourages a healthy politics followed by the freeing of slaves, because this move turns slaves into the subjects of the king. Raynal adds a concluding sentence to this introductory sketch of the rise of modern civilization. In discussing the geography of India and the civilization of its inhabitants, Raynal wrote (I, 38): "Telle est la liaison entre les lois physiques et morales, que le climat a jetté partout les premiers fondements des systèmes de l'esprit humain, sur les objets importants du bonheur."

Book nineteen of the tenth volume of the *Histoire philosophique et politique* (Neuchâtel, 1783–1784, 10 vols.) is a sort of philosophical summary of the work. Raynal claims that he has disclosed the condition of Europe before the discovery of the two Indias and that he has followed the uncertain, tyrannical, and bloody establishments founded in these faraway lands. Now he promises to develop "l'influence des liaisons du Nouveau Monde sur les opinions, les gouvernements, l'industrie, les arts, les mœurs, le bonheur de l'Ancien." He begins with religion. Raynal points out that each man has tried to explain the enigma of his existence. First, he adopted polytheism as an explanation, then manicheism, then Deism. During all this time, human sacrifice abounded. What confounded the people of the time was the suffering of the virtuous, the triumph of the wicked, and the success of the legislators in enslaving the people. A "théocratie sacrée" is established in which there is no justice except what pleases the ruler and no injustice except what displeases him. Judaism does not differ from this system, he states. Christianity first succeeded with its superstitions. Constantine, however, wrecked the Empire by creating an ecclésiastical despotism. The rise of Protestantism followed. Out of the ruins created by the Catholic-Protestant quarrels, philosophy arose and atheism was established: "Par une impulsion fondée dans la nature même des religions, le catholicisme tendait sans cesse au protestantisme, le protestantisme au socinianisme, le socianianisme au déisme, le déisme au scepticisme." Raynal proposes a single code for everybody in religion, claiming that the results have been fantastic wherever it has been tried, despite the "fanatisme des prêtres," "enthousiasme des peuples," a tendency towards tolerance. What has aided greatly in this movement are the multiplicity of sects in America and, of course, foreign trade.

He asserts that (X, 11) "on a vu qu'il y avait partout de la morale, et de la bonne foi dans les opinions, partout du dérèglement dans les mœurs, et de l'avarice dans les âmes." Hence, the public concluded that what modified the nature of man were climate, the government, and social interest. The result of this development was an indifference toward religious salvation, a revolution in the mœurs, and a rapid transformation in political thought.

In the section on government, Raynal begins by questioning whether sociability is as natural to the human species as it was thought. He first examines the state of nature without legislation, without formal government, without leaders, without magistrates and courts, and without laws. With the establishment of the state, a veritable state of war has been inaugurated. He concludes that man "tend naturellement à la sociabilité." From the necessity of living together arises the need for laws. He confesses that he is puzzled by the succession of different governments (p. 14): "Toujours la police commence par le brigandage, et l'ordre par l'anarchie." He rejects the idea that there are two (physical and moral) worlds. There is, he thinks, only the physical "qui mène tout." He guesses that from anarchy arises monarchy and from monarchy comes democracy, which is naturally unstable. He approves it, but notes that "partout les révolutions, dans le gouvernement, se succèdent avec une rapidité qu'on a peine à suivre." He has contempt for Moses's type of government and his theocracy. He admits, though, that the threat of slavery is the source of the spirit of patriotism. Raynal follows these struggles which appear hopeless. Neverthless, he writes (X, 19): "Le peuple, qui n'a rien gagné dans le gouvernement d'un seul homme ou de plusieurs, fut toujours écrasé, mutilé, foulé par ces démembrements de l'anarchie féodale." He continues: "Cependant, une fermentation continuelle conduisait les nations à prendre une forme, une consistance."

In his opinion, the struggles between state and church wreck government. Commerce is what saves it. Luther and Columbus arrived: "L'un de ces hommes ranima tous les esprits, l'autre tous les bras. Depuis qu'ils ont ouvert les routes de l'industrie et de la liberté, la plupart des nations de l'Europe travaillent, avec quelque succès, à corriger, ou à perfectionner la législation d'où dépend la félicité des hommes."

The rise and fall of the Ottoman world was countered by the rise of the Western world. He urges the citizens to prevent their rulers even from doing good without insisting that it be in conformity with the general will. He considers that it is all the more important to forestall the establishment of any arbitrary power and the calamity which can be expected to follow, all the more since the remedy for such great evils is impossible for the despot himself. His is the opinion that the civilization has been more the result of events than of the wisdom of the rulers. He states that it will be impossible to civilize Russia because it is lacking in "bonnes mœurs." He asks himself if it would be possible to have a civilization without justice. Notwithstanding his pessimism in this regard, his judgment of Catherine's government seems to me very shrewd (X, 30): "S'il est très difficile de bien gouverner un grand empire, civilisé, ne l'est-il pas davantage de civiliser un grand empire barbare?" He notes the presence of tolerance at Saint-Petersburg, but he notes also a great disparity between the capital and the provinces where the priests foment superstitions. These priests are "plongés dans la crapule et dans l'ignorance, sans en être moins respectés." Then he proposes one of his leading questions: "Civilise-t-on un état sans l'intervention des prêtres, qui sont nécessairement misérables s'ils ne sont utiles?" He seems convinced that in this matter of civilization "le climat dispose de tout," but corruption is the result of "mauvaises mœurs."

There follows an analysis of many of the European nations, short but considered sketches which will explain the position which each holds in the European family of nations. Sweden, he thinks, has just passed from slavery to anarchy. Everyone cries for freedom, but the surrounding nations have spread more confusion.

Poland is a government ten centuries behind Europe. Travel around its vast territory, what do you encounter? Royal dignity, with the name of republic, the magnificence of a king who has no authority to make himself obeyed; an excessive desire for independence with all the depravity of slavery, liberty with avarice, laws with anarchy, the wildest kind of luxury with deep poverty, the fertile soil of the countryside untilled, a love of the arts but with no art. They are the amazing contrasts you will see throughout the land. Under these conditions, one can readily understand the partition of Poland. Raynal concludes (X, 38): "C'est dans la sécurité de la paix, c'est sans droits, sans prétexte, sans griefs, sans un ombre de justice, que la révolution a été opérée par le terrible principe de la force."

Germany is a country where each member is a separate body. It is a nation of "petits états," which together compose a "république fédérative." The people have always been enslaved, deprived of everything, and held in misery by ignorance. Maximilian, however, has attempted to remedy this situation. He has been offering to the Germans "tous les germes de bonheur que le temps et les événements avoient amenés dans son siècle." Raynal calls this submitting each state to law. What interests him more is the desire to see all of Europe broken up into these petty states, but united into a European federation, which, says Raynal, was the great dream of the Abbé de Saint-Pierre. Such an act would guarantee the reign of wisdom in this world. Raynal notes that Europe owes to Germany the progress of all international legislation. And yet, the Germans themselves do not possess either tranquillity or consideration of others. Raynal attributes this to the obscurity of the laws, and the lack of patriotism. Each prince exceeds his means, and there is always a tendency to slavery and tyranny.

England in its past was subjected to a whole series of invasions, first by Rome, then by the Scandinavians, then from William and his Normands. After these upheavals, England recovered its freedom with the Magna Carta. The whole movement was toward freedom for all groups and representation of all groups. Little by little, the rights of all came to be respected. Raynal concedes that absolute monarchy is a tyranny and democracy tends to anarchy and aristocracy floats between the two. The English government is a mixed government, that is, all three kinds. The first peculiarity of this government is that it has a king who is hereditary. Moreover, the government is subject to a periodic review. Finally, separation of powers helps protect and preserve liberty. Despite his admiration for the openness of English government, he states that it is not perfect. The structure can be used to intimidate the monarch. A division between the legislative and the executive is a perpetual division. The struggle between the three powers can result in anarchy. Nonetheless, he admits that England has been a model government to other European nations. What could cause trouble is excessive luxury followed by excessive corruption.

The government of Holland has been planned in a most intelligent way, but it is nonetheless more defective than those governments which have been allowed to form themselves by chance. The main defect of the government of Holland is due to the fact that the sovereignty is too dispersed. Authority does not reside in the *Etats-Généraux* at The Hague. Each deputy must ask for his orders from his province. The action taken is thus public and slow. Each province has the same authority. Moreover, unanimity is required for all decisions. At times, when important decisions are required (the suppression of office of Stadthouder, for instance) the government almost became an aristocracy. "A ces époques . . . sont arrivés de grands changements. Les auteurs de la révolution se sont hardiment partagé tous les pouvoirs. Une tyrannie intolérable s'est partout établie avec plus ou moins d'audace . . . Le gouvernement est devenu presque aristocratique." Raynal foresees that Holland will eventually become a monarchy.

France is depicted as an anarchy until 1490. Then, under Louis XI, France changed. From "une complication d'états" which she had been in the middle ages, she now became a great monarchy. But she lost her liberty, slowly, and by erosion. Nonetheless, as the government changed slowly and almost in an imperceptible way, the individual Frenchman preserved a sort of personal dignity. All the other monarchies on the continent were more despotic. Raynal nonetheless condemns all these monarchies as arbitrary. His only exception is Venice, but he states that Venice was ruined by the discovery of America.

In Switzerland, Raynal finds that the revolutions are "faciles et fréquentes." But the inhabitants of the thirteen Cantons are in his opinion better informed as to their own interests than any other government in Europe. They form the people, says Raynal, "le plus sensé de notre politique moderne." They are not a republic, he explains, as Holland is; not a simple confederacy, as Germany is, but a league. "Chaque Canton a sa souveraineté, ses alliances, ses traités à part." They sell troops to the surrounding nations and thus preserve themselves from the ruin of their freedom. Raynal predicts for them a more permanent situation. He praises them for the simplicity of their morals, and the tranquillity of their bodies. Raynal now turns from the characterization of each country of Europe to the brief consideration of a special problem in all these countries—the relationship of church and state. He sketches the rise of Christianity to power in one page where he presents the development of the Church throughout the centuries from a true democracy to a government *semi-civil, semi-ecclésiastique*, and eventually to a *Monarchie universelle*. And thence, says Raynal, it became a *despotisme absolu*, followed by utter *anarchy*. Having traced the history of the Church in such succinct fashion, he feels that he is now in a position to deduce from the history of Christianity three principles. (1) "L'état . . . n'est point fait pour la religion, mais la religion est faite pour l'état." (2) "L'intérêt général est la règle de tout ce qui doit subsister dans l'état." (3) "Le peuple, ou l'autorité souveraine dépositaire de la sienne, a seule le droit de juger de la conformité de quelque institution que ce soit avec l'intérêt général." The state thus has the right to judge and proscribe any established cult, or decide whether it wishes a cult at all. "L'Etat a la suprématie en tout." Raynal does make a great distinction between "la religion extérieure," which he condemns here, and "la religion intérieure" more or less as Jean-Jacques had done in the *Contrat social*, where each man owed his allegiance to God alone.

Raynal now attempted to sum up all his conclusions concerning the political status of Europe (X, 92 ff.). He states that if we will now go back with him and review his present presentation, we will find that all types of possible governments will be included. But each has also been modified by what he calls "la situation locale," that is "attendant circumstances": the mass of the population, the extent of the territory, the influence of opinions and occupations, the external relations, and something which he calls "les vicissitudes des événements qui agissent sur l'organisation des corps politiques . . ." (X, 92). Thus, using the political theory as it had developed in France from Montesquieu to Raynal in what we have called a bit indiscriminately the relationship between "mœurs" and "lois," Raynal has changed, it seems to me, the concept of the state. He now defines it as (X, 93) "une machine très-compliquée, qu'on ne peut monter ni faire agir sans en connaître toutes les pièces." This would appear to be a counsel of caution. The danger which lies therein all comes from not heeding the appeal to caution. Raynal certainly does not do so. He immediately makes three general statements which require some very serious deliberation before accepting them in their generalization (X, 95-98): (1) "Il est toujours plus dangereux d'étouffer la liberté de penser, que de l'abandonner à sa pente, à sa fougue." (2) "Un état ne doit avoir qu'un objet, et cet objet est la félicité publique. Chaque état a sa manière d'aller à ce but, et cette manière est son esprit, son principe auquel tout est subordonné." (3) "C'est un bonheur pour une nation, que le commerce, les arts et les sciences y fleurissent." Raynal insists that it is not war but commerce which decides the preponderance of a nation. He notes that the countries of Europe are stupid not to organize into *one* Europe (p. 107). His idea is that if the countries could unite, apparently in a league, there could be a balancing between industry and manufacturing, on one hand, and foreign commerce, on the other. It was certainly a sort of vision of the possibilities of a European economic community. We should quote Raynal here in full:

Si les lumières étoient assez répandues en Europe, et que chaque nation connût ses droits et ses vrais biens, ni le continent ni l'océan ne se feroient mutuellement la loi; mais il s'établiroit une influence réciproque entre les peuples de la terre et de la mer, un équilibre d'industrie et de puissance, qui les feroit tous communiquer ensemble pour l'utilité générale.

This step would not only increase the activity of each country, it would also give a more balanced activity to each; above all, it should also do away with some of the causes of instability in a government. Raynal now lists what he considers these causes to be: (1) weakness and hesitation in a ruler; (2) jealousy in the "dépositaires de l'autorité royale"; (3) in a republican government, one has to act in accordance with an "esprit général"; (4) there is also a "crainte" of the contrast in political maxims which has to be dispelled.

The remainder of Raynal's treatise is devoted to a number of particular economic problems. The first is the creation of a national marine for the sake of world commerce. It is, says Raynal, what has assured the power of commerce. It is a new sort of power which has delivered the whole universe to Europe: "Cette partie si bornée du globe a acquis par ses escadres un empire absolu sur les autres, beaucoup plus étendues. Elle s'y est emparée des contrées qui étaient à sa bienséance, et a mis dans sa dépendance les habitants et les productions de toutes." The development of a military marine has led to the possibility of a vast commercial marine. This leads Raynal to a discussion of the advantages of commerce. First, he again gives a succinct account of those who since the Phoenicians have played a significant role in this development—Greeks, Romans, Carthaginians, Crusaders, Portuguese, Spanish, and Dutch. Thereupon he stops for a short conclusion: which is more of a criticism of what this commerce was supposed to do (X, 147): "cependant les nations conquérantes des deux Indes négligèrent les arts et la culture, pensant que l'or devoit tout leur donner, sans songer au travail qui seul attire l'or, elles apprirent un peu tard, mais à leurs depens, que l'industrie qu'elles perdoient, valait mieux que les richesses qu'elles acquéroient; et ce fut la Hollande qui leur fit cette dure leçon." Holland, having become a prosperous state because of its foreign trade, became also the haven of the persecuted of Europe because of religion and politics. It was the center of European tolerance. Raynal then suggests an idea which does not seem entirely in line with this Dutch tolerance (X, 149): "Enfin la présentation commerçante sut tourner à son profit tous les événements et faire concourir à son bonheur les calam-

ités et les vices des autres nations." Finally, other European nations—
England, France, and Germany followed the lead of Holland.
Raynal ends with a song of praise for the merchant who enriches and
honors his country; he places the merchant alongside the philosopher
who seeks the truth, the magistrate who holds the scales of justice, the
soldier who defends his country. He warns though that all foreign
monopolies must be avoided and all trade barriers must be suppressed. Thus, world tranquillity will be assured.

He next adopts the view, held by the Physiocrats, that agriculture
is the foremost source of wealth of the state. In France, though, he
finds that the farmer is taxed beyond his means and, for that reason,
agriculture has not made the same progress as the other arts. He
agrees with D'Alembert that, since the Renaissance, the genius of
man has made great strides in the advance of science, but he deplores
that it has but rarely turned its attention to agriculture. Raynal echoes
the Physiocratic view with: "Tout, en effet, dépend et résulte de la
culture des terres." His thesis is that the other arts take their origin
in agriculture. He adds, nonetheless, that manufactures are also
important for the arts.

Raynal has some severe words for the nobles and the clergy.
Nobility, he remarks, is only an odious distinction when it is not
justified by real and useful services to the state. As for the clergy,
it is only a sterile profession as far as the land is concerned, even
when it devotes itself to prayer. But, in addition, it practices scandalous morals. It preaches a doctrine which its example and its ignorance render doubly unbelievable and impracticable. And after having
dishonored, denounced, and overthrown religion by a pack of abuses,
sophistries, injustices, and usurpations, it sets out on a round of
persecutions. That is the time when this privileged body becomes the
most cruel enemy of the state and nation. Raynal, however, makes
an exception for the working priests of his day: "Il ne lui reste de
sain et de respectable que cette classe de pasteurs, le plus avilie et la
plus surchargée, qui, placée parmi les peuples des campagnes, travaille, édifie, conseille, console et soulage une multitude de malheureux."

One of the strange things about this work is that every condemnation seems to carry a commendation. Raynal is utterly negative
toward religion, but he is highly in favor of the arts. He proclaims

that the arts are always favorable to freedom. They encourage that "esprit de société" which assures the happiness of living in a community. They are dependent, he maintains, upon the climate, but this climate is broadly conceived, since it incorporates the "caractère national" and the government which contributes to the economic prosperity of the community. Above all, these arts are favorable to an increasing population.

About population, Raynal, as are all the Physiocrats from Goudar to Mirabeau, is very concerned. He concedes that there are difficulties in determining accurate statistics in world population, and he confesses that he does not know how to evaluate influence of various types of climate upon early populations. It is his opinion that the only way to judge is by the history of the development in human industry. He doubts that the population was formerly greater in the earlier periods than now. However, though he seems to come to no definite conclusions, he does lay down some criteria which will have to be applied: "Pour décider si notre continent (Europe) était anciennement plus habité que de nos jours, il faudrait savoir si la sûreté publique y étoit mieux établie, si les arts y étoient plus florissants, et la terre y étoit mieux cultivée." After some reflection he concludes that in former times, the political institutions were "très-vicieuses," unstable, and there was much civil war; the arts were no more dynamic than the laws; commerce was limited; manufactures were crude and restricted; and agriculture was barely adequate. The consequences of all this was that Europe had a small, restricted population. Moreover, constant wars, which were cruel, killed many. Most governments were despotic or aristocratic. Neither favors increased population. There were very few democracies which have a tendency to favor an increase in population. Raynal notes that there has been a great dread of depopulation in his day. He expresses a final conviction that the decline in feudalism and the increase in urban life will bring about "d'autres villes, moins monstrueuses, mais pourtant très considérables, se sont aussi élevées dans chaque province à mesure que l'autorité suprême s'affermissait. Ce sont les tribunaux, les affaires, les arts qui les ont formées, et le goût des commodités, des plaisirs, et la société qui les a de plus en plus agrandies." He also has a good word for modern policing. Contemporary morality and municipal politics contribute to an increase in population. So does accumulation of wealth. But he cautions that, at a certain point, wealth also halts the increase in population. A couple of reforms, which he proposed, were much discussed at the time: cut down the amount of land occupied by the clergy and the nobles, and do something about the poverty of the people. He also urges the abolishment of celibacy in the clergy, and a greater effort to suppress intolerance and to reduce luxury. Raynal worked out a curious theory that at a given moment the factors which favored population can become so successful that they become unfavorable to population. Nonetheless, his conclusion is consistent with his advocacy of international trade. "Une nation galante, ou plutôt, libertine, ne tarde pas à être défaite au dehors et subjuguée au dedans. Plus de noblesse, plus de corps qui défende ses droits, ni ceux du peuple; parce que tout se divise et qu'on ne songe qu'à soi . . . Cependant il faut aujourd'hui porter les hommes au commerce, parce que la situation actuelle de l'Europe est favorable au commerce, et que le commerce est lui-même favorable à la population."

The greatest danger comes from the unreasonableness of the taxing system. Raynal insists that any tax on necessities is cruel and inhuman. A tax on imports from abroad is normally unjustifiable also. The most reasonable tax is the tax on the land, just as the Physiocrats maintained. But he admits that there is not a nation in Europe which could change over to this system: "Peut-être n'y a-t-il en ce moment aucun peuple de l'Europe, à qui sa situation permette ce grand changement. Partout les impositions sont si fortes, les dépenses si multipliées, les besoins si pressants, partout le fisc est si obéré, qu'une révolution subite dans la perception des revenus publics, altéreroit infailliblement la confiance et la félicité des citoyens." He insists that all land without exception must be subjected to this tax and that nobles and clergy must pay as well as others. He opposes the "Dîme ecclésiastique" as a system of taxation. He accepts that the best means is to divide up the fixed assignment among the inhabitants of a community. Finally, he insists that not only must it be collected justly and equally and imposed with moderation, but it must be proportioned to the needs of the state.

MABLY

PROFESSOR Lecercle seems to me to have presented the most consistent biography of Mably in his critical edition of the *Des Droits et des devoirs du citoyen*. (See J. L. Lecercle, ed., *Des Droits et des devoirs du citoyen*, édition critique avec introduction et notes, Paris, 1972.) He stresses that little is known about Mably's life. It is a curious coincidence that but little is known also about the biography of Morelly or that of Raynal. In Mably's case, it is very strange, seeing that others in his family became well known in the world of letters. Mably was born at Grenoble in a middle-class family trying to enter into the nobility. One of his brothers became Condillac. Another, in whose family Rousseau was preceptor for a year or so after leaving Mme. de Warens, was "grand prévôt de Lyon." Rousseau became well acquainted with Condillac in Paris, where the two were on intimate terms in the early forties. Jean-Jacques mentions in the *Confessions* that they and Diderot would dine together at the Tour du Pin in the Palais-Royal. Mably's education had been directed toward the religious sphere, but the actual area of the educational program has been variously interpreted. Biographers have wavered between a strong scholasticism, deeply rationalist, and a dualism in philosophy which is at the same time highly mystical and symbolical. At all events, it seems all his early training was aimed at a thorough preparation for taking orders. On concluding this training, though, he devoted himself to history with a work entitled *Parallèle des Romains et des Français* (1740), where the influence of Montesquieu's *Considérations sur les causes de la grandeur et de la décadence des Romains* is very strong. In this early work, however, his ideas in politics are presented straightforwardly and conservatively; he favors absolute monarchy, justifies inequality, approves the right of sovereigns to put the interest of their state before the rights of humanity, speaks favorably of conquests, and condemns the presence of luxury in large monarchies. Eventually, he recanted every one of these beliefs. In Paris, he attended Mme. de Tencin's salon, where he knew apparently Marivaux, Prévost, Duclos, and the Abbé de Saint-Pierre, and perhaps Bolingbroke and Lord Chesterfield. Mably also became secretary-consultant for the Cardinal de Tencin. It was because of this position that Mably eventually became actively interested in the political treaties of his day among the European governments. However, there were others who brought out large collections of these treaties also, notably Rousset de Missy, who published a *Recueil historique d'actes, négociations, mémoires et traités, depuis la paix d'Utrecht jusqu'au second congrès de Cambray inclusivement* (La Haye, 1728–1754, 21 tomes en 23 volumes, in-8°). Mably's *Droit public de l'Europe*, published in La Haye (1746, 2 vols.), was borrowed by Voltaire along with Rousset de Missy's lengthy compendium from the Bibliothèque Royale.

It was around this time that Mably broke with Mme. de Tencin and her brother, and devoted himself henceforth to the life of a scholar intermingling history, politics, psychology, and philosophy. What dominates is undoubtedly history. In the collected works of a much later date can be found a whole set of *Observations—Sur l'histoire de France, Sur les Grecs* which was published in 1749, and *Sur les Romains* which appeared for the first time in 1751. The emphasis falls in all these histories upon "observations." It is a type of erudite history not far removed from that of Voltaire. What interested Mably, for instance, in the early history of France were such items as (1) "Des mœurs et du gouvernement des Francs en Germanie. Leur établissement dans les Gaules"; (2) "Quelle fut la condition des Gaulois et les autres peuples soumis à la domination des Francs"; and (3) "Des causes qui contribuèrent à ruiner les principes du gouvernement démocratique des Francs. Tyrannie des grands. Etablissement des seigneuries." These subjects recall Montesquieu's Appendix in the *De l'Esprit des lois*.

Mably in these chapters seems to be interested in the reasons why certain historical phenomena can be seen as so similar to those being repeated in France: such things, for instance, as the weakening of royalty and the rise and power of the nobility, an event which confirmed, according to him, the enslaving of the "peuple." In Book VII of this work there is a curious Chapter I which is entitled "De la révolution arrivée dans la politique, les mœurs, et la Religion de l'Europe depuis le regne de Charles VIII jusqu'à Henri II." This relationship between religion, politics, and *mœurs* is, as we have shown, characteristic of the "new" history. Mably pursues the same kinds of interest in the observations on the Greeks and the Romans.

We should note, though, that, in addition to this interest, so characteristic of Voltaire's approach to history, Mably has also adopted Montesquieu's interest in the relationship between *mœurs* and *lois* and in the whole area between duties, rights, and legislation, which we have already studied in Montesquieu's projected *Traité des devoirs*. Indeed, Mably has a whole volume entitled *Des Droits et des devoirs du citoyen* which was written around 1758, although it was not published until 1789. In connection with this volume, to which we shall return, there was also a volume entitled *De la Législation ou principes des lois*. It is in this second work that Mably takes up certain conditions of political life which are to become fundamental to the Revolution. For instance, in Chapter I, the author insists that one must know the happiness to which man is destined by nature and the condition under which nature permits him to be happy in order to judge what laws are the most useful to a society. Mably adds: "Le devoir du législateur est de faire sentir les qualités sociales par lesquelles nous sommes invités à nous unir en société." Chapter II maintains that nature has willed that equality in wealth and the condition of the citizen is an absolute requirement for the prosperity of states. Finally, Chapter IV discusses the insurmountable obstacles which prevent the reestablishment of equality once it has been destroyed. The author adds: "Dans l'ordre des choses où nous nous trouvons, le législateur doit avec prudence tourner toutes ses forces contre l'avarice et l'ambition."

Book IV in this work on *Législation* is an interesting development on the relationship between laws and education. It is significant in that from Montesquieu through Morelly, Mably, Raynal, Rousseau, Helvétius, and Holbach, there is agreement that a vital region in political thought is that in which legislation, *mœurs*, manners, and education meet with morality and religion and together build up a harmonious conception of life. Mably had added to these elements the role of religion in this very section on education. He opposes atheism outright, and urges the desirability of a cult. He also insists upon the necessity of a religion which is neither "superstitieuse" nor "fanatique." Mably has succinctly summarized these elements in one sentence in a little essay "Du Développement, des Progrès, et des Bornes de la Raison" (XV, 12): "En faut-il d'autres preuves que cette prodigieuse harmonie qu'on rencontre entre les mœurs, les lois, les usages, les coutumes, et les morales mêmes des différentes nations, et même des différents siècles chez le même peuple?" Thus from the arbitrary, conservative statement upon politics, morality, religion, and legislation which appeared in the first of his historical works to the little essay upon progress and the role of the human mind at the end of his career, Mably had undergone, thanks to the effective way he had integrated the political thinking of Montesquieu, Rousseau, and Voltaire, a complete turnaround in which he rejected every one of his original political beliefs. This development is very significant, but there is just no way of ascertaining to what extent it is typical of public opinion in the area of political thought from 1750 to 1789.

At all events, these ideas were the source of *Des Droits et des devoirs du citoyen* which contained the explosive aspects of a shift from arbitrary conservative thought to integral liberalism. The book consists in eight letters reporting six "entretiens" the author had with "Milord Stanhope." Three problems are proposed: (1) Letters I through IV present the question: Do citizens have the right and duty to start a revolution? (2) Letters V through VI examine the question: What means do they have to start one? (3) Letters VII through VIII discuss the proposition: Once freedom has been revived, how can it be strengthened? Mably offers two general statements (p. xxiii): "among men, reason and the moral sense have developed before the social state"; (p. xxv): "Les bonnes lois ne vont pas sans bonnes mœurs." Mably adds that he opposes absolute monarchy, but he criticizes "pure democracy" also. In fact, he is equally suspicious of both kinds. He feels that a "régime mixte" would be the best kind of government. Lecercle (p. xxvii) notes that Stanhope finds that Voltaire shares this view, since the latter is inclined to defend the principles of a limited monarchy while declaring his adherence to republican ideas. It was what was understood to be the "régime anglais." What should be stressed in Mably's political point of view is less his wavering between monarchy and democracy, characteristic of everybody at the time save Rousseau, but rather the way that point of view combined principles from Montesquieu, Voltaire, and Rousseau. Indeed, Lecercle stresses that Mably's great merit consists in the clear, outspoken way he had of describing the practical problems of the Revolution thirty years before it took place.

Lecercle fully approves this tendency on Mably's part to face the problems of a revolution rather than its dogma, even the very important problem: "Le citoyen a-t-il le droit de se révolter, si la loi est injuste?" Lecercle summarizes provisionally (p. xlvi) that Mably's treatise cannot be regarded as a cause for subsequent revolutionary revolt. The remarkable aspect about the work, though, is that a full generation before the outburst of events, he thought out the problems which the Revolution was to bring up.

Lecercle is nonetheless inclined to regard Mably's stance of an advanced revolutionist as exaggerated, and much of his analysis of Mably's position is placed in the context of twentieth-century communism. Seen in these terms, Lecercle seems very aware of a serious flaw in Mably's political ideas. It had already been brought out by Lecercle in an article (*SVEC*, vol. 26, 1963, pp. 1049-1070) entitled "Utopie et Réalisme Politique chez Mably." Briefly put, Lecercle sees in the Enlightenment an eternal debate between a realistic and the utopian politics together. "Lui est réaliste et uto- as that of Morelly. The originality of Mably consists in bringing the realistic an dthe utopian politics together. "Lui est réaliste and utopiste à la fois." He explains that it is this contradiction of the two opposing aspects in Mably which complicates the revolutionary movement in the philosophy of the Enlightenment.

Lecercle presents a Mably who in his work as a whole is self-contradictory and apparently often confused. For instance, despite some very obvious repetitions of Jean-Jacques Rousseau's political ideas ("bonté naturelle" and "contrat social," which he rejects; equality, which he accepts; property rights upon which he wavers, only to end by supporting the suppression of all property), he opposes the Physiocratic notion of a "despote légal" but is suspicious of a "pure democracy." One of his principal ideas is that in a country where the *mœurs* are corrupt, there is no possibility of having "good" laws. He nonetheless wrote a chapter entitled "Là où l'injustice des lois est la première cause de tous les biens et de tous les maux de la société."

Lecercle adds that critical opinion about Mably's communism differs greatly. Some think he is a utopian communist after the fashion of Plato. Others see him as a defender of the "tiers" who has the merit of mapping out the steps in the early stages of the Revolution. Lecercle seems to feel that the best method of weighing Mably's hesitations and variations in interpreting them is to start with an examination of his sources (Condillac, Locke, Montesquieu, Morelly, Rousseau, but especially the ancients such as Plato). Lecercle thus sees him as an idealist who despairs of any possible reform, who is doubled by a realist who maps out with precision the way the Etats généraux will have to be recalled in order to revive the freedom of the individual and the destruction of the despot. The place where this can be best seen is in the *Des Droits et des Devoirs*, especially in the last letters.

Mably defines the best government as that one which produces the maximum of happiness. He opposes luxury because it humiliates the poor. He asserts that every government whose magistrates are appointed for life or who have hereditary positions is to be condemned. And he adds that the passions are the eternal enemies of public order. He affirms his confidence (p. 40) in revolution, asserting that a good citizen should work to make all revolutions useful and possible. A good citizen must also correct the abuses of his government. He maintains that despotism will always profit from revolution by increasing the burden upon "sots et ignorants."

Mably selected as the epigraph of his treatise a paragraph from Cicero's *De Republica*: "Est quidem vera lex, recta ratio, naturae congruens, diffusa in omnes." The one true law is right reason, which is, conform to nature, given to all men, unchanging and eternal. Its orders command us to fulfill our duties, its prohibitions can turn us away from evil actions; its voice never speaks in vain to the upright, but it is powerless with the wicked. Cicero notes nonetheless that this law of justice can never be suppressed, neither in part nor in its entirety. Neither the senate nor the people can excuse us from obeying it, nor can anyone explain it or interpret it in a partisan way. God alone who has promulgated it, knows the full extent of its power. He who disobeys its call will become a stranger to himself, and, for having sinned against human nature—his own nature—will have called upon himself the eternal curse of mankind, and the everlasting torture of the damned.

Mably succinctly comments that his treatise is but a commentary upon this Ciceronian passage which those who have written upon natural right and the principles of government should never have lost from view. He has attempted throughout the eight letters which relate the dialogue he had with Stanhope to reestablish the power of natural right—or God-given reason—in the affairs of man. He notes that it is absurd to think that the quality of citizen should destroy the dignity of man (p. 14). He concedes nonetheless that this human dignity has been impaired by the struggle between man's reason and his passions. In this struggle, man often forgets to apply philosophy to the study of politics ("droit naturel," p. 15). Thereby one withdraws from the orders of nature into a consequential disorder. Under those conditions, the only remedy is to return to a rigid examination of man's nature. There, it will be seen that reason is man's most essential trait. It is the only guide to happiness. And freedom is the second attribute of humanity.

In this return to natural right and the resumption of one's civic duties, Mably urges (p. 44) that every step should be planned: "Il faut étudier et connaître la marche de l'esprit humain, et le jeu des passions, pour ne leur rien proposer d'impracticable." The first thing the French have to do is "aspirer à liberté," that is, to reesablish the assemblies of Etats généraux. Lecercle has noted that this was more or less the thinking of Parlement in the 1750s. In a rather lengthy note (p. 50, n. 1) he has traced the struggles between royalty and Parlement from 1753 on, that is, from the scandals of the "billets de confession." In this episode, Mably expresses a total lack of confidence in the people, stating that they must be led, not just instructed in the doctrine. He even foresees that civil war is possible, but he excuses it with the remark that "la guerre civile est quelquefois un grand bien." He accepts that sovereign power resides originally in the people and they can accord it to whom they wish, take it back when they wish, "établir un nouvel ordre des choses." He keeps repeating that the great difficulty is not to know the truth, but to know how to carry out what it orders. However, he concedes that the truth is sometimes obscure ("Autant d'hommes, autant d'opinions différentes," p. 91).

But, he argues, there has to be a universal, common reason; that is, the law which conciliates all these opinions, since every citizen possesses this right reason and consequently the right to examine every law and power to reject it if it is unreasonable. Hence, his conclusions (p. 102) tend to be somewhat radical. (1) The state must be its own legislator. (2) An aristocracy and a monarchy can hardly be expected to make just and reasonable laws. (3) Love of liberty suffices to give birth to a republic, but it requires love of the laws to preserve it. Consequently both love of liberty and love of the law are fundamental to politics. (4) Even then, the republic will hardly succeed, unless there is a strict rapport between morality and politics: "Les bonnes mœurs veillent, pour ainsi dire, comme des sentinelles, devant des lois, et empêchent qu'on n'ose même songer à les violer" (p. 107).

The principal source of all misery which afflicts humanity is property. Property rights introduce luxury which develops in the nobles "l'esprit de tirannie." They degrade the multitude and serve to enslave them. Sumptuary laws are insufficient to prevent these evils. Mably admits that Europe's chaos discourages him to the point where he would like to hie to some faraway land and create a golden age. The people of Europe have lost their liberty, but he reaffirms that (p. 114) "nous pourrions encore être libres, si nous le voulions."

Letter V takes up the duties of a good citizen in a free state. This particular formula, it will be recalled, was chosen as Rousseau's political ideal by Vaughan in his introduction to the *Political Writings of Jean-Jacques Rousseau*. Mably selects as model states for the recapture of freedom Sweden, England, and Switzerland. To restore normal justice, the good citizen must have the courage to attack the government; he should fear repose, he should be up and doing, "semer de bonnes maximes dans le public." He must attack all forms of luxury. Switzerland, he says, will remain free as long as it rejects luxury. Holland, too, retains its freedom, but the government is changing its form. The good citizen must attack all prejudices, particularly feudal prejudices. Here, Mably excoriates, particularly in France, men of letters who prostitute themselves by flattering the government. He points out that history is frivolous unless it teaches "la morale" and "la politique." And he concludes by rejecting Montesquieu's *L'Esprit des lois* which he says has "bien des défauts, les idées fondamentales de son système sont fausses, tout y est décousu, rien n'y est lié . . . Son ouvrage mérite cependant une grande considération; il fait haïr le pouvoir arbitraire par la multitude même qui le lit . . ."

Mably approves the *Remontrances* of Parlement, since they proclaim the need for freedom. He insists, however, that "s'il est du devoir des corps et des compagnies, de tout tenter pour soutenir leurs droits, ce ne doit être que dans la vue de secourir, de servir, de protéger la nation entière." Mably cites the clergy as an example, not Parlement, for refusing to pay the "Vingtième."

The sixth letter is offered as a blue-print for the return of freedom in France. Stanhope urges opposition to the progress of despotism in all possible ways (encouraging nobles to oppose royalty, supporting the Parlements in their opposition to royalty, painting the misery of the people who are being taxed to death. He here gives a succinct account (p. 156, n. 1) of the conflict between royalty, Parlement, and the princes in 1758, when the princes demanded an Assemblée générale which was, to be sure, not the Etats généraux, but an assembly of counselors (enquêtes, requêtes, peers, princes) to deliberate upon the right to convoke the peers. Mably urges (through Stanhope) that all these judicious quarrels should be used to upset the despotic authority of the king. To see the full significance of these recommendations, it should be recalled that the letters are themselves dated 1758 (p. 159): "Pour moi," he wrote, "ce dont je suis très convaincu, c'est que dans ces conjonctures tout acte de rigueur ne servirait qu'à embarrasser le gouvernement et mettre sa faiblesse dans un plus grand jour." Mably insists that the time has come to choose between revolution and slavery: "La noblesse seroit puissante, si elle était réunie . . . Le Clergé . . . est aussi nécessaire que vos Parlements."

This call to arms between 1758 and 1771, as Lecercle has pointed out, was in reality a powerful revolutionary act. It is true that Parlement does not compare itself with the Etats généraux. It compares itself with the powers of the king, while admitting that the king actually possesses them. What is important to note is that Mably's revolt is contemporary with the revolt of the Paris Parlement between 1756 and 1770, which culminated in a demand for the recall of the Etats. It was not the Paris Parlement which issued the demand, however, but the Parlement of Rouen in a letter to the king of 8 February 1771. Mably insists upon the widespread corruption but he comments at once that "l'amour de la patrie et de la liberté commence à murmurer dans notre cœur" (p. 172). He flatters himself that France is sufficiently enlightened now to recognize its needs (p. 173): "Aujourd'hui qu'on ne croupit plus dans une ignorance monstrueuse, qu'on a la méthode d'étudier et de raisonner, qu'on connaît les sources où il faut puiser les vérités historiques et politiques, mille brochures paraîtront sur le champ pour instruire le public de ses intérêts." Mably is not terribly consistent in the way he passes from deep pessimism to mild optimism, but who was at the time? He seems overwhelmed by the loss of liberty which has led to the loss of morals. Vice he finds rampant everywhere. But he actually calculates that this confusion of the passions will only serve to stir up more the stability of the nation and during a long period will prepare a revolution, which will have to come at the appropriate moment. In the new division of power, the Etats généraux must control the finances; declaration of war must be made by the nation as a whole. Royal prerogatives must be severely reduced, while the power of the nobility must be increased. The king, though essential, is only leader of his army and the foreign ministers. Mably concludes (p. 212): "La Royauté est sans doute un vice, dans un gouvernement, mais quelque soit ce vice, il est nécessaire dans une nation, dès qu'elle a perdu les idées primitives de simplicité et d'égalité qu'avaient autrefois les hommes, et qu'elle est incapable de les reprendre."

To understand fully the conclusions of the *Droit et Devoirs* of 1758, one has to add some observations drawn from Mably's *Doutes proposés aux philosophes économistes sur l'ordre naturel et essentiel des sociétés politiques* (La Haye, 1768), also written in the form of letters. Mably had read the *Ordre naturel et essentiel des sociétés* of the Physiocrat Lemercier de la Rivière, and he now proposes to test his firmest beliefs against the Physiocrats' most fundamental doctrine. He himself subscribes to many of these ideas. He praises them, for instance, for their views upon taxation, for the unqualified support they accord agriculture, and even for their proposals to further trade. He expresses the opinion that, whereas in the past economics has been largely a matter of guesswork, thanks to the Physiocrats, firm principles in these matters have been established. Now, however, they have turned their attention to the first principles of a society, and they proclaim that "philosophie rurale" serves as the foundation of political order which they interpret as that which most contributes to man's happiness. They proclaim: "Happiest are those whose fields are best tilled." Mably, who is prepared to accept this principle, confesses that he is perturbed by their views on property rights. He would like to know why the Physiocrats maintain that "propriété personnelle, nobiliaire et foncière" (that is to say, the property of one's person, the right which one has to the necessities of life, and the right one has to the ownership of the land) are three sorts of ownership which are so closely united that they should be understood to form but one single ownership. Why do they assert that to detach one of these from the other two may cause the destruction of all three? For instance, if in a society one establishes a community of property, why should that endanger the ownership of one's person? When the increased population produced the division of the land, why should that necessitate the destruction of the property of one's person? Mably suggests that what is implied in this point of view is whether the individual would wish to toil if he were not encouraged by the ownership of the land. He confesses that the "ordre naturel" seems to him actually against nature (p. 13). For him, property is always the source of unequal fortunes. This inequality results if differing, opposing interests exist and ultimately it produces all the vices of riches, poverty, "l'abrutissement des esprits, corruption des mœurs civiles, tous les préjugés et toutes ces passions." Immediately, there will spring up unjust, tyrannical government and partial, oppressive laws. Mably absolutely condemns this inequality (p. 12). "Ouvrez toutes les histoires, vous verrez que tous les peuples ont été tourmentés par cette inégalité de fortune. Des citoyens, fiers de leur richesse, ont dédaigné de regarder comme leurs égaux, des hommes condamnés au travail pour vivre. Sur-le-champ vous voyez naître des gouvernements injustes et tyranniques, des lois partiales et oppressives, et, pour tout dire en un mot, cette foule de calamités, sous laquelle les peuples gémissent." That will always be the source of all disorder in a society. Nature in fact destined every one to be the equal of others. We all have the same needs. It must be noted, though, that Mably, like Rousseau, accepts that once inequality has entered into society, no one can reestablish equality. He nonetheless states that "la philosophie peut encore employer pour adoucir du moins et diminuer les maux que nous fait la propriété foncière" (p. 15). But he still asserts that there is no human force which can reestablish equality without causing greater disorder still.

Mably concedes that the inequality of riches produces a greater abundance in production, but he insists that it makes men unjust, fraudulent, and violent. It also contributes to foreign wars. He has no patience with those who maintain that inequality is perfectly natural to mankind. Such an assertion, he says, makes of force and ruse a veritable right. He concedes nonetheless that (p. 22) the physical and moral qualities are not equal in all individuals. He argues, however, that the reasonable thing to do is to try to overcome this physical and moral inequality. Still, he asserts (p. 24) that evil is now too deeply rooted to be cured. He maintains that it is not necessary to destroy personal property which may very well exist without possession of the land. This argument seems to justify the right to be one's self (that is, individualistic) and even to own objects (that is, all movable things which one may purchase) but denies the right to own the land.

It is evident Mably was caught in a dilemma. He had to decide upon a means of preserving the rights of the individual to the ownership of himself and of the normal, personal possessions, while denying that same individual the right to possess the land. Rousseau had a similar dilemma when he was faced with the necessity of solving the conflict between the individual and the general will. This problem has been vigorously debated by every critic of Rousseau from Vaughan to Cobban, as we have already seen. Vaughan decided that Rousseau began as an individualist but after the second *Discourse* became a collectivist, and Cobban concluded, even after the long debate, though with some difficulty, that Rousseau was at the beginning and even unto the end an individualist. (See *Rousseau and the Modern State*, p. 239.) It would thus seem that both Rousseau and Mably handled this particular problem in the same way with the intent of safeguarding the individual's right to be himself and the state's right to distribute the land. But what does not seem to have been considered by any of the critics is that this problem is part of a larger consideration, namely, how to preserve the spiritual forces of individual man and give what is due to the physical forces of nature. It was this larger aspect which was present in Morelly, Raynal, and Helvétius, but above all in Rousseau and Diderot.

It seems that although the problem is constantly reappearing in all these exponents of the natural law theory of the state, it shows up in its simplest form in the debate between Mably and the Physiocrat

Lemercier de la Rivière. Mably attacks Lemercier's notion that everything is physical in nature and consequently the natural order of
which the social order is a part is nothing more and can be nothing
more than the physical order. Mably insists that Lemercier contradicts himself when, in Chapter I, he speaks of man's "qualités
morales" which have led to the formation of society, and when, in
Chapter VI, he insists upon a "machine physique," having stated
that society is the result of "causes morales." Mably's position is that
social causes are "moral causes." He states (p. 30) that although one
cultivates the land to obtain subsistence, mœurs, laws, and institutions are more essential to one's happiness, and they are therefore
moral not physical causes. His stand (p. 32) is thus: "Le physique et
le moral étant unis dans l'homme, ils doivent l'être également dans
la société." He adds that it is all right to desire abundant crops,
"mais il faut commencer par avoir d'excellens citoyens." He concedes that agriculture is the fruit of a good government, but it does
not create it. And he concludes: "Ne transposons pas les choses, c'est
la culture des hommes, c'est-à-dire ce sont les vertus sociales qui
serviront de base au bonheur de la société. Voilà le premier objet de
la politique, nos champs viendront après."

Mably is convinced that the secret underlying the making of good
citizens can be found not in the physiocratic doctrine of enlightened
despotism nor in their assertion that the best way to institute good
laws in a state is to bring them into conformity with natural laws
(what the Physiocrats called "évidence"), but in the development of
the best relationship of the legislative and executive, or mixed government. Mably always conceives of society in terms of development.
To understand that development, one must start with man's condition
"tel qu'il était en sortant des mains de la nature." He continues: "Il
faut ensuite rechercher par quels moyens malheureux nous sommes
parvenus à changer les qualités sociales que Dieu nous a données
qui ont avili l'intelligence humaine." This, in Mably's opinion came
from the ownership of the land. This one move has created the
inequalities of conditions which have given rise to a limitless number of needs—avarice, ambition, prodigality, luxury, large fortunes,
extreme misery, pride on the part of the great, fawning on the part
of the poor. Mably urges mankind to seek diligently whether it is
at all possible to return to the road of true happiness. Is man's state

now desperate? Or can he return to the community of property and the equality of conditions? If it is no longer possible to obey the simple laws of nature, can we at least find the resources to remedy a part of the inequality which wealth has introduced? At this point, Mably hesitates, as Rousseau did in the *Second Discourse* (cf. "Mais la nature humaine ne rétrograde pas ... Peut-être voudrais-tu revenir ... "). Indeed, he hardly differs one bit from Jean-Jacques in his despair that the fatal step having been taken, man's fall has been irretrievably consummated. And yet, there is also in both a certain latent hope, an indefinable optimism that persists. Jean-Jacques Rousseau still hopes that his *Contrat social* will restore a balance in the state. As for Mably, he maintains that the great enemy is strong passions—those of the princes which are to be found in a despotism, those of the people in which are found a *pure* democracy, or those of the nobles which are found in an aristocracy. He adds, though, that "les seuls qui aient réussi à rendre la société florissante, ce sont ceux qui ont imaginé de faire en quelque sorte un mélange de divers gouvernements et d'établir par de sages tempéraments une administration modérée qui prévient les abus ou les excès du pouvoir et de la liberté." Therefore, the problem which he has to consider throughout the remainder of his treatise concerns the search for a means to reestablish this balance, what had come to be known in Mably's time as the theory of the mixed state, and what Mably called the doctrine of counterforces. Mably notes that the Romans and several contemporary societies stress the need for an equilibrium in government ("que le pouvoir se balance réciproquement et que ce n'est que par ce balancement que tous les citoyens, malgré l'inégalité de leur fortune, peuvent se rapprocher de l'égalité naturelle, et jouir de la sûreté pour laquelle ils se sont réunis en société").

Hence, Letter X is entitled: "Examen des raisonnements de notre auteur sur la nature du gouvernement mixte, ou sur ce qu'il appelle le système des contreforces." Mably states that if this doctrine of balance of power (mixed government) is accepted one will also have to accept the *Despotisme légal*, and reject the Greek and Roman system of democracy, those who have worked against tyranny, and those who have adopted a temperate monarchy with fundamental laws, Mably explains (p. 289): "Il n'est question ni de contreforces d'ignorance, ni de contre-l'évidence ... il s'agit d'établir des contreforces

entre les magistratures, pour qu'on ne soit pas la victime de l'ignorance et des passions des magistrats." He adds that Rome had these
counterforces. They are also essential to English government. They
prevent despotism, pure aristocracy, or pure democracy. On the other
hand, Mably seems to think the system of counterforces would be
impractical if one force absolutely balanced another (p. 295): "Les
contreforces, en politique, sont établies, non pas pour priver la puissance législative et la puissance exécutrice de l'action, qui leur est
propre et nécessaire, mais afin que leurs mouvements ne soient ni
convulsifs, ni peu médités, ni trop rapides, ni trop prompts."

Finally, Mably explains that a mixed government is established,
so that no one is exclusively occupied with his own interests. Thus,
being obliged to conciliate them with the interests of others, each
member of the state works despite himself for the public good.
However, Mably thinks that it is in a republic that these counterforces work best. What he opposes in the Physiocrats is their idea
that the counterforce is an enemy force. He thinks it a moral force
used to produce harmony in all the pieces of government. He accuses
the Physiocrats of failing to understand this notion of balance of
power. However, his conclusion (p. 309) is the important thing:
"Si ces réflexions sont vraies, vous en concluerez, Mr., que les mœurs
méritent la principale attention de la politique, et que bonnes ou
mauvaises elles décident du sort des états."

THE IMPACT OF THE AMERICAN REBELLION

ISTORIANS of the French Revolution have often stressed the impact which the American Revolution had upon public opinion in France, but we still do not have a clear notion as to the scope and effect of that influence. One of those who served as liaison between the Americans and the French was Raynal. In 1782, he brought out a small essay of around 200 pages upon the *Revolution in America*, which attempted to bring together his views upon the nature of that Revolution and the manner in which it was developed. Raynal noted from the beginning of his treatise that the principles which justified the Revolution were drawn from many dispersed sources. He conceded that the American colonies were indebted to Europe for those principles and especially to England from whence they had been translated into America through philosophy. Raynal gave them in order. (1) Care must be exercized never to confuse the concept of a society with the notion of a government. (2) Society is formed by the necessity, which each man recognizes, of uniting with other men for mutual protection. (3) Thus, society originates in the needs of men; government originates in their vices. (4) Society is independent and free; government was instituted to give it stability and coherence. (5) The organization of society led to the creation of public power. It is essentially good, while government is all too often an evil. (6) It is an error to assume that all men are born equal or that they all possess equal rights. Raynal meets this prejudice squarely with the statement: "There is amongst men an original inequality which nothing can remedy." For this reason legislators have been forced to create an artificial equality, the consequence of which is that man's history is but an account of his misery. (7) There is no form of government which enjoys the prerogative of immutability, nor is there any political power which cannot at any moment be abrogated. Further, there is no prescription in favor of tyranny against freedom. Nonetheless, all power tends towards despotism, despite the fact that no man can barter away his right to liberty. At this point, Raynal stops to give a brief summary of Thomas Paine's *Common Sense* followed by a short history of revolutions ("Remember Holland, and all her sons"). These principles can be traced straight back to Diderot

(*Droit civil, Droit naturel*), Rousseau (*Contrat social*), and Voltaire (*Essai sur les mœurs*).

Raynal notes, apparently with approval, that the Americans gave themselves a "federate" court which united the interior advantages of a republican form of government to the powers of a monarchy. He insisted, though, that the "Federate Republic of America" differed greatly from the republics of Holland and Switzerland. What constitutes a significant difference is that these two are small, as are the republics of Greece.

Raynal does not totally condemn the English just because he favors the American cause. He stresses, for instance, English "public spirit," just as Voltaire had long since done, and remarks that although they have so much impetuosity in party matters, they are usually cool and collected in other matters and are agitated only by violent passions. When these passions are not actively driving them, they govern themselves by the temper of their mind, which in general, with the exception of arts of imagination and taste, is in everything else methodical and wise. He concedes that the military can be cruel, but he notes "in all the monarchies of Europe, the soldier is but an instrument of despotism" (p. 118).

These observations, fairly inconsequential, nevertheless lend authority to his judgment, but they are unimportant in comparison with his main thesis, which consists in maintaining that none of the obvious events which caused so many revolutions in the past existed in the so-called revolution in North America. In the colonies, neither religion nor the laws have been "outraged." The blood of martyrs and patriots had not flowed from the scaffolds. Morals had not been flaunted. Manners, customs, and habits—dear to nations—had become the sport of ridicule. Arbitrary authority had not been exercised unjustly, since no one had been torn from the bosom of his family and the arms of his friends, and dragged into some dreary dungeon. Public order had not been subverted. Nor had the principles of administration been changed. The maxims of government which had obtained in the past had remained untouched (p. 127). "The whole question was reduced to knowing whether the mother country had, or had not, the right to lay directly, or indirectly, a slight tax upon the colonies," wrote Raynal. The implication is all too clear that all the evolution of French Enlightenment thought which could conceivably produce a revolution in France had no part in producing a rebellion in America. Raynal, in fact, asserts that (p. 155) philosophy's first sentiment is the desire to see all governments just and all people happy; that, in casting her eyes upon the (Franco-American) alliance of a monarch with a people who are defending their liberty, philosophy is curious to know its nature. He concludes, though, that France sees only too clearly that the doctrine of universal happiness, to which all the thought of the French Enlightenment leads, has nothing to do with this rebellion.

Raynal, who clearly sees in this treatise, at least by implication, the need for a revolution in Europe, predicts that the day (p. 165) must come when the New Hemisphere must necessarily be detached from the old. Already "this grand scissure" is being prepared in Europe by the collision and fermentation of public opinion; by the deprivation of citizens' rights; by the luxury of the royal courts and the misery of the masses; by the endless hatred of heartless, dishonorable men who possess everything, and robust, virtuous men who possess nothing. And while the great struggle of revolution is being prepared in Europe, another kind of evolution is shaping itself in America, prepared by the increase in population, the increase in industrial productivity, the augmentation of knowledge. Raynal literally chants his final prophecy: "Everything forwards this rupture between the old and the new world, as well the progress of evil, in the old world, as in the new the progress of good."

Raynal concludes with a list of exhortations. For America he urges: fear the corrupting influence of gold; fear luxury, and the corruption of manners; fear a too unequal distribution of riches. Fight against the spirit of conquest. Develop the arts and the sciences, which distinguish the civilized from the savage man. Practice a widespread education. Assure freedom by wise laws. Remember always there must be no legal preference among the different forms of religious worship.

Two years after Raynal's little work on *Revolution in America*, Mably brought out in Amsterdam his *Observations sur le gouvernement et les lois des Etats-Unis d'Amérique*. Mably's *Observations* consisted in four rather lengthy letters purported to have been addressed to Adams in 1783 during the period from 24 July to 20

August. The first letter is devoted largely to an expression of good will on Mably's part toward the thirteen colonies. Mably notes with obvious approval that in the thirteen constitutions the one thing which is invariably stressed is the dignity of man, and he concludes that the authors of these constitutions must have gone back to the wisest philosophers as the sources of their task. He acknowledges with sympathy that the colonists have been the victims of the British government, and that they have been sacrificed to the interests of the motherland. He deems them wise to have created a federated republic rather than an empire, since he judges this form will be less likely to stir up jealousies. Mably likens it to the Swiss form. He expresses the conviction that the Americans understand well the rights of man and the rights of nations. He feels certain that since the colonies are more extensive and more populated than the ancient city states, the common people will be less fickle. He approves of the organization of the local governments and the appointment of representatives to the central government. In addition, he notes that the separate constitutions have respected the rights of the people, they have performed a neat task in providing means whereby slaves may one of these days become citizens. He commends the jury-system: "Vous avez assuré à chaque citoyen cette première sûreté et la plus essentielle, de ne pouvoir être opprimé par un ennemi puissant." Mably winds up his expression of commendation with the remark that surely European justice is not as good, and he urges that the legislature be careful to correct laws which are too severe, and particularly those not adjusted to the crime.

However, with all his commendations, Mably confesses that he has some reservations. He accepts that democracy must serve as basis to every government which wants to get the best results from its citizens. But he insists that "cette démocratie veut être manisée, tempérée et établie avec la plus grande prudence." He expresses the fear that the masses have neither time nor talent to understand the nature of democratic government (what he calls "principes d'une sage politique") and consequently each will pursue only his personal interest. He further feels that it is a mistake to always shape the laws after the English pattern, because the laws in America have a different history. He approves that the colonies have accepted Locke's

principle of natural freedom and his theory of government. He nonetheless fears that the passage from English jurisprudence to American justice could be too brusque.

What disturbs the most, though, is a tyranny which comes from
the ignorance of the masses. He dreads just as much a tendency
toward the formation of an aristocracy. He thinks these two tendencies can "mettre en contradiction les lois et les mœurs." He proposes to curtail aristocracy and "faire des lois pour empêcher les
riches d'abuser de leurs richesses." Mably stops at this point to stress
the fact that contemporary "mœurs" will no longer justify the love
of freedom, the love of the fatherland, and the love of glory which
existed in ancient Rome. The Europe of his time has long since
abandoned these incentives to the good life and has become established upon money and commerce. Trade has, in his opinion, put
an end to the ancient virtues. He openly doubts that anything has
been done to revive those ancient virtues. He anticipates rather that
the rich will seize all the authority, thereby giving occasion to rebellion (which is what precisely happened in France six years later).

The second letter is devoted to an analysis of the constitutions of
Pennsylvania, Massachusetts, and Georgia. Mably approves of
Georgia's constitution because the population is relatively small
(40,000) and the manners are simple and uncorrupted. Moreover,
it is a farming country, and he, with his inclinations towards the
Physiocrats, states that "les hommes n'ont de véritables richesses que
les productions de la terre." That, however, does not seem to be the
principal purpose of this letter. In the early part, Mably analyzes most
carefully the relations between *government* and *citizens, mœurs*, and
lois, character and *prosperity*. He explains that only by understanding
these relationships can one arrive at the comprehension of the "fundamental laws" of each state. He interprets: "J'entends par ces mots la
forme que chacune de vos Republiques a donnée à son gouvernement." That's the origin of the character of each people and the
source of its *génie*. "Si ce gouvernement pourvoit à tous ses besoins,
si toutes les parties en sont faites les unes pour les autres; si elles tendent toutes à la même fin, qu'au lieu de s'embarasser et de se
nuire, elles se prêtent un secours mutuel; je suis sûr que de jour en
jour la prospérité de la République s'affermira d'avantage." In that

way the citizen will have the *mœurs* of his government and the society will be as perfect as it can be.

That does not mean that in his opinion the result will be a "pure démocratie." As Mably uses the term, a democracy which is not pure is tainted with a bit of aristocracy. He states outright that a "pure démocratie" is an excellent government in a society which has good manners and customs, but it would be awful in a society whose *mœurs* were as degraded as the French. He thinks that America is destined to become an aristocracy, and consequently it would be an error to establish "une égalité de droits entre les citoyens contraire à tous leurs préjugés . . ." He insists the "Démocratie demande beaucoup de mœurs," although he can conceive of a democracy where the wealth may be very disproportionate among the citizens as in the Florence of the Medicis, for instance. He therefore feels that the provisions made for protests in the Pennsylvania constitution will produce not a remedy for inequality, but anarchy. Besides, he notes that new needs, new *mœurs*, will always require new laws. Failure to respond to these "new" things will break down respect for the legislature. Moreover, the way nature has distributed its favors to each individual indicates that it is responsible for the subordination of the individual to the group which society must always require. He therefore concludes that "C'est donc en se conformant à ses loix que nous devons établir les nôtres" (p. 67). In general, he foresees that as the manners and customs degenerate, the laws and the power will have to be concentrated in the hands of a few. It is this belief which makes him deem that a democracy which has become corrupt transforms itself consecutively into an aristocracy, an oligarchy, and eventually a monarchy. Not that he approves. He states (p. 73): "Une aristocratie, sans un conseil où se conservent et se perpétuent continuellement les mœurs, l'esprit, le caractère et les principes de l'état, est un véritable monstre en politique."

Letter III is devoted to a set of observations concerning the legislation in the new republic. He suspects that the legislators, despite the wisdom which they have displayed up to the present, will neglect to create constant rules in favor of good manners and customs. They seem, on the contrary, preoccupied with the establishment of trade and thereby open the gates to avarice. Mably feels that commerce is the great enemy of equality. He therefore urges the establishment of sumptuary laws, once more because it is the only way to keep the proper balance between manners and laws. "Sans le secours des *mœurs*," he wrote, "toutes les lois sont superflues." Mably stresses the importance of the role which morality has to play in the preservation of democracy, all the more since in the past it was supplied by the sense of religion, and he foresees that at the present time religion can no longer serve that purpose: "Je prierai les E. U. de faire attention qu'ils ont d'autant plus besoin des secours de la morale et des établissements pour lesquels elle sait rendre agréable et chère aux citoyens la pratique des vertus les plus nécessaires; que vous ne pouvez presque tirer aucun avantage de la Religion, que la politique de tous les peuples a cependant regardée comme un des plus puissans ressorts qui font mouvoir le cœur humain, et dirigent notre esprit." Mably acknowledges that the colonies in America were founded when religious controversy was rampant in Europe. Indeed, the colonists fled Europe because of these religious wars. Hence freedom of religious conscience has been engrained in the morals of the society. Mably believes that this extreme religious tolerance, unless it be compensated in some other way, can be deleterious to the state. It can lead, for instance, from deism to atheism and thence to the destruction of the *mœurs*. This was, it will be recalled, Voltaire's great fear. For these reasons, Mably is inclined to question the freedom of religion permitted in the South Carolina constitution, for fear of causing more religious controversy. To remedy the situation, he proposes a common religious catechism containing also the principles of morality. This was, it will be recalled, Rousseau's proposal in the *Contrat social*. Mably wrote (p. 122): "Après avoir fait connaître les devoirs de l'homme comme homme, on le considérerait comme citoyen, et de ce nouveau rapport, on verrait naître de nouvelles vertus à la tête desquelles seroit l'amour des lois, de la patrie et de la liberté. Je ferais voir ensuite par des images et des exemples sensibles comment ces vertus ont besoin les unes des autres pour conserver toute leur dignité." The object would be to develop better magistrates and to make better citizens. Mably also thinks that it can be used to unite more closely the thirteen colonies.

He perceives a risk in exaggerating the freedom of the press in a country just beginning its freedom. He approves the freedom of thought and he concedes this cannot be developed without freedom of the press and consequently a situation occurs where *mœurs* and "progress" cannot be assured. But he thinks that it can be carried too far in a recently created state. In reality Mably has little confidence in the common sense of man. "Combien est petit," he wrote, "le nombre des hommes capables de penser par eux-mêmes et de discuter une opinion." This constant return which he shows to the theory of *mœurs* he defends by reference to Brown's *Mœurs anglaises* (see Vol. I, " 'Mœurs,' 'Lois,' and Economics"). Mably adds (p. 121): "Je ne connais point d'ouvrage plus profond en politique." And he comments upon its great success in England with the additional statement that the American Legislators can get from Brown's treatise most useful suggestions, not to forget his principles and his method (p. 123).

He does suggest some minor criticisms: he does not approve of Supreme Court judges for life. He does not seem to agree that the judiciary should be entrusted with interpreting the laws. When laws are obscure the legislature should clarify them. He does approve the division and control of riches by the Constitution. The standing army should be subordinated to civil laws. A more serious defect he perceives in the constitutions is that he does not find anything which will bring together the citizens into a closer harmony, or give to the body of citizens a common spirit. Finally, he suggests that laws should restrict personal wealth. He concludes this section with the suggestion that the Americans should study the way these things have been treated by the Swiss. He judges that the latter have organized things better and more simply. What he seems to fear most is that the Americans will become increasingly wealthy and threaten the whole basis of organization.

F. Mazzei, who calls himself a "Citoyen de Virginie," brought out in 1788 his *Recherches historiques et politiques sur les Etats-Unis de l'Amérique* (4 vols.) in which he criticized very severely and at great length both Raynal's work on commerce and Mably's on the American government. Volume I of Mazzei's presentation is an historical account of the thirteen colonies; Volume II is entitled *Réponse aux observations de l'abbé de Mably*. Volume III is entitled *Observations sur l'Histoire philosophique des deux Indes relativement aux Etats-Unis d'Amérique*. Volume IV is a *Continuation des recherches politiques*.

Mazzei's objections to Mably and Raynal were summarized in the

Introduction to Volume I (p. viii). He accuses Raynal of inexactitude, and although he concedes that the author of the *Deux Indes* is eloquent in his invocations to truth, he asserts that Raynal shows but little regard for it in the work. As for Mably, Mazzei grants that he is animated, as he asserts, by zeal for America and a desire to be useful, but he finds that the *Observations* have been composed at a time in life when one is no longer open to new experiments. As a consequence, the *Observations* have been established upon false principles. Indeed, Mazzei deplores that the United States are now less well-known than before the American Revolution. He blames Mably in part for these misconceptions, although he does not question the friendliness and enthusiasm of the French author, and he concludes that the Mably *Observations* are more accurate than the Raynal *Deux Indes*. Mazzei then states his own aim: "Mon but principal est de donner l'idée la plus précise et la plus claire de la situation des affaires dans les treize Etats-Unis, et surtout de leurs gouvernements." The interesting thing about Mazzei's book is that in his account of the founding of the early colonies, he always finds time to stop at some point to quote from the so-called constitutions of each colony and to point out therein the tendencies toward liberty and other innovations. Since this work was published in 1788 in France, it presumably had some effect in informing the French at the proper moment about the background to the American revolt. An example of this tendency occurs on p. 38 while speaking of the constitution of Massachusetts: "les lois des premiers émigrans furent conformes à l'austérité de leur Religion et de leur mœurs." Mazzei insists (pp. 111–112) that knowing the relations of the colonies with England will make it easy to grasp the real cause of the Revolution. He points out that religion was one of the major reasons of emigrating to America. But he vigorously stresses that settling condemned criminals in the colonies as a means of increasing the population had practically no importance whatever. Indeed, it was this kind of allegation on Mably's part which had raised the righteous indignation of the "citoyen de Virginie." Mazzei's explanation of the cause of the Revolution is a plausibly historical account (p. 123). He thinks the veritable cause was the decapitation of Charles I and the assuming of the royal power by the English Parliament and their usurpation of the king's right to sovereignty over the colonies. It all goes back, he said, to 1650 when Parliament passed an act to forbid the colonies to carry on trade with any nation except England. Thus Parliament claimed the right to dictate to the colonies.

Mazzei gives a brief account of the way the colonies organized themselves into watch-committees and thence into committees of public safety and how eventually a convention was called at Williamsburg. He remarks that at this time (5 September 1775) the power of Congress, the assemblies, the convention, and the committees was limitless. He publishes the Declaration of Rights drawn up by the "bon peuple de Virginie" on 1 June 1776, with its Article 1, so important to the French (p. 158):

Tous les hommes naissent également libres et indépendans, et ont des droits naturels et inhérens à leurs personnes dont ils ne peuvent, par quelque convention que ce soit, priver ni dépouiller leurs déscendans, tels sont la vie et la liberté, avec tous les moyens d'acquérir et de posséder des biens, de chercher et d'obtenir le bonheur et la sûreté.

Mazzei's objections to Mably's *Observations* seem at first more like quibbling than real objections. Often, they turn upon the meaning of some word, usually to bring out a trait in American character. For example, at Mably's mention of "superiors" Mazzei notes (II, 19): "That would be impossible in America, the people being sovereign cannot have superiors." They admit only obedience to the laws which are equal to all. Those who enforce the laws are agents of the people, not superiors. Those who make them are likewise the peoples' agents; chosen by the people and when they are dissatisfied with these agents they dismiss them. When the agents are assembled legally they represent the sovereign power. The focus of Mazzei's objection at this point was to Mably who had expressed concern about the danger inherent in giving too much power to the people. Mazzei attacked Mably's remark about "démocratie trop pure." His comment at this point is very important: since we do not accept any distinction in rank or personal privilege, he asserts, since no citizen is excluded from any office in the Republic, and since, finally, the citizens entrust to their agents almost all the power which they exercise in democratic governments, we do not believe in limiting democracies.

On the problem whether the American people (which Mazzei

insists is classless) differs from people in other countries and whether this difference is attributable to the soil or to the climate, Mazzei concludes: "La différence vient du moral, non du physique." And he adds: "Il n'a jamais existé de république où la masse du peuple ait autant influé dans le gouvernement, et à qui les routes ayent été aussi ouvertes à tous les honneurs et avantages de la patrie que dans les Etats-Unis." He insists, that being classless, the popular disorders which occur in other countries, cannot occur in the United States. Also he insists that the American public is "passablement instruit" and rather indifferent to "vains honneurs."

Mazzei condemns Mably's views on the control of the press, insisting that nothing is more important for this kind of government than freedom of the press. He suggests that Mably has "aristocratic principles" and he appears to make no distinction between the executive and the judiciary. He accuses the Frenchman of being unduly suspicious of the people. Although there is much to be admired by the European of the time, there is already apparent a certain amount of misunderstanding between the European in general and the American. For instance, despite the good will expressed by the Europeans towards the Americans and a genuine enthusiasm, the latter are inclined to respond with a certain contempt for European manners and customs. In this view, not only the French but all Europeans are filled with corruption. While the Europeans fear that European corruption will enter into American *mœurs*, the Americans express complete confidence in their ability to avoid this corruption. What upsets the Americans the most was the fact that Europeans, although genuinely enthusiastic for American ideals, ultimately speak only as Europeans. Mazzei sums up Mably's views as follows (II, p. 180):

Le but de ses conseils est que l'on proscrive le commerce et les arts, que l'on défende les richesses, que l'on enchaîne la presse, que non seulement on ne souffre point de liberté de religion, mais même que l'on prenne garde d'étendre trop la tolérance, qu'on interdise aux citoyens la faculté de se rassembler et de consulter sans la permission d'un magistrat, enfin qu'on fasse renaître le pouvoir des censeurs pour veiller sur la conduite des citoyens.

CONDORCET AND PROGRESS

I N the relationship between "lois" and "mœurs," there is implied the notion that if the connection is understood, much can be done to modify the conditions of life, either by improving these conditions or by corrupting them. The assumption is made, of course, that we should want to improve them. In Montesquieu's opinion, that can only be achieved by comprehending the nature of laws and the nature of man. Laws he defined as the "rapports nécessaires qui dérivent de la nature des choses." What defines man's nature are "manières, esprit, mœurs"; what are capable of modifying these things are climate, understood in the broadest way, government, and religion, that is to say, the outside world of nature, the society of man, and the world of God. Since man can exercise some control over two of these factors, nature and society, there is a final assumption that he is responsible for improvement or corruption.

There had been in the last half of Louis XIV's reign and the first two decades of Louis XV's several events which encouraged a greater belief in the possibility of progress. The most important was the outcome of the Quarrel of the Ancients and the Moderns where arguments had been adduced to show that while certain things may have been superior in antiquity, others were decidedly inferior. The partisans of the ancients insisted that the arts were superior in antiquity in their fidelity to truth and beauty, while Fontenelle and other moderns retorted that the moderns with Descartes had much better rules for reasoning, and consequently that philosophy of the present was far superior. But there was always, even in these fields where the ancients were admittedly superb, possibilities that the moderns were equally good. National pride in France asserted that even if Sophocles was a great dramatist, Racine is likewise great, and that although Aristophanes and Menander are excellent, so, too, is Molière. Fontenelle proposed the modern argument that one often respects the past because it is far away and denigrates the present because it is close at hand. It carried some conviction. The most significant argument proposed by Fontenelle and Perrault was the statement that when a decline occurs, it can be shown that attendant circumstances—wars, pestilence, great disasters—have occasioned it. Conceding that a temporary decline is possible carries with it the inference that changing the conditions of the decline may bring about an amelioration and if such amelioration is possible, then there can be no limits to improvements in other circumstances.

The quarrel was only one of the factors which operated in favor of a possible belief in progress. What had been going on in the field of religion was fully as meaningful. The wranglings between the religious groups had done much to discredit the traditional hold which they had exercised: the fight between the Catholics and the Protestants; the bitter discussions between the Jansenists and the Jesuits; and the quarrel between Bossuet and Fénelon over Quietism had all contributed to the weakening of religion, but so had the political moves of Louis XIV. The Revocation of the Edict of Nantes, the persecutions of both Protestants and Jansenists, and the absurdity of the Unigenitus Bull had played a role in this weakening, too. A religion whose head is the Prince of Peace cannot fight its way to glory. The important point to make there is that the weakening of religion in general brought about a breakdown of religious dogma, particularly the dogma of Providence, free will, original sin, and the problem of good and evil. Every one of these points was taken up by Pierre Bayle (who incidentally did not believe in progress, but thought that every age conducted itself as if it was the first to appear). Nonetheless, Bayle's assault against the dogmatic function, the moral function, and the police function of the church left but little room for orthodoxy.

This undermining of the doctrine of Providence and consequent decline in other religious doctrines led to a shift in favor of that view (so strong with Voltaire) that man was responsible for the making of his world.

We have already seen that certain other developments had tremendously encouraged that point of view: confidence in the ability of the human mind to reason succinctly (see C. Frankel, *The Faith of Reason,* New York, 1948) and logically upon the data of human experience, a faith which was expressed very aptly from the 1720s to the 1740s by Fontenelle, Saint-Pierre, and Espiard. This confidence in the innate ability of the human mind was confirmed by a successful development in the natural sciences. This enthusiasm was expressed best by Voltaire and Mme. du Châtelet, as we have attempted to show, around the late 1730s and throughout the 1740s.

But it was likewise visible in Fontenelle, Maupertuis, La Mettrie, Réaumur, Nollet, and in the Dutch trio of Newtonians: Bœrhaave, Musschenbrœck, and 'sGravesande. The confidence in the ability of the human mind to shape the fortunes of mankind was underscored by the growth in the natural sciences and by the inauguration of a whole group of human sciences. The impact given by the development of Newtonian astronomy was followed by a whole series of life sciences beginning with Réaumur and his studies of insects, continuing with Maupertuis and his treatise on the progress of science, and with La Mettrie and the development of medical science. By 1749, one witnessed the beginning of Buffon's *Histoire naturelle*, the most popular of eighteenth-century works, according to an inventory conducted by Mornet. (See D. Mornet, "Les Enseignements des bibliothèques privées [1750–1780]," *RHL* 17 1910: 449–496.) By that time, all the natural sciences (mathematics, astronomy, botany, zoology, geology, and psychology had been developed to the point that each science had now a particular area in nature to exploit; each had its place in revealing the inner forces of nature, in presenting a common experimental scientific method, and in coordinating the sciences of nature with the sciences of man. The first results of this evolution was a reaffirmation of the doctrine of final causes, but very soon this doctrine was challenged by those who felt that in the forces of nature were material forces which could just as easily explain the phenomena. Coincident with this movement, there was a parallel movement in the human sciences, also operating in the 1730s and 1740s. Two events are clearly causes for this new orientation of science. One was the breakdown in the anthropocentric hypothesis which consisted in seeing in the natural phenomena of the universe events which worked for the benefit of man. One can see a clearcut turn from the doctrine of final causes to a new assertion that man does not occupy any preferential place in the scheme of things. He is a part of nature like everything else, not any more important than any other part. As a consequence, many now deemed foolish the belief that things happened for man. Such a view ran, of course, contrary to the doctrine of Providence, but it did not negate the possibility that man could make for himself a position of importance in the scheme of things. This belief was encouraged by the whole development of the human sciences, beginning with Biblical criticism, which established clearly the two principles of the power of God-given reason to shape the destiny of man and the superiority of natural religion over all man-made religions. Criticism thus had a very active role in the development of a universal religion and in the fostering of tolerance, but also a negative role in the movement toward the suppression of all formal religions including Christianity. This latter effect was of great importance for the development of all the human and social sciences: psychology, history, economics, politics, primitive anthropology, and sociology.

These separate subjects were understood nonetheless to be parts of the general field of knowledge: mathematics, astronomy, plant biology, animal biology, geology, and chemistry were all "natural sciences" called by the generic term "la physique," while Biblical criticism, history, politics, economics, and psychology became "sciences morales et politiques," and remained in fact under that rubric far into the twentieth century, but they were known under the generic name "la morale." In fact, "physique" and "morale" were the two large divisions of knowledge: together they formed "la Philosophie." Everyone seems to have agreed that science, that is knowledge, is a "unity." Indeed, it formed not only a unity among the particular fields of learning, but science, which was the combination of all the sciences, united with arts and letters in the closest possible way. De Jaucourt expressly gives the example of Greece and Rome to substantiate this point. But he goes much further in insisting upon the unity. He insists that the union of sciences and arts is what assures progress in a society. This concept is so central to the doctrine of progress that we must quote his remark: "J'ose dire sans préjugé en faveur des sciences et des lettres que ce sont elles qui font fleurir une nation, et qui répandent dans le cœur des hommes les règles de la droite raison, et les semences de douceur, de vertu, et d'humanité si nécessaire au bonheur de la société." Moreover, for the *Encyclopédie*, progress is not guaranteed by the solidarity of the sciences, and the integration of sciences and arts; there is a "law of total effect" to which many of the thinkers of the time refer which consists in stating that happiness of society not only depends upon arts and sciences but also upon institutions and above all upon manners and customs. The institutions which are stressed in this connection are government, religion, economics, and education. It is affirmed often that of the four, religion and politics—church and state—are crucial to this "bonheur," but so is the economic welfare of man and the development of his mind. All of these aspects of living are now brought together, and in accord with this law of total effect, there is enunciated the conviction that progress is a cultural matter, an urge to civilization, that it involves always sciences and arts, political and social institutions, manners and customs, that these things are realities which have to work together if one is to achieve the goal which mankind has delineated as the happiness of man.

It would be wise to keep constantly in mind that this was now the basic concept of philosophy. Everything was declared to be "philosophical"—meaning practically all of man's intellectual, social, and institutional activities and including not only his thought but also his judgment of its worth and the way he proposed acting upon it. Each man was inclined thus to regard himself as a philosopher and to justify the procedure because it was the sum total of his life. So that the life of the mind became absolutely identical with the life of the spirit, that "esprit."

There was much idealism in this conception of progress as Enlightenment, and during the nineteenth and twentieth centuries it has often been subjected to much unfavorable criticism. What should be stressed is the way the doctrine of progress became a religious view which in many respects supplanted the service which had been rendered by religion. It had, indeed, become a lay religion which had its dogma, its beliefs, and its ultimate goals. One believed, for instance, that nature's laws are immutable, that all the sciences form a unit, that truth has a utilitarian value for man, and that when rightly applied, knowledge leads to the improvement of the individual, because individual man is thought to be perfectible. He responds to the influence of climate, of government, of education. He therefore can be trained to perfect himself in accordance with the impact of these conditions and institutions. They naturally mold him in accordance with the goals set. And this accord between man and society, between his capabilities and his aspirations, will lead naturally to the happiness of the individual, which is the admitted goal of civilization. There are, however, essentials which must be respected; it is this knowledge which offers stability in an ever-changing universe. As De Jaucourt explains in his article "Vicissitude" quoting Bacon: "La matière est dans un mouvement perpétuel et ne s'arrête jamais." De Jaucourt adds: "C'est ainsi que tout naît, s'accroît, change et dépérit, pour recommencer et finir encore, se perdant et se renouvellant sans cesse dans les espaces immenses de l'éternité." As Diderot expresses the idea in the *Rêve*: "Tout change . . . tout passe . . . il n'y a que le tout qui reste." Finally in this flux there is a latent perfectibility, a possible "bonheur," but only on condition that the individual accept some hard truths; one must distinguish between truth and the préjugé, one must ever seek the right relationship in human phenomena, one must also be seeking the origins of things, must be always open to reforms, and must constantly search for directions.

We should stop for a little to listen to those who were deeply preoccupied with the doctrine of progress. Naturally, the *Encyclopédie* became the core around which were grouped those who were to become its defenders. D'Alembert celebrated their activities in the *Discours préliminaire* as he traced the history of the progress of the human mind and elaborated upon the goals set, the outstanding contributors to its development, and the classification of the fields of knowledge. Thereafter, D'Alembert returned on occasion to enumerate the outstanding features of the whole intellectual movement to the middle of the eighteenth century—what he entitled the "Tableau de l'esprit humain au milieu du XVIIIᵉ siècle." Cassirer, in the opening pages of his *Philosophy of the Enlightenment*, has quoted one of these statements. The other, appearing in Volume V of the *Mélanges de littérature, d'histoire, et de philosophie* (Amsterdam, 1764) and entitled "Essai sur les éléments de philosophie, ou sur les principes des connaissances humaines," is fully as provocative. After noting that the middle of a century seems destined, since the last three hundred years, to be the epoch of a revolution in the human mind, D'Alembert remarks that if one will consider carefully the middle of the eighteenth century, the events which attract the active attention, the "mœurs," the works, and even the daily conversations, he will be struck that there has taken place a remarkable change in thought which promises a greater change yet. D'Alembert adds that only posterity will better understand its drawbacks and its accomplishments. He nonetheless affirms that any analysis of the present state of knowledge will show a great progress in philosophy. The sciences of nature have become extraordinarily rich, geometry has been greatly expanded, the true system of the universe is now known. Knowledge of the movements of the celestial bodies has been supplemented by the further knowledge of those things which surround us. In short, "Depuis la terre jusqu'à Saturne, depuis l'histoire des cieux jusqu'à celle des insectes, la physique a changé de face. Avec elle presque toutes les autres sciences ont pris une nouvelle forme, et elles le devoient en effet." In a note to the fermentation of minds brought about by the contemporary developments, D'Alembert remarks that everything concerning human life has been put in question:

Ainsi depuis les principes des sciences profanes jusqu'aux fondemens de la Révélation, depuis la métaphysique jusqu'aux matières de goût, depuis la musique jusqu'à la morale, depuis les disputes scholastiques des théologiens jusqu'aux objets de commerce, depuis les droits des Princes jusqu'à ceux des peuples, depuis la loi naturelle, jusqu'aux lois arbitraires des nations, en un mot, depuis les questions qui nous touchent davantage jusqu'à celles qui nous intéressent le plus faiblement, tout a été discuté, analysé, agité du moins.

Around the same time (1749) the Soissons Academy announced a competition for the best essay upon the subject of "Les Causes des progrès et de la décadence du goût dans les arts et les sciences." Turgot assembled a certain number of fragments on the subject which are now published in Volume I of his *Œuvres complètes* (Paris, 1913, 5 vols.). Among the causes listed by Turgot are the rise of geniuses; the formation of the language; the progress of philosophy, the mechanical arts, and the speculative sciences; printing, the fine arts, and chance. Turgot suggests that they may be reduced to three: the condition of the language, the nature of the government, the presence of geniuses. He notes that "la nature sème dans tous les temps et dans tous les lieux un certain nombre de génies." The problem is to discover what circumstances best contribute to their development, that is, those which are essential. For instance, poets of genius can flourish only when the language is completely formed. In addition, a new invention, such as printing, can be immensely important to arts and letters.

Turgot remarks that the proper sphere of universal history is to assemble the phenomena of successive periods of progress in the human race and to seek the causes which have contributed to it. What one must examine with care are the early beginnings of men, the formation and intermingling of nations, the origins and the evolutions of governments, the progress which has taken place in the development of languages, in the study of nature, in the creation of a morale, in the organization of manners and customs, and in the expressions of all these activities in the sciences and the arts. Turgot is inclined to regard all human phenomena from the historical point of view. What has a fascination for him is the rise and fall of empires. What intrigues him, as well as Montesquieu and Voltaire, are the causes underlying these revolutions. What lies behind all these revolutions which have made empires follow empires into oblivion, nations succeed other nations, religions yield to other religions? Turgot envisages the "genre humain toujours le même dans ses bouleversements, comme l'eau de la mer dans les tempêtes, et marchant toujours à sa perfection." Nonetheless, for him, as for Montesquieu and Voltaire, decline was as possible as advance. It is not a matter of historical pessimism, as twentieth-century historians have been saying, it is a matter of philosophical speculation, the problem being to detect those causes which make for progress and separate them from the phenomena which make a decline inevitable. The eighteenth-century historians make no effort to conceal the possibility of decline; if anything, they have a rather exaggerated fear of it. Nor do they shut their eyes to the undesirable events of universal history. Turgot calmly notes (I, 303) that "les progrès, quoique nécessaires, sont entremêlés de décadences fréquentes, par les événements et les Révolutions qui viennent les interrompre." Voltaire in his *Essai sur les mœurs* is more explicit still. Since Morize, we have all been inclined to believe that his conclusions tend to the pessimistic. Indeed, Morize suggested that the writing of universal history was one of the important factors in turning Voltaire to the pessimism of *Candide*. It is true that in his conclusions of the *Essai* he confesses that, in general, all this history is a "ramas de crimes, de folies, et de malheurs," but he adds in characteristic manner that there can be discovered in it "quelques vertus, quelques temps heureux." He commends Pope Alexander III for having liberated the serfs, for having revived the rights of society, and for having repressed the crimes of kings. He deplores the civil wars, conspiracies, crimes, and follies, but he observes that amidst all these undesirable things, a lot of people cultivated the useful and agreeable arts in Italy and elsewhere. And with more than piety, he notes that "au milieu de ces saccagements et de ces déstructions que nous observons dans l'espace de 900 années, nous voyons un amour d'ordre qui anime en secret le genre humain." In a moment of unusual generosity, he comments that "il y a partout un frein imposé au pouvoir arbitraire, par la loi, par les usages, et par les mœurs." Finally, his ultimate conclusion is that of practically all his contemporaries who speculated on the possibilities of civilization: "trois choses influent sans cesse sur l'esprit des hommes: le climat, le gouvernement, et la religion; c'est la seule manière d'expliquer l'énigme de ce monde." It would certainly be difficult to deduce from these concluding remarks that Voltaire has become an unbridled optimist, but to any impartial critic they would seem fair, judicious, reasonable, and moderately well balanced.

Turgot's attitude does not differ greatly from Voltaire's, in fact. In the *Tableau philosophique des progrès successifs de l'esprit humain*, he wrote (*Œuvres complètes*, I, 215):

On voit s'établir des sociétés, se former des nations, qui dominent tour à tour et obéissent à d'autres nations; les Empires s'élèvent et tombent; les lois, les formes du gouvernement se succèdent, les unes aux autres, les arts, les sciences tour à tour se découvrent, se perfectionnent; tour à tour retardés et accélérés dans leurs progrès, ils passent de climats en climats; l'intérêt, l'ambition, la vaine gloire changent à chaque instant la science du monde, inondent la terre de sang: et au milieu de leurs ravages, les mœurs s'adoucissent, l'esprit humain s'éclaire, les nations isolées se rapprochent les unes aux autres; le commerce et la politique réunissent enfin toutes les parties du globe, et la masse totale du genre humain par des alternatives de calme et d'agitation, des biens et des maux, marche toujours, quoiqu'à pas lents, à une perfection plus grande.

Turgot points out that there are differences in the qualities of the human mind. There are noteworthy inequalities in souls which will always be a puzzle to us. But he argues that much can be corrected by a well-directed education. Like Voltaire, he finds that many of the differences which appear between peoples can be explained by the differences in climates. He explains that these physical causes operate only on the hidden principles which contribute to the formation of our mind and our character, and not on the results which we only see. The point he stressed is that in the immense expansion of science, the development of philosophy, and progress in artistic taste, it is the duty of the historian to describe them. The preferred method, he said, would be to follow step by step the human mind as it makes its discoveries and to integrate them into the body of truths already collected.

The *Encyclopédie*, which was so favorably disposed to the advance in philosophy, in the arts, and in the sciences, nonetheless gave considerable thought to those factors which were obstacles to their development. In the *Discours préliminaire* itself there is a section devoted to an enumeration of those causes which prevent progress in arts and sciences and philosophy. Among those mentioned are: attachment to "le faux bel-esprit," an exaggerated tendency to bring out abridgements in the different literary genres, and an overabundance of dictionaries and journalistic articles. The writers also are somewhat responsible in that they pretend to an importance which they can with difficulty justify. Moreover, they are often satisfied not to use their talents to the maximum of their powers. A great hindrance is the diversity of languages. But a greater hindrance still is the contemporary trend toward luxury and idleness. Cases are cited (IX, 763[b and c]; XIV, 789[a and b]) to elucidate the peculiar effect luxury has had on the decline of letters in Paris. Moreover, there is lacking a good supply of elementary works, and the influence of the various academies has not worked altogether for the excellence of arts or science. The manner of instructing in both areas in the educational institutions has been subject to an excessive authority, while too much time is spent in building too many hypotheses, and there is an inordinate fondness for the "esprit de système." A whole section (V, 284[a]; XII, 499[b]) is devoted to those causes which have particularly impeded the advance in philosophy.

The contributors offer a fair number of suggestions and recommendations. Not all of them think, for instance, that the academies are necessarily deleterious to progress. D'Alembert further stresses that the various dictionaries have contributed to rather than hindered the general enlightenment which has spread throughout society. Ways should be devised (V, 284[b]) for contemporary philosophers to work for the perfecting of the arts, and those authors who have gained a reputation for their works should spend some of their time in training the coming generation. The government, it is asserted, could do much more in encouraging progress both in science and the arts, seeing that their development is of inestimable value to the rulers. Finally, ways should be devised to encourage communication among the scholars of the various countries.

The outstanding exponent of progress at the end of the century was Condorcet who, in the midst of the Revolution while he was in hiding in the quarries of Montrouge to escape the police, found time to write a large volume which he entitled *Esquisse d'un tableau historique du progrès de l'esprit humain.*

Condorcet had been trained in part by Voltaire and as a consequence many of his views grew out of the *Essai sur les mœurs.* They were, however, more theoretical and, curiously, more optimistic in their tendencies. Nonetheless, if one takes time to look beneath the surface, he will find that despite the "marche à pas lents" to which Turgot constantly referred, Condorcet always found that there was something dreadfully wrong. In the Introduction, he affirms that "ce progrès est soumis aux mêmes lois générales qui s'observent dans le développement des facultés chez les individus." He insists, however, that in the history of progress, the present always takes its direction from the momentum of the past and transmits this momentum to future times. In this evolution there is no halt. Condorcet recognizes that "la perfectibilité de l'homme est réellement indéfinie." In a curious way, though trained by Voltaire, Condorcet has an inclination to adopt Rousseau's views on the rise of primitive societies, and offers a justification for these views in contemporary studies of primitive societies.

To the origins and evolution of these primitive societies, which he endeavors to trace, Condorcet promises to add "le tableau de nos espérances" which will outline "ces progrès qui sont réservés aux générations futures," seeing that the laws of nature will always remain constant. Condorcet's faith in the immutability of natural law is as unshakable as Fontenelle's almost a century earlier. To this general march of mankind along the road of indefinite progress, Condorcet promises to bring out in what way nature has indissolubly united progress in enlightenment with the advance of freedom, virtue, and respect for the natural rights of man. This can only be done, he adds, when knowledge has reached a certain perfection in a number of nations and when it will have spread to the masses. Finally, he states his intention to stress the history of the errors of mankind which have impeded or delayed the march of reason. These errors are prejudices, especially "le préjugé qui rejetterait avec orgueil les leçons de l'expérience." He promises in conclusion that "tout nous dit que nous touchons à l'époque d'une des grandes révolutions de l'espèce humaine" (p. 12).

Condorcet has divided the history of humanity into ten epochs from the rise of a feeling for justice and a mutual affection among the members of a society to the moment of the Ascent of Man. The first and the tenth are periods which are relatively free from the evils of society. The others seem always to have been subjected to a constant struggle between the forces which tend to impede progress and those which urge it to its goal. Condorcet, like Turgot, Voltaire, D'Alembert, and all the other encyclopedists, all defenders of progress, does not conceal that there are problems which threaten a decline at every moment of human history. Nor does he forget that what he is proposing is progress of the human mind as it strives through knowledge to achieve an advance in thought, in the penetration of the phenomena of nature, in an enrichment both in thought and expression, that is, in art and philosophy. It is for this reason that the locus of progress is in the human mind, while the fact of progress is in philosophy, science, and art.

What characterizes the first epoch is a sense of justice and mutual love. What typifies the second was the development of agriculture, but what marked it was "l'art de tromper les hommes, pour les dépouiller," and the effort of a few to dominate the opinions of the group, along with the invention of cults. What Condorcet stresses is that the formation of society made apparent the cruelty, the corruption, and the prejudices of the individual. He refuses, however, to subscribe to Rousseau's idea that the organization of society produced "la dégénérescence de l'espèce."

The third epoch was distinguished by the division of labor and the formation of classes. The community was now divided into proprietors, domestic servants, and slaves. In this period, there were the beginnings of conquests and the rise of despotism. The *mœurs* of the community now converted into empires have become an example of all the villainy, corruption, and superstition humanity is capable of. But there are compensations. Man begins to feel the urge to create. He begins to be aware of the need for new ideas, new sensations. It was the beginning of arts and trades, the invention of mathematics. Man thus discovered the means of doubling the capacity of the human mind. In truth, although progress could have been made, despotism and superstition prevented it. An age of darkness ensued in which the human mind "livré à l'ignorance et aux préjugés, fut condamné à une honteuse immobilité dans ces vastes empires." Still, the alphabet, exploited by the Greeks, was discovered.

The fourth epoch was the Grecian Age, characterized by freedom and independence and, thanks to Socrates, wisdom. It was he who taught the Greeks to limit their desires to their capacities; to be sure of the step taken before risking another; to study the world surrounding man before leaping into unknown realms. Condorcet approved of this, but there was another side to the picture. What actually happened was the formation of limitless sects and the promotion of all kinds of errors. They failed to realize, in fact, that society must be founded upon reason, upon the rights which all men have received from nature, and upon that universal justice without which no society of free and equal men can be maintained. They did see, though, that there was an organic relationship among agriculture, industry, commerce, the constitution of a state, and its legislation, and that this organic quality had a tremendous importance upon the state's prosperity, its power, and its freedom. Naturally, these important insights could not escape a people as clever as the Greeks, especially as they were interested in public welfare. In fact, freedom, art, and enlightenment have contributed to the amelioration of manners and customs. Their vices, often attributed to the progress of their civilization, really came from earlier untutored centuries, and their culture of the arts have restrained them. Condorcet adds that as a general rule progress in virtue has always accompanied progress in enlightenment just as the advance of corruption has always followed or foreboded a decline.

The fifth epoch embraced the second age of Greece and the rise of Rome. It was the age of mathematics, rational mechanics, scientific inventions, and technology. But it was lacking in technical language.

In Greece, it was represented by the rise of skeptics. In Rome, it was characterized by the founding of jurisprudence which, adds Condorcet, is the only new science which we owe to the Romans. On the other hand, there was a plethora of new religions, along with the establishment of Christianity, and a scorn for human science and philosophy. As a consequence, sciences declined in importance, a decline which Condorcet attributed to the rise of Christianity. He suggests also that the flourishing of the arts, letters, and sciences was incompatible with the Roman, and even with the Greek, temperament, which statement seems totally incomprehensible to a schoolboy today. "Jamais à Rome," he wrote, "l'étude des lettres, l'amour des arts, ne fut un goût vraiment populaire." In his opinion, both Romans and Greeks lacked "cet esprit de doute, qui soumet à l'examen sévère de la raison, et les faits et les preuves" (87). Condorcet's presentation of the fifth epoch is unacceptable. One would think that the establishment of mathematics and rational mechanics, which he stresses in Greece, and the great strides made in jurisprudence would have given him ample opportunity to celebrate the union of natural sciences with the human sciences. On the contrary, he stresses that, despite the advance in mathematics and natural mechanics, scientific inventions and technology were not encouraged. Despite the rise of skepticism in Greece, the Greeks and the Romans were deficient in "esprit de doute," he finds. What repels him especially is the rise of Christianity with its scorn for science and philosophy.

This fifth epoch, unacceptable as it is, is not as roughly treated as the sixth which extends from the early Middle Ages to the Crusades. In the opinion of the author, this was a deplorable epoch. Here Condorcet can find no redeeming feature, no successful achievements to balance the deficiencies. One quote will give the tone: "Des rêveries théologiques, des impostures superstitieuses sont le seul génie des hommes; l'intolérance religieuse est leur seule morale; et l'Europe, comprimée entre la tyrannie sacerdotale, et le despotisme militaire, attend dans le sang et dans les larmes, le moment où de nouvelles lumières lui permettront de naître à la liberté, à l'humanité, et aux vertus." This statement can be found duplicated in one form or other in the works of Holbach or Helvétius. This shows that the antireligious propaganda had done its work. Condorcet does not seem to suspect, as did many of his predecessors in the eighteenth century—Fontenelle, Espiard, Turgot, and Voltaire—that no age is totally unworthy, that the decline of one thing can be compensated by the rise of something else, that when there is a serious setback, there may be multiple causes for the catastrophe. Condorcet himself had written in his life of Voltaire (1787): "Plus la civilization s'étendra sur la terre, plus on verra disparaître la guerre et les conquêtes, comme l'esclavage et la misère." This latter statement is probably closer to the general philosophical thinking upon progress in his time.

It has not, in fact, been sufficiently noted that the *Esquisse* is intimately connected with the *Essai sur les mœurs*. Everyone knows that Condorcet was trained in part by Voltaire and that he repaid the Patriarch by directing after Voltaire's death the Kehl edition of his works. He also wrote one of the early biographies of the author (1787). We have been insisting during the past decade that Voltaire began with the writing of the *Lettres philosophiques* a new kind of history. Long before that, however, Lanson in his *Voltaire* (1909) had already tried to characterize that history in a chapter of his biography, but without establishing the intimate connection which exists between the *Histoire de Charles XII*, the *Siècle de Louis XIV*, the *Essai sur les mœurs et sur l'esprit des nations*, and the *Lettres philosophiques*. Lanson did stress Voltaire's concept of the relationship of history and culture, but he failed to note the same relationship between culture, "mœurs" (manners), and progress. This was understandable: Voltaire could hardly insist on the interrelationship between culture and civilization until he had worked out that connection in the *Philosophie de l'histoire*. There were two underlying principles of this concept. (1) For Voltaire, there was a clear application in the *Siècle* and *Essai* of the elements which he had discovered in the *Lettres philosophiques*. Having discovered and arranged these categories which entered into the making of a civilization, he now applied the method of analysis which he had learned to apply in the criticism of literature: the principle of beauties and defects. And so the *Siècle* is a set of *Lettres philosophiques* on France and the *Essai* is a set of *Lettres philosophiques* on all nations which had played a key role in the making of Western history. Voltaire judged, though, that the early ages of that history are too remote to be well known or understood or really of vital interest to the present world in which we live. For this reason, he first established the doctrine of the Four Superior Ages of man: Pericles, Augustus, the Medici, and Louis XIV; two from the distant past, two from the immediate past. Eventually, he adopted the view that the part of history which has the most meaning for us began with the two great ages from the immediate past.

Condorcet devised his *Esquisse* with Voltaire's principles fully in mind. That is why history is demonstrably a long list of crimes. That is why the task of the historian is to balance the beauties against the defects of history. That is to say, Condorcet succeeds only moderately well in the early epochs, in tracing the coherence, continuity, and consistency of history. That, finally, is the reason why progress only is the true theme of the last four epochs which occupy the last half of the treatise.

The seventh epoch extends from the revival of learning to the invention of printing. Condorcet presents it as the restoration of science in the West. He gave credit for inaugurating these sciences to the Arabs, whose love of poetry, he says, along with the study of Aristotle and the reintroduction of Greek science into the West renewed what Condorcet called the "génie de l'esprit humain." There was, to be sure, the revolt of the Westerners themselves against "l'intolérance des prêtres," especially in the south of France. But there was the rise of the Spirit of Freedom, particularly of freedom of thought, among its devotees—Frederick II, suspected of having composed a *Trois imposteurs* which Condorcet believes apochryphal and a Boccaccio. Condorcet still presents the struggle as a combat between "ceux qui avoient un esprit plus juste" and the priests. This free-thought was likewise aided by the quarrels between royalty and the nobles, between the rulers and their foreign enemies, and between kings and popes. The greatest change was brought about by the Crusades, because it brought the West in contact with Arab culture. "Ces guerres, enterprises pour la superstition, servirent à la détruire." Condorcet doesn't forget either the rise of the city-states in Italy and their tendency to imitate in organization the republics of the Greeks. There were also the free cities of the north along the Baltic and the people of Helvetia, who broke with feudalism and kings. Finally, there was the Magna Carta in England, followed by Charters which aided the cause of freedom everywhere. They now stand as the ancestors of the present declarations of the rights of man. Commerce flourished in the Mediterranean, in the Baltic, the Levant, and around the Black Sea. Politics, legislation, and public economy were in their infancy, but "on rassembloit les observations qui pouvoient y conduire . . ." Even scholasticism made its contribution to freedom in all its different senses. But scholasticism impeded progress in the natural sciences which was dominated by astrology rather than by astronomy. There was, however, development in the mechanical arts; for instance, the invention of the compass, which eventually opened up so many unknown lands. Gunpowder transformed war and rendered it "moins meurtrière." In Italy language reached its perfection and literature (Boccaccio, Petrarch) flourished along with painting. Other countries of Europe followed Italy. What was definitely lacking, Condorcet concluded, was the authority of reason. "Ainsi partout, l'autorité des hommes étoit substituée à celle de la raison. On étudiait les livres beaucoup plus que la nature et les opinions des anciens plutôt que les phénomènes de l'univers." There was no "critique éclairée," no method, but it was apparent that the human mind had now been prepared for the revolution which the discovery of printing would bring.

The eighth epoch extended from the invention to printing to the work of Descartes, characterized, said Condorcet, by the overthrow of arbitrary authority by science and philosophy. Condorcet goes to some length to bring out the power of the press to expand thought, to evade censure and the suppression of ideas. It was printing, he feels sure, which assured the triumph of reason. Moreover, coinciding with the invention of printing, was the fall of Constantinople and the discovery of America opening up to Europe, Asia, Africa, and eventually America. Condorcet stops his paean of praise to lament the cruelty with which the conquistadores treated the American natives: "Les ossements de cinq millions d'hommes ont couvert ces terres infortunées." They will proclaim forever, wrote Condorcet, against the doctrine of the political utility of religions. But on the positive side is that mankind now knew the whole globe and all its countries and humankind in all their diversity, "modifiée par la longue influence des causes naturelles ou des institutions sociales" (p. 196). And thence came an expansion in navigation, commerce, and industry, which led "par un enchaînement nécessaire" to a flourishing of all sciences and all the arts, and perforce to freedom. Unfortunately, all these advantages brought national jealousies, and excesses in tyranny. The Church fell into the sale of indulgences, giving rise to Luther who "annonçait aux peuples étonnés que ces institutions révoltantes n'étaient point le Christianisme." The reform would have delivered the people from the yoke of Rome, had the latter not been seconded by the powerful kings and emperors, who, thought Condorcet, not only defended the Church but the despotic rule of kings. Thus religious intolerance became common to all sects. Happily, "quelques savants cherchaient à établir un système déstruc- teur de toute idée religieuse." They are the martyrs of free-thinking, opposed by all sects, all governments, all authority. Even philosophy was corrupted by their opinions. Worse still, the Reform held in contempt the doctrine of the equality of man. Condorcet conceded that the reformers should have been normally the allies of the free- thinkers, but Protestantism, in his opinion, "ne conduisait pas à la véritable liberté de penser." In a few European countries, though, the multiplicity of sects led to a kind of tolerance. Some generous souls among the free-thinking Protestants, Althusius, for instance, succeeded in revealing to mankind that freedom is an inalienable right, that there can be no prescription in favor of tyranny, no con- vention in favor of a royal family, and that the magistrates are the officers of the people, and not its masters.

Condorcet insists (p. 210) nonetheless that history shows little progress of freedom among the common people during this period, but "plus d'ordre, et plus de force dans le gouvernement, et dans les nations un sentiment plus fort et surtout plus juste de leurs droits." The laws are better combined. The popular agitations and revolu- tions attract the attention of philosophers, who study more carefully to foretell the effects which constitutions, laws, and public institutions have upon the freedom of the masses, upon prosperity, upon the power of the state, the preservation of their independence, and the form of the government. Economics became a science. Rules of an international order between states were formulated, giving rise to international law. Condorcet notes that (p. 213): "La science de la morale ne pouvoit sans doute exister encore," since priests were the official interpreters of good and evil. He adds, though, that the Reform "épura les principes de la morale." At the same time, hypocrisy and fanaticism were rampant. On the contrary "la marche des sciences devient rapide et brillante" (p. 215). Condorcet details with some satisfaction the specific progress made in mathematics, physics, and chemistry, but he cannot omit the long list of the errors of his time and of his country. He attributes the major portion of these prejudices to the vices of public education. Nonetheless, detailing the intellectual benefits derived from Bacon, Galileo, and Descartes, he confesses: "Nous sommes arrivés au point de civilisation, où le peuple profite des lumières, non-seulement par les services qu'il reçoit des hommes éclairés, mais parce qu'il a su s'en faire une sorte de patrimoine, et les employer immédiatement à se défendre contre l'erreur à prévenir ou satisfaire ses besoins, à se préserver des maux de la vie, ou à les adoucir par des jouissances nouvelles" (p. 227).

The ninth epoch extends from Descartes to the formation of the French Republic. Condorcet notes that he has shown how man's mind has slowly formed itself throughout the eight previous periods due to the natural advance of civilization and despite the inroads of superstition and the degrading effects of despotism. Only one people, however, escaped the pernicious effects of these scourges. There the human mind marches to truth in the name of freedom. This ninth epoch is thus the period of the mind's deliverance from tyranny. At the beginning of the epoch, the nations reputed free were far from achieving those rights natural to mankind. There were all kinds of derogations from the right of equality, although laws now guarantee individual and civil liberty. In other nations, political liberty was restricted. The first requirement for these nations was to perfect their constitutions. Those which had adopted a kind of enlightened despotism had already enjoyed a certain progress. Manners became gentler; prejudices lost their ferocity; commerce, industry, and ideas spread. Religious intolerance still exists, but it has become milder, Condorcet summarizes (p. 240): "Ainsi le tableau des progrès de la philosophie et de la propagation des lumières . . . va nous conduire à l'époque où l'influence de ces progrès sur l'opinion, de l'opinion sur les nations et sur leurs chefs, cessant tout à coup d'être lente et insensible, a produit dans la masse entière de quelques peuples, une révolution, gage certain de celle qui doit embrasser la généralité de l'espèce humaine."

The rights of man have finally been found, deduced from one simple truth: "Man is a sensible creature, capable of forming rational thoughts and acquiring moral ideas." From this one observation (this capacity to build moral ideas) was deduced the notion that men assembled in society for the sole purpose of preserving their rights in perfect equality. This state is guaranteed by the adherence of each to the rights of all. The consequences of this doctrine are clearly marked. Man rejects henceforth that a small group is destined to govern a large group which is condemned to obey. Rather, it is understood now that the efforts of each should contribute to the welfare of all. Thus, man must henceforth be free to use his faculties, dispose of his wealth, and provide for his needs. Condorcet remarks that there are public works, establishments, and institutions useful to all members of a society. They should be established, inaugurated, and defended. In this way, the progress of politics and economics is a good for all. Condorcet intimated that this view was fundamental to Descartes, by the enhancement of reason, and to Locke by the method of analysis. The application of these methods to morality, politics, and public economy brought into the human science a firmness as great as that in the natural sciences: "cette méthode devint en quelque sorte un instrument universel: on apprit à l'employer pour perfectionner celles des sciences physiques pour en éclaircir les principes, pour en apprécier les preuves." It became a new kind of metaphysics, applying itself to all the objects of human intelligence. Condorcet notes that Leibniz is the main inventor of this new metaphysics, but he accords much credit also to the Scottish philosophers. What he insists is of primary importance is the effect of this metaphysics upon the opinion of the masses and thus it became proper and fitting to proclaim the right of each man to submit his opinion to his own reason, that is, to employ the only instrument capable of grasping truth.

This was the task performed by the philosophes—a class of men, said Condorcet, more engaged in spreading truth than in discovering and penetrating it, who devoted themselves especially to the suppression of prejudices and the destruction of popular errors. The leaders in France were Bayle, Fontenelle, Voltaire, and Montesquieu. They employed all the arms of erudition, philosophy, wit, and style; they adopted all tones; they employed all forms of expression and all

genres of literature; they demanded freedom of the mind and freedom of the press; they rebelled against all the crimes of fanaticism
and tyranny, adopting as their war-cry reason, tolerance, and humanity. This was the nature of that "new" philosophy.

This philosophy spread throughout Europe, thanks to the universal use of the French language, thanks also to the widespread use of
printing. As a result there arose the doctrine of the indefinite perfectibility of the human species. And in time, despite the same old
attempts to seduce the inhabitants of the new colonies by arguments
for keeping the status quo, these colonials rebelled in the name of
their human rights. It was then one saw "pour la première fois un
grand peuple délivré de toutes ses chaînes se donner paisiblement à
lui-même la constitution et les lois qu'il croyait les plus propres à
faire son bonheur" (p. 272). They thus created thirteen different
republican constitutions. Condorcet remarks that the thirteen
achieved the idea of the necessity of establishing and regulating by
law a normal peaceful means of reforming a constitution. In time,
the American revolt came to France where "la maladresse de son
gouvernement a précipité cette révolution, la philosophie en a dirigé
les principes, la force populaire a détruit les obstacles qui en pouvoient en arrêter les mouvements." Here Condorcet stops to show
that the French Revolution was fuller than the American because
it embraced the political, civil, and criminal laws. The French had
to attack "l'économie toute entière de la société, changer toutes les
relations sociales, en pénétrer jusqu'aux derniers anneaux de la
chaîne politique." They attacked the despotism of kings, the political
inequality, the pride of the nobility, the domination, intolerance,
riches of the priesthood, and the abuse of feudalism. Hence in
Condorcet's opinion, the principles upon which the constitution of
French laws have been created are more precise, more profound, and
more pure than those of the Americans.

Condorcet traces the whole revolution in theory back to the moment when Descartes imprinted upon the human mind a notion of
its mission, its power, and its duty. He marks its progress from the
"impulsion générale," which he calls the first principle of a revolution in the destiny of the human species, to the happy moment of a
thorough social freedom. Between these two moments, Condorcet
envisages a long period of slavery and misfortune, preceding Des-

cartes. It was eventually conjured by the progress introduced in the mathematical and physical sciences. It was this activity which introduced the "impulsion générale" and the "impulsion" which led to the revolution. Specifically, Condorcet names it the application of algebra to geometry. In due time, the principles of calculus were invented by Leibniz and Newton, and the laws of movement were followed by the law of gravitation—the first time man ever knew a universal law, added Condorcet. Newton also taught mankind how to be absolutely precise in its calculations. Due to this instruction, a large number of problems in statics are now solved. What ultimately is understood is that all these universal laws, which are known in science and derive from mathematics, redound to a new insight into the eternal order of the universe and belong to the field of philosophy. The one supreme law of philosophy is that all bodies are subject to necessary laws which tend to stabilize and maintain order in the universe. This was first observed in astronomy, then in physics, then in chemistry, all of which Condorcet discusses in detail. Their importance lies in the way these general laws destroy superstition and establish the authority of the human mind in the building of a true philosophy. The physical laws unite with moral laws; physical and moral sciences unite with the arts and with the mechanical arts. With the creation of new sciences, there cluster around them whole groups of new arts. Chemistry, botany, and natural history "répandaient une lumière féconde sur les arts économiques." Condorcet names these "economic arts": farming, animal husbandry, the art of perfecting the different races, pharmacy, surgery, and medicine. The movement from the abstract theory to the "savantes et délicates" applications is of great importance. Condorcet insists tremendously upon the practical uses of these scientific theories, even to the point of suggesting a number of specific research problems: "recherche sur la durée de la vie des hommes," the influence exercised upon this longevity by the differences in sex, climate, temperature, profession, government, habits, human mortality caused by diseases. He admits, as does Voltaire, that there are natural limits to these discoveries. What intrigues him greatly is the nature of "genius." It was a major problem of the Enlightenment. His greatest interest, however, lies in the advantages which man can obtain from all these intellectual activities. Here, without hesitation, he proclaims that the great service the advance in science has produced is the destruction of errors in politics, in morality, and in philosophy. "Il n'existe," he wrote (p. 309), "ni un système religieux, ni une extravagance surnaturelle, qui ne soit fondé sur l'ignorance des lois de la nature." Moreover, true facts serve to destroy erroneous superstition and the manner of reasoning acquired in science is useful in solving problems in life. What has been learned in a particular field about solving scientific problems may be used in the solution of problems encountered in other fields. Condorcet, once launched, is tireless in his enumeration of advantages from the advance in the sciences: the establishment of journals and periodicals, the rise of dictionaries and encyclopedias, the proliferation of scientific societies, the encouragement given by the government. The final result can be measured in the fine arts (in music, in drama, in painting), enriched by the progress in philosophy. Condorcet gives a summary of great importance which we always persist in ignoring (p. 318), although it defines superbly his law of total effect.

Ainsi, toutes les occupations intellectuelles des hommes, quelque différentes qu'elles soient par leur objet, leur méthode, ou par les qualités d'esprit qu'elles exigent, ont concouru aux progrès de la raison humaine. Il en est, en effet, du système entier des travaux des hommes, comme d'un ouvrage bien fait, dont les parties distinguées . . . avec méthode, doivent être cependant étroitement liées, ne former qu'un seul tout, et tendre à un but unique.

Condorcet explains (p. 319) how this organic unity between reason, science, method, and order works in raising humanity from knowledge to utility, from one's prejudices and superstitions to liberty, from the enlightened few to a large number of enlightened nations. This movement of ideas is what has established the principles of true philosophy: the maxims of freedom, the knowledge of the rights of man, and man's recognition of his interests. Condorcet's refrain is a veritable battle hymn of the republic. In enlightenment there is power, power because man now knows freedom, freedom because it is the natural right of every human being. Still, much remains to be done (p. 321):

Nous voyons que les travaux de ces derniers âges ont beaucoup fait pour le progrès de l'esprit humain; mais peu pour le perfectionnement de l'espèce humaine; beaucoup pour la gloire de l'homme, quelque chose pour sa liberté, presque rien pour son bonheur.

Man's task has just begun, his mission shines before him, his destiny lies way into the future. Hence the necessity for a tenth epoch, the ascent of man, or rather, the ascent of all men. The science and philosophy of the happy few must be made available to all men, and each must conquer his happiness while guaranteeing the happiness of all. Condorcet states very categorically that the human problem is in reality a problem in political history (pp. 324–25):

C'est à cette partie de l'histoire de l'esprit humain, la plus obscure, la plus négligée, et pour laquelle les monuments nous offrent si peu de matériaux, qu'on doit surtout s'attacher dans ce tableau, et, soit qu'on y rende compte d'une découverte, d'une théorie importante, d'un nouveau système de lois, d'une révolution politique, on s'occupera de déterminer quels effets ont dû en résulter pour la portion la plus nombreuse de chaque société car c'est là le véritable objet de la philosophie, puisque tous les effets intermédiaires de ces mêmes causes ne peuvent être regardés que comme des moyens d'agir enfin, sur cette portion qui constitue vraiment la masse du genre humain.

Progress thus as a reality still remains in the future, in the tenth epoch, where the past progression of the human mind must be carried on with coherence, consistency, and continuity. This coherence is assured only by the orderly unity between thought, expression, personality, and existence. What one is is what one thinks: his existence, expression, and his action are all modes of his thinking. It is true that Condorcet as well as all his contemporaries are still vague about the origin of that thought, its means of development, the consequences to which it leads, and its meaning to the person thinking. But mankind has had ultimately to guess about the origin and end of all things. Condorcet seems convinced nonetheless that the laws of nature are necessary and constant in physical matters and should be equally constant in moral, that is to say, eternal matters. Coherence, continuity, and consistency derive from this constancy of nature's laws. Moreover, all human beings live through the same existential experience of every other human creature, not at the same pace, to be sure. It can be expected, therefore, that all peoples will follow the same road to progress which some have already trod. That assumption is backed by two ideas in Condorcet. (1) The principles of the French constitution are already fully recognized by the enlightened few. (2) It is the mission of France to enlighten Europe. The accomplishment of this mission should make the rights of man a reality. This can only be done by establishing equality, otherwise there will always be forces which can destroy liberty. These forces are inequality of riches, of inheritance, and of knowledge. There are, Condorcet admits, other dangers: the revolt of the masses constitute a menace, and overpopulation can disrupt all these advances made by civilization. These serious threats can be averted only by constant instruction of the masses, by a policy of constant democratization of man: what Condorcet calls the "perfectionnement de l'espèce humaine." He concedes that the human mind is limited and will never exhaust all the facts of nature, nor will it measure precisely the meaning of existence. It is nonetheless the only instrument we have which can help carry the human mandate.

THE RESULT

THE one result of the movement of Enlightenment which I find incontrovertible is the French Revolution. It was followed by an age of revolutions, which has continued from 1776 to the present day. Startling as this fact is, the most stupendous fact still is that the age was an era of democratic revolutions. The revolutions to which I refer are not those which consist in change or reform. Change and reform may play a role in the movement and there are many cases since 1776, or since 1680 for that matter, where they have taken place for the better. But the general march of civilization can hardly be defended after the past two hundred years in terms of human progress, human happiness, or even human reason. Not that we would find it at all difficult to point out many areas of intellectual activity which have produced an advance in living and in learning. Lanson, for instance, makes the point that Voltaire's ideal of economic and political progress could have been successfully achieved had Turgot remained in charge of the government for a generation instead of remaining in power for eighteen months. I am afraid this is a completely unrealistic remark, especially in the France of the Enlightenment.

We make remarks of this sort all the time, though. I have often heard mentioned that the reforms in medical education have produced almost miraculous improvements in the field of medicine, surgery, and even in the life-span of the individual. I would feel that much could be said in defense of that view. Having lived through fairly disastrous wars since 1914 where it is not any longer unusual to kill as many as forty million in a single war, and where that end can now be achieved, if anybody wants to do so, in a single planned attack, one wonders what is the advantage in preserving an individual from yellow fever if he is to be presumably annihilated with atomic energy. Sending a man to the moon is certainly a great technological exploit, but I have heard many inquire just what advantage will accrue from that imaginative act for those who are destined to slow starvation in the overpopulated regions of this little world which we are accustomed to call "our" world. I confess, perhaps too ingeniously, that I do not know what is the solution to these problems. I do not even know whether this is the context in which the problems should be put. Under these circumstances, I must plead ignorance and leave well enough alone, as my friend Voltaire did.

I cannot offer the same plea when it comes to the nature of the Enlightenment and its meaning for us. It would hardly be acceptable to claim so much for that age and then suddenly adopt that point of view that it, like all other ages, really produced so little in terms of stabilization, order, human progress, comfort, or happiness. I have often rejected the view offered by many of my historian colleagues that it just happened that way; that there is in reality no accounting for it; that it was at best a happy or unhappy incident in man's affairs. I am reminded of a remark in Professor Palmer's very fine book where he stated, "Events seemed to run away with ideas," which I interpret to mean that the age may have been a *democratic* revolution, but certainly no *intellectual* one. Indeed, I find it very hard to envisage just what happens when an idea runs away with an event. Then, too, it may be impossible to produce an intellectual revolution. However, since I am attempting to prove that the basic situation of all Enlightenment is its thought, since we all agree that practically everything became "philosophique," and since I invariably revert to what I hope is a basic principle—what one thinks and says is what he is and does—I am mildly disconcerted to discover at the end that such was not the case, that it just happened, period. I could possibly adjust myself to that point of view, were it not that the Enlightenment held out so many promises of intellectual achievements that I am nonplussed to realize that it ended guillotining people, creating ten-fold all the intolerance and corruption it was supposed to eradicate, and sent armies across Europe in the name of liberty, equality, and fraternity, spreading deicides, regicides, and suicides, not to insist upon the many who were put to death in the general mêlée. I certainly do not approve of this indiscriminate holocaust which, I am afraid, goes on all the time. Despite that sad confession, we must not forget that the Enlightenment has at least one merit. It seems to have created the most important idea of modern times in its concept of civilization, although, at the same time, it also created the concept of revolution which is designed to tear civilization to pieces. And that is man's destiny since 1789. It was his destiny before 1789, too, I suspect. However, let us not exaggerate.

What we should do here is recapitulate just what did happen, not forgetting the subsequent consequences. The best account I know was given by G. Lefebvre, *La Révolution française* (P U F, Paris, 1968, 6th ed., Introduction). The Revolution precipitated evolution of the nation, but did not modify its general direction. Begun by "patriciens," it appears as the last episode in the struggle between the aristocracy and the monarchy and closes the past history of the kingdom. Completed by "plébéiens," it effected the rise of the bourgeoisie, thereby inaugurating the modern history of France. Lefebvre insists that France was only one of the European countries (and not the first) that went through this development. He claims that it should be envisaged in the general movement of civilization. Seen thus, it is a continuation of the age-old struggle to subject the forces of nature, to dominate this planet, and to discipline society, manners, and economy for the happiness of the individual and the perfecting of the species.

The general event of the Revolution he describes as follows. The bourgeoisie could have increased its power and taken its place in the new government without breaking with aristocracy. It did so in England after the two revolutions in the seventeenth century. Gentlemen and bourgeois united to share the power with the monarch. In France, though, the bourgeois responded by demanding equality of rights. The popular force intervened in their favor and the *Ancien Régime* collapsed: the king lost his crown; the aristocracy lost its privileges, its wealth, and its authority. The Revolution ended in a Terror and a political democracy.

Lefebvre describes very carefully the relations of Europe and the newly discovered worlds; they are characterized by the revival of a renewed outburst of exploration and a competitive race to acquire possession of as much of the globe as possible. There was nevertheless a lag between the new discoveries and the ability to colonize the New World. America was divided between Spain and Portugal, France and England, the East between England and Holland, but more slowly. These countries had difficulty in retaining their possessions. Portugal held only Brazil; Holland, mostly the East Indies; France, chiefly the West Indies; Spain was more successful in clinging to its positions in the two Americas; England was more successful still in the American colonies and in the Indian Ocean. Practically the whole operation was one of domination; the European countries tended to enslave the natives; there was in addition a subsidiary slave trade and even a steady tendency on the part of the European mother country to oppress the settlers from Europe. Raynal's *Histoire philosophique des deux Indes* violently denounced the situation. There was, on the other hand, much to be said for the progressive development of the colonies, also, which in a way were an expansion of the qualities of the mother country and a repetition of their problems and their difficulties.

Everyone will concur that from the fall of the Bastille in 1789 and at least until 1794, when the Terror finally was spent, there was a total collapse of the Old Regime. It is possible even to argue that it had been effected between 14 July 1789 and the flight of the king to Varennes on 20 June 1791. However, beyond the confines of these encompassing dates, there would be wide divergences of opinion as to what brought on these events and even what happened of consequence because of them. It is even questionable just what meaning to assign to the term "breakdown." The Old Regime has been defined in the Cambridge *History* (p. 592) as "a monarchical bureaucracy working amid the survivals of a mediaeval society." It had undoubtedly often shown signs of weakness; but it was taken for granted by both conservatives and revolutionaries. Conservatives, of course, opposed the growing bureaucracy, while the "radical" thinkers conceived of a royal power served by an enlightened bureaucracy, both governing for the common good. The state was expected to be moderately despotic and more or less corrupt, serving to collect the taxes and to provide for peace and justice. All the political thinkers of the Enlightenment thought of the state in terms of the least government possible. There had developed throughout the eighteenth century the feeling that the local community could be mildly liberal while the royal power had to be more arbitrary, more despotic, and less personal. Still, there persisted also the feeling that the king could be expected to look after the welfare of all his subjects. When the taxation became unbearable, or the "corvée" system too onerous or the military recruitment absolutely unfair, or when a failure in the crops produced widespread starvation and misery, there could be revolts. These were mostly local, although sometimes they spread throughout the province as a whole. The most troublesome of these revolts occurred apparently in Paris where some concerted action was always possible. In these moments of threatened rebellion or actual revolt, the fragility of peace and justice and the utter impossibility of happiness became very evident in a society which had been told for over sixty years that peace, justice, and happiness were all possible and desirable goals in life. On these occasions something was done to "reform" the situation, depending mostly upon the seriousness of the revolt. However, these reforms had been going on, both in theory and in practice, over a half-century. They had been discussed in every conceivable way in the literature, the journals, the salons, and the cafés of the time, as well as in the higher institutions of learning, the academies, and the social assemblies. The result of all this discussion and activity was first of all the creation of a widespread, fairly enlightened public opinion which, despite the censorship, could now make itself heard and felt.

Nonetheless, the king and his administrative staff were not always in a position to respond adequately to these demands for reform. One source of constant embarrassment was the depleted state of the public treasury. One reason for this was the fact that France, though economically prosperous from 1725 to 1775, really never did recover from the disastrous and costly wars of Louis XIV. Its fiscal policy, in addition, has been declared inept by those who have studied these problems. Its system of taxation, which fell upon the *tiers état* almost exclusively, was so manifestly unjust that it constantly invited riots among the peasants and the lower bourgeoisie. Moreover, it now appears that the suggested reforms were largely extensions of Colbert's time. In general, they had been more or less moderate, and had been largely of the order proposed by Colbert. To a great extent, they were opposed by some vested interest or by some favored group. The greatest difficulty lay in the apparent incompetence of the finance ministers. The only outstanding one was Turgot, who was granted eighteen months to reform the fiscal policy by Louis XVI. Turgot had been preceded by a long line of contrôleurs-généraux extending back to the late years of Louis XV (Orry, Machault, Bertin, D'Invau, and Terray). Indeed, all during the reign of Louis XV, there had been need for serious adjustments in this area of the state. However, each minister had undertaken the task only to see himself thwarted either by the magistracy or by the privileged. Terray was the last ahead of Turgot to try to adjust matters, but for the most part he adopted the reforms of Machault, a predecessor. He had but limited success, though, because he was a manipulator, and merely shifted the difficulties from one area to another. Indeed, it now appears that he knew very little about the true financial situation; in addition, he squandered money freely as a means of staying in power. Both procedures he concealed in his reports to the king by falsifying the true position of the treasury. When it is recalled that it was this particular situation which was not remedied, thereby causing the return of the Etats généraux which eventually launched the Revolution, its importance looms rather large in the history of Europe.

There was, however, another proposed reform which was not without great importance also—the reform in the judiciary. This need for reform went back also to the last years of Louis XIV's reign, where his attempt to suppress Jansenism in France was met by the opposition of Parlement. From then on, it was clear that a reform of Parlement was indicated, some accord between the Crown and Parlement was to be reestablished. The opposition reached a peak around 1751 over the scandalous affair of the "billets de confession." Nothing was done of consequence to bring about a reconciliation of Crown and Parlement until the period from 1765 to 1770, when Choiseul made some attempt to appease Parlement by his opposition to the Jesuits. He was, however, not very successful. Only after his fall, in 1770, was a serious effort made. The Parlement was largely exiled, six judicial councils were established to carry on the work of the judiciary, and a Grand Conseil was retained (now called the Parlement Maupeou) to act as a tribunal for Crown affairs and as a Court of Peers. Maupeou abolished both the Cour des aides (dealing with fiscal affairs) and the Châtelet (dealing with criminal cases). The intention behind this move was a desire to break the authority of the judicial aristocracy. It was consequently not looked upon with favor by the aristocracy as a whole, who were inclined to regard it as an episode in the struggle between the Crown and Parlement. Voltaire, curiously, approved the move, but the philosophes, as a group, did not. Consequently, the full plan which included the sup-

pression of the provincial parlements and a thoroughgoing over-
hauling of the whole judicial system was never carried out since
Maupeou fell from power and the old Parlement was recalled in
1774. Many of these reforms did not get into the French judicial
system until the days of Napoleon's Code.

The breakdown in this judiciary reform led to some dire consequences. It not only heightened the opposition of Crown and Parlement, but it exasperated a dissension between the Crown and the
aristocracy, which had been building up since the reform movement
assembled around the duke of Burgundy in the days when he was
expected to succeed his grandfather. It now included not only the
true aristocracy but also the princes of the realm. When it is recalled
that this aristocracy forced Louis XVI to summon the Etats généraux, one begins to wonder if things could not have been different.
The point to stress here, however, is that the Leviathan State, which
had become so monolithic, now had developed some very serious
cracks.

The effect of the Revolution was so cataclysmic that historians of the
nineteenth century, and even more recent ones, have experienced
some difficulty in understanding just what did take place. In general, it was thought that the underlying cause of the outburst must
be attributed to the intolerable conditions of life: hunger, suffering,
and the misery of the peasants. There was an inclination to cite
Arthur Young's picture of France in his voyages as evidence of that
widespread misery, and in due time a considerable amount of supplementary evidence was added to Young's. Gradually there was built
up a kind of official view of the Revolution which was thought to
have been expressed by Tocqueville in his *Ancien Régime* and in
Taine's *Ancien Régime*. Each historian had conducted his investigation in an entirely different way. Tocqueville largely used the
archives of the state, while Taine was more inclined to draw his
material from the *Memoirs* of the time. In both cases, the result
does not seem to differ greatly—what each depicts is a civilization
in ruins.

At the beginning of the twentieth century, this picture was challenged by two other historians, Jean Jaurès and J. Mathiez. The

latter, in *La Révolution française*, conceded that there had occurred at the time of the outbreak a cleavage between reality and the laws, between the institutions and manners and customs, and between the letter and the spirit of the law. He admitted further that the king had suddenly been deprived of his subject's obedience, that public opinion became a ruling power, that there was a breakdown in the feudal taxing system, and that government had become totally incoherent. He denied, however, that these things could be explained by the poverty, misery, and hunger of the peasants. Indeed, he pointed out that there was solid evidence to support the view that the nation's wealth was rising, that the population was increasing rapidly, and that the prices of foodstuffs, of the land, and of dwellings were constantly rising throughout the century. He cited cases to show that the comfort of life characteristic of the upper bourgeoisie was beginning to appear in the lesser and even the lowest middle class. And he added: "On s'habille mieux, on se nourrit mieux, surtout on s'instruit." He concluded that there is no way to justify the Revolution on the grounds that the country was exhausted, when, on the contrary, affairs seem to be flourishing. He added that, in his view, misery can result in revolt, but it could never have produced a revolution of this magnitude. This can only occur in the breakdown of class structure. Mathiez insisted that the bourgeoisie, which possessed the larger part of the national wealth while the privileged class was steadily ruining itself, began to be more and more conscious of its social inferiority and eventually rebelled against that situation. Little by little, the middle class seized the moral power. Since, in general, the writers belonged to this group, they saturated the public with their writings. "Ils écrivent maintenant pour le grand public qui les lit, ils flattent ses goûts. Ils défendent ses revendications. Leur plume ironique persifle sans cesse toutes les idées sur lesquelles repose l'édifice ancien et tout d'abord, l'idée religieuse." Mathiez insisted, just as Mornet and Hazard did at a later date, that religion is "la clef de voûte du régime." He concludes that these writers attacking religion weakened the state and thereby prepared slowly the explosion. "Que vienne l'occasion et toutes les colères accumulées et rentrées armeront les bras des misérables excités et guidés par la foule des mécontents" (p. 14).

Since the views of Mathiez and Jaurès there have been more precise studies made especially by E. Labrousse, in *Esquisse du mouve-ment des prix et revenus en France au XVIIIe siècle* (Paris, 1933), and by R. Mousnier, *Progrès scientifique et technique au XVIIIe siècle* (Paris, 1958). These studies have been discussed vigorously by three different critics since the middle of the present century: La-brousse, Mousnier, and Bouloiseau (in *Le XVIIIe siècle, Révolution intellectuelle, technique, et politique, 1715–1815*, Paris, 1953); by A. Soboul, in *La France à la veille de la Révolution* (Paris, 1966), and *La Société française dans la seconde moitié du XVIIIe siècle* (CDU, Paris, 1969); and by F. Furet, and D. Richet, in *La Révolution française* (Paris, 1970, 2 vols.).

Soboul's synthesis may be taken as a broad summary of the com-bined findings of these works. He notes that the characteristic trait of the Old Regime was a feeling of permanence in the traditional structures of agriculture, industry, and commerce. This permanence, however, was threatened by the introduction of a capitalistic develop-ment in this economic tradition. Agriculture was the most important of the three sectors, four-fifths of the population being still rural. There were, however, in the area of agriculture, restrictions which could become troublesome: the obligatory rules for the shifting of crops and the laws against enclosures. On the other hand the peasant had compensating rights: the right of open pasture, of "glanage," and of collecting firewood. In general, there was no freedom of cultivation, and the production was very limited because of the weakness in farming techniques. Likewise, commerce and industry were more or less subject to restrictions, traditions, and correspond-ing weaknesses. The new school of economists (the Physiocrats) loudly criticized these restrictions and advocated economic freedom. Soboul recalls that the general impression has normally been that social and economic conditions were bad especially among the peas-ants and the lower bourgeoisie. He concedes that this was probably correct, but he adds that the thought now is that these unfavorable conditions could not conceivably produce a revolution. He suggests that the judicious view now is that France, though far behind Eng-land in economy, commerce, and industry, was developing a progres-sive economy. Big industry was just beginning, though timidly; in-dustrial capitalism was making some headway, and there was a rising economy from 1724 to 1774. A depression occurred, however, during the reign of Louis XVI (1775–1788).

Soboul concludes this part of his investigation with the remark that at the end of the Ancien Régime, the French economy is steadily rising. Despite this progression, one must remember that only certain sectors of the economy and certain classes were able to benefit from the advance. The commercial class profited more than the industrial class and the landowners fared much better than the farmers. However, while there were reasons for some satisfaction, there were other situations which were less promising: salaries had not kept up with the rise in prices, the peasants had in reality profited but little from the increase, and even the commercial and industrial bourgeoisie began to feel that it was difficult to operate within the framework of the Ancien Régime.

Along with the rise in the economy, there was also an increase in the population, which advanced from twenty to twenty-six millions. It came not so much from an increase in births (they actually, it appears, decreased), but from a decline in mortality rates. The change most affected the peasant and artisan groups. Hence, while France as a whole profited, these two particular groups found their difficulties increasing. Some of these difficulties explain certain aspects of the origins of the revolution. It was probably this fact which originally gave rise to the belief that the misery of the peasant and artisan was what occasioned the explosion.

The situation which has to be examined with great care is the interrelationships between the different orders of French society, since in the early months of the Revolution practically the whole activity turned upon the position and obligations and rights of each social group. In 1759, French society was essentially aristocratic, though composed of three orders: the nobility, the clergy, and the third estate. There were roughly about 140,000 nobles; 130,000 clergy; and the rest of the 26 or 27 millions formed the "tiers." None of the three groups was really homogeneous. The nobility was of two sorts: the old feudal, military nobility and the new, administrative nobility. From Louis XIV on, it was possible to purchase one's nobility as well as earn it or inherit it. The clergy was divided into the upper clergy of about 3000 of the very highest nobility and the remainder was recruited from the other orders. In one sense of the word, it was more representative of the whole of France than any of the other orders. The "tiers" comprised the bourgeois group and the peasant group, but the bourgeois group itself comprised an upper, a middle, and a lower bourgeoisie. It was naturally difficult to draw the lines of demarcation of these groups and harder still when there was an urban group that was relatively small in comparison with the rural group, which was vast.

The aristocracy thrived on money, furnished to a great extent by the royal treasury. It was essentially a landowner class, and it had special privileges which derived in part from feudal rights as well as exemption from taxation. As a class, it attempted in the early years of Louis XV's reign to combine with the upper bourgeoisie in marriage, but it was said not to have been too successful. Montesquieu has scathing remarks in the *Lettres persanes* directed against this custom. Finally, we should note that the aristocratic group jealously guarded its rights. Hence, it was often in opposition with the upper bourgeoisie and rather contemptuous of its achievements. This was one of the serious sources of friction after 1770 when the bourgeoisie was pursuing its ambitions to rise in the social scale and found the insulting and inconsiderate aristocracy blocking the way. The greatest source of trouble was the ideological opposition of the aristocracy to royalty itself. It had begun in the last part of Louis XIV's reign when the so-called Fénelon-Saint-Simon-Boulainvilliers group gathered around the duke of Burgundy in order to institute a reform in the government. Thereafter, it had a tendency to work through the princes on the one hand, and Parlement on the other. It should be remembered that Boulainvilliers was the representative of the feudal opposition to Louis XIV, and that Montesquieu's *De l'Esprit des lois* was said by Brunetière to have been written in part as a satire of Louis XIV. Soboul notes that the aristocratic opposition came to a head in the *De l'Esprit des lois*, and states that it represents, particularly in the Appendix, the doctrine of "droit historique" of the nobility in contrast with the doctrine of "droit naturel" of Voltaire and Rousseau. Soboul further adds that the whole of the appendix of the *Esprit des lois* justifies the pretensions of the nobility (p. 82): "*L'Esprit des lois* est, à sa date, une réfutation très nette des écrivains bourgeois à tendance monarchiste. Si Montesquieu est un libéral en politique, un adversaire déterminé du despotisme, il n'en reste pas moins que son livre a constitué, jusqu'en 1789, la *Bible* de l'Aristocratie, où puiseront les Parlements pour leurs remontrances et les nobles pour leurs attaques contre l'absolutisme."

This remark explains in part the dominance of Montesquieu's political theories in the early years of the revolution. We should not forget, though, that although the aristocracy used Montesquieu constantly in their tendencies toward reform in government, those belonging to that order demanded that the reform be carried out to their advantage. The aristocracy was hostile to all rights of equality with the upper bourgeoisie. It was, in fact, this hostility to all equality of rights which precipitated the Revolution. And it can be argued, as G. Lefebvre has done in *Quatre-vingt-neuf* (tr. Palmer, pp. 209–212, 214–220) that it was really the aristocracy that precipitated the Revolution by forcing the king to call the Etats généraux. Lefebvre asserts that the court turned to the use of force to protect the aristocracy, thus driving the third estate to choose between resistance or surrender. The third estate chose resistance. Lefebvre notes that in reality, many things came to a head all at once: the clash in class interests (the nobility, for instance, refused to grant equality to the upper bourgeoisie), the individual interest which prevailed, the humbled pride, mass suffering, and widespread philosophical propaganda. Lefebvre insists that the third estate actually believed in an aristocratic conspiracy, because the bourgeoisie had laid the foundation for this belief in the declaration of the *Rights of Man* on 26 August 1789. He notes that it came to France via Lafayette and Jefferson and was an imitation of the Bill of Rights of the Virginia constitution. But Lefebvre argued that it was also an off-shoot of the whole philosophical movement in France during the Enlightenment. Montesquieu, Rousseau, and Voltaire had contributed to its making while both England and France had assembled a body of ideas which constituted a common ideal summarizing the evolution of Western civilization.

The problem which has to be considered is how the "esprit philosophique" became in time the "esprit encyclopédique" and this latter "esprit" was transformed into the "esprit révolutionnaire." The first transformation does not seem to offer too much difficulty. The organization of the "esprit philosophique" into "esprit encyclopédique" was effected in a perfectly normal way through the development of the *Encyclopédie*. The very steps followed were traced in fact by

D'Alembert on two occasions (first in the *Discours préliminaire* and, in a modified way, in his *Mélanges*) and by Diderot in the article "Encyclopédie." Cassirer has used one of D'Alembert's presentations as an introductory statement in his *Philosophy of the Enlightenment*. However, in addition to these general statements on the role of the human mind in the making of human history, there is a more explicit way of tackling the problem which consists in analyzing the seven categories of man's thought. If this is done with precision, we ought to be able to show how this thought became readjusted to a new way of thinking as there was developed a new way of intellectually approaching each category. There is thus created a new philosophy of religion, of esthetics, of morality, of politics, of economics, of man's history, of science, of the science of man, and even of philosophy itself. The sum total of these discrete philosophies is what constitutes the philosophy of the *Encyclopédie* around 1765. It is what we usually call the "esprit encyclopédique." There are still many gaps in our knowledge about the organic quality and the interrelationships of these separate philosophies. We do not know really, except in a general way, the sequence of their development. We can, however, when challenged, give a fairly lucid account of the first of the two main transformations. That is what Cassirer's *Philosophy of the Enlightenment* and Hazard's *Crise de la conscience européenne* were designed to do. For the most part, these general all-embracing syntheses of the Enlightenment break down, though, whenever the author is faced with the problem of the organic unity of the philosophy of the Enlightenment. That is what I think has happened to both Cassirer and Hazard, who are certainly the two of the very best we have. For instance, neither Cassirer nor Hazard face the transformations of the twelve seventeenth-century philosophers into the "esprit philosophique" nor the change which took place when this "esprit philosophique" was molded into the "esprit révolutionnaire." They both studiously avoided the evolution of this "esprit encyclopédique" into the "esprit révolutionnaire." Others who deal with this problem usually reduce it to one of the categories—morality, religion, politics, sciences, etc., and write very informative syntheses on this one aspect of their choice. Any one of us could name between a dozen and a score of titles of works which have been excellent in that they have covered the aspect which interested each particular author. They did not in any sense of the word attempt to cover the subject as a whole. The two who came closest, in my opinion, were Taine and Mornet. I am afraid, though, that my opinion in this matter is not worth very much, seeing that Mornet long ago absolutely rejected Taine's interpretation, although his own seems to me ultimately very similar to Taine's.

For Taine, the revolutionary spirit is formed somewhere between 1760 and 1770; it is a social spirit derived from Rousseau's *Contrat social*, from Mably, Holbach and a dozen or so books which are similar in nature. It expresses itself in abstract statements. Man is now enslaved. Freedom is man's right. Men are all equal by nature. Men are entitled to equal rights. Men are naturally good. Society is what has corrupted them. Man freed from the corruption of society would be happy. Men should live in peace with their fellow men. There is, of course, no evidence that these statements are correct. In Taine's opinion, they invite the society intellectuals to attempt the destruction of the old system, firmly convinced that reason will not lead them astray. Naively, this revolutionary spirit proceeds; it is never supported by facts, only by abstractions and remarks upon nature, reason, tyrants, and freedom. Taine draws these remarks from a selected body of texts, predominantly *Memoirs*.

Mornet, of course, rejects this interpretation for two reasons: in the first place, it is substantiated only by a selected number of statements; secondly, these statements give only a small sample of what was thought in the Enlightenment. The so-called petits faits which Taine insisted upon are often not necessarily true simply because the body of documents from which they are drawn is too restricted and because the interpretation is far too casual. Mornet reproaches Taine for presuming that the historian can always speculate on the origins of the Revolution by what actually occurred in the Revolution, very often much later. He forgets, insists Mornet, that what happened was not planned. Mornet concludes: "Les origines de la Révolution sont une histoire, l'histoire de la Révolution en est une autre." Mornet, however, never asks himself, insofar as I know, whether there is any demonstrable correlation between the origins and the history of the Revolution.

These remarks of Mornet are but the logical consequences of his own way of regarding things. He is an excellent bibliographer and, for his time, a very good statistician. His importance in the scholarship of the Enlightenment lies in his widespread acquaintance with a vast body of writings. For most of us, a lot of it is trashy, but in reality it is unknown to us. It was not only known to him, but he diligently studied its editions, and insofar as the conditions permitted, he traced its history, organized it into collections, and inscribed it in a vast collection of "fiches." He judged that he was able therefrom to state by the number of editions or by the number of private libraries which possessed a particular work how popular the work was, and since he was well read in these works, he was competent to judge what were the significant ideas and how far they could have permeated the society of the time. He was inclined to diminish the importance of the *Contrat social* on the grounds that it was not widely read, since it did not occur in any large number of private libraries which Mornet sampled (see "Les Enseignements . . . ," *RHL* 17, 1910: 449–496). In fact, he found only one copy in the catalogues of five hundred libraries. However, while Mornet's judgment certainly was founded upon evidence which he could interpret statistically, having read the work under consideration, his method of interpretation is not without its limitations. Who read the *Contrat social* is just as important as how many read it. If Robespierre read it, or if one priest read it to a score or so of peasants in a village square, these facts could outweigh the fact that only one of 500 catalogues of private libraries listed it. Moreover, we must not forget that Mornet, despite his unquestioned merit, fell into the same error which he condemned in Taine—he, too, made up his mind as to the nature of the French Revolution before presenting his evidence. In the introduction, for instance, of the *Origines intellectuelles de la Révolution française*, he recognizes three kinds of revolution: (1) revolution of hunger and wretchedness, (2) revolution of a well-organized small minority, intelligent and daring, which seizes the power and directs the activities, (3) revolution of a large minority, if not of an actual majority, more or less enlightened, which recognizes defects of the political regime, decides upon the reforms it wishes, and develops a public opinion which justifies the revolutionary movement. In Mornet's view, the French Revolution is of this third order. But isn't there in the French Revolution something of all three of these orders? In this Introduction, he makes a second statement which should also be underscored—he confesses that his study ends with the conviction that, in a way, ideas have been the determining factors in the French Revolution (p. 3). When this statement is compared with Professor Palmer's remark (R. R. Palmer, *The Age of Democratic Revolutions*, I, 286): "but real events in Europe, as distinguished from the stirring up of ideas, seemed to be going the opposite way," one becomes more than a little mystified.

Despite this assertion of principles, Mornet then ventures to analyze the Spirit of the Enlightenment as the origin of the Revolution. This "esprit" is above all hostile, he states along with Hazard, to religion. He insists that the effect of the clandestine manuscripts was necessarily limited. After 1750, the attack against the Church was more widespread. The Church organization was condemned for its intolerance. Mornet finds public opinion in this matter practically unanimous. In time, it embraces the state, which seems to support the intolerance of the clergy. Thus the battle against religious fanaticism became a battle against the political situation. Along with the condemnation of Church and state, there was an increase in unbelief, represented by a widespread condemnation of dogma, the scriptures, and the Catholic ritual. Mornet admits that this attack has not "dechristianized" France, but he maintains that it spread religious indifference among much of the aristocracy, among the young students, and even among the clergy. From the hostility to the Church, one passed by 1770 to a hostility to the state. Before that, there were rumblings, but no intention to change the principles of government. Reform was proposed for cleaning house, not for sweeping out the state. Mornet concedes, though, that they have their importance in procedures of justice, in administration, in taxation, in public charity, in special privileges, in the "Corvée" system of road-building; in all the subjects proposed by the local academies for their annual competitive essays. By 1770, though, the writers become more urgent. Thus, a strong movement of religious incredulity developed, and a similar movement of political uneasiness extended from the writers to some of the aristocracy, to the middle classes, and thence to the students, eventually creating a public opinion of protest. Mornet interprets this as, "La France tout entière se met à penser." This had been going on, of course, since the sixteenth century; now, however, in his opinion, it became more widespread, more general, better or-

ganized. Mornet finds it best expressed in the memoirs just as did
Taine, and in the correspondence, but better still in the transformations in education, in provincial academies, in literary societies, in
public libraries, and in newspapers. In the end, it turned into a
genuine movement of Enlightenment. Mornet admits that in this
development, the outstanding writers—particularly Voltaire and
Rousseau—played their role. The editions of their works were multi-
plied almost fabulously. The periodicals of the time constantly make
reference to them. Mornet stresses, notwithstanding, that though
popular and constantly in the eye of the public, they are not at all the
initiators of the revolutionary movement. In the religious field, the
clandestine manuscripts had reported all the criticisms which Voltaire was to repeat over and over. In political matters, says Mornet,
Montesquieu, Rousseau, Voltaire, and Diderot were neither revolutionary nor even radical reformers. Mornet even stresses that the
role of Rousseau has been seriously exaggerated, since his *Contrat
social* was little read. Mornet concludes that "les grands philosophes
ne révèlent pas des pays inconnus." Besides, in his opinion, the role
of intelligence in man's history is now of minor consequence. His
last word is "assurément, s'il n'y avait eu que l'intelligence, pour
menacer effectivement l'Ancien Régime, l'Ancien Régime n'aurait
couru aucun risque." What it took to organize this revolutionary
movement was the misery of the people and the political uneasiness.

Mornet nevertheless stresses (p. 675) that all of France began to
read and that there was a tremendous fermentation of intellectual
interests. He calls it "cet éveil si vaste, si actif, si ardent de l'intelligence." There is no doubt that these are what he considers the
intellectual origins of the Revolution. Further, he grants that the
influence of the great writers has been "considérable." He stresses
that the importance especially of Voltaire and Rousseau has dominated the thought of the century. On the other hand, these assertions seem strangely modified in the conclusion by another line of
thought. As for the importance of the great writers, he fails to
mention Montesquieu or Diderot, and he can't overlook that in five
hundred catalogues of libraries of the period, only one listed the
Contrat social. He notes that neither Voltaire, Rousseau, nor the
other great writers of the time had revolutionary intentions. Finally,
he has a tendency to play down the role of speculative ideas and

philosophical thought in any political, social, and moral movement (p. 475): "Si l'ancien régime n'avait eu contre lui les assembleurs de nuage, il ne se serait sans doute écroulé—s'il s'était écroulé—ni aussi vite, ni de la même façon."

This point of view is so self-contradictory in its details and the impression which he leaves is so ambivalent that we are at a loss to know how it should be assessed. Was it because he was trying deliberately to discredit Taine's interpretation which he thought exaggerated that he somewhat distorted his own interpretation? Was he attempting to strike some sort of reasonable balance between his own views and those of the Marxist historians of his time, whom he deemed more or less reasonable? Or did he place so much confidence in the statistical, historical method that he himself had practiced? I naturally do not know the answers to these disturbing questions. It is nonetheless true that though he wrote his work to trace the "intellectual origins" of the Revolution, he finally seemingly abandoned the notion that ideas played a very important role in the coming of the Revolution and adopted rather the view that the Revolution just happened in some inexplicable way. Some of the difficulty is caused by the failure to distinguish between the "esprit philosophique," the "esprit encyclopédique," and the "esprit révolutionnaire." Mornet just didn't believe in the consistent, coherent development of these "esprits" throughout the Enlightenment. There are others also, such as the "esprit critique" and the "esprit moderne," which merged right at the beginning of the eighteenth century to form the original "esprit philosophique." I doubt whether he could understand that there is a deep reality to these "esprits," that they represent validly the livingness of man, of his ideas, of his aspirations, and finally of his meaning. Indeed, I am not sure that Mornet has ever heard of Dilthey and his *Geist* and its function in the building of the *geistige Welt*. I am sure, however, that he has never given one moment to pondering the relationship between *esprit* and *geist*. Anyone who dared suggest that all this had definitely some bearing upon the concept of *erleben* would have been treated with a kindly, but firm skepticism. He would be told that there are really two ways in which one can easily go astray. One is to attach to these notions a higher content of mysticism than the actual event will justify. The other is to deny any spiritual content whatever. In that respect, the present

writer would be inclined to agree with Mornet. It would help perhaps if we would keep in mind that "esprit" and "morale" are
spiritual and at the same time rational faculties. They are, indeed,
the only spiritual faculties we are sure to possess. Moreover, it will
not hurt to recall that the *philosophique, encyclopédique*, and the
révolutionnaire form a progression derived from philosophy and
poetry (*i. e.* creation). We might for the time being, while attempting
to obtain an acceptable perspective on this intellectual development,
keep in mind just what we understand by each of these *esprits* or
even what we understand by *esprit*. In other words, we must
formulate some sort of working hypothesis on the relationship between what man knows, what he thinks, what he says, and what
he does, especially in the religious, political, economic, esthetic, scientific, moral, and social spheres. I suspect we will have to scrupulously
renounce some of those "préjugés" which the Enlightenment abom-
inated, and which unfortunately are not all traditional.

Some of these activities are already going on. I quoted above a
passage from Cobban in an article which he wrote on "How Revolutionary was the Revolution?" (*The French Revolution: Conflict
or Continuity*, ed. Steven T. Ross, New York, 1971, pp. 33–44) in
which he returns to the importance of ideas in the making of the
Revolution. Cobban (p. 44) seems to believe that the Revolution
adopted some of the ideas of the Enlightenment while it rejected
others. He attributes it to the fact that the people of that time stood
on the threshold of a new world between the romantic and rational
ages, the Enlightenment and the religious revival, humanitarianism
and the terror, the ecumenical ideal and the rise of nature, universal
brotherhood and the Napoleonic wars. These remarks are all too
true, but somehow they do not seem to me to touch the significant
things in the changeover. Peyre also wrote a significant article on
these matters in the *JHI* (1949, pp. 63–87), in which he heartily
commends Mornet because of the extensiveness of his research. He
states that Mornet broadened the makers of the Enlightenment by
including a larger group of philosophes and by studying the contribution of the salons, the academies, the colleges, and particularly
the *Cahiers de doléances*. Still, he adds that even after Mornet we
know "very little about the influence of Montesquieu, Voltaire, or
Rousseau himself, or the way in which they influenced certain actors

in the great drama." He notes that everybody seems to agree now that "pure historical materialism does not explain the Revolution." He, as did Gay much later, judged that the philosophes taught the public to know that it was wretched. In his opinion, it was the propaganda of the philosophes which spread discontent with the existing state of things. And he, as did Mornet, seems willing to concede that the writers prepared the way for the Revolution, without wishing for it. They did so by weakening the traditional religion; by teaching a secular code of ethics, a code which stressed love of humanity and urged the development of a critical spirit and a spirit of analysis; and, finally, by creating through a new type of history, a sense of progress and a desire for liberty. That statement seems to me eminently fair. Indeed, I feel, or at least I hope, that this treatise functions partly as a footnote to Peyre's succinct remark.

However, there are two further factors both extraordinarily important, which have been brought into the picture since Mornet and Peyre presented their views. The first is a definite trend among the more recent critics of the Revolution to stress that it is by nature an "Atlantic" revolution. This view has been best developed by Professor Godechot in his *France and the Atlantic Revolution of the Eighteenth Century, 1770–1799*. The central point made by Professor Godechot is that France was not the first country to revolt: there was a decided restlessness in the American colonies, in Geneva, and in the Low Countries. In each case, the uneasiness was expressed in a revolt. Indeed, the only place where the disquiet was not manifested in an open rebellion was Great Britain. There was, however, an Irish uprising and the Pugachev revolt in Russia. Godechot has noted that if historians can tie all these revolutions into a common Atlantic Revolution, it could be more difficult to defend the position that their underlying cause can be found in the writings of Montesquieu, Voltaire, Diderot, Rousseau, and other French philosophes. Professor Godechot has given some attention to the common causes. He admits, though, that some of the causes are not at all common. "They were," he says, "bound up with transformations in the social structure itself." The basic change was from some feudal-organized society toward a freer ownership. Godechot admits that there were variations in the ownership of the land. Moreover, "everywhere in Western Europe there existed a rich and active bourgeoisie." It was a wealthy class and readily prepared to take an active part in industrialization. Their rise to power was "one of the principal causes of social disturbances." In addition to the bourgeoisie as a cause for social unrest, Godechot cites the increase in population, which produced problems in food distribution and problems in employment. Despite the rising prices throughout the century from 1725 to 1774, the rise in salary did not keep up with them.

Godechot notes (p. 19) that "it was in this atmosphere of uncertainty and economic and social difficulties that the ideas of the philosophes began to spread." This point seems to contradict the other idea that if such a thing as an Atlantic phenomenon existed, the importance of the philosophes would be necessarily diminished. Be that as it may, Godechot adds that the French were the most active. They were naturally the most numerous (but why "naturally"?) and the most brilliant. They were the heirs of Bacon, Locke, and Spinoza, those "who had demonstrated the possibility of dominating nature by means of science and had substituted the results of experience and the conclusions of reason for the authority of tradition not only in the realms of science but also in the area of religion, morality, economics, and politics." Unfortunately, they were not in agreement, Godechot adds. There were in fact three schools. (1) Those (Locke and Montesquieu) who thought that government was founded upon contract and that it should be composed of three separate powers. This "school" was favorable to the aristocracy. (2) Those (Voltaire, the Physiocrats, and so on) who wanted monarchy to be enlightened by the philosophes. They wanted reforms, not revolution. (3) Those (Rousseau, Morelly, and so on) who insisted upon equality, abolition of luxury, and curbing of civilization. They placed sovereignty in the people. Finally, Godechot finds (p. 22) that "this intellectual movement of the second half of the eighteenth century was so unified and coherent that it has been given a characteristic name in every language." He concedes that the Atlantic Revolutions have political causes, fiscal causes, and constant wars. Aristocracy was organized in most countries. In all of them aristocracy formed a front against the claims of the sovereign. Sovereigns sought the support of the people; so did the aristocracy.

Godechot grants that each country had its own causes for revolt.

He insists, though, that they all wanted "to establish a new regime in which the citizens would enjoy greater equality and liberty and participate more fully in central government and local administration" (p. 27). He seems, however, to make some exception when it comes to the problem of the American Revolution (p. 33): "Was the struggle of the U. S. against England only a war of independence? Or was it at the same time a revolution?" Godechot states that the question has been debated by American historians who are deeply divided on the answer. Three attitudes have been taken by these historians. (1) The American Revolution was even more radical than the French. (2) It was a war of independence and also a political, economic, and social revolution, but very moderate in character. (3) It did not produce profound economic and social transformations. Godechot concluded that the middle view is now prevailing.

A second factor which now has to be considered and which vitiates to some extent all previous thinking upon the relationship of the encyclopedic doctrine and the French Revolution is the interpretation proposed by Professor J. L. Talmon in his *Rise of Totalitarian Democracy* (Boston, 1952).

The starting point of Mr. Talmon's thesis is that two types of democracy, liberal and totalitarian, emerged from the same premises in the eighteenth century and these two types have existed side by side ever since. The essential difference between the two schools of political thought is not in the affirmation of the value of liberty by one and its denial by the other, but in their differing attitudes toward politics. The liberal assumes politics to be a matter of trial and error and political systems to be contrivances of human ingenuity and spontaneity. For liberal democracy, therefore, other categories which may be completely outside the political sphere have an existence of their own. For totalitarian democracy, truth lies only in politics, which embraces all the other categories. Talmon calls it political Messianism, which postulates a preordained, harmonious, perfect scheme of things. For totalitarian democracy, economics, morality, religion, psychology, and sociology are integral parts of politics. Together they form a definite ideology which is called ultimately a philosophy. The thing to stress is that this philosophy is not spontaneous, subject to trial and error, and ultimately harmonious; it is completely and willfully planned in the light of a precisely defined goal to which everyone is summoned to conform. Presumably, if one refuses to conform, he is immediately liquidated. Talmon does not say so, but this is the ultimate effect of Rousseau's remark in the article "Economie politique" that "tout tient à la politique" and it is carried to its logical extreme by Jean-Jacques in his theory of state religion in the last chapter of the *Contrat social*.

Talmon explains that the two interpretations of politics which occurred were the result of the change of the state of mind in the last half of the eighteenth century. He asserts that the conviction spread that the conditions under which men and their forefathers had been living were unnatural and had to be replaced by deliberately planned uniform patterns, which would be natural and, at the same time, rational. What convinced the public of this necessity was a decline of the traditional order in Europe in which religion lost its intellectual and its emotional hold, feudalism collapsed under the impact of social and economic factors, and "the older conception of society based on status came to be replaced by the idea of abstract, individual man." Thus the areas in which the world drama was unfolded were religion, politics, economics, and morality, but the center was firmly political.

It is Talmon's contention that the origin of this totalitarian democracy is extracted, not from the organic and diverse quality of Enlightenment thought, but rather from the thought of a certain number of writers—Morelly, Mably, Condorcet, Helvétius, Holbach, Rousseau—which led directly, says Talmon, to Robespierre and Babeuf. The concept upon which that thought was centered was the postulate of natural order. Talmon finds that the situation which brought the concept to the fore was the analogy drawn since Montesquieu's day between the laws which govern the phenomena of nature and those which govern the phenomena of man. Succinctly put, these thinkers avowedly sought to equate the postulate of natural law with the postulate of the nature of man. They started out on a search for the one dominating law of natural morality which would correspond with Newton's law of attraction in natural sciences. It is true, although Talmon makes no mention of the matter, that Descartes in his *Discours* had precisely excluded the human sciences from his method, because of the danger of upsetting religion, politics, and morality. Notwithstanding this exclusion, under the combined in-

fluence of the seventeenth-century philosophers, the efforts throughout the Enlightenment were directed to isolate the one controlling
law of both human and natural sciences. It was avowed by Voltaire
in the *Traité de métaphysique,* the *Lettres philosophiques,* and the
Essai sur les mœurs; by Montesquieu in the *Esprit des lois*; by
D'Alembert in the *Encyclopédie*; by Diderot in all his work; and
by Rousseau in the *Contrat social.* The point to stress, however, is not
the widespread search for the one uniform law of man and of nature
which was even so central to all the thinking of the Physiocrats with
their concept of *ordre social,* but the failure of everybody, even the
Physiocrats to identify that law. Hence, while it is reasonable to see
in Morelly's *Code de la nature,* Mably's *Droits et devoirs,* Helvétius's
De l'Esprit, and Rousseau's *Contrat social* tendencies toward political
radicalism, some stress should be placed upon the fact that much
effort is expended also toward the establishment of political utopianism. Whereas it is undoubtedly true that Babeuf derived from this
group, particularly in his defense at Vendôme, even Talmon shows
that there was already present an awareness that this utopianism was
incompatible in a society which was far from perfect.

These remarks, however, do not vitiate Talmon's analysis of
eighteenth-century thought. His view that it prepared the ground
for the Revolution seems to me eminently sound. His insistence (1)
that it criticized the Ancien Régime and its abuses and absurdities,
(2) that it brought forth more positive suggestions for a more
rational, freer political adminstration (the separation of powers, the
place of the judiciary, the system of taxation) seems to be acceptable.
But these moves tended more toward reform than toward revolution.
I am not sure, however, about the unyielding opposition which the
philosophes offered to religion. It is a fact, nonetheless, that all the
philosophes could find reasons for criticizing the effect of religion
upon society. But there was a wide divergence of opinion in the
Enlightenment as to the possibility of creating a sound ethical society
divorced from some religious practice.

Talmon notes that Rousseau influenced Robespierre, Mably influenced St. Just, and Morelly influenced Babeuf. He draws a distinction between the French Revolution compared with the American Revolt, finding that the American Revolution had been an event
on quite a different plane. The French Revolution had been a total

revolution in the sense that it had left no sphere and aspect of human existence untouched, whereas the American Revolt had been a purely political changeover.

Concluding Remarks

Having gathered together as much of the evidence as to what actually happened as I have been able to find, I would now like to add a few concluding remarks. The Enlightenment as it developed clearly showed not only the flaws in the Ancien Régime but also the permanent defects in the nature of things. The critical spirit was acutely active in finding defects in every category of life, but the philosophes also often recognized that in many respects much progress was being made. The comment was widespread that in the areas of religion, morality, and politics, much reform was necessary; in the areas of natural science, humanism, and the arts, there was confidence that progress could be noted. However, there seems to have developed a general feeling that a struggle between tradition and modernism was causing misery in all the categories. This battle between respect for the past and a desire for change was also introducing confusion in all the categories, but it was most acutely felt in religion, morality, and, to a lesser extent, in art. It was likewise bothersome in politics and economics, but no longer a serious issue in natural science. The evidence clearly indicates, nevertheless, that the power of ideas, thought, and learning in all its broad aspects was now rightly encyclopedic, propagandistic, and vital to the good life. The fundamental notion which directed the whole movement of Enlightenment was that enlightenment was the indispensable means of assuring that good life. The human mind, enlightened by awareness of the phenomena of the universe, could be trusted to guide the individual man and his society to a richer, more enjoyable future. Happiness was now thought very possible.

Of course, this reason for optimism was countered by a keen awareness of the flaws which still endured, and a good deal of exasperation was expressed at their presence. Moreover, between utopia and the realistic assessment of life, the forces of realism were obviously winning out, but not without some very difficult moments. The sense of human limitations was ever-present, countered by the vague yearning for a world of dreams. There were some real human achievements; tolerance, humanitarianism, political and civil freedom, and a desire for justice were plainly noticeable in the midst of some intolerance, much class hatred, some despotic acts, and injustices. There was a strong feeling on the part of many that reform was the way of the world. Many accepted Voltaire's assessment that man, though capable of continual improvement, is nonetheless limited by his humanity. Just as many felt that Rousseau's tightly wrought search for identity in a world consciously trying unmercifully to suppress that identity had achieved in all the spheres of human activity new ways to release human forces. Though tightly wrought, Rousseau's approach to the meaning of his world was as rationally fashioned as Voltaire's and far more spiritually expressed. The grave tendency on our part to perceive in Rousseau's thought a new drive toward utopia is undoubtedly a mistake. It is a drive toward self-realization in which the yearning for the ideal fulfills the role of the human mind in Voltaireanism. It is thus fully as rational, but it unveils a new form of idealism which increases existence and elevates idealism to a world of dreams far beyond Voltaire's world of common sense, but not necessarily opposed to it. Rousseau, for all his difficulties with Diderot, is the connecting link between the prudence of Voltaire and the drive to esthetic self-realization by Diderot.

On the other hand, there was a strong and widespread feeling that religion was the common enemy. This belief often turned into a fanaticism against Christianity which was unbelievably strong. Mornet, Hazard and, indeed, practically everybody else who studies this moment, note this opposition to religion with some astonishment. It was certainly a genuine opposition. There were many at the time who believed sincerely that it would be possible to replace it with a simple natural law which was looked upon as a natural religion. The feeling was widespread that obedience to God's will, love of one's fellow man, and a charity which expressed itself in human justice were possible without a cult, a formal Church hierarchy, and a complicated greed. I know many who had a deep hatred of Catholicism, chiefly because of the religious persecutions. There were few who really were true atheists in the modern sense of the term. There is some evidence, however, that even the deists and many of the critics of Christianity felt that there was something monolithic in religion which could not be reformed. History after the Revolution proved that such an opinion was premature, but not until much damage had been caused in the area of religion.

It is evident that this opposition to religion had been going on since the beginning of modern times in the very early Renaissance. After the middle of Louis XIV's reign, the movement was accelerated, but after 1750, it was swifter still. Everybody agrees that the big break which occurred was brought about by a savage attack against Christianity. Less evident is the fact that the decline of respect for Christianity brought about changes in all the other categories. The one which suffered the most, after religion, was the area of morality, despite a constant effort to protect that area while attacking religion. The reason, to be sure, is fairly clear. It was the function of the Church to control morality. Bayle thought that the Church could return that function to the state and morality would not suffer. That idea proved to be untenable. It was thought also by many that the state should control the organization of the Church. That idea produced greater confusion in the state. Nonetheless, politics as a category became, with the weakening of religion, enormously important and in time threatened to take over religion. It is evident that in the Enlightenment proper, it was the most active of the categories. It was not by accident that Rousseau decided that "tout tient à la politique" and that the Abbé de Saint-Pierre invented the notion of "la politique complète."

Thus at the moment of disintegration of the Enlightment ideal, what really collapsed first was religion and morality. The forces which dominated were political and economic, scientific and esthetic, individualistic and collectivist.

I have assumed that it would be wise, if possible, to adopt one particular philosophe from among the group of outstanding ones as the leader of the whole philosophical movement. That is what we have been inclined to do in the past, due in large part to the sheer impossibilty of investigating the operations of all of them. I quickly learned that it would be an injudicious move to select the world of any one of these giants to the exclusion of the concept of the worlds of the others. I judge that the most far-reaching achievement of the Enlightenment was Voltaire's assertion of what Renan, over a century later, defined as the goal of the world. "Le but du monde,"

Renan wrote, "c'est le développement de l'esprit, et la première condition de ce développement, c'est sa liberté." Acknowledging that this was his attitude, Voltaire concluded that the human mind was responsible for the making of civilization—total civilization. I judge this conclusion the most significant of all those proposed during the Enlightenment. It was at the core of the notion that enlightenment opens up awareness of the surrounding universe and leads to an augmented happiness. It was literally the blueprint of the *Age des lumières*. But significant though it was in the making of the Enlightenment, Voltaire was unprepared to carry it out without the notion of Rousseau that civilization always springs, not from the mind, but from the heart of man. What must first be accomplished is that a new science must be created: the science of man. To understand the importance of these categories, one must first seek what is the dynamic relationship of man with all the categories of his existence. Diderot would agree undoubtedly with both of these interpretations, but he would assert that what was more indispensable still was a more profound recognition of the power of change, in which all human possibilities are contained. Really, in his eclectic interpretation of the world, the maker, the supreme poet, is the Great God Change. Change is the full esthetic act. That act demands the human mind of Voltaire ("son esprit"), the human heart of Rousseau ("son sentiment"), and finally, the human creativity of Diderot ("son esthétique"). The heirs of this new era (this insight into the limitless human possibilities) must incorporate these three insights into an essential new human vision of man's world. The incorporation of any one of these three new worlds requires as much "suspension of disbelief" as the acceptance of God's world. That very act is simultaneously a philosophical and a poetic act, and probably the religious act also. It was, if I have seen things aright, the essential and ultimate human act—terrifyingly complicated, ambiguous, self-contradictory. Voltaire foresaw that the goal is reached through "philosopher" and "poétiser"; through them, one arrives at the making of an acceptable human civilization. Though responsible for the making of the blueprint, Voltaire alone couldn't succeed in putting it into effect. For that, he needed the active collaboration of both Rousseau and Diderot to achieve the ultimate goal.

Did the three of them and all their many followers achieve their goal? Obviously, the answer depends upon the way each of us assess success. I opened this conclusion with the remark that we all agree that the Enlightenment terminated in the French Revolution. I added as quickly as I could that the dominant trait of Enlightenment thought was its discovery that the ultimate goal of man was the making of a satisfactory civilization in this world. Now I add that two ingredients are most necessary to that end: "*philosopher*" and "*poétiser*"—rational penetration of reality and creative art. Further, every category of human existence is characterized by thought, change, and poetry. If one will learn how to live with ideas (living ideas) and with poetry (harmonious, creative ideas), if he will carefully and scrupulously make an effort to organize (Diderot's great word), order (Rousseau's great word) and examine (Voltaire's great word) he could presumably succeed in making for himself and his society a very enjoyable place to live out quietly his meaning. However, he has not done so yet, not even in "his" world.

BIBLIOGRAPHY

GENERAL BIBLIOGRAPHIES

Cioranescu, A. *Bibliographie de la littérature française du dix-huitième siècle.* Paris, 1969. 3 vols.

Cabeen, D. C. general editor. *A Critical Bibliography of French Literature.* Vol. IV: *The Eighteenth Century.* Edited by G. R. Havens and D. F. Bond. Syracuse, 1951.

Supplement. Edited by R. A. Brooks. Syracuse, 1968.

BIBLIOGRAPHICAL GUIDES

Diderot

Dieckmann, H. Bibliographical data on Diderot. In *Studies in Honor of F. W. Shipley.* Washington University, St. Louis, 1942, pp. 181–220.

———. *Diderot und die Aufklärung.* Stuttgart, 1972.

———. *Inventaire du fonds Vandeul et Inédits de Diderot.* Geneva, 1951.

Montesquieu

Cabeen, D. C. *Montesquieu, A Bibliography,* New York, 1947.

———. "Montesquieu, A Partial Bibliography." *FAR* 2 (1949): 22–29.

———. "Montesquieu, A Supplementary Bibliography." *R. Int. Phil.* 9 (1955): 409–439.

Rousseau

Dufour, T. *Recherches bibliographiques sur les œuvres imprimées de Jean-Jacques Rousseau.* Paris, 1925. 2 vols.

Schinz, A. *La Collection Jean-Jacques Rousseau de la bibliothèque J. Pierpont Morgan. Lettres, notes, manuscrits et éditions.* Paris, 1925.

Sénelier, J. *Bibliographie générale des œuvres de J. J. Rousseau.* PUF, Paris, 1949.

Voltaire

Alekseev, M. P., and Kopreeva, R. K., eds. *Bibliothèque de Voltaire: Catalogue des livres.* Moscow, 1961.

Barr, M. M. *A Century of Voltaire Study: A Bibliography of Writings on Voltaire, 1825–1925.* New York, 1929.

Barr, M. M., and Spear, F. A. *Quarante années d'études Voltairiennes: Bibliographie analytique des livres et des articles sur Voltaire, 1926–1965.* Paris, 1968.

Bengesco, G. *Voltaire. Bibliographie de ses œuvres.* Paris, 1882–1890. 4 vols.

COLLECTED CORRESPONDENCE, WORKS, AND STUDIES

Diderot

Correspondance de Diderot. Édition établie, annotée et préfacée par Georges Roth. Les Editions de Minuit, Aubanas (Ardèche), 1955–1975. 16 vols.

Diderot, D. *Œuvres politiques.* Textes établis par P. Vernière avec introduction, bibliographies, notes, et relevé de variantes. Garnier edition. Paris, 1961.

———. *Œuvres philosophiques.* Textes établis par P. Vernière. Paris, 1956.

———. *Œuvres esthétiques.* Textes établis par P. Vernière. Paris, 1959.

———. *Correspondance inédite.* Publiée d'après les manuscrits originaux avec des introductions et des notes par A. Babelon. Paris, 1931. 2 vols.

Diderot studies. Edited by Otis Fellows. Librairie Droz, Geneva, 1949–. 18 vols.

Rousseau

Correspondance complète de Jean-Jacques Rousseau. Édition critique établie et annotée par R. A. Leigh. Institut et Musée Voltaire, Les Délices, Geneva, 1965–. 25 vols.

Annales de la société Jean-Jacques Rousseau. Geneva, 1905–. 37 vols. Table of vols. 1–35, 1905–1962, edited by A. Jullien.

Voltaire

Voltaire's Correspondence. Edited by Theodore Besterman. Institut et Musée Voltaire, Les Délices, Geneva, 1953–1975. 108 vols.

The Complete Works of Voltaire. The Voltaire Foundation, Thorpe Mandeville House, Banbury, Oxfordshire. 1975–.

Studies on Voltaire and the Eighteenth Century. Edited by Theodore Besterman. The Voltaire Foundation, Thorpe Mandeville House, Banbury, Oxfordshire, 1955–1975. 165 vols.

WORKS ATTEMPTING A GENERAL SYNTHESIS OF THE ENLIGHTENMENT

Braudel, F. *Civilisation matérielle et capitalisme.* Vol. I: XVe-XVIIIe siècles. Paris, 1967.

Braudel, F., and Labrousse, C. E. et al. *Histoire économique et sociale de la France.* Vol. II: *Des Derniers temps de l'âge seigneurial aux préludes de l'âge industriel (1660–1789).* Paris, 1970.

Cassirer, E. *The Philosophy of the Enlightenment.* Princeton, 1951.

Chaunu, P. *La Civilisation de l'Europe des lumières.* Paris, 1970.

Crocker, L. G. *Cahiers d'histoire mondiale.* See "Recent Interpretations of the French Enlightenment," vol. 8 (1964–1965), pp. 426–456.

Crocker, L. G. *An Age of Crisis: Man and World in Eighteenth-century French Thought.* Baltimore, 1959.

———. *Nature and Culture: Ethical Thought in the French Enlightenment.* Baltimore, 1963.

Dieckmann, H. "An Interpretation of the Eighteenth Century." *MLQ* 15 (1954): 295–311.

Ehrard, J. *L'Idée de nature en France dans la Première moitié du XVIIIᵉ siècle.* Paris, 1963. 2 vols.

Gay, P. *The Enlightenment: An Interpretation.* Vol. I: *The Rise of Modern Paganism.* Vol. II: *The Science of Freedom.* New York, 1968.

Goyard-Fabre, Simone. *La Philosophie des lumières en France.* Paris, 1972.

Gusdorf, G. *Introduction aux sciences humaines.* Publications de la Faculté des lettres de l'Université de Strasbourg, fascicule #140. Paris, 1960.

———. *Les Sciences humaines et la pensée occidentale.* Vol. I: *De l'Histoire des sciences à l'histoire de la pensée.* Vol. II: *Antiquité, moyen âge, Renaissance.* Vol. III: *La Révolution galiléenne.* Vol. IV: *Les Principes de la pensée au siècle des lumières.* Vol. V: *Dieu, la nature, l'homme au siècle des lumières.* Vol. VI: *L'Avènement des sciences humaines au siècle des lumières.* Paris, 1966.

———. *La Science de l'homme au siècle des lumières.* Vol. 3 of Gusdorf's *De l'Histoire des sciences à l'histoire de la pensée.* Paris, 1966.

Hazard, P. *La Crise de la conscience européenne.* Vol. I, Part 1: Les Grands changements psychologiques; Part 2: Contre les croyances traditionnelles. Vol. II, Part 3: Essai de reconstruction; Part 4: Les Valeurs imaginatives et sensibles. Vol. III: Notes et références. Paris, 1935.

———. *La Pensée européenne au XVIIIᵉ siècle.* Vol. I, Part 1: Le Procès du Christianisme; Part 2: La Cité des hommes. Vol. II, Part 3: Désagrégation. Vol. III: Notes et références.

Mauzi, R. *L'Idée du bonheur dans la littérature et la pensée française au XVIIIᵉ siècle.* Paris, 1960.

Mornet, D. *Les Origines intellectuelles de la Révolution française.* 6th ed. Paris, 1967.

Palmer, R. R. *The Age of Democratic Revolutions: A Political History of Europe and America, 1760–1800.* Vol. I: *The Challenge.* Vol. II: *The Struggle.* Princeton, 1959.

Préclin, F., and Tapié, Victor L. *Clio.* Vol. 7: *Le XVIIIᵉ siècle.* Vol. I: *La France et le monde de 1715 à 1789.* Vol. II: *Les Forces internationales.*

Proust, J. *Diderot et l'Encyclopédie.* Paris, 1962.

Roger, J. *Les Sciences de la vie dans la pensée française au XVIIIᵉ siècle; la génération des animaux de Descartes à l'Encyclopédie.* Paris, 1963.

Trénard, L. *Histoire sociale des idées.* Paris, 1958.

Studies

Adam, A. "Rousseau et Diderot." *RSH*, 1949, pp. 21–34.

———. *Le Mouvement philosophique dans la première moitié du XVIIIe siècle*. Paris, 1967.

Alengry, F. *Turgot*. Paris, 1942.

Alexander, I. W. "Philosophy of Organism and Philosophy of Consciousness in Diderot's Speculative Thought." *Studies in Romance Philology and French Literature Presented to John Orr*. Manchester, 1953.

Alquié, F. *La Découverte métaphysique de l'homme chez Descartes*. Paris, 1950.

Annales. Numéro spécial à l'occasion du deuxième centenaire: *L'Encyclopédie Française*. Paris, Oct. 1952.

Ascoli, G. *La Grande Bretagne devant l'opinion française au XVIIe siècle*. Paris, 1930. 2 vols.

Babelon, A. *Diderot: Lettres à Sophie Volland*. Paris, 1930. 3 vols.

Barber, E. G. *The Bourgeoisie in Eighteenth-century France*. Princeton, 1955.

Barber, W. H. *Leibniz in France from Arnauld to Voltaire*. Oxford, 1955.

Barckhausen, H. *Montesquieu, ses idées, et ses œuvres*. Paris, 1907.

Belaval, Y. *L'Esthétique sans paradoxe de Diderot*. Paris, 1950.

———. "Note sur Diderot et Leibniz." *RSH*, 1963, pp. 435–451.

Belin, J. P. *Le Mouvement philosophique de 1748 à 1789*. Paris, 1913.

———. *Le Commerce des livres prohibés à Paris de 1750 à 1789*. Paris, 1913.

Berr, H. "Le Rôle des idées dans la Révolution." *RDS* 17 (1939): 19–198.

Bertaud, J. F. *Les Origines de la Révolution Française*. Paris, 1971.

Bien, D. D. *The Calas Affair*. Princeton, 1960.

Bloch, C. *L'Assistance et l'Etat en France à la veille de la Révolution*. Paris, 1908.

Boisguilbert, P. *Pierre de Boisguilbert ou la naissance de l'économie politique*. Paris, 1966, 2 vols.

Bonno, G., *La Culture et la civilisation britannique devant l'opinion française de la paix d'Utrecht aux Lettres philosophiques (1713–1734)*. Philadelphia, 1948.

Bray, R. *La Formation de l'esprit classique en France*. Paris, 1927.

Brooks, R. A. *Voltaire and Leibniz*. Geneva, 1964.

Brown, H. *Scientific Organizations in Seventeenth-century France*. Baltimore, 1934.

Brumfitt, J. H. *Voltaire Historian*. Oxford, 1958.

Brunet, P. *Maupertuis, Etudes biographiques*. Paris, 1929. 2 vols.

Brunetière, F. *Etudes critiques*. Paris, 1910–11. 8 vols.

———. "Huit leçons sur les origines de l'esprit encyclopédique." *Revue hebdomadaire*, 1905.

Buffon, J. L. de. *De l'homme*. Edited by Michèle Duchat. Paris, 1971.

Burgelin, P. *La Philosophie de l'existence de Rousseau*. Paris, 1952.

———. Introduction. In *Œuvres complètes de Rousseau*, Pléiade edition. Paris, 1969. Vol. IV, pp. 88–102.

———. "L'Unité dans l'œuvre de Rousseau." *RMM*, 1960, pp. 199–209.

Busson, H. *La Religion des classiques*. Paris, 1948.

Cadet, F. *Histoire de l'économie politique*. Reprint ed. New York, 1970.

Callot, E. *La Philosophie de la vie au XVIIIe siècle*. Paris 1965.

Caillaud, E. *Les Idées de Condorcet*. Reprint ed. New York, 1970.

Carcassonne, E. *Montesquieu et le problème de la constitution française au XVIIIe siècle*. PUF, Paris, 1927.

Carré, J. R. *La Philosophie de Fontenelle, ou le sourire de la raison*. Paris, 1932.

———. *Fontenelle: De l'Origine des Fables*. Critical edition. Paris, 1932.

———. *La Consistance de Voltaire le philosophe*. Paris, 1939.

Cassirer, E. *The Question of Jean-Jacques Rousseau*. Translated by P. Gay. Princeton, 1958.

Caussy, F. *Voltaire, Seigneur de village*. Paris, 1912.

Cavallucci, G. *Vauvenargues dégagé de la légende*. Paris, 1939.

Ceitac, S. *Voltaire et l'affaire des natifs*. Geneva, 1956.

Charbonnaud, R. *Les Idées économiques de Voltaire*. Angoûleme, 1907.

Chaunu, P. *La Civilisation de l'Europe des lumières*. Paris, 1970.

———. *La Civilisation de l'Europe classique*. Paris, 1960.

Chouillet, J. *La Formation des idées esthétiques de Diderot*. Paris, 1973.

Church, W. F. *The Influence of the Enlightenment on the French Revolution*. Boston, 1964.

Cobban, A. *Rousseau and the Modern State*. Hamden, Conn., 1961.

———. *The Social Interpretation of the French Revolution*. Cambridge, 1968.

———. *Aspects of the French Revolution*. New York, 1968.

———. *Causes of the French Revolution*, 1946.

———. *In Search of Humanity*. London, 1960.

———. *The Eighteenth Century*. New York, 1969.

———. Review of R. Derathé, *JJR et la Science politique de son temps*. *PSQ* 66 (June 1951): 272–284.

Conlon, P. M. *Voltaire's Literary Career from 1726 to 1759*. SVEC, Vol. XIV. Geneva, 1961.

Cournot, A. *Considérations sur la marche des idées et des événements dans les temps modernes*. Paris, 1872. 2 vols.

Crocker, L. *Two Diderot Studies: Ethics and Esthetics*. Baltimore, 1952.

———. *Diderot's Chaotic Order*. Princeton, 1974.

Crowley, F. J., ed. *Voltaire's Loi naturelle*. Critical edition. Berkeley, 1938.

Daire, E. *Economistes français du XVIIIe siècle.* Paris, 1843.

Dakin, D. *Turgot and the Ancien Régime in France.* London, 1939.

Daumas, M. *Histoire de la science.* Paris, 1957.

Dédéyan, C. *Rousseau et la sensibilité littéraire à la fin du XVIIIe siècle.* CDU, Paris, 1966.

————. *Voltaire et la pensée anglaise.* CDU, Paris, 1958.

————. *Diderot et la pensée anglaise.* CDU, Paris, 1958.

————. *Montesquieu et l'Angleterre.* CDU, Paris, 1958.

Dedieu, J. *Montesquieu et la tradition politique anglaise en France: les sources anglaises de l'Esprit des lois.* Gabalda, Bordeaux, 1909.

Delbèke, F. *L'Action politique et sociale des avocats au XVIIIe siècle.* Paris, 1927.

Deloffre, F. *Une Préciosité nouvelle: Marivaux et le marivaudage.* 2d ed. rev. Paris, 1967.

Derathé, R. *Jean-Jacques Rousseau et la science politique de son temps.* Paris, 1950.

————. "The Civil Religion of Rousseau." *Annales JJR,* 1963, pp. 161–164.

————. *Le Rationalisme de Rousseau.* Paris, 1948.

————. "L'Unité de la pensée de Jean-Jacques Rousseau." *Jean-Jacques Rousseau.* Université ouvrière et Faculté des lettres de l'Université de Genève. Neuchâtel, 1962, pp. 203–218.

Deslex, M. G. "L'Aggettivazione nei 'Contes' di Voltaire: da Zadig a Candide." *Pubblicazioni della Facoltà de Magistero,* vol. 30.

Diaz, F. *Voltaire storico.* Turin, 1958.

Dieckmann, H., ed. *Le Philosophe. Texts and Interpretation.* St. Louis, 1948.

————. "Zur Interpretations Diderot's." *Rom. For.,* 1939, pp. 46–87.

————. *Cinq Leçons sur Diderot.* Geneva, 1959.

————. "L'Encyclopédie et le Fonds Vandeul." *RHL,* 1951.

————. "Diderot's Conception of Genius." *JHI* 2 (1941): 151–182.

————. "Themes and Structure in the Enlightenment." *Essays in Comparative Literature.* Washington University, St. Louis, 1961.

Dix-huitième Siècle. No. 5, Paris, 1973. Numéro special: *Problèmes actuels de la recherche.*

Dommaget, M. *Le Curé Meslier.* Paris, 1965.

Doolittle, J. "Hieroglyph and Emblem in Diderot's *Lettre sur les sourds et muets.*" *DS,* vol. II (1952), pp. 148–166.

————. "Criticism as Creation in the Work of Diderot." *YFS* 2 (1949): 14–23.

Drouet, J. *L'Abbé de Saint-Pierre.* Paris, 1912.

Dubosq, Y. Z. *Le Livre français.* Amsterdam, Paris, 1925.

Ducretet, P. R. *Voltaire, Candide, étude quantitative.* Toronto, 1974.

Ducros, L. *Les Encyclopédistes.* Paris, 1900.

Duprat, P. *Les Encyclopédistes.* Paris, 1866.

Durdent, R. J. *Histoire littéraire de Voltaire.* Paris, 1818.

Echeverria, D. *Mirage in the West.* Princeton, 1957.

Egret, J. *Louis XV et l'opposition parlementaire.* Paris, 1970.

Ehrard, J. *L'Idée de nature en France, à l'aube des lumières.* Paris, 1970.

———. *Politique de Montesquieu.* Paris, 1965.

Ellis, M. B. *Julie, A Synthesis of Rousseau's Thought, 1749–59.* Toronto, 1949.

Ellul, J. *Histoire des institutions.* Paris, 1956.

Fabre, J. *Stanislas-Auguste Poniatorski et l'Europe des lumières.* Strasbourg, 1952.

Faguet, E. *Politique comparée de Montesquieu, Rousseau et Voltaire.* Paris, 1902.

———. *Le Dix-huitième siècle, études littéraires.* Paris, 1890.

———. *Voltaire.* A series of articles published in the *RCC* between 3 May 1900 and 30 May 1901 dealing chiefly with Voltaire's literary and poetic ideas.

Faure, E. *La Disgrâce de Turgot.* Paris, 1961.

Fellows, O. "The Theme of Genius in Diderot's *Neveu de Rameau.*" *DS,* vol. II (1952), pp. 168–199.

Fitch, R. E. *Voltaire's Philosophical Procedure.* New York, 1935.

Folkierski, W. *Entre le classicisme et le romantisme.* Paris, 1925.

Francastel, P. *Utopie et institutions.* Brussels, 1963.

Frankel, C. *The Faith of Reason.* New York, 1948.

Free, J. P. Rousseau's Use of the *Examen de la Religion* and of the *Lettre de Thrasybule à Leucippe.* Unpublished manuscript deposited in Firestone Library, Princeton, 1935.

Funt, D. *Diderot and the Aesthetics of the Enlightenment.* Geneva, 1968.

Gay, P. *The Party of Humanity.* New York, 1964. See "The Unity of the French Enlightenment," pp. 114–132.

———. *Voltaire's Politics.* Princeton, 1959.

———. *Voltaire, Dictionnaire philosophique.* Translation with an Introduction and Glossary. New York, 1962. 2 vols.

Gillot, H. *Denis Diderot, l'homme, ses idées philosophiques, esthétiques, littéraires.* Courville, 1937.

Gilman, M. "The Poet According to Diderot." *RR,* Feb. 1946, pp. 37–54.

———. *The Idea of Poetry in France.* Cambridge, Mass., 1958.

Godechot, J. L. *France and the Atlantic Revolution of the Eighteenth Century, 1770–1799.* New York, 1965.

Gordon, D., and Torrey, Norman. *The Censoring of Diderot's Encyclopédie.* New York, 1947.

Gouhier, H. *Les Méditations métaphysiques de Jean-Jacques Rousseau.* Paris, 1970.

Green, F. C. *Jean-Jacques Rousseau, A Critical Study of his Life and Writings.* Cambridge, 1955.

Grimsley, R. *Jean-Jacques Rousseau, A Study in Self-Awareness.* Cardiff, Wales, 1961.

Groethuysen, B. *Philosophie de la Révolution française.* Paris, 1956.

Grossman, M. *The Philosophy of Helvétius, With Special Emphasis on the Educational Implications of Sensationalism.* New York, 1926.

Hampshire, S. *The Age of Reason.* Boston, 1956.

Hampson, N. *A Social History of the French Revolution.* London, 1963.

Havens, G. R. "Voltaire's Micromégas (1739–52), Composition and Publication." *MLQ* 33 (1972): 113–118.

———. "Voltaire's Marginal Comments upon Pope's *Essay on Man.*" *MLN* 43 (1928): 429–439.

———. "Candide Returns." *DS*, vol. XVI (1973), pp. 347–359.

———. "Voltaire's *Ingénu*: Composition and Publication." *RR* 63 (1972): 261–271.

———. "Voltaire's Pessimistic Revision of the Conclusion of his Poème sur le Désastre de Lisbonne." *MLN* 44 (1929): 489–492.

Hazard, P., *Quatre Etudes* (containing "L'Homme de Sentiment"), New York, 1940.

———. *Etudes critiques sur Manon Lescaut.* Chicago, 1929.

Hendel, C. W. *Rousseau Moralist*, Oxford, 1934. 2 vols.

Hermand, P. *Les Idées morales de Diderot.* PUF, Paris, 1923.

Hibben, J. G. *The Philosophy of the Enlightenment.* New York, 1910.

Hubert, R. *Rousseau et l'Encyclopédie.* Paris, 1928.

———. *Les Sciences sociales dans l'Encyclopédie.* Paris, 1923.

Hufton, O. H. *The Poor in Eighteenth-century France, 1750–1789.* Oxford, 1974.

Jamieson, R. K. *Marivaux, A Study in Sensibility.* New York, 1941.

Jones, H. M. *Revolution and Romanticism.* Cambridge, Mass., 1974.

Josephs, H. *Diderot's Dialogue of Gesture and Language: Le Neveu de Rameau.* Columbus, O., 1969.

Kafker, F. A., and Laux, J. M. *The French Revolution: Conflicting Interpretations.* New York, 1968.

Kaye, F. B., ed. *The Fable of the Bees, by B. Mandeville.* Oxford, 1924.

Keim, A. *Helvétius.* Paris, 1907.

Kiernan, C. *Science and the Enlightenment in Eighteenth-Century France. SVEC.* Geneva, 1968.

Knight, I. *The Geometric Spirit*. New Haven, 1968.

Krauss, W. *Fontenelle und die Aufklärung*. Munich, 1969.

Labrousse, C. E. *Esquisse du mouvement des prix et des revenus en France au XVIIIe siècle*. Paris, 1933

———. *La Crise de l'économie française à la fin de l'Ancien Régime*. Paris, 1944.

———. *Histoire économique*, vol. I. Paris, 1970.

Lallemand, L. *La Révolution et les pauvres*. Paris, 1898.

Lanson, G. *Voltaire*. Paris, 1909.

———. "L'Eveil de la conscience sociale et les premières idées de réforme politique." *Revue du Mois*, 1910.

———. "Origines et premières manifestations de l'esprit philosophique dans la littérature française." *RCC*, 1907–1910.

———. "Questions diverses sur l'histoire de l'esprit philosophique en France avant 1750." *RHL*, Jan.–June, 1912.

———. "L'Unité de la pensée de J. J. Rousseau." *Annales JJR*, vol. 8 (1912), pp. 1–30.

———. *Le Marquis de Vauvenargues*. Paris, 1930.

———. "Voltaire et les *Lettres philosophiques*." *RDP* 4 (1908): 367–386.

Lauer, R. Z. *The Mind of Voltaire*, Westminster, Md., 1961.

Laufer, R. *Style Rococo, style des lumières*. Paris, 1963.

Lecercle, J. L., ed. *Des Droits et des devoirs du Citoyen*. Edition critique avec introduction et notes. Paris, 1972.

———. "Utopie, et réalisme politique chez Mably." *SVEC*, vol. 26 (1963), pp. 1049–1070.

Lefebvre, G. *La Révolution française. Peuples et Civilisation*. PUF, Paris, 1968.

———. *Quatre-vingt-neuf*. Paris, 1939.

Le Gras, J. *Diderot et l'Encyclopédie*. Amiens, 1928.

L'Encyclopédie et le progrès des sciences et des techniques. Paris, 1952.

Leroy, M. *L'Histoire des idées sociales en France*. Vol. I: *De Montesquieu à Robespierre*, Paris, 1946.

Libby, M. *The Attitude of Voltaire to Magic and the Sciences*. New York, 1935.

Lichtenberger, A. *Le Socialisme au XVIIIe siècle*. Paris, 1895.

Lough, J. *An Introduction to Eighteenth-century France*. London, 1960.

———. *Essays on the Encyclopédie of Diderot and D'Alembert*. London, 1968.

———. "The Contemporary Influence of the *Encyclopédie*." *SVEC*, vol. 26 (1963), pp. 1071–1083.

Lovejoy, A. O. *Essays in the History of Ideas*. Baltimore, 1948.

Lupporini, C. *Voltaire et le "Lettres philosophiques."* Firenze, 1955.

Luxembourg, I. *Bacon and Diderot.* Muntesgaard, 1967.

Macary, J. *Masques et lumières au XVIIIe siècle. André-François Deslandes "Citoyen et philosophe," 1689–1757.* La Haye, 1975.

McDonald, J. *Rousseau and the French Revolution, 1762–1791.* London, 1965.

Maday, A. "Rousseau et la Révolution." *Annales JJR,* vol. 31 (1938), pp. 169–207.

Maestro, M. *Voltaire and Beccaria as Reformers in Criminal Law.* New York, 1942.

Malvaux, Abbé de. *Résumé des mémoires qui ont concouru pour le prix accordé en l'année 1777, par l'Académie des sciences, arts et belles-lettres de Châlons-sur-Marne et dont le sujet étoit: Les moyens de détruire la mendicité en France en rendant les mendiants utiles à l'Etat sans les rendre malheureux.* Châlons-sur-Marne, impr. de Seneuze, 1779, in-8°. 2d ed., 1780.

Manuel, F. E. *The Age of Reason.* Ithaca, 1957.

Martin, K. *French Liberal Thought in the Eighteenth Century.* Boston, 1928.

Mason, H. *Pierre Bayle and Voltaire.* Oxford, 1963.

Masson, P. M. *Religion de Rousseau.* Paris, 1916. 3 vols.

Mathiez, A. *La Révolution française.* Paris, 1959.

Mauzi, R. *L'Essai sur le bonheur de Mme du Châtelet.* Paris, 1960.

May, G. "The Influence of English Fiction on the French Mid-Eighteenth Century Novel." *Aspects of the Eighteenth Century.* Edited by E. R. Wasserman. Baltimore, 1965.

———. *Le Dilemme du Roman au XVIIIe siècle.* Paris, 1963.

———, ed. *Hemsterhuis: Lettre sur l'homme et sur ses rapports, 1772.* New Haven, 1964.

———. *Quatre visages de Diderot.* Paris, 1951.

Mayer, J. *Diderot, Homme de science.* Rennes, 1959.

Mazauric, C. "Sur une nouvelle conception de la Révolution." *Annales historiques de la Révolution française.* Paris, 1967, pp. 339–368.

Meyer, A. *Voltaire, Man of Justice.* London, 1951.

Meyer, P. H. *Diderot: Lettre sur les sourds et muets.* Edition commentée. *DS,* vol. VII (1965).

Momdjian, K. N. *La Philosophie d'Helvétius.* Moscow, 1959.

Monglond, A. *Le Préromantisme français.* Grenoble, 1930. 2 vols.

Monod, A. *De Pascal à Chateaubriand.* Reprint ed. New York, 1971.

Morehouse, A. *Voltaire and J. Meslier.* New Haven, 1936.

Morelly. *Code de la Nature.* Abbeville, 1755. Critical edition. Edited by G. Chinard. Paris, 1950.

Morize, A. *Le Mondain et l'apologie du luxe au XVIIIe siècle.* Paris, 1909.

———, ed. *Voltaire: Candide ou l'optimisme.* Edition critique avec une introduction et un commentaire par André Morize. Paris, 1913.

Morley, J. *Voltaire*, London, 1913.

Mornet, D., ed. *Jean-Jacques Rousseau: La Nouvelle Héloïse*. Critical edition. Paris, 1925. 4 vols.

———. *Les Origines intellectuelles de la Révolution française, 1715–1787*. Paris, 1932.

———. "Les Enseignements . . . des bibliothèques privées (1750–1780)." *RHL* 17 (1910): 449–496.

———. *La Pensée française au XVIIIᵉ siècle*. Paris, 1929.

———. *Diderot: L'homme et l'œuvre*. Paris, 1941.

———. *Sentiment de la nature en France de Jean-Jacques Rousseau à Bernardin de St.-Pierre*. Paris, 1907. Reprint ed., 1971.

Mortier, R. "Diderot et le problème de l'expressivité." *CAIEF* 13 (1961): 283–297.

Mousnier, R. *Le XVIIIᵉ siècle, révolution intellectuelle, technique et politique*. Paris, 1953. In collaboration with Labrousse and Bouloiseau.

———. *Progrès scientifique et technique au XVIIIᵉ siècle*. Paris, 1958.

Naves, R., and Benda, J., eds. *Voltaire: Dictionnaire philosophique*. Paris, 1935–1936. 2 vols.

———. *Voltaire, l'homme et l'œuvre*. Paris, 1942.

———. *Voltaire et l'Encyclopédie*. Paris, 1938.

———. *Le Goût de Voltaire*. Paris, 1938.

Naville, P. *Paul Thiry d'Holbach et la philosophie scientifique au XVIIIᵉ siècle*. Paris, 1967.

Neymarck, B. *Turgot et ses doctrines*. Paris, 1885, 2 vols.

Niklaus, R. "Présence de Diderot." *DS*, vol. VI (1964): 13–28.

Nixon, E. *Voltaire and the Calas Case*. New York, 1961.

Palmer, R. R. *The World of the French Revolution*. New York, 1971.

Pappas, J. N. *Voltaire and D'Alembert*. Bloomington, Ind., 1962.

Patterson, H. T., ed. *Voltaire's Traité de métaphysique*. Manchester, 1937.

Paultre, C. *De la Répression de la mendicité*. Paris, 1906.

Perkins, Jean A. *The Concept of the Self in the French Enlightenment*. Geneva, 1969.

Perkins, M. L. "Voltaire and the Abbé de Saint-Pierre." *FR* 34 (1960–1961): 152–163.

———. *Voltaire's Concept of International Order*. *SVEC*, vol. XXXVI (1965).

Peyre, H. "The Influence of 18th-Century Ideas on the French Revolution." *JHI*, 1949, pp. 63–87.

Philips, E. *The Good Quaker in French Legend*. Philadelphia, 1932.

Pierron, A. *Voltaire et ses maîtres*. Paris, 1866.

Pintard, R. *Le Libertinage érudit dans la première moitié du XVIIᵉ siècle*. Paris, 1943.

Piveteau, J., ed. *Corpus général des philosophes français*. Vol XLI: *Œuvres philosophiques de Buffon*, Paris, 1954.

Poitrineau, A. *Le Premier XVIII⁰ siècle, 1680–1750.* Paris, 1971.

Pomeau, R. *L'Europe des lumières.* Paris, 1966.

——, ed. *Rousseau's Julie ou la Nouvelle Héloïse.* Paris, 1960.

——. "Nouveau Regard sur le dossier Calas." *Europe*, June 1962, pp. 57–72.

——. *La Religion de Voltaire.* Paris, 1956.

——. *Diderot, sa vie, ses œuvres, avec un exposé de sa philosophie.* Paris, 1967.

——, ed. *Voltaire's Essai sur les Mœurs.* Paris, 1963. 2 vols.

——. *La Politique de Voltaire.* Paris, 1963.

Proust, J. "L'initiation artistique de Diderot." *Gazette des Beaux-arts*, April 1960, pp. 225–232.

——. *L'Encyclopédie.* Paris, 1965.

Quesnay, F. *La Physiocratie.* Paris, 1958. 2 vols.

Rang, Martin. *Rousseau's Lehre vom Menschen.* Göttingen, 1959.

Raymond, M. "Jean-Jacques Rousseau et le problème de la connaissance de soi," *Jean-Jacques Rousseau: La Quête de soi et la rêverie.* Paris, 1962, pp. 187–219.

Rihs, C. *Voltaire, Recherches sur les origines du matérialisme historique.* Geneva, 1962.

——. *Les Philosophes utopistes.* Paris, 1970.

Robertson, M.E.I., ed. *Mémoires et avantures d'un homme de qualité.* Book V. Paris, 1927.

Roche, D. "La Diffusion des lumières: Un Exemple, L'Ac. de Châlons-sur-Marne." *Annales* (1964), pp. 887–922.

Rocheblave, S. *Vauvenargues, ou la symphonie inachevée.* Paris, 1934.

Rocquain, F. *L'Esprit révolutionnaire avant la Révolution.* Paris, 1878.

Roger, J., ed. *Buffon: Les Epoques de la nature.* Edition critique avec le ms., une introduction, et des notes. Paris, 1962.

Rosenfield, L. *From Beast-machine to Man-machine.* New York, 1941.

Ross, S. T. *The French Revolution: Conflict or Continuity?* New York, 1971.

Rothkrug, L. *Opposition to Louis XIV: The Political and Social Origins of the French Enlightenment.* Princeton, 1965.

Sabine, G. H. *A History of Political Theory.* New York, 1937.

Sagnac, P. "Les Origines de la Révolution: La Décomposition de l'Ancien Régime." *RHM*, 1910.

——. *La Formation de la société française moderne.* Vol. I: *La Société et la Monarchie absolue, 1661–1715.* Vol. II: *La Révolution des idées et des mœurs et le Déclin de l'Ancien Régime.* PUF, Paris, 1946.

Sainte-Beuve, C. A. *Portraits littéraires.* On Diderot, see vol. I, pp. 239–264.

Sampson, R. V. *Progress in the Age of Reason*. London, 1956.

Schinz, A. *La Pensée de Jean-Jacques Rousseau*. Northhampton, Mass., 1929. 2 vols.

Schneider, J. *The Enlightenment*. New York, 1965.

Schwartz, J. *Diderot and Montaigne: The Essais and the Shaping of Diderot's Humanism*. Geneva, 1966.

Sée, H. *La France économique et sociale au XVIIIe siècle*. Paris, 1925.

──────. "Les Idées philosophiques et la littérature révolutionnaire." *RSH*, 1925.

──────. *L'Evolution de la pensée politique en France au XVIIIe siècle*. Paris, 1925.

Seznec, J. *Diderot: Sur l'art et les artistes*. Paris, 1967.

Sgard, J. *Prévost romancier*. Paris, 1968.

Shackleton, R., ed. *Fontenelle: Entretiens sur la pluralité des mondes* and *Digression sur les anciens et les modernes*. Oxford, 1955.

──────. "Montesquieu." *FS*, 1949–1950.

──────. *Montesquieu, A Critical Biography*. Oxford, 1961.

Shapiro, M. "Diderot on the Artist and Society." *DS*, vol. V (1964), pp. 5–11.

Shepherd, R. P. *Turgot and the Six Edicts*. New York, 1903.

Soboul, A. *La Civilisation et la Révolution française*. Vol. I: *La Crise de l'Ancien Régime*. Paris, 1970.

──────. *La France à la veille de la Révolution*. CDU, Paris, 1964.

──────. *La Révolution française*. PUF, Paris, 1964.

──────. *La Sociéte française dans la 2nde moitié du XVIIIe siècle*. CDU, Paris, 1969.

──────. "Notes pour une définition de la philosophie (XVIIIe siècle)." *L'Information historique* 26 (March–April, 1964): 47–52.

Sonet, E. *Voltaire et l'influence anglaise*. Rennes, 1926.

Spengler, J. J. *L'Economie et population. Les Doctrines françaises avant 1800*. Paris, 1954.

Spink, J. S. *French Free-thought from Gassendi to Voltaire*. London, 1960.

──────. "Le *Théophrastus Redivivus*." *RHL*, 1937, pp. 248 ff.

──────. *Jean-Jacques Rousseau et Genève*. Paris, 1934.

Starobinski, J. *Jean-Jacques Rousseau: La Transparence et l'obstacle*. Paris, 1957.

Strowski, V. *La Sagesse française*. Paris, 1925.

Strugnell, A. *Diderot's Politics: A Study of the Evolution of Diderot's Political Thought after the Encyclopédie*. Archives internationales d'histoire des idées, no. 62. The Hague, 1973.

Talmon, J. L. *The Rise of Totalitarian Democracy*. Boston, 1952.

Teyssendier de la Serve. *Mably et les Physiocrats*. New York, 1971.

Thielemann, L. "Diderot and Hobbes." *DS*, vol. II (1952), pp. 221–278.

Thomas, J. *L'Humanisme de Diderot*. Paris, 1938.

Tilley, A. *The Decline of the Age of Louis XIV*. Cambridge, 1929.

Tobiassen, R. *Nature et Nature Humaine dans l'Emile de Jean-Jacques Rousseau*. Oslo, 1961.

Torrey, N. *Voltaire and the English Deists*. New Haven, 1930.

——. "Voltaire's Reaction to Diderot." *PMLA* 50 (1935): 1129 ff.

——. "Voltaire's English Notebook," *MP* 26 (1929); 307–325.

——. *The Spirit of Voltaire*. New York, 1938.

Trahard, P. *Les Maîtres de la Sensibilité française au XVIIIᵉ siècle*. Geneva, 1931–1933. 5 vols.

Trenard, L. *Histoire sociale des idées*. Paris, 1958. 2 vols.

——. "Pour une histoire sociale de l'idée du bonheur." *Annales historiques de la Révolution française* 35, nos. 173, 174 (1963).

Van den Heuvel, J. *Voltaire dans ses contes de Micromégas à l'Ingénu*. Paris, 1967.

Vartanian, A. *Diderot and Descartes*. Princeton, 1953.

——. *La Mettrie's L'Homme machine*. Princeton, 1960.

Vaughan, C. E. *The Political Writings of Jean-Jacques Rousseau*. Cambridge, 1915. 2 vols.

Venturi, F. *La Jeunesse de Diderot*. Paris, 1939.

Venturi, L. *A History of Art Criticism*. New York, 1936.

Vernière, P. *Spinoza et la pensée française avant la Révolution*. Paris, 1954. 2 vols.

Vial, F. *Une Philosophie et une morale de sentiment, Luc de Clapiers*. Paris, 1938.

Voltaire, *Le Philosophe ignorant*. Edited by E. H. Carr. London, 1965.

Vreeland, W. U. *Etude sur les rapports littéraires entre Genève et l'Angleterre jusqu'à la publication de la Nouvelle Héloïse*. Geneva, 1901.

Wade, I. *Voltaire and Candide*. Princeton, 1959.

——. *Intellectual Development of Voltaire*. Princeton, 1968.

——. *The Intellectual Origins of the French Enlightenment*. Princeton, 1971.

Waldauer, J. L. *Society and the Freedom of the Creative Man in Diderot's Thought*. *DS*, vol. V (1964).

Waldinger, R. *Voltaire and Reform in the Light of the French Revolution*. Geneva, 1959.

Wallas, M. *Vauvenargues*. Cambridge, 1928.

Wasserman, E. R., ed. *Aspects of the Eighteenth Century*. Baltimore, 1965.

Watts, G. B. "The *Encyclopédie méthodique*." *PMLA* 73 (1958): 348–366.

Weulersse, G. *La Physiocratie sous les ministères de Turgot et de Necker*. Paris, 1950.

——. *La Physiocratie à la fin du règne de Louis XV, 1770–1774*. Paris, 1959.

Weulersse, G. *Les Physiocrates*. Paris, 1936.

White, R. J. *The Anti-philosophes*. Macmillan, 1970.

Wilson, A. "Sensibility in France in the Eighteenth Century." *FQ*, March 1931, pp. 35–46.

————. *Diderot*, New York, 1972.

Yolton, J. W. *Locke and the Way of Ideas*. New York, 1956.

Texts

Abbé de la Porte. *L'Esprit de l'Encyclopédie ou choix des articles*. Paris, 1768. 5 vols.

————. *Supplément à l'esprit encyclopédique*. 1772. 2 vols.

André, le père Y. *L'Essai du beau*. Paris, 1741.

Arbuthnot, J. *Essai des effets de l'air sur le corps humain*. 1733.

Barclay, J. *Le Tableau des esprits*. Paris, 1625.

Batteux, C. *Les Beaux-arts réduits à un même principe*. Paris, 1746.

Bayle, P. *Dictionnaire historique et critique*. 1697. 4 vols.

Beausobre, I. de. *Histoire du Manichéisme*. Amsterdam, 1734–1739. 2 vols.

Berkeley, G. *Essay towards a new Theory of Vision*. 1709.

————. *Treatise on the Principles of Human Knowledge*. 1710.

Boulainvilliers, H. *L'Etat de la France*. 1727. 3 vols.

Boulanger, N. *L'Antiquité dévoilée*. 1766. 3 vols.

————. *Essai sur le despotisme oriental*. 1762.

Brown, J. *An Estimate of the Manners and Principles of the Time*. 1756.

Brucker, J. *Historia critica philosophiae*. 1742–1744. 5 vols.

Burlamaqui, J. J. *Principes du droit naturel*. Geneva, 1747.

————. *Principes du droit politique*. Geneva, 1754.

Cantillon, R. *Essai sur la nature du commerce en général*. Paris, 1952.

Castilhon, M. L. *Considérations sur les causes physiques et morales de la diversité du génie, des moeurs et du gouvernement des nations*. 1769.

Châtelet, Mme. du. *Institutions de physique*. 1741.

————, tr. *Newton's Principia*. 1759. 2 vols.

Clairaut, A. C. *Exposition abrégé du système du monde, et explication des principaux phénomènes astronomiques tirés des principes de M. Newton*. 1759.

Condillac, E. B. de. *Dissertation sur la liberté*. 1754.

————. *Œuvres philosophiques*. Edited by LeRoy. Paris, 1947–51. 3 vols.

Condorcet, A. *Œuvres*. Edited by A. C. O'Connor and F. Arago. Paris, 1847–49. 12 vols.

Crousaz, J. P. de. *Traité du beau*. 1725.

D'Argenson, Marquis. *Considérations sur le gouvernement ancien et présent de la France*. Amsterdam, 1764.

Deslandes, A. F. *Histoire critique de la philosophie.* Amsterdam, 1756. 4 vols.

———. *Nouveau voyage en Angleterre,* 1717.

Desmaizeaux, P. *Dissertations meslées.* 1720. 2 vols.

D'Holbach. *Le Christianisme dévoilé.* 1767.

———. *Système de la nature.* 1770.

Diderot, D. *Pensées sur l'interprétation de la nature.* 1753.

———. *Œuvres complètes.* Edited by Assézat and Tourneux. Paris, 1875–1877. 20 vols.

D'Ivernois, F. *Les Révolutions de Genève.* Geneva, 1782.

Dubos, J. B. *Réflexions critiques sur la poésie et la peinture.* 1719.

Duclos, C. P. *Considérations sur les mœurs de ce siècle.* 1761.

Dupont de Nemours. *La Physiocracie.* Leyde, 1768.

Dutot. *Réflexions politiques sur les finances et le commerce.* La Haye, 1738. 2 vols.

Espiard, F. I. d'. *Essais sur le génie et le caractère des nations.* Brussels, 1743. 3 vols.

———. *L'Esprit des nations.* Geneva, 1752. 2 vols.

Fontenelle, B. B. *Œuvres de Monsieur de Fontenelle.* Amsterdam, 1764. 12 vols.

Forbonnais, V. de. *Eléments du commerce.* Leyde, 1754. 2 vols.

———. *Recherches et considérations sur les finances.* Bâle, 1758. 2 vols.

Formey, S. *Concise History of Philosophy.* London, 1756.

———. *Mélanges philosophiques.* 1754.

Gordon, T. and Trenchard. *Cato's Letters.* London, 1748.

Gordon, T. *Discours sur Tacite.* 1728.

———. *Discours historiques et politiques sur Salluste.* Geneva, 1759.

Goudar, Ange. *Les Intérets de la France mal-entendus.* Amsterdam, 1756. 3 vols.

Grimm, F. M. et al. *Correspondance littéraire, philosophique et critique.* Edited by M. Tourneux. 1877–82. 16 vols.

Grotius, H. *Le Droit de la guerre et de la paix.* Translation by Jean Barbeyrac, avec les notes de l'auteur même, qui n'avaient point encore paru en François, et de nouvelles notes du Traducteur. Amsterdam, 1724.

Hartley, D. *Observations on Man.* 1749. Reprint ed., Gainsville, Fla. 1966.

Helvétius, C. *De l'Esprit.* 1758, in-4°.

———. *De l'Homme, de ses facultés intellectuelles, et de son éducation.* 1772. 2 vols., in-8°.

Histoire générale des dogmes et opinions philosophiques. London, 1769. 3 vols.

Holbach, Paul Thiry, Baron d'. *Le Système de la nature.* 1770. 2 vols.

Hume, D. *Treatise on Human Nature.* 1738.

Hutcheson, F. *Recherches sur l'origine des idées que nous avons de la beauté et de la vertu*, 1725.

Isnard, A. N. *Observations sur le principe qui a produit les révolutions de France, de Genève, et d'Amérique, dans le dix-huitième siècle.* A. Evreux, Oct. 1789.

Justi, J. I. *De la Nature et de l'essence des corps politiques, ou principes fondamentaux de la politique, de la police, et de toutes les sciences qui appartiennent au gouvernement particulier.* Leipzig, 1760.

Lacombe, J. *La Poétique de Voltaire.* Paris, 1766.

Lambert (Abbé). *Recueil d'observations sur les mœurs, les coutumes, les usages, les différentes langues, le gouvernement, la mythologie, la chronologie, la géographie ancienne et moderne, les cérémonies, la religion, etc., de différents peuples, de l'Asie, de l'Afrique, et de l'Amérique.* Paris, 1749. 4 vols.

La Mettrie, J. O. de. *L'Homme machine.* Leyde, 1748.

———. *Histoire naturelle de l'âme.* In *Œuvres philosophiques de la Mettrie.* 1796. 3 vols.

———. *L'Anti-Sénèque ou Discours sur le bonheur.*

———. *Système d'Epicure.* 1750. In *Œuvres philosophiques de la Mettrie.* Amsterdam, 1774. 3 vols.

La Mottraye. *Voyages.* 1727.

Lemercier de la Rivière. *L'Ordre naturel et essentiel des sociétés politiques.* 1767.

L'Encyclopédie ou Dictionnaire raisonné des sciences, des arts et des métiers. 1751–1765. 35 vols., in-fol.

L'Encyclopédie méthodique. Panckoucke edition. 1780–1832. 166½ vols. of text.

L'Esprit de Voltaire. 1759, 1761, 1765.

Letrosne. *La Liberté de commerce des grains toujours utile et jamais nuisible.* 1765.

Mably, Abbé G. B. de. *Des Droits et des devoirs du citoyen.* Critical edition. Edited by J. L. Lecercle, Geneva, 1973.

———. *Observations sur le gouvernement et les loix des Etats-Unis.* Amsterdam, 1784.

———. *Recherches historiques et politiques sur les Etats-Unis.* Paris, 1788.

———. *Parallèle des Romains et des Français.* 1740.

———. *Droit public de l'Europe.* La Haye, 1746. 2 vols.

———. *Observations sur l'histoire de France.* 1749.

———. *Observations sur les Grecs.* 1749.

———. *Observations sur les Romains.* 1751.

———. *Doutes proposés aux philosophes économiques sur l'ordre naturel et essentiel des sociétés politiques.* La Haye, 1768.

Maillet, B. de. *Telliamed.* 1748.

Mandeville, B. *Pensées libres sur la religion.* Translated by Van Effen. 1723. 2 vols.

Malebranche, N. de. *De la Recherche de la vérité.* Introduction et texte établi par Geneviève Lewis. Paris, 1945. 2 vols.

Maupertuis, P.L.M. de. *Lettre sur le progrès des sciences.* 1752.

———. *Discours sur les différentes figures des astres.* 1732.

———. *Essai de cosmologie.* 1741.

Melon, J. F. *Essai politique sur le commerce.* N.p., 1736.

Mirabeau, V. R. *L'Ami des hommes.* Avignon, 1756–58.

———. *Théorie de l'impôt.* N.p., 1760.

———. *Philosophie rurale.* Amsterdam, 1763. 3 vols.

Montesquieu, C. de Secondat, Baron de la Brède et de Montesquieu. "Notes sur l'Angleterre." *Œuvres complètes.* Garnier, 1879. Vol. VII, p. 195.

———. *Œuvres complètes de Montesquieu.* Publiées sous la direction de M. André Masson. Paris, 1950. 3 vols.

Morellet. *Mémoires de l'abbé Morellet sur le XVIIIe siècle et sur la Révolution.* Précédés de l'éloge de l'Abbé Morellet par Lemontey. Paris, 1821. 2 vols.

Morelly. *Le Code de la nature.* 1755.

———. *L'Essai sur l'esprit humain.* 1743.

———. *La Physique de la beauté.* Amsterdam, 1748.

———. *L'Essai sur le cœur humain.* 1743.

———. *Le Prince.* 1751.

———. *La Basiliade.* 1753.

———. *L'Hymen vengé.* 1778.

Mounier, J. J. *De l'Influence attribuée aux philosophes.* Tübingen, 1801.

Muralt, B. *Lettres sur les Anglais et sur les Français et sur les voyages.* N.p., 1725.

Naigeon, J. A. *Recueil philosophique.* London (Amsterdam), 1770. 2 vols.

———. *Encyclopédie méthodique; Philosophie ancienne et moderne.* Paris, 1791. 3 vols.

Newton, I. *Philosophiae naturalis principia mathematica.* 2d ed. Prefacée par Roger Côtes. Amsterdam, 1714, in-4°.

Nollet, Abbé J. *Leçons de physique expérimentale.* Paris, 1743–48. 6 vols.

Paulian, Abbé. *Traité de paix entre Descartes et Newton.* Avignon, 1763. 3 vols.

Pemberton, H. *Introduction to Sir Isaac Newton's Philosophy.* 1728.

Pichon, T. J. *La Physique de l'histoire, ou considérations générales sur les principes élémentaires du tempérament et du caractère naturel des peuples.* La Haye, 1765, in-12°.

Pluche, Abbé Antoine. *Le Spectacle de la nature, ou entretiens sur les particularités de l'histoire naturelle qui ont paru les plus propres à rendre les jeunes gens curieux et à leur former l'esprit.* Paris, 1732–1744. 8 vols.

Prévost, A. F. *Histoire générale des voyages, ou nouvelle collection de toutes les relations de voyages par mer et par terre qui ont été publiées jusqu'à présent dans les différentes langues.* Paris, 1745–70. 21 vols.

——. *Pour et contre, ouvrage périodique d'un goût nouveau, par l'auteur des Mémoires d'un homme de qualité.* Paris, 1733–40. 20 vols.

Pufendorf, S. *Le Droit de la Nature et des Gens, ou Système général des principes les plus importants, de la Morale, de la Jurisprudence, et de la Politique, traduit du latin de feu M. le Baron de Pufendorf, par Jean Barbeyrac, avec des notes du traducteur et une Préface qui sert d'introduction à tout l'ouvrage.* Amsterdam, 1706. 2 vols.

——. *Les Devoirs de l'homme et du citoyen tels qu'ils lui ont été prescrits par la loi naturelle. Traduits du latin de feu M. le Baron de Pufendorf, par Jean Barbeyrac. Avec quelques notes du Traducteur.* Amsterdam, 1707.

Quesnay, F. *Tableau économique, avec son explication et des maximes générales du gouvernement économique.* Versailles, 1758.

Raynal, G. *Histoire philosophique et politique des établissements et du commerce des Européens dans les deux Indes.* Geneva, 1780. 10 vols.

——. *Histoire philosophique et politique.* 1776. 7 vols.

——. *Histoire philosophique et politique des établissements et du commerce.* Neuchâtel, 1783–1784. 10 vols.

——. *Tableau et révolutions des colonies anglaises dans l'Amérique septentrionale.* Amsterdam, 1781. 2 vols.

Réaumur, R.-A. *Mémoires pour servir à l'histoire des insectes.* Paris, 1734–1742. 6 vols.

Robinet, T. B. *De la Nature.* 1761–63. 2 vols.

Rousseau, J.-J. *Œuvres complètes* (Pléïade edition). Published under the direction of Bernard Gagnebin and Marcel Raymond. Paris, 1959–1964.

Savary, J. *Dictionnaire universel de commerce.* Paris, 1723–1730, in-fol. 3 vols.

Savérien, M. S. *Histoire de la philosophie moderne.* 1762. 8 vols.

Shaftesbury, A. C. *Characteristics of Men, Manners, Opinions, Times.* 1711.

Sorbière, S. *Relation sur l'Angleterre.* 1664.

Stanley, T. *Historia philosophiae, vitas, opiniones, resque gestas, et dicta philosophorum sectae cuijusvis complexa autore Thoma Stanlejo.* 1731, 3 vols.

Turgot, A.R.J. *Œuvres complètes.* Paris, 1913. 5 vols.

Voltaire, A. de. *Eléments de la philosophie de Newton.* 1738.

——. *Œuvres complètes.* Edition Moland. Paris, 1877–85. 52 vols.

INDEX OF NAMES

INDEX OF IDEAS

I would like to organize in some useful way the contents which can be found in this lengthy presentation. It is the problem with which I have been faced during the last twenty-five years. The only way which appears feasible to me is to make, in brief outline form, a statement of the theory which I think the Enlightenment originated, organized and developed. In support of this view, I offer in this *Index* special references where these points have been introduced, suggested, or discussed. The French Enlightenment accepted:

The identity of life, civilization, and inner meaning.

The identification of each individual with each phenomenon which enters into each concept.

The key which opens the door to this meaning is the human mind working with the *données* of existence.

Hence:

An intellectual response to all human phenomena is required.

When given, this response capable of producing

1. Ideas
2. Movements in ideas
3. Actions
4. Reforms
5. Restructuring
6. Revolt
7. Organization or reorganization
8. Creation or re-creation.

Thus, in the Enlightenment, what one thinks is what one says, what one says is what one does, what one does is what one has become. *Moi suis un autre* does not seem a bit absurd. What is further required to guarantee this effect is:

1. Clarity of definition.
2. Correctness of organization.
3. Awareness that the human understanding, though limited, possesses
   a. The power of metaphor. The intelligent man as well as the poet has the ability to use these perceived analogies. He thus acts as poet.
   b. The further ability to grasp the necessity of establishing necessary relationships in the "nature of things." *Rapports* and *la nature des choses* are essential ingredients of life and the constitution of reality. The awareness of correct *rapports* is what produces the correct organization.

The intelligent man must remember that the correct organization can be expressed only in terms of the poetic act. It can therefore be understood in terms of symbolism.

Enlightenment is consequently at the same time a *myth* and a *reality*, a *poem* and a *system* of philosophy, an "idea" clear and distinct and a "meaning" which is neither clear nor distinct, but ambiguous and even at times paradoxical.

Our only chance of grasping these things and realizing their usefulness is to reduce them to a certain number of key people, categories, ideas, concepts, movements of thought, metaphors, and conclusions. Our only chance of keeping these elements together in some sort of clear, consistent, continuous and coexistent order is through the concept of organic unity. That is to say: all these things are alive and they work together to produce the same unified life, the same unified society, the same orderly civilization.

The key people, in my opinion, are

1. Montesquieu
2. Voltaire
3. Diderot
4. Rousseau.

The key work which organizes people, work, ideas into a unity is *L'Encyclo-pédie, ou Dictionnaire raisonné des sciences, des arts, et des métiers.*

The seven categories of existence are

1. Religion
2. Ethics
3. Esthetics
4. Politics
5. Economics
6. Science
7. The self.

I have used them for my analysis of changes in views in each category during the Enlightenment. I have wanted to show in each case that the factors which determine these views are men, works, and ideas, which bring about a new way of organizing them and a consequent new interpretation of life and civilization. The result is always a new structure given to the category, and new conclusions given to its meaning. I make no distinction between the meaning and the form of a human phenomenon. Ideas, theories, intellectual structures, and philosophies, have the same living, human qualities as a person, people, nations, societies. They all lead to the establishment of a "spirit."

These key ideas, concepts, and words are not easy to assemble accurately because we never start from scratch, nor are we ever sure that we have organized them in the correct way. Despite this obvious difficulty, I have assumed that each category carries within itself its own key idea and an inner organization. In addition, I have observed as scrupulously as I could the three concepts of God, Nature, Man as the French Enlightenment understood those terms. To the seven categories of existence, and these three concepts, I have tentatively added the following "ideas," which are really of the order of "ideals":

1. *Bonheur*
2. Brotherly love (*charité*)
3. Freedom
4. Democracy
5. Law
6. *Mœurs*
7. Reason
8. Imagination
9. *Esprit*
10. Society
11. Revolution
12. Natural Law.

I would like now to give a few examples of these things. The most important word in this whole work is *Esprit*, especially as it takes on the following forms: *Esprit philosophique* (Part I), *Esprit Encyclopédique* (Part II), *Esprit Révolutionnaire* (Parts III and IV).

In the Introduction, I started with

The role of sight and light and meaning, p. xiv

Enlightenment as an awareness, a being, a meaning, a self, pp. xiv, xv, xvi

The Paduan movement in Italy in the Renaissance, p. xvi

The philosophes as an integrated group of scientists, moralists, and artists, xvi-xix

The key categories

The key groups: poets, philosophes, free-thinkers, xxi-xxii

The key ideas, xxi-xxiii

The key institutions: religion, state, education, and social order;

An analysis of the Paduan Movement in terms of

1. Major conditions
2. Major developments
3. Readjustments of institutions
    a. Church
    b. State
    c. Social order, pp. xii-xiii.

Importance of *rapports*, xvi

Building of categories, xvii, xviii

Importance of some groups: (a) philosophers, (b) free-thinkers, (c) scientists, (d) poets, xix

Key men of Paduan School, xx

Building of art, literature and philosophy, xxi-xxiii

Key group: philosophes, 3-23

The search for pleasure, happiness, 118
Voltaire analyzes the British Civilization in terms of the seven categories.
He shows that when merged, the categories constitute a civilization, 123
Voltaire analyzes the seven categories of life in the *Lettres philosophiques*,
as a means of understanding the relationships between the categories, 141

Part II is devoted to showing how each of the four key Philosophes make
their personal contribution to each category, to the key work—the *Encyclopédie*—and to the key ideas devoted to restructuring the seven categories of
existence. Here, I have taken up each category one after the other. I have
analyzed in each category the leading man in that category: Voltaire for religion, Diderot for esthetics, Rousseau for politics, Montesquieu for jurisprudence, the *Encyclopédie* for the social category. Whenever occasion demanded,
I have used people who are important but obviously of lesser rank: Espiard,
St. Pierre, Grosley, Pichon, Castilhon. They all operate in the area of *Mœurs*
and *Lois*, that is, civilization. The statement on the way we have proceeded is
explained in the Foreword, 175.

The importance of these categories and ideas in restructuring, reforming, or
rebuilding the present organization of life, 256-310.

I kept two other problems in mind, while bringing together the contributions of each outstanding philosophe, or each philosophe of a lesser order but
nonetheless important:

What were the interrelations of one category with another—religion with
ethics, ethics with politics, or politics with economics?

What were they achieving working together in a unified way? Were they
really working together in unity or in impossible confusion? Was there a break
between the procedures of the natural sciences and the human sciences? Answers to this last problem are elusive. However, as shown at the end of Part II,
the *Encyclopédie* became essential for organic intellectual unity. The problem
of organic unity thus became the all-important problem of Part III, and the
relationship between structure and form became paramount.

Key statement about relationship between human and natural sciences, 313
Superiority of politics as the dominant human science, 326
The problem of structure in the relationship of *lois* and *mœurs*, 339
This relationship between *lois* and *mœurs*, proposed by Montesquieu, 349
Organic unity in Montesquieu, 250
Further consideration of *mœurs* and *lois*, 351-354
Key definition: "enlightened despotism" in Voltaire, 359
Key ideas in Voltaire, 361
Form as a part of structure in Rousseau, 416

Form and structure in Rousseau, 425

The interrelationships of ideas with history, philosophy, science of nature,
and the life sciences in Voltaire, 441

Voltaire's affirmation of organic unity in the making of a life-style, a spirit,
a civilization, 441

Grosley gives the same sort of analysis as Voltaire, 446

Espiard best expresses the theory in his *Essais sur le génie, et le caractère des
nations*, 1746, and *L'Esprit des nations*, in 1752.

Despite my emphasis on organic unity, I have not neglected insofar as I
know either the impossible diversity nor the deep resemblances between these
makers of the French Enlightenment. I took them one by one, giving a section
on the organic unity of each. While desirous to have each organize the material
as he sees fit, I nonetheless searched diligently for the principle of organization in each case. With Voltaire, for example, I showed how he struggled
from the first to write an outstanding play. He was still trying to write that
play after some fifty-four attempts. In the meantime, all his plays had become
mélanges just as everything else. Everything had been merged (*mélangée*)
with everything else.

After all, the only difference between life and death is one more breath, one
more heartbeat, one more idea. Seen in terms of outer reality, this doesn't
seem very significant, since these things go on all the time, with us or without
us, with no perceptible consequences. However, in terms of inner meaning,
they seem to us of the greatest consequence, since they solicit our attention
with the urgency of some mysterious, absolute, categorical imperative, always
tugging at our elbow and always saying: "Now, look here, you, you listen to
me!" It's the only knowledge we are permitted to know. No wonder we call it
Esprit and when we think nobody is looking, we add the little adjective
humain: *l'Esprit humain*.

Library of Congress Cataloging in Publication Data

Wade, Ira Owen, 1896-
  The structure and form of the French Enlightenment.

  Bibliography: v. 1, p.   v. 2, p.
  Includes index.
  CONTENTS: v. 1. Esprit philosophique.—v. 2.
Esprit révolutionnaire.
  1. Enlightenment. 2. Philosophy, French—18th
century. I. Title.
B1925.E5W33   194   77-72139
ISBN 0-691-05256-5 (v. 1)
ISBN 0-691-05257-3 (v. 2)